THE SACRAMENTARY

When the newly consecrated monk-Archbishop of Milan visited his seminary in 1929 he was invited to explain Benedictine spirituality. "There is no such thing," he replied. "It is nothing other than the spirituality of the Church: the praying of the Sacred Liturgy." For Blessed Ildefonso Schuster—monk, abbot, cardinal and archbishop—that reality was a constant. The Sacred Liturgy was the source and summit of his entire Christian life and work, as these volumes testify.

Scholarship has progressed in the century since higher duties called Schuster from the classroom, certainly. Yet in these pages his thirst for learning is as palpable as is the true liturgical spirit—indeed sanctity—that animates his exposition of the nature of the liturgy and his meditations on the seasons and feasts of the liturgical year. From these we can learn a great deal, not only in respect of our approach to liturgical study and celebration, but also regarding the fundamental nature of Christian life and spirituality. That these volumes are once again in print is a singular grace.

—DOM ALCUIN REID, Prior, Monastère Saint-Benoît, Fréjus-Toulon, France, Author, *The Organic Development of the Liturgy*

In addition to having been a worthy son of Saint Benedict and, later, successor of Saint Ambrose, Blessed Ildefonso Schuster (1880–1954) was a notable figure of the early Liturgical Movement, one whose scholarship deserves to be better known in the anglophone world. Arouca Press has done a great service toward that end by republishing the English translation of his long out-of-print seminal work. Although scholarship has progressed in some areas in the last century, it remains a valuable commentary on the living tradition that is the older Roman Rite, on a par with Dom Guéranger's magnum opus, *The Liturgical Year*.

—FR. THOMAS KOCIK, KHS, Author, *Singing His Song: A Short Introduction to the Liturgical Movement*

The achievement of Blessed Ildefonso's Schuster *Liber sacramentorum* was to build a bridge between liturgical scholarship and spiritual commentary on the Mass. The reprint of this great contribution to liturgical renewal in the twentieth century is most welcome at a time when the older form of the Roman Rite is rediscovered by new generations of Catholics. Anyone diving into this monumental work of erudition and piety will find it an inspiring guide to the riches of the liturgical year.

—FR UWE MICHAEL LANG, Cong.Orat., Mater Ecclesiae College, St Mary's University, Twickenham, London

Ildefonse Schuster was among the towering figures of the Liturgical Movement in its healthy phase, where the overriding concern was to study the family history in the spirit of descendents keen to know their glorious heritage, so that they might carry on long-standing customs with grateful understanding, and rediscover lost, forgotten, or neglected treasures. In his own life, he combined a scholar's diligent attention to primary sources with a pastor's warm-hearted embrace of all the gifts the Holy Spirit has bestowed on the Church over the ages. This carefully limned commentary, spacious and leisurely, plunges us into the pure font of tradition and intensifies our participation in the life-giving mysteries of Christ.
 —DR. PETER KWASNIEWSKI, author of *Noble Beauty, Transcendent Holiness: Why the Modern Age Needs the Mass of Ages*

The Sacramentary
(LIBER SACRAMENTORUM)
Historical & Liturgical Notes on the Roman Missal
BY ILDEFONSO SCHUSTER
Abbot of the Monastery of St Paul's Without the Walls. Translated from the Italian by ARTHUR LEVELIS-MARKE, M.A.
Translation completed by Mrs. W. FAIRFAX-CHOLMELEY

VOLUME V
(Parts 8 and 9)

Volume 5 originally translated from the Italian
by Arthur Levelis-Marke and completed
    by Mrs. W. Fairfax-Cholmeley
© Burns Oates & Washbourne Ltd.
1930

Reprinted by Arouca Press 2020

All rights reserved
No part of this book may be reproduced or transmitted,
in any form or by any means, without permission

ISBN: 978-1-989905-11-1 (pbk)
ISBN: 978-1-989905-12-8 (hardcover)

Arouca Press
PO Box 55003
Bridgeport PO
Waterloo, ON N2J3G0
Canada
www.aroucapress.com

Send inquiries to info@aroucapress.com

NIHIL OBSTAT:
INNOCENTIUS APAP, S.Th.M., O.P.
Censor deputatus.

IMPRIMATUR:
EDM. CAN. SURMONT,
Vicarius generalis.

WESTMONASTERII,
die 26a Junii, 1930.

First published 1930

Made and Printed in Great Britain

CONTENTS

PARTS VIII & IX

THE SAINTS IN THE MYSTERY OF THE REDEMPTION

(THE FEASTS OF THE SAINTS FROM AUGUST 14 TO ADVENT)

INTRODUCTION

	PAGE
CHAPTER I. THE SANCTUARIES OF THE BLESSED VIRGIN MARY IN MEDIEVAL ROME	1
CHAPTER II. THE PORTRAITS OF THE BLESSED VIRGIN MARY VENERATED AT ROME	22
CHAPTER III. THE FESTIVAL OF THE ASSUMPTION INTO HEAVEN OF THE BLESSED VIRGIN MARY IN THE ANCIENT ROMAN LITURGY	31
SANCTAE ROMANAE ECCLESIAE FERIALE	43

THE FEASTS OF THE SAINTS FROM AUGUST 14 TO NOVEMBER 28

FEASTS IN AUGUST

AUGUST 14. VIGIL OF THE ASSUMPTION OF THE BLESSED VIRGIN MARY	50
,, 15. THE ASSUMPTION OF THE BLESSED VIRGIN MARY	52
,, 15. ST TARCISIUS, ACOLYTE AND MARTYR	55
,, 16. ST JOACHIM, FATHER OF THE BLESSED VIRGIN MARY	56
,, 17. OCTAVE DAY OF ST LAWRENCE	58
,, 18. ST AGAPITUS, MARTYR	59
,, 19. ST MAGNUS, MARTYR	60
,, 20. ST BERNARD, ABBOT, CONFESSOR AND DOCTOR	61

The Sacramentary

		PAGE
AUGUST 21.	ST JANE FRANCES FREMIOT DE CHANTAL, WIDOW	62
,, 22.	ST TIMOTHY, PRIEST AND MARTYR	63
,, 22.	ST HIPPOLYTUS "QUI ET NONNUS"	65
,, 22.	ST SYMPHORIAN, MARTYR	66
,, 22.	OCTAVE DAY OF THE ASSUMPTION	66
,, 23.	SS ABUNDIUS AND IRENAEUS, MARTYRS	67
,, 23.	ST PHILIP BENIZI, CONFESSOR	68
,, 23.	VIGIL OF ST BARTHOLOMEW, APOSTLE	69
,, 24.	ST BARTHOLOMEW, APOSTLE	69
,, 25.	ST GENESIUS, MARTYR	71
,, 25.	ST LOUIS, KING AND CONFESSOR	72
,, 26.	ST ZEPHYRINUS, POPE	74
,, 27.	ST JOSEPH CALASANCTIUS, CONFESSOR	75
,, 28.	ST HERMES, MARTYR	77
,, 28.	ST AUGUSTINE, BISHOP, CONFESSOR AND DOCTOR	78
,, 29.	ST SABINA, MARTYR	80
,, 29.	THE BEHEADING OF ST JOHN THE BAPTIST	81
,, 30.	SS FELIX AND ADAUCTUS, MARTYRS	84
,, 30.	ST ROSE OF LIMA, VIRGIN	88
,, 31.	ST RAYMUND NONNATUS, CARDINAL AND CONFESSOR	89

FEASTS IN SEPTEMBER

SEPTEMBER	1. THE TWELVE HOLY MARTYRS OF BENEVENTUM	89
,,	1. ST GILES, ABBOT	91
,,	2. ST STEPHEN, KING OF HUNGARY, CONFESSOR	91
,,	3.	93
,,	4.	93
,,	5. SS ACONTIUS, NONNUS, HERCULANUS AND TAURINUS, MARTYRS	94
,,	5. ST LAWRENCE JUSTINIAN, PATRIARCH OF VENICE	95
,,	6.	95
,,	7. VIGIL OF THE BIRTHDAY OF THE BLESSED VIRGIN	96
,,	8. DEDICATION OF ST ADRIAN, MARTYR	96
,,	8. BIRTHDAY OF THE BLESSED VIRGIN	97

Contents

		PAGE
SEPTEMBER	9. St Gorgonius, Martyr	99
,,	9. St Hyacinth, Deacon and Martyr	100
,,	10. St Nicholas of Tolentino, Confessor	101
,,	11. SS Protus and Hyacinth, Martyrs	101
,,	12. Feast of the Holy Name of Mary	105
,,	14. SS Cornelius, Pope, and Cyprian, Martyrs	106
,,	14. The Exaltation of the Holy Cross and the Dedication of the "Martyrium" on Calvary	108
,,	15. St Nicomedes, Martyr	111
,,	16. St Euphemia, Virgin and Martyr	113
,,	16. SS Lucy and Geminianus	114
,,	16. SS Abundius, Priest, and Abundantius, Deacon, Martyrs	116
,,	16. St Martin, Pope and Martyr	117
,,	17. The Imprinting of the Stigmata on the Body of St Francis	117
,,	18. St Joseph of Cupertino, Confessor	120
,,	19. St Januarius, Bishop, and his Companions, Martyrs	122
,,	20. St Eustace, Bishop and Martyr	124
,,	20. The Holy Vigil of St Matthew, Apostle and Evangelist	125
,,	21. St Matthew, Apostle and Evangelist	125
,,	22. St Basilla, Virgin and Martyr	128
,,	22. St Merita, Martyr	129
,,	22. SS Maurice and Companions, Martyrs	130
,,	22. St Thomas of Villanova, Bishop and Confessor	131
,,	23. St Thecla, Virgin and Martyr	132
,,	23. St Liberius, Pope	133
,,	23. St Linus, Pope	137
,,	24. Our Lady of Ransom	138
,,	26. St Eusebius, Pope and Martyr	139
,,	26. SS Cyprian and Justina, Martyrs	140

		PAGE
SEPTEMBER 27.	SS COSMAS AND DAMIAN, MARTYRS	141
,, 28.	ST STACTEUS, MARTYR	143
,, 28.	ST WENCESLAS, DUKE AND MARTYR	143
,, 29.	DEDICATION OF THE BASILICA OF ST MICHAEL THE ARCHANGEL ON THE VIA SALARIA	144
,, 30.	ST JEROME, PRIEST, CONFESSOR AND DOCTOR OF THE CHURCH	146

FEASTS IN OCTOBER

OCTOBER	1. TRANSLATION OF ST REMIGIUS, BISHOP	151
,,	2. FEAST OF THE HOLY GUARDIAN ANGELS	151
,,	3. ST CANDIDA, MARTYR	154
,,	4. ST BALBINA, MARTYR	155
,,	4. ST FRANCIS OF ASSISI, CONFESSOR	155
,,	5. ST PLACIDUS AND COMPANIONS, MARTYRS	158
,,	5. ST PLACIDUS, DISCIPLE OF ST BENEDICT, ABBOT	158
,,	6. ST BRUNO, CONFESSOR	160
,,	7. ST MARK, POPE	161
,,	7. SS MARCELLUS AND APULEIUS	163
,,	7. SS SERGIUS AND BACCHUS, MARTYRS	163
,,	7. THE MOST HOLY ROSARY OF THE BLESSED VIRGIN MARY	165
,,	8. ST BRIDGET, WIDOW	169
,,	9. SS GENUINUS AND COMPANIONS, MARTYRS	170
,,	9. SS DENIS, RUSTICUS, AND ELEUTHERIUS	170
,,	10. ST FRANCIS BORGIA, CONFESSOR	172
,,	12. ST AEDISTUS, MARTYR	173
,,	13. ST EDWARD, KING AND CONFESSOR	174
,,	14. ST CALLISTUS, POPE AND MARTYR	175
,,	15. ST TERESA, VIRGIN	179
,,	16. ST SOSIUS, DEACON AND MARTYR	180
,,	17. ST HEDWIG, WIDOW	180
,,	18. ST LUKE, EVANGELIST	181
,,	19. ST ASTERIUS, MARTYR	183
,,	19. ST PETER OF ALCANTARA, CONFESSOR	184

Contents

	PAGE
OCTOBER 20. ST JOHN OF KENTY, CONFESSOR	185
,, 21. ST HILARION, ABBOT	187
,, 21. ST URSULA AND HER COMPANIONS, MARTYRS	187
,, 24. ST RAPHAEL, ARCHANGEL	189
,, 25. SS CHRYSANTHUS AND DARIA, MARTYRS	192
,, 26. ST EVARISTUS, POPE	195
,, 27. VIGIL OF THE HOLY APOSTLES SIMON AND JUDE	195
,, 28. SS SIMON AND JUDE, APOSTLES	197
SUNDAY BEFORE THE FEAST OF ALL SAINTS. THE FEAST OF THE KINGSHIP OF OUR LORD JESUS CHRIST	200
OCTOBER 31. VIGILIARY MASS OF ALL SAINTS	204

FEASTS IN NOVEMBER

NOVEMBER 1. ST CAESARIUS, DEACON AND MARTYR	206
,, 1. FEAST OF ALL THE SAINTS	208
,, 2. COMMEMORATION OF ALL THE FAITHFUL DEPARTED	213
THE FIRST MASS	221
THE SECOND MASS	228
THE THIRD MASS	229
THE LITURGY AT THE GRAVESIDE IN CHRISTIAN ANTIQUITY:	231
HOLY MASS FOR THE DAY OF DEATH AND BURIAL OF THE DEPARTED	233
ON THE THIRD, SEVENTH AND THIRTIETH DAY AFTER BURIAL	236
ON THE ANNIVERSARY OF THE DEPARTED	237
DAILY MASSES FOR THE DEAD	237
ANOTHER MASS FOR THE ANNIVERSARY OF THE DEPARTED	239
FOR THE PARENTS OF THE CELEBRANT	239
FOR ALL THE DEPARTED LYING IN A CEMETERY	240
AT THE BURIAL OF AN ABBOT	241
NOVEMBER 2. DEDICATION OF THE GREATER BASILICA OF ST LAWRENCE	241
,, 3. ST SYLVIA, WIDOW	242
,, 4. SS VITALIS AND AGRICOLA, MARTYRS	245

The Sacramentary

		PAGE
NOVEMBER	4. ST CHARLES BORROMEO, BISHOP AND CONFESSOR	246
,,	6. ST LEONARD, CONFESSOR	248
,,	7. ST WILLIBRORD, BISHOP, APOSTLE OF FRISIA	249
,,	8. THE HOLY CROWNED MARTYRS	249
,,	8. OCTAVE DAY OF ALL SAINTS	252
,,	9. ST THEODORE, MARTYR	253
,,	9. DEDICATION OF THE LATERAN BASILICA OF THE SAVIOUR	254
,,	10. SS TRYPHO AND RESPICIUS, MARTYRS, AND ST NYMPHA, VIRGIN AND MARTYR	262
,,	10. ST ANDREW AVELLINO, CONFESSOR	263
,,	11. ST MENNAS, MARTYR	264
,,	11 (or 12). ST MARTIN, BISHOP OF TOURS	266
,,	12. ST MARTIN, POPE	271
,,	13. ST BRICE, BISHOP	272
,,	13. ST DIDACUS, CONFESSOR	273
,,	14. ST JOSAPHAT, BISHOP AND MARTYR	273
,,	15. ST GERTRUDE, VIRGIN	276
,,	17. ST GREGORY THAUMATURGUS, BISHOP AND CONFESSOR	279
,,	18. DEDICATION OF THE BASILICAS OF THE PRINCES OF THE APOSTLES, PETER AND PAUL	280
,,	19. ST PONTIAN, POPE AND MARTYR	287
,,	19. ST ELIZABETH, WIDOW	288
,,	20. ST FELIX OF VALOIS, CONFESSOR	289
,,	21. PRESENTATION OF THE BLESSED VIRGIN MARY	290
,,	22. DEDICATION OF THE TITULUS CAECILIAE IN THE TRASTEVERE	291
,,	23. ST CLEMENT, POPE	294
,,	23. ST FELICITAS, MARTYR	297
,,	24. ST CHRYSOGONUS, MARTYR	299
,,	24. ST JOHN OF THE CROSS, CONFESSOR AND DOCTOR	301
,,	25. ST CATHERINE, VIRGIN AND MARTYR	302
,,	26. ST PETER, BISHOP OF ALEXANDRIA AND MARTYR	303

Contents

		PAGE
NOVEMBER 26. ST SYLVESTER, ABBOT	- - - - -	304
,, 27. ST OPTATUS, BISHOP	- - - - -	305
,, 28. ST GREGORY III, POPE AND CONFESSOR	-	306

HOLY MASS IN VARIOUS PUBLIC AND PRIVATE CIRCUMSTANCES OF CHRISTIAN LIFE :   308

    I. FOR THE CONSECRATION OF A POPE - - - 317
    II. THE NUPTIAL MASS - - - - - - 320
    III. IN TIME OF WAR - - - - - - - 324
    IV. MASS FOR THE SICK - - - - - - 327
    V. THE EUCHARISTIC SACRIFICE ON OCCASIONS OF PUBLIC PLAGUE - - - - - - - - 331

EUCHOLOGICAL APPENDIX

PRAYERS TO THE BLESSED VIRGIN FROM THE BYZANTINE LITURGY   337
BYZANTINE PRAYER IN FORM OF A LITANY - - - - 337
INVOCATIONS TO THE MOTHER OF GOD - - - - - 338
PRAYER OF ST MARTIN FOR HIS PEOPLE - - - - 339
BYZANTINE TROPES FOR SUNDAYS, COMPOSED BY ST METROPHANES OF SMYRNA, FOR THE UNION OF THE CHURCHES - 340

PART VIII

THE SAINTS IN THE MYSTERY OF THE REDEMPTION

(THE FEASTS OF THE SAINTS FROM THE VIGIL OF THE ASSUMPTION TO THE DEDICATION OF ST MICHAEL)

In the Baptistery of San Lorenzo.

Adsp]ICE · QVI · TRANSIS · QVAM · SIT · BREVIS · AC[cipe vita
Atqu]E · TVAE · NAVIS · ITER · AD · LITVS · PARAD[isi
Rell]EGE · QVO · VVLTVM · D̄NĪ · FACIAS · TIBI · PO[rtum
Percipias gra]TIAM · QVIS · QVIS · HAEC · SACRA · PERH[auris
Glor]IA · SVMMA · D̄S · LVMEN · SAPIENTIA · VIR[tus
Ver]VS · IN · ALTARI · CRVOR · EST · VINVM · QVE · [videtur
Is]Q · TVI · LATERIS · PER · OPVS · MIRAE · [pietatis
Unde]POTENTER · AQVAM · TRIBVIS · BAPTI[smate lotis

(*5th cent. inscription in the sepulchral basilica of S Lawrence.*)

Reflect, O thou who passest here, how short is this life.
Turn back, steer for the shore of Paradise, that thy bark may find harbour with the Saviour.
Receive grace, thou who partakest of these holy mysteries.
It is God, the supreme glory, light, wisdom, power, who at the Altar appears as wine, yet is in truth Blood.
This miracle of infinite love flows from thy side, O Christ,
Whence thou pourest also the waters of baptism to save our souls.

INTRODUCTION

CHAPTER I

THE SANCTUARIES OF THE BLESSED VIRGIN MARY IN MEDIEVAL ROME

JUST as we find Mary as the central figure in the symbol of the Christian Faith, so love for her and devotion towards her cause to leap for joy the very heart of the Catholic Church, which from the city of the Seven Hills impresses its supernatural rhythm upon the whole world. It is an obligation on Christian Rome, inherent in her office and dignity, to take the lead before any other country in love for her who called down to earth eternal Love itself. Is it not indeed in Rome that revealed dogma is first realised in its entirety, before this great heart of the Church sends forth its life and its energy throughout the rest of the mystical body of Christ?

It is, then, with perfect right that Catholic Rome which guards intact the deposit of dogma entrusted to her by Peter and Paul, addresses the Blessed Mother of God with singular complacency, as *Salus populi Romani*, and as if a special pact exists between her and the later descendants of Romulus and Remus, the latter have now for many centuries invoked her as *Romanae portus securitatis.*

This devotion of the city of Rome to Mary has left throughout the centuries a number of artistic, literary and liturgical records which might well be formed into an imposing collection. Leaving this task, however, to other hands, it must suffice us to touch lightly upon this vast theme, merely passing in review, as it were, the more ancient basilicas of Rome dedicated to the great Mother of God. In this manner the subject-matter is brought into close connection with the Liturgy, and it will prove of advantage to us to penetrate still farther into the spirit of those early generations of Christians who enriched the Roman Missal with so many festivals in honour of the Blessed Virgin.

* * * * * *

For the sake of brevity we must limit our researches to the Middle Ages only between the fifth and the thirteenth centuries, therefore we shall refrain from descending into the extra-mural cemeteries in order to wander through their labyrinths and there retrace among the passages of the apostolic age the first signs of the devotion to Mary which was brought from Palestine to the banks of the Tiber by the Apostles, Peter, Paul and John, the disciples Luke, Mark, Epaphroditus, Clement, Aquila and others.

Otherwise in the cemetery of Priscilla we should find the earliest representation of the Blessed Virgin which has yet been discovered. It is not later than the beginning of the second century, for it still retains all the freshness which we associate with Pompeian art. Mary is seated on a throne, her head covered with a veil, and holds in her arms the Child Jesus, whilst a figure wearing a *pallium* stands respectfully before her, pointing upwards to a star which shines in the sky above the head of the Infant.

The figure is generally supposed to be the Prophet Isaias, in whose writings, however, there is no prophecy concerning a star. Some have suggested that it represents the soothsayer Balaam who foretold, it is true, that a star should arise upon the house of Jacob. Yet this association of a pseudo-prophet with the Mother of God seems to us very strange, and would hardly have been understood by the faithful of the second century.

Does the holy Gospel really need to appeal to the testimony of false and lying religions? In interpreting ancient paintings, especially those in the catacombs, we must reject too ingenious theories in favour of that explanation which first occurs to the mind of the student well versed in his catechism and in sacred history. For the art of the catacombs was intended to appeal especially to the popular Christian mentality.

Let us therefore put aside any far-fetched explanation taken from the prophecies of Isaias or from the Book of Numbers, and instead let us open the New Testament and see who it was that stood before our Blessed Lady when she sat with the Infant Jesus on her lap, and when a mysterious star came and rested over the *domus* at Bethlehem. Who but the Magi? *Stella quam viderant (Magi) in Oriente, antecedebat eos, usque dum veniens staret supra ubi erat Puer.*[1] The picture represents then the Adoration of the Magi, a scene constantly depicted in the first four centuries.

If the painter of the catacombs of Priscilla has merely outlined the episode by showing one only of the wise men of the East, and not three or four as we sometimes see in the catacombs, this has been so not only because of the lack

---

[1] Matthew ii, 9.

of available space, but also for an aesthetic reason, namely for the sake of symmetry to which the early painters clung very much. As a matter of fact the painting forms part of a frieze which adorns the arch of a tomb.

Now on the side opposite to the Adoration of the Magi another scene confronts us, the meaning of which is the subject of still greater controversy. It consists, like the first, of three persons only, that is, a man, a woman and a little child, who may represent the deceased persons for whom the sepulchral *arcosolium* was prepared.

Early Christian art did not aim at being realistic, nor did it claim to possess the quality of a photograph. Its tendency on the contrary was to simplify as far as possible the scriptural scenes which it sought to represent. In every picture it chose the characteristic moment of the mystery portrayed, and reproduced that, leaving on one side every other secondary object.

The earliest picture of the Blessed Virgin in the cemetery of Priscilla, may be included then in the series of representations of biblical subjects, but the *cultus* of our Lady is, however, indirectly confirmed by it, since the painters of those very early days would certainly not have reproduced with such frequency that Gospel scene in which Mary must necessarily occupy the principal part of the picture, if veneration for her had not from that time been intimately associated with the *cultus* of her divine Son.

The following apparent anomaly arouses some wonder: whilst during the first four centuries of the Christian era the scene of the adoration of the Magi is that one which is most frequently found on the walls of the catacombs and on the Roman sarcophagi, the temporal birth of Christ, on the other hand, and his infantile cries in the crib of Bethlehem only appear towards the fourth century and in a very few instances.

The Liturgy itself, however, gives us the explanation of this seeming anomaly. The feast of January 6, wholly Eastern in its origin, and having many significations (the baptism, the marriage-feast of Cana, the adoration of the Magi, the birth of Jesus in the stable, all commemorated under the single title of *Theophania*, that is to say revelation, or appearance of the Lord to the world), dates from the second century and takes root especially in gnostic surroundings. These heretics indeed recognised in the descent of the Holy Ghost upon Jesus in the waters of the Jordan nothing less than his real birth to the nature conferred upon him at that moment by the Father because of his supreme merits.

The Catholics in their turn, in opposition to this anti-evangelical *gnosis* upheld the dogma of the hypostatic union to which the human nature of Jesus was raised from the moment of his conception, in consequence of which the Word was made flesh, and God was born in Bethlehem of the Virgin Mary. For controversial reasons the " great Church " by means of the Liturgy and of Art rendered the Messianic significance of the Adoration of the Magi familiar to the people rather than the baptism in the Jordan, and this occurrence, even in preference to the crib of Bethlehem, was chosen by all the theologians together, by the painters and sculptors of the catacombs, as being that which best expressed the divine nature and the human nature together of him who, whilst remaining God eternal, yet deigned to be born in all things like unto us.

The wise man from the East of the catacombs of Priscilla points out, therefore, the star which shines in the heavens above the head of the Child, and the star, in classical Roman art also, is always the symbol of the deity.

At a very early period of which we may perhaps find some trace in the writings of Hippolytus, when Rome, too, celebrated on January 6 with rites almost equal to those of Easter, the feast of the Epiphany, that is, the first appearing of Christ to the world, it is not surprising that it should also have been so favourite a subject with painters and that they should so often have reproduced it on the *arcosolia* and sarcophagi of the catacombs. The faithful who beheld these representations at once grasped their significance with regard to Christian doctrine, so that if we were able to-day to question a Christian of the second century standing before the figure of the Blessed Virgin in the cemetery of Priscilla whom we see being saluted by the person in the *pallium* who points to a star in the heavens, as to the meaning of the picture, he would reply without hesitation that it represents the *Theophania*, that is the first appearing of the Saviour of the world.

Passing from this first *parousia* in the cemetery of Priscilla of Jesus in Mary's lap, before arriving at the second and last coming of the supreme Judge, who will indeed appear to us again in his Mother's lap, even in that tremendous office, in a painting at the cemetery of Commodilla, we meet another intermediate representation of our Lady to which we might give the title of *speculum justitiae*.

This is to be found in the same cemetery of Priscilla and is of very great importance because in it the Virgin appears not merely as an historic person who forms part of a scene from the Bible but who is represented singly as a special object of veneration. We are alluding here to the well-known painting of the third century depicting a *velatio virginis* in which the bishop is pointing out to the candidate the holy Mother seated on a throne with the Child Jesus in her arms, as a model of virginal purity for her imitation.

We know, indeed, from St Ambrose and other Fathers of the Church that this reference to Mary as the mirror of immaculate virginity was then almost a commonplace theme in the many addresses given by the bishops on the occasion of the consecration of virgins. So that the third century painting in the *cubiculum* of Priscilla with its allusion to the rite of the consecration of virgins, is not only a witness to the early devotion of the Romans to our Lady, but also confirms a fact which on the other hand was already known to us, that even at that time bishops and preachers proclaimed the praises of the incomparable virtues of Mary just as we all still do in our churches.

In view of such fervent devotion to the Blessed Virgin during the first four centuries of the Church, it is hardly wise to speak of a development of this devotion in the Middle Ages and in times nearer to ourselves.

The conception of the eminent dignity of our Blessed Lady is also beautifully expressed in the third painting existing in the cemetery of Commodilla which we have mentioned above. It belongs, however, to the sixth century and refers to the *parousia* of Christ in judgement after death. A certain deceased person, Turtura by name, is introduced into the hall of divine judgement by the saints who are her advocates, the local martyrs SS Felix and Adauctus. The latter, who is of youthful aspect and has the clerical tonsure, places his hand kindly with a gesture of protection on the shoulder of the deceased, who, on her part, seems hardly to venture to approach the throne of her Judge.

A singular air of peace and confidence pervades the whole scene, and its chief feature is that he who has to pronounce the sentence is no longer represented as seated on a throne, with his usual majestic aspect emanating from imperial Rome, with a young and beardless countenance, and clothed in a toga adorned with the *clavus latus*; here on the contrary we have something very different, which makes this painting of the tomb of Turtura unique. The throne from which Christ on this occasion is to proclaim judgement is nothing else than the virginal lap of Mary who holds her Son tenderly in her arms.

She, who is Blessed among women, occupies therefore the central place in the picture, and sits majestically upon a high bejewelled throne, with her feet resting on a footstool. But as though all this imperial pomp seemed insufficient to the Roman artist who was striving to express his conception of the eminent greatness of the Mother of God, he has even placed in her hand the insignia of the highest dignity of the imperial republic : that is, the consular *mappula*, the emblem which is always given to the successors of Brutus and Collatinus in the *diptycha* which inaugurate their term of office.

Some time before this, the distinction of the *mappula* from being exclusively confined to the Consuls had been extended to the Pope, to the deacons of the city, and to a few other privileged ecclesiastics, who, however, usually wore it only during the offering of the Holy Sacrifice. Christian art was more generous, and sometimes conferred the *mappula* and the royal diadem also upon her who was blessed among all creatures, as we can see in the mosaic at Sta Maria *in Domnica*.

We have announced our intention of not going down into the extra-mural cemeteries and must therefore resist the temptation to break our resolution. Let us then seek above ground the monuments of devotion to our Lady in the classical ways and medieval quarters of the Eternal City.

Which then is to be our starting point ? There are three churches, each of which claims above all others to be the most ancient building in Rome dedicated to the Blessed Virgin, and these are : Sta Maria *in Trastevere*, Sta Maria *Maggiore*, and Sta Maria *Antiqua*.

This last *diaconia*, however, by the very fact of never having been a presbyterial *titulus*, and also because it was adapted somewhat late within the hall of an abandoned imperial building, clearly shows its later origin, and must not, therefore, enter into competition with the others. So we have to deal only with the two basilicas, of the Esquiline and of the Trastevere, both of which support their claims with solid arguments.

The Church of our Lady in the Trastevere maintains that it is connected with the ancient *taberna emeritoria*, which was removed thence by Alexander Severus, out of consideration for the Christians. The name of its first founder, Callixtus, given from the fourth century to the surrounding district, which was consequently known as the *Area Callisti*, is undoubtedly a proof of the influence once exercised in the Trastevere by the former manager of the people's bank, who became later an energetic and enterprising Pope.

The inhabitants of the Trastevere of to-day, not less than those of the fourth century, separated as they are from the rest of the city by the course of the Tiber, still show some inclination to regard Sta Maria *in Trastevere* as their own particular cathedral. Indeed, in olden times, when dissensions arose amongst the Romans over the choice of a successor to the Apostolic See, we find that in the very century of the

Peace of Constantine, the schismatic factions more than once made the Basilica beyond the Tiber their headquarters.

There Felix II established himself against Pope Liberius, later the electors of Ursinus assembled there in opposition to Damasus, and lastly, in 418, Boniface I was elected in Sta Maria *in Trastevere*, whilst the opposing party stirred up tumults and secessions in the city. All this happened within a period of not much more than fifty years.

In those days, however, the church across the Tiber was known as the *Basilica Iulii trans Tiberim, regione XIII iuxta Callistum*, taking its name from that Pope Julius who had built it. We use the word "built" intentionally, for the *Liber Pontificalis* bears witness to the fact, and distinguishes the work of Pope Callixtus from the *Basilica Iulii iuxta Callistum*, which was, therefore, close to the constructions of the former. The two buildings are not to be confused, for the first, that of Pope Callixtus, was probably a charitable institution, a *diaconia*, adjoining which Julius I erected a church.

When did this Julian Basilica, which by the Middle Ages had appropriated the history and the glory of the third century building of Pope Callixtus, assume the name of the Blessed Virgin Mary? It appears for the first time in documents of the seventh century, but it must have been in general usage before this, since the tendency to dedicate to the saints the various urban titles which originally had borne only the name of their founder, had increased in Rome in the fifth century. At any rate in the seventh century the basilica on the other side of the Tiber was commonly known among the people by two titles, the one relatively new, and the other primitive, but still used by the Roman populace: *Basilica sanctae Mariae quae Callisti vocatur*.

Let us now enter the magnificent sanctuary. The noble vaulting of the apse, executed by order of Innocent II, which rises so majestically above the sepulchre of SS Cornelius, Callixtus, Julius and Calepodius chants as it were a hymn of praise to Mary. Surrounded by a retinue of saints she is seated in triumph on a throne beside her divine Son, who in the usual semblance of the *Pantocrator* throws his arms about her neck and draws her to himself in a tender embrace.

Lower down, in the left-hand corner, the scene is completed by the interesting figure of Jeremias, the tearful prophet of the Lamentations, who as one that has himself had much experience of imprisonment points to a caged bird and holds up a scroll with the words: *Christus Dñus captus est in peccatis nostris*. "The Lord Jesus became captive through our iniquities." This strange allegory of Jeremias in prison and of the caged bird is very rarely seen in ancient Christian art. From the artistic point of view, the small pictures in the lower part and on the sides representing scenes from the life of the Blessed Virgin are much more important. The action, the drapery and especially the spirit which inspires those scenes make us realise at once that by the influence of Pietro Cavallini the *dolce stil nuovo* has been inaugurated also in the art of painting, whilst the epoch of the Byzantines and of the Cosmati is closed in Italy for ever.

Now in order to go from Sta Maria *in Trastevere* to the Liberian Basilica on the Esquiline, but first glancing for a moment at Sta Maria *Antiqua* in the Forum, we are obliged to traverse a great part of the city. This is just as well, for in this way we shall be able to notice a large number of ancient monuments connected with Mary scattered everywhere through the streets of the city by the pious devotion of the Popes and of our forefathers.

Indeed, as soon as we leave the Basilica of Pope Julius and turn in the direction of the Sublician Bridge, by which we shall cross the Tiber in front of the title of St Cecilia, we come at once upon two ancient little churches dedicated to Mary : the one, Sta Maria *ad Pineam*, now named *in Cappella*, recalls the piety and devotion of *Madonna Francesca dei Ponziani* (St Frances of Rome), the other, Sta Maria *in Turri*, now " *del buon Viaggio*," is a last remaining relic of the towers and fortifications formerly built along the banks of the river by Leo IV as a defence against the Saracens.

We will now cross the bridge under the smiling hill-side of Monte Verde in which is hidden away the cemetery of Pontianus with its martyrs Abdon, Sennen, Pollio, Vincent, Pigmenius and Milix. On the opposite bank of the river we see at once the façade of the ancient *statio annonae*, turned into a deaconry and almost rebuilt by Adrian I, under the Byzantine name of Sta Maria *in Cosmedin*. The Christian charitable institution in this, as in several other quarters of the city, merely took the place of *frumentatio* which the Roman State carried on here under the Empire, when it had to fulfil the arduous duty of providing for the glorious *plebs romulea : panem et circenses*.

When the State ceased to care for the people in Rome the public granaries near the landing-stage were entrusted to the care of a deacon. Thus a deaconry was established which was placed under the patronage of the Mother of God, as was fitting, because she, after having cared for Jesus with maternal solicitude at Nazareth, showed herself at Cana the special providence of the bridal pair in their need.

This instance of the *statio annonae* having become simply

the church of Sta Maria *in Cosmedin* must often have been repeated at Rome, for example in the case of Sta Maria *Antiqua*, Sta Maria *in Portici*, Sta Maria *in Cyro*, Sta Maria *in Xenodochio* and others. It is practically a rule that the Roman deaconries are named after the Blessed Virgin, so that, besides those already mentioned, we have also Sta Maria *in Domnica*, Sta Maria *iuxta Callistum*, Sta Maria *in Via Lata*, Sta Maria *Nova*, etc.

If the length of the way did not deter us we might, after leaving Sta Maria *in Cosmedin*, ascend the Aventine, and go as far as Sta Maria *in Monasterio*, the seat of the Priory of the Knights of Malta, which dates from the time of Alberic I. In that monastery the great Hildebrand, then in his early youth, dedicated himself to God by monastic vows. But, avoiding the tiring climb up the cosmopolitan hill and keeping instead along the banks of the Tiber beneath the Aventine and the Palatine, let us make our way to Sta Maria *in Porticu Gallae*. As we look around during this short walk to get our bearings, we catch sight of the little façade of Sta Maria *in Secundicerio*, where the unfortunate Pontiff Paschal II once took refuge. We notice, too, the apse of Sta Maria *in Curtae domnae Micinae*, and the bell-turrets of Sta Maria *de episcopio* and of Sta Maria *in Ambrosii*. For lack of time we must, however, omit to visit these three small but important churches, in order to betake ourselves directly to the deaconry of the *Porticus Gallae*, or *Gallatorum*, the origin of which is hidden in the midst of a prehistoric era.

In that church, which has been many times renovated from its foundations, and which in the seventeenth century was despoiled of its marbles and of the ancient enamelled representation of the Blessed Virgin which was venerated there, we shall see an exceedingly interesting monument which may perhaps help us to reconstruct the past history of that building. It consists of a classical marble *cippus* adorned with the emblems of the worship of Cybele, used at a later time as a support for an altar. On that marble may be read an inscription of the eleventh century which records the dedication of the church performed by Hildebrand only a few months after he was raised to the Papacy.

Now, it is well known that the future Gregory VII had spent his early boyhood in the neighbouring palace of the Pierleoni, near S Nicolas *in Carcere*. Is there any connection between the wealthy family from which Hildebrand sprang, the rebuilding of the *titulus* of Sta Maria *in Portico*, and the enamelled picture which must from that time have adorned the marble top of the *tegurium* or canopy over the new altar?

These are questions which we have not time to discuss, but

we may remark that the dimensions of the highly venerated *ikon* of the ancient deaconry *in Porticu*, now preserved in the neighbouring church of Sta Maria *in Campitelli*, are far too small for the artist ever to have intended it originally for an altar in a public church. Therefore it was probably designed for a small oratory or private chapel, and in that case it appears most likely that it was the Christian family of the Pierleoni or Hildebrand himself who presented this family treasure to the newly-restored deaconry church of the *Porticus Gallatorum*.

The *ikon*, as a matter of fact, has many characteristics of the art of the eleventh century, the period in which Hildebrand lived. The trees which surround the Blessed Mother of God recall vividly that one sacred to Cybele, which is carved also on the *cippus* that was used as a support for the altar. Moreover the two heads of SS Peter and Paul, Paul on the right and Peter on the left, following the Roman custom, harmonise well with the spirit of Gregory VII, who, in his vigorous defence of the liberty of the Church, identified himself as it were with the two Princes of the Apostles, acting and speaking always in their name and by their authority.

If this hypothesis which we are now considering is true, then the charming legend must be abandoned which relates that the enamelled picture was brought in the fourth century by the hands of the angels themselves to Galla, daughter of Symmachus, but the value of the precious treasure, on the other hand, is increased, for it becomes connected with the memory of one of the greatest of the sons of Rome, of whom, alas! we have hardly any memorials, with the exception of a few personal objects which are preserved in his Abbey of St Paul.

We must now leave the *diaconia* of the *Porticus Gallatorum*, but before directing our steps towards the Capitol, let us spend a little more time by the Tiber, in order to see the other sanctuaries of our Lady, which are to be found scattered about there.

In the tenth century the *Arenula* and the *Scorticlaria* were regarded as localities in which the Lombard influence was paramount, being subject, as they were, to a great extent to the authority of the famous Abbey of Farfa in the *Sabina*. It is not surprising then, if those monks of Sancta Maria, as they proudly called themselves, should have spread and extended the *cultus* of their patron the Blessed Virgin also in their Roman dependencies.

Besides Sta Maria *in Monticelli*, we find in the neighbourhood of the Farfensian *prepositum* of San Salvatore *in domno Campo*, the churches of Sta Maria *in Cacabis*, Sta Maria in

Sanctuaries of the Blessed Virgin Mary

publicolis, Sta Maria *in Iulia*, and Sta Maria *de Cellis*. This last church, which is now part of the offices of the Senate, formed in the centre of the *Scorticlaria* a second source whence the monastic influence of Farfa was spread throughout the Eternal City.

The Church of Sta Maria *in Cacabis* took its name from the coppersmiths whose workshops were in that neighbourhood. Sta Maria *in Monticelli*, which was reconsecrated by Innocent II, still contains the relics of the martyrs Ninfa, Mamilian and Eustace.

Sta Maria *de Cellis* or *de Thermis* on the ruins of the Baths of Severus, near the palace of the Crescenzi, came into the possession of the monks of Farfa during the second half of the tenth century. The celebrated painter Antonazzo Romano was buried in this church.

The sanctuaries dedicated in the name of Mary at Rome are so numerous that they are like a closely woven network interlacing the whole city, and if we were desirous of enumerating them all, we should not find our task an easy one. But as it is so near Sta Maria *in Cellis* we are absolutely obliged to make mention of the church of Sta Maria *ad Martyres* or, as it is called in ancient documents, Sta Maria *Martyra*. The Rotunda of Agrippa, converted into a Christian church by Boniface IV, entered almost at once into competition with the *Apostoleion* of Narses at the foot of the Quirinal, so that it attained to the honour of having four solemn stations in the Roman Liturgy in the course of the year. These occurred in the Octave of Christmas, during the two weeks following Easter and Pentecost, and on the Sunday after the Ascension.

On this last occasion, during the papal Mass, showers of white rose leaves descended on the people from the circular opening in the centre of the dome, and the Pope, addressing them, explained that this was a symbol of the imminent coming of the Holy Ghost. In this church during the early Middle Ages there was preserved in a chest locked with thirteen keys, the famous Vatican *ikon* afterwards known as the *Veronica* or the *Volto Santo*.

Not far from the Pantheon are the churches of Sta Maria *sub Minervium* and the deaconry of Sta Maria *in Cyro*.

As to the first, it once belonged to the Greek nuns of Sta Maria *in Campo Marzio*, but in 1370 it was given over to the Dominican monks. There, beside the tomb of St Catherine of Siena, the following Popes sleep their last sleep: Urban VII, Paul IV, Leo X, Clement VI, and Benedict XIII, thus forming a little papal cemetery of their own.

Then, as to Sta Maria *in Aquiro*, we know that before the

time of Gregory III there existed in that place a *diaconia et parvum oratorium*, as the *Liber Pontificalis* tells us. The *diaconia*, or distributing centre for the poor, was originally quite distinct from the *parvum oratorium*, which was for domestic use and was almost entirely private, as must have been the case in all the deaconries, so much so that no titular presbyters were attached to them. It was only in the eighth century that the charitable institution of Sta Maria *in Cyro* lost its earlier character and became like other churches.

Such, too, must have been more or less the history of the not very distant *diaconia* of Sta Maria *in Xenodochio* founded by Belisarius on the Via Lata, *ob culpae veniam*, that is to say in atonement for the sacrilegious deposition of Pope Silverius, and the substitution of an antipope in the person of the intriguing deacon Vigilius. An inscription in Leonine verses on the exterior wall of the church still reminds passers-by of the expiatory act of the famous Byzantine general, and invites them to pray for the peace of his soul: *date obulum Belisario*.

Under the *collis ortorum*, where the Flaminian Way begins, a medieval legend told of evil spirits and devils that danced and capered with joy every night around the tomb of Nero. At length Paschal II resolved to purify the district, so he erected there an oratory dedicated to our Lady, which in the thirteenth century was transformed into the present vast edifice. In order to make it the more venerable, Gregory IX brought thither from the Lateran the picture of the Blessed Virgin which is now over the high altar. Pinturicchio, Caracci, Caravaggio, Fra Sebastiano del Piombo, Raphael, Sansovino, and others contributed by their genius to the decoration of this magnificent sanctuary of our Lady, so that it has become one of the most interesting monuments of Christian Rome.

Besides Sta Maria *del Popolo* two other churches dedicated to Mary adorn the great square which opens out within the Flaminian Gate: Sta Maria *de Monte Sancto* and Sta Maria *dei Miracoli*. This latter designation owes its origin to a miraculous picture of the Blessed Virgin which was painted in one of the internal arches of the city wall, near the Porta del Popolo, and which in 1325 was transferred to a small chapel. In process of time this simple oratory developed into the present graceful little church.

But it is now time to retrace our steps in order to return to the Capitoline Hill. Following the ancient Via Lata, we must leave on one side the Greek convent of the nuns of Sta Maria *in Campo Marzio*, which dates from the time of Pope Zachary. Nor can we stop before the deaconry of Sta Maria

Sanctuaries of the Blessed Virgin Mary 13

in Via Lata, constructed about the seventh century within the dilapidated porticos of the *septa Iulia*, where in the tenth century there arose a celebrated convent dedicated to St Cyriacus.

A little farther on—leaving behind us, for lack of time, the church of Sta Maria *in Augusta*, mentioned in the time of John IX—there arose Sta Maria *in Posterula* (Sta Maria dell' Orso) where there was originally venerated that most devotional Byzantine *ikon*, known by the name of Our Lady of Perpetual Succour, which is now preserved at St Alphonsus on the Esquiline.

In this way we soon arrive at the foot of the Capitoline, on which has stood since the ninth century at least the majestic Abbey of Sta Maria *in Capitolio*, passing in 1250 into the hands of the Minorites. These walls are full of historical associations, for within them have lived in turn Greek cenobites, Benedictines, Friars Minor, and, during the time of the Communes, the *Patres Conscripti* who held here their parliament.

We now cross the level ground of the triumphal hill of Rome to descend at once into the opposite valley of the Forum by means of the *clivus capitolinus*. At the foot of the hill we find another *diaconia* also dedicated to the Blessed Virgin and to the Eastern martyrs Sergius and Bacchus. The building consists of various oratories stretching from the western corner of the Julian Basilica to the Arch of Septimius Severus, which rises in front of the Senate.

A few steps farther on, beside the fountain of Juturna and the classical *statio aquarum*, we finally reach the *diaconia* of Sta Maria *Antiqua* erected towards the seventh century in a hall of the imperial palace itself. As we have already seen in the *Rione Elephantus* how Mary takes the Place of Cybele, so here too the Immaculate Virgin is a substitute for Vesta, whose shrine with the sacred fire and the Palladium stood beside the *Regia* close to the *atrium* of the *diaconia*.

Ancient legends told of the *Lacus Curtius* which was on this spot, and of chasms and dragons which swallowed up human victims. Now the evil beast Idolatry has been driven back into the infernal pit by Mary who is enthroned as Queen on the verge of the abyss, so that Satan shall never again raise his head: " *Cunctas haereses sola interemisti in universo mundo.*" This is the meaning of the picture of *Maria Regina*, which we see painted in the vestibule of the church, and in which she is clothed in robes sparkling with precious stones, crowned with a diadem, seated on a rich throne, and surrounded by a retinue of saints.

The *diaconia* of Sta Maria *Antiqua* cannot, however, lay

claim to any privilege arising from age over the other basilicas of our Lady at Rome, for it belongs to a relatively later period.

The importance of this building, besides the artistic treasures which it contains, is derived above all from the place where it stands, and from the special signification connected with that fateful spot. For there on the very site where for many centuries the Vestal Virgins fed the sacred flame, the symbol of the pagan State, Mary Immaculate now crushes the head of Vesta, Christianity conquers Idolatry and takes its place.

By an association of ideas, the mind goes back at once to the time of Pope Sylvester, and we understand how it was that by a logical chain of thought and an easily explained example of historical anticipation, the foundation of Sta Maria *Antiqua* was antedated in the Middle Ages, by at least two centuries, in order to attribute it to the great Sylvester, the reputed baptiser of Constantine. As in the picture of *Maria Regina* which we noted in the portico of the *diaconia*, so a number of ancient churches dedicated to saints surround that of Maria *Antiqua* which seem to mount guard with her over the *lacus leonum*, lest the savage beast of idolatry shall once more spring out from his den.

These sanctuaries which surround the Forum like a necklace are : Sta Maria *in foro*, SS Sergius and Bacchus, Sta Martina, St Adrian, St Lawrence *in Miranda*, SS Cosmas and Damian, and lastly, on the *summa Sacra Via*, Sta Maria *Nova*. This deaconry took the place of Sta Maria *Antiqua* in the time of Leo IV, when the latter church had become unfit for use on account of the damp, and the constant danger of being overwhelmed by landslides from the Palatine Hill.

Sta Maria *Nova* is now more commonly known by the name of Sta Francesca Romana, for it was there that the noble matron dedicated herself as an oblate of St Benedict, and there she desired to be buried.

This venerable basilica of the *Summa Sacra Via*, enriched by the possession of several bodies of martyrs, holds a special place in the papal Liturgy of the Middle Ages, because it was there on the night before the feast of the Assumption that the procession of the clergy and people of Rome stopped to wash with aromatic essences the feet of an ancient *ikon* of the Saviour and to sing the Matins of the festival.

A visit to Sta Maria *in Pallara* on the Palatine where Pope Gelasius II was elected, would be interesting but would take us too much out of our way ; for the same reason we must also refrain from going as far as the Coelian to visit the *diaconia* of Sta Maria *in Domnica* and the neighbouring

Sanctuaries of the Blessed Virgin Mary

monastery of St. Andrew *ad clivum Scauri*, where Gregory the Great became a monk.

In that sacred retreat of prayer under an ancient representation of Mary, the monks of the early Middle Ages reproduced the magnificent hymn by Andrew the Orator in honour of the Mother of God. As, however, the last verse of the poem referred to Rusticiana the daughter of Boethius, the good monks without disturbing themselves for so small a matter calmly adapted the verses *Invita Minerva* to suit their own purposes, so instead of the line:

Protegat ille tuum, Rusticiana, genus

they substituted:

Protegat ille tuum, Gregori Praesule, genus.

In order to reach the Esquiline without further delay we must leave behind us these ancient churches and keep to the direct road. Therefore, crossing the Forum near the Basilica of Antoninus and Faustina, where there was also a monastery in the early Middle Ages, we find ourselves in the Roman district of the *Carinae*, the name of which was preserved to us in the Middle Ages in the title of the church Sta Maria *in Carinis*, rather than in that of the modern Piazza *delle Carrette*.

In this neighbourhood, according to some archaeologists, must have stood the Oratory of Sta Maria *in monasterio de Lutara* mentioned in the life of Leo III, if this monastery was not, indeed, identical with that one entitled Sta Maria *in monasterio* which arose on the level ground of the Esquiline opposite the title of Eudoxia. The valley over which stretches the Roman Forum divides us from the fateful site of the *Roma quadrata* of Romulus which alone constituted the *inquilinus*. That which was outside this limit was *exquilinus* or foreign.

A few more steps on the Esquiline and we are at St Mary Major, but before entering we must stop at least for a minute or two at the neighbouring *titulus Praxedis*, in order to admire a beautiful chapel in honour of the Blessed Virgin. It owes its origin to Paschal I, who had it decorated with rich marbles and mosaics in memory of his mother, who was buried there.

From an inscription, we learn the name of the deceased lady: *domna Theodora*: but as she was the mother of the *episcopus*, she is styled *episcopa* as a title of honour, just as in other inscriptions where the wife of a presbyter, married, that is, before the elevation of her husband to Holy Orders, assumes the title of *presbytera*.

Now we have at last reached the Basilica of St Mary Major.

The history of the building is well known. The ancient hall of Sicininus was converted into a place of Christian worship under Pope Liberius, as is attested by Ammianus Marcellinus: *In basilica Sicinina, ubi ritus Christiani est conventiculus*. Later, however, Sixtus III caused it to be restored from the foundations, so that to this day it is possible to distinguish work of two different periods in the mosaics which adorn the triumphal arch and the lateral walls of the nave.

The principal arch belongs to the time of Sixtus III, whilst the pictures on the side appear older than that period, and perhaps did not even occupy the same place originally, for they are too high up to be seen distinctly by the people. They come probably from the Liberian edifice, if they did not indeed form part of the hall of Sicininus, which, in that case, may have been covered with small mosaic pictures, just as the neighbouring hall of Junius Bassus which afterwards became the Basilica of St Andrew, was incrusted with marble carvings representing mythological subjects.

That which for the moment chiefly attracts our attention, however, is not the Gospel story reproduced on the walls of the nave of the basilica, but the mosaic of the triumphal arch of Sixtus III, where we see depicted what may be described as an *Evangelium infantiae* of the divine Saviour. Such a subject was indeed well chosen for a basilica which took its name from the crib of Bethlehem and the Virgin *Theotokos*. But a special circumstance makes those ancient mosaics precious to us, for in them the artist shows himself to have been under the influence of the apocryphal Gospels, and particularly of the so-called *Protevangelium Jacobi*, or *Evangelium infantiae*.

Those who call to mind how rigorously the Roman Church guarded herself in early times from the acceptance of such legends—*apocrypha nescit ecclesia*, as St Jerome declared—will certainly be surprised that Sixtus III should show so much toleration towards the artist of the triumphal arch of the Liberian basilica. We do not know what the reason for this may have been, but we must note that it is not an isolated case, for just at that time the apocryphal writings found their way also into the Roman Liturgy and they have remained there to this day. It happened in a moment of surprise, as it were, when the enthusiasm of the Latins for the Byzantine churches which had defended so well the honour of the Mother of God at Ephesus, made them less distrustful of Oriental wares.

Let us examine these precious mosaics more closely. In the centre we see the customary *etimasia* or celestial throne prepared and adorned for the final *parousia* of Jesus, whilst at the sides Peter and Paul have already taken their places to act as assistants at the divine judgement. The lateral scenes are divided into four partitions so as to form nine small pictures in which, however, the artist has sacrificed the chronological sequence of the events to the symmetry of his squares.

First comes the Annunciation of the Blessed Virgin in the upper division on the left. Besides St Gabriel three other angels approach her reverently, eager to behold her and to greet her as their Queen. It is at once apparent here that the artist has wished his work to contain both exegetical and theological teaching. The four celestial messengers, therefore, come from that heavenly temple of God which is often mentioned in the ancient Liturgies. On the opposite side is another temple, the front of which is supported by two columns and crowned by a *tympanum*. It is the temple of Jerusalem before which—still in the same left-hand division—the priest Zachary also receives the message of the Archangel, announcing the birth of the Baptist.

The artist is obviously obsessed with the idea of symmetry. The division which we have described has a temple at each end, and on the other side he reproduces a third. This scene shows the Presentation of the Child Jesus in the Temple. The Virgin, accompanied by St Joseph and by two angels, comes forward with her divine Son in her arms towards a kind of portico supported by columns, where she is reverently met by the prophetess Anna, and the aged Simeon.

We note that the latter stretches out his arms underneath his *pænula* in order to receive the Saviour of the world with due respect—for in olden times those who received any sacred object, such as the Gospel, or a book of praise, and in the case of women also the Holy Communion, always had their hands covered with a cloth—whilst in front of the Temple, which closes the scene, there appears a group of priests who prepare to perform in the case of the Child Jesus all the rites prescribed by the Law for his Mother's purification.

Coming down now to the lower division we see, on the right, the wise men adoring Jesus. Here the artist abandons altogether the traditional Roman forms of the first three centuries and within a *domus* shows us Jesus already grown into a comely lad, seated on a throne furnished with a richly decorated footstool, and having an escort of four attendant angels by his side.

To the right and the left are seated, also on high thrones, two female figures—the Blessed Virgin and Salome, or according to others, the two churches *ex circumcisione et ex gentibus*—while from a city seen in the background of the picture come two Oriental figures, distinguished by the characteristic Phrygian cap, who approach our Lord.

The scene represented on the same level but on the opposite side of the arch is certainly taken from the *Protevangelium* of James, and the artist has intentionally connected it with that of the Adoration of the Magi. As the divine nature of the Babe of Bethlehem was recognised by these, so too his majesty was acknowledged by the Egyptians who adored him when he was an exile in the land of the Pharaohs. King Aphrodisius with a chosen band of courtiers comes forth from his capital and goes to meet Jesus, who, as in the scene with the Magi, is no longer an infant in swaddling clothes in his Mother's arms, but a gracious youth, clad in a tunic and walking along the sandy road of the desert. Mary and Joseph accompany him with the usual four attendant angels.

The desire for symmetry in the two scenes has caused the artist of the time of Sixtus III to sacrifice the chronological order of the events, but he comes back to it in the next division, where, however, we must study the pictures from left to right. First we see the Magi appearing before the Sanhedrim, presided over by Herod. The priests confer with one another in order to find out from the Scriptures where the Christ is to be born. It is decided that Bethlehem is the place, and Herod—who in deference to his royal rank is always represented with a *nimbus* like Justinian and Theodora in the mosaics of San Vitale at Ravenna—when sending forth the Magi bids them return to him at Jerusalem in order to give him an account of the result of their quest.

The jealous king awaits the return of the Wise men of the East in vain, wherefore, being filled with anger at having been deceived by them, he causes in the next scene on the right all the mothers of Bethlehem with their babies to be brought before him, and orders the massacre of the Innocents.

There is one peculiarity in the mosaics of St Mary Major. The artist, who probably came from the East and who took the legends of the so-called *Protevangelium* of James seriously, was evidently a lover of detail, and therefore pedantic and narrow. He altogether disregarded the solemn and majestic proportions of the building in which he was working, which required sober and simple themes, but such as were at the same time expressive of noble ideas on broad and powerful lines. Moreover, he has transferred to the lofty walls of the basilica the miniatures from an illuminated Missal which were his models, with the result that his pictures, hardly visible from the nave and aisles of the church, have not exercised any influence on later Roman art.

Sanctuaries of the Blessed Virgin Mary

It is well to draw attention to one characteristic of the triumphal arch of Sixtus III. The scenes here represented are not scenes chosen casually from the Gospels, but have especial reference to our Blessed Lady. In the mind of the Pope who caused them to be executed they form a kind of distant echo of the acclamations which had resounded a few years before at Ephesus, when Mary was saluted by the whole council of bishops with the title of *Theotokos* or *Deipara*, that is, Mother of God.

If it were possible for any doubt on this subject to arise, the well-known epigraph of Sixtus III in commemoration of the work accomplished would suffice to dispel it:

> *Virgo Maria, tibi Xystus nova tecta dicavi*
> *Digna salutifero munera ventre tuo.*
> *Te Genitrix ignara viri, te denique foeta,*
> *Visceribus salvis, edita nostra salus.*
> *Ecce tui testes uteri sibi praemia portant,*
> *Sub pedibus iacet passio cuique sua.*
> *Ferrum, flamma, ferae, fluvius saevumque venenum,*
> *Tot tamen has mortes una corona manet.*

The great work of Sixtus III, therefore, included besides the triumphal arch the vault of the apse which is now covered by the mosaics of Nicholas IV. Originally the central position must have been occupied by the picture of the Blessed Virgin with the divine Infant, to whom a succession of martyrs presented their crowns according to the description in the Apocalypse. There was, however, one special point to be noticed. As is well known, ancient Roman art, less so that of the East, shunned that severe realism which has found so much favour in our day. It had therefore a great aversion from representing the martyrs in the midst of their sufferings or with the instruments of their tortures. In the concave of the apse of St Mary Major under each martyr:

> *Sub pedibus iacet passio cuique sua.*

We do not know which nor how many were these *tui testes uteri*, as Sixtus III translates in Latin form the Greek name of martyr, but we may perhaps guess them by their respective symbols:

> *Ferrum, flamma, ferae, fluvius, saevumque venenum.*

There were, then, four or at most five figures, amongst whom may have been Matthias with the poison swallowed by him, Sixtus II with a sword, Lawrence with a fiery gridiron, Ignatius of Antioch with the lions, and Clement who was cast into the sea.

Surroundings so full of devotion to Mary and so magnificently ornamented seemed, in the Middle Ages, to be the place best suited to the celebration of the solemn festivals in the liturgical cycle in honour of Mary. The *Ordines Romani*, in fact, describe them for us with every particular.

How and when the four original feasts of the Blessed Virgin —those of her Nativity, of the Annunciation, Purification, and Falling asleep—first formed part of the Roman Liturgy is still uncertain. They already existed in the time of Sergius I (687–701), who, Oriental as he was, desired to surround them with the greatest splendour, and ordered therefore that on these days a great torchlight procession should go either at night or in the early morning from St Adrian *al Foro* to St Mary Major.

The meeting place was the ancient senatorial hall, which, still adorned with rich marbles, stood untouched before the famous *rostra* of Cicero. The night preceding the feast of the Assumption was, however, an exception to the rule. As on that occasion the vigil was celebrated in the Liberian basilica, so in order to make the nocturnal procession more imposing, the cortège returned from the Esquiline to the Lateran where the cardinals brought out the celebrated picture of the Saviour which was usually kept in the Oratory of St Lawrence.

The procession was then reformed. The seven cross-bearers took their places among the people, each one raising aloft his processional cross. At short intervals there followed eighteen deacons carrying in their arms as many *ikons* of the Blessed Virgin from amongst the most ancient of the city. Then followed an interminable crowd of the faithful and of the clergy, singing psalms, often walking barefooted and wearing mournful-looking black *pænulas* as a sign of penitence.

When the procession reached St Mary Major the dawn of our Lady's feast was fast approaching, and the first rays of the rising sun were about to kiss the face of the Virgin in the mosaic of Sixtus III. At the foot of that gracious picture lighted up and transfigured by the renascent day-star, was offered the eucharistic sacrifice, during which the people of Rome received from a golden chalice held by the deacon that precious blood of redemption which Christ had drawn from the heart of Mary.

This is indeed the result of the devotion to Mary which has spread from Rome through the whole world by the labours of the Popes and of the missionaries, together with the faith preached by the holy Apostles. Already in the second century Bishop Abercius of Geropolis united these two devotions, that of the Eucharist and that of Mary, when on his sepulchral *stele* he spoke of the divine 'ΙΧΘΥΣ which is caught by the chaste Virgin, who serves it up to her friends, offering them wine at the same time. When, therefore, in Holy Communion we receive the blood of God made man, that blood brings us into closer relationship, so to speak, with the Blessed Virgin who was the fount and source from which it was drawn.

At that solemn moment Mary recognises in us something which belongs to her. We become her sons then in the most perfect and highest sense of the word, for it is her own blood which flows in our veins.

CHAPTER II

THE PORTRAITS OF THE BLESSED VIRGIN MARY VENERATED AT ROME

ROME possesses a number of pictures of the Mother of God, which, without claiming to be true portraits, are proofs that this devotion dates from the time of the Apostles. As, according to the early Fathers, we do not possess a real likeness of Jesus Christ, so, too, we have none of Mary who, even outwardly, must have very greatly resembled Jesus, and have been endowed with great beauty as befitted a masterpiece of the Holy Ghost.

It may have been that the same sense of the impossibility of conveying in a painting the reflection of the Godhead in the countenance of the Saviour, also prevented any painter from attempting to portray the virginal features of Mary, so that we have in Rome from the first years of the second century, only imaginary representations of her.

The earliest of these portraits is certainly that in the catacombs of Priscilla, in which a star shines above the head of the divine Infant, and which may go back to the beginning of the second century. She who is blessed amongst women has a veil upon her head and is seated full of dignity on a throne, whilst the prophet or the wise man, wearing a pallium, stands respectfully before her. The little Child whom his Mother appears about to suckle, turns his back upon the robed figure of the seer, so that the latter is addressing not Jesus, but Mary, who in the intention of the artist was therefore to be the central figure of the picture.

Another painting of our Blessed Lady, which is to be found in the cemetery of Domitilla, is worthy of mention. The picture dates from the third century, and represents the Wise Men, who, four in number, advance towards the Blessed Virgin bearing gifts. Here, too, Mary is veiled as a mark of her maternal dignity. She is seated in majesty upon a throne and instead of clasping the holy Child to her breast, she holds him upon her knee.

We must also note a third portrait of the Blessed Virgin, painted on an *arcosolium* in the *coemeterium maius* on the

Via Nomentana. This work seems to belong to the first half of the fourth century and represents the Virgin, who, veiled and adorned with a necklace of pearls, is in an attitude of prayer before her divine Son, *Advocata nostra*.

In order that there should be no doubt of the scene represented being a religious one, the artist has added two Constantinian monograms, one on the right and the other on the left of the Saviour, indeed the P on the left has the curve or loop inclined towards the central figure as though to indicate that it really does represent Christ.

We have already spoken of the picture of the Mother of God on the tomb of *Turtura* in the cemetery of Commodilla. That portrait of *Maria Regina* is of the fourth century and is important not only from the artistic point of view, but because the painter, in order to express the great dignity of our Blessed Lady, has surrounded her with such symbols of pre-eminence and veneration that there can be no manner of doubt concerning the thought which inspired him. The throne with the footstool, the consular *mappula*, the central place in the picture, the two saints on the right and on the left, both of them standing, all bear witness to the greatness of her regal dignity.

It is quite evident that the generation for whom the painter of *Turtura* executed his picture was accustomed to venerate the Blessed Virgin as Queen of the Saints, and advocate of men before the tribunal of her divine Son.

In the cemetery of St Valentine on the Via Flaminia we find another picture of Mary. In the historical crypt of the famous martyr, at the back of a small niche may be seen our Lady with the Child Jesus at her breast. Her head is surrounded by a circular *nimbus*, whilst her divine Son has a halo in the shape of a cross, which is a veiled symbol in his crucifixion. The work seems to be of the time of Honorius I (625–638), and may be regarded as the last representation of the Blessed Virgin in the Roman catacombs.

After the subterranean cemeteries come the mosaics of the churches dedicated to Mary at Rome. We have already mentioned those of Sta Maria *in Trastevere*, and of the Liberian Basilica, with the dedicatory inscription of Sixtus III ; we now notice those no less celebrated of the Vatican Oratory of John VII, which at present are scattered, some of them being in the crypt of St Peter's, some at Sta Maria *in Cosmedin*, and others even at San Marco in Florence. The figure of Mary which we find in the apse of the Oratory of St Venantius *in Laterano*, in that of the *titulus de fasciola*, of Sta Maria *in Domnica* and of Sta Maria *Nova*, is also worthy of mention.

The mosaic of St Venantius was executed under the

Dalmatian Pope John IV (640–642). In it the Virgin, robed in a *pænula*, and in the attitude of an " orante " occupies the chief post of honour in the centre of a band of eight other saints.

We see on the vaulting of the apse in the *titulus de fasciola* dating from the ninth century the same Eastern influence of the *Protevangelium Jacobi*, just as in St Mary Major. Indeed in this church of the Via Appia the central scene is that of the Transfiguration, as in Justinian's Basilica on Sinai, whilst on either side we find a representation of the Blessed Virgin. In the one on the right our Lady is seated in a chair working with her needle, when the Archangel Gabriel appears before her and announces to her the mystery of the Incarnation of the Word. In that on the left this mystery has already taken place, for we see the Virgin again with the Child Jesus in her arms whilst Gabriel stands reverently at her side.

The mosaic at Sta Maria *in Domnica* is only of the ninth century. In the centre of the apsidal vaulting the Blessed Virgin appears with the *mappula* in her hand and the Infant Jesus on her lap. At her feet, but on a smaller scale in order to imply humble subjection, we see Pope Paschal I, who on his knees dedicates to her the works carried out by him in this church.

VIRGO · MARIA · TIBI · PASCHALIS · PRAESVL · HONESTVS
CONDIDIT · HANC · AVLAM · LAETVS · PER · SAECLA
MANENDAM

The Mosaic of Sta Maria *Nova* is later, for it possibly only goes back to the time of Alexander III.

It recalls to some extent that of Sta Maria *in Trastevere*, for here, too, in the *summa sacra via* Mary, full of dignity and majesty, is seated on her throne of glory and clasps in her arms that Child who is the Master of the Apostles Peter, Andrew, James and John, who stand around her to do her honour.

Under this picture the following lines might once be read:

CONTINET · IN · GREMIO · CAELVM · TERRAMQVE · REGENTEM
VIRGO · DEI · GENITRIX · PROCERES · COMITANTVR

The Roman Churches contain several *ikons* of the Blessed Virgin of the so-called Byzantine type, some of which are said to date back to the time of St Gregory the Great, if not actually to St Luke himself and the age of the Apostles.

The fact, however, remains that originally pictures and *ikons* did not form part of the liturgical ornaments of the Roman basilicas. These were indeed decorated, as we have seen, by paintings and mosaics upon the walls, but in those days when a feeling opposed to the idolatry of the past was still very strong, sacred pictures were placed in the apse and on the walls of the holy place more by way of decoration and for the instruction of the unlearned than as objects of direct veneration. This preventive measure taken by the Church was necessary at that time lest the new converts to the Faith who had only lately been rescued from paganism should slip back into idolatry through veneration of sacred paintings.

Therefore the ancient basilicas had their altar isolated in the centre of the *bema*, under the vaulting of the apse, and the priest when offering the holy sacrifice did not face some sacred painting attached to the wall, as he does now, but faced the assembly of the people who thronged the three, or sometimes five, aisles of the hall. When, however, towards the seventh century, it became the custom to celebrate several Masses each day in the same church, these were said at different altars which were therefore placed against the walls in the side aisles. These walls had been already decorated with pictures of the saints, and thus it was that the priest began to have before him when he offered the holy sacrifice a sacred *ikon*, not as yet moveable, but fixed to the spot, which in that form came to be regarded as part of the official furniture of a Christian altar.

Having, then, shown that moveable pictures and *ikons* must not be regarded as forming part of the liturgical ornaments of the Roman basilicas in the early Middle Ages, we must now endeavour to ascertain at what subsequent period of distinctly Byzantine influence such pictures were introduced into the Roman churches. Already under Sixtus III we find in the Lateran baptistery a group representing the Lamb of God, the Saviour and St John the Baptist in pure gold. According to the *Liber Pontificalis* Gregory III covered with silver the cross-beam of the *pergula* that separated from the nave the Vatican *Confessio* of St Peter's, on which he caused to be represented on one side the Saviour with the Apostles, and on the other the Blessed Mother of God between two rows of holy virgins.

Long before the Pontificate of Stephen II there were to be seen in front of the altar of St Mary Major two pictures representing on a groundwork of silver, the Mother of God. This Pope had a third one made on a sheet of purest gold, which according to the custom of the time in the East, he caused to be decorated with pearls, jacinth, and emeralds. The picture represented the Blessed Virgin with the Child Jesus on his Mother's knees.

In the same Liberian basilica Adrian I had the altar-stone

covered with a cloth of woven gold adorned with jewels, and on it was embroidered a representation of the Assumption of our Lady into heaven.

As a rule almost all the donations of a liturgical nature given by the Popes to the Roman basilicas between the seventh and the ninth centuries take the form of pictures painted on plates of gold or silver, or of vessels of goldsmith's work and hangings on which were embroidered sacred scenes. Judging by the catalogues of the *Liber Pontificalis* the art of needlework must have been held in great esteem at Rome at that time, but no mention is made of pictures or *ikons*.

Yet paintings on wood cannot have been altogether unknown in the Eternal City. They did not, it is true, form part of the liturgical furnishings, and because of this they are rarely mentioned in the *Liber Pontificalis*, but they certainly existed, and we have an indication of this, not only in the hymn of Andrew the Orator to Rusticiana already quoted, but also in the history of the mission of St Augustine and the forty Roman monks to England. When they first landed on British soil they formed themselves in procession and advanced, preceded by a silver cross and a picture with the representation of the Saviour.

In the life of St Benedict Biscop too, it is related that on each of the four occasions when he, like a true Anglo-Saxon, journeyed from England to Rome, he always returned with a large number of codices, relics and sacred pictures which were evidently paintings. This occurred about the middle of the seventh century when the war of the Iconoclasts was already about to break out in the East.

Moveable *ikons*, unlike the biblical and hagiographical representations painted, or executed in mosaic, on the walls of the basilicas, were according to Roman usage chiefly venerated in private houses or were carried triumphantly in solemn processions as had once been done with the portraits of the Emperor. It is therefore easy to understand that the greater number of these paintings must have represented the Saviour or his Blessed Mother.

We have already spoken of the two pictures of the Redeemer and of our Lady which were carried in procession on the night preceding the feast of the Assumption. The *Ordo Romanus* of Benedict the Canon relates that in the twelfth century, on the feasts of the Purification and of the Annunciation, not merely two, but as many as eighteen sacred pictures were carried in the procession by the deacons between lighted double candles. These pictures are precisely those ancient *ikons* of the Blessed Virgin which are still preserved in many Roman basilicas, and around which many pious legends have grown up.

Some of these paintings are attributed in good faith to the time of Gregory the Great, and it is even asserted that they used to be carried processionally in the famous *litania septiformis* itself, which that holy Pope commanded to be held at the beginning of his Pontificate in order to obtain the cessation of the plague. It is said that when the procession arrived at the bridge before the mausoleum of Hadrian, a group of angels descended from heaven to salute the blessed effigy of the Mother of God, chanting the Antiphon: *Regina coeli, laetare*, etc. St Gregory listening to the celestial choir learnt from them that beautiful hymn to our Lady, and added to it the last hemistich: *Ora pro nobis Deum. Alleluia.* Hence the friars of *Ara Coeli* and one of the other Roman basilicas obtained the privilege of singing the *Regina Coeli* when the papal procession passed over the Ælian Bridge.

It is not improbable that during the Iconoclastic persecution many sacred images were brought from the East and placed in safety in Italy and especially at Rome. This would explain the great number of Byzantine images of the Blessed Virgin which exist in the Eternal City, although not all of these date back to the eighth century, for the relations between the Italian and the Greek artists were friendly during the whole of the Middle Ages, so much so that all art in Italy before Cimabue and Giotto is commonly known as Byzantine.

The *Liber Pontificalis* tells us of the arrival at Rome about the year 854 of Lazzarus, monk and confessor, *picturiae artis nimirum eruditum*, Legate of the Emperor Michael Porphyrogenitus, with a great quantity of gifts. Another embassy from Constantinople reached Rome in the time of Nicholas I, sent by the same Emperor, and once more treasures of Oriental jewellery and embroideries went to enrich the sacristies of the Lateran and of St Peter's. In this latter basilica there is still preserved a sacred *ikon* representing the Saviour between the two Princes of the Apostles, which was presented in the ninth century by SS Cyril and Methodius, the Apostles of the Slavs.

A list of these Greek or Byzantine *ikons* existing in Rome would be too long, since we find them almost everywhere: for instance at San Domenico e Sisto, St Mary Major, St Boniface on the Aventine, at Ara Coeli, SS Cosmas and Damian in the Forum, Sta Maria *Nova*, St Alphonsus on the Esquiline, at Sta Maria dell'Itria, Sta Maria in Cosmedin, Sta Maria del Popolo, at Sta Maria in Campo Marzio, St Lawrence in Damaso, St Augustine, and at San Francesco a

Ripa. Others, such as the *Mater Domini* in the Basilica of St Paul, the *ikon* of Sta Maria in Cosmedin, that of Sta Maria in Aquiro, etc., seem to be of local workmanship, and belong to the period between the thirteenth and the fifteenth century.

One entry which we find in an early list of the Roman churches of the seventh century is remarkable : *Basilica quae appellatur sancta Maria Transtiberis, ibi et imago sanctae Mariae quae per se facta est.*

We know from Pietro Mallio that in his time, that is to say in the thirteenth century, lamps were kept perpetually burning in the Vatican Basilica *ante imaginem beatae Mariae quae est de mosibo, post Veronicam . . . ad sanctam Mariam de cancellis . . . in sancta Maria in Oratorio . . .* Hence we have here three distinct shrines of our Lady besides that of Sta Maris *de Turre* which was in the atrium of the church.

The *Mater Domini* in the Ostian Basilica also *est de mosibo*, that is, in mosaic and goes back perhaps to the time of Honorius III. It was before this image that on April 22, 1541, St Ignatius of Loyola and his first companions pronounced their solemn vows, and that the holy founder was elected to be the first general of the new Society of Jesus.

Not a few of these venerated effigies have been crowned with a golden crown by the Vatican Chapter. The origin of this pious custom dates back to the time of Count Alessandro Sforza, who in his testament of July 3, 1636, left his property to the Canons of St Peter on condition that they should place golden crowns upon those images of the Blessed Virgin which were the most renowned for their antiquity and for the miracles wrought through them. The first to receive a crown was the so-called *Madonna della febbre*, which from the ancient Basilica of St Peter had been translated after many changes to the *secretarium* to the " grotte vecchie," and to the Chapel of the Holy Column, and finally, under Pius VI, had found a definite resting place in the new sacristy of the Chapter.

But previous to the pious legacy of Sforza, Clement VIII had already crowned with a jewelled diadem the celebrated image of the Virgin which is so greatly honoured at St Mary Major, in the Borghese Chapel. And because afterwards, on one of the various occasions when that basilica had been sacked, this crown was stolen, Gregory XVI in 1837, in reparation for the outrage, with great solemnity placed a new diadem on the forehead of the Mother of God.

Pius IX on December 8, 1854, on the occasion of the proclamation of the dogma of the Immaculate Conception, followed his example and crowned the effigy of Mary Immaculate which is venerated in the choir of St Peter. Fifty years

The Portraits of the Blessed Virgin Mary

later, under Pius X, during the magnificent festivities which were being celebrated at Rome in commemoration of that great event, the crown given by Pius IX was wholly adorned with precious stones.

On July 9, 1796, a rumour spread throughout Rome that several of the sacred images of the Blessed Virgin in the churches and streets of the city had been seen to move their eyes and even in some cases to shed tears, as a sign of great grief and as a portent of coming disasters.

These wonders continued to occur until the month of January in the following year, so the ecclesiastical authorities had plenty of time during which to examine closely into them. Pius VI was so deeply impressed that he at once declared special fasts and penitential processions, and had missions preached in six of the principal open spaces of Rome.

From the legal documents we learn that the wonders were proved to be genuine in the following instances:

The Madonna dell' Archetto.
Our Lady of Sorrows in the Chiesa degli Agonizzanti.
The Madonna in the Vicolo delle Muratte.
Our Lady of Sorrows near Sant' Andrea delle Fratte.
Mary Immaculate in Sant' Andrea dei Lorenesi.
Our Lady of Sorrows near the Chiesa Nuova.
Mary Immaculate in San Silvestro *in Capite*.
Our Lady of the Assumption in the Chiesa Nuova.
Sta Maria delle Grazie in the old church of the Hospital della Consolazione.
Our Lady of Mount Carmel in San Martino.
The Madonna in the Piazza dell' Olmo.
The Madonna under the Arch of Grottapinta.
Our Lady of the Rosary at the Arch of the Ciambella.
Our Lady of Sorrows in Piazza Madonna.
The Madonna of Guadeloupe in San Nicola in Carcere.
Our Lady of Sorrows at the corner of Piazza del Gesù.

The ninth of July, the anniversary of the miracle, was appointed as a special feast, called *prodigiorum B. Mariae Virginis*, in memory of the marvellous event.

On January 20, 1842, Alphonse Ratisbonne, a Jew, happened by chance to be standing before the altar of Mary Immaculate in the church of Sant' Andrea delle Fratte, when the Blessed Virgin appeared to him, all radiant with light which illuminated his soul, and he was immediately converted to the Faith. The Vatican Chapter in 1892 girded the forehead of the venerated figure with a golden crown.

There was a time when Protestant heresy declared that

Catholic devotion to the Mother of God was a corruption of the Christian Faith which only began in the Middle Ages. The Mother Church, that of Rome, answers in the name of all, and by merely indicating the memorials to Mary which we have here passed in review, gives the history of the veneration shown by all generations towards her, the new Eve, whom Christ upon the cross presented to the whole human race with the words: *Ecce Mater tua*.

We have seen in Rome proofs of this filial affection towards the Madonna in the miraculous pictures of July 9, 1796, and in that which converted Ratisbonne. But this devotion is expressed artistically in exactly the same way in the long series of images of our Lady of the Renaissance, in the so-called Byzantine *ikons*, in the mosaics of the early Middle Ages, and finally in the paintings of the catacombs, until we come to that of Priscilla which at the latest may belong to the first half of the second century. The generation which first saw that Madonna with the star above her head was the same one or at least the offspring of that which had known John under that same roof, which had heard Paul preach, which had received baptism from Peter, and had been witness to the living torches of Nero in the Vatican Gardens. Farther back than the favourite disciple, beyond Peter and Paul, we can find only the Blessed Mother of God herself and only Christ our author, our teacher and the object of our holy Faith.

CHAPTER III

THE FESTIVAL OF THE ASSUMPTION INTO HEAVEN OF THE BLESSED VIRGIN MARY IN THE ANCIENT ROMAN LITURGY

THE feast of the "Dormition" or Assumption of the Mother of God into heaven is probably the most ancient of all the feasts of Mary, since, long before the Councils of Chalcedon and Ephesus, it appears to have been commonly and widely celebrated, not only among Catholics, but also among the schismatical sects and the very ancient national Churches such as the Armenian and the Ethiopian.

It is probable that the dedication in Rome itself of the Basilica *maior* of the Blessed Virgin on the Esquiline on August 5, in the time of Pope Liberius (352–66), or in that of Sixtus III, had some connection with the feast of the Assumption, which, even if it was kept in the Gallican rite on January 18, and in that of the Copts on January 16, yet it was celebrated by the Byzantines in the middle of the month of August, on a date which the Emperor Maurice fixed definitely in the time of St Gregory the Great.

Whatever may have been the origin of its introduction, it is certain that the festival was kept at Rome long before the Pontificate of Pope Sergius, for, as we have already said, this Pontiff, in order to surround it with greater splendour, ordained that a solemn procession should take place every year on this occasion, starting from the Basilica of St Adriano *sul Foro*, and proceeding to St Mary Major, where the Pope celebrated the stational Mass.

He also prescribed that the same ceremony should take place on the Purification, the Nativity, and the Annunciation of the Mother of God, and in this he was probably influenced by the custom of the Byzantines, who had already been keeping these festivals for several centuries.

Leo IV, about the year 847, ordered that the feast of the Assumption should be preceded at Rome by a solemn vigil, to be kept by the clergy and the people in the Basilica of St

Mary Major, and he also appointed that on the day of the Octave the station should be celebrated outside the Porta Tiburtina in the Basilica *Maior* dedicated to the Blessed Virgin, which had been built by Pope Sixtus III in front of the apse of the Constantinian Church of St Lawrence.

The order of the solemn stational procession introduced in the time of Sergius I is still known to us. Early in the morning, the people, carrying lighted candles and to the singing of antiphons and of solemn litanies, went in procession to the Church of St Adrian, where they awaited the coming of the Pontiff. As soon as he had arrived, having come on horseback from the Lateran, both he and his seven deacons exchanged their usual garments for sombre penitential *pœnulas*, and the procession set off.

First walked seven crossbearers with their crosses, the people followed praying aloud, then came the clergy attached to the palace with the Pope escorted by two acolytes, carrying candelabra with lighted torches according to the Roman imperial custom. A subdeacon came next, swinging a thurible with incense, then two more crossbearers the one behind the other, each bearing a precious stational cross, and finally the procession was closed by the *schola* of the choir, composed of the boys of the Orphanage, who sang alternately with the clergy the antiphons and litanies appropriate to the occasion.

When this interminable procession at length reached St Mary Major at the break of dawn, the Pope with his deacons withdrew to the *secretarium* in order to change their garments and prepare for the celebration of the Mass, while the rest of the clergy together with the people, humbly prostrate before the altar, as is still the custom on Holy Saturday, sang for the third time the Litany *ternaria* of the Saints, that is to say each invocation was repeated three times.

In course of time this vigiliary ceremony, comprising nocturnal processions with crosses, candles and antiphons, which is so different from the customary Roman *pannuchis* and which consequently at once betrays its Eastern origin, developed very considerably and became one of the most characteristic ceremonies of medieval Rome. In the tenth century the Pope, together with the College of Cardinals, on the morning of the Vigil of the Assumption, went barefooted to the Oratory of San Lorenzo, now called *Sancta Sanctorum*, at the Lateran, where among other relics was preserved the ancient likeness of the Saviour which was said to have been formerly rescued from the fury of the Iconoclasts at Constantinople.

This picture was greatly venerated at Rome, so the Pontiff,

before opening the doors of the tabernacle in which it was kept, made seven genuflections before it, as did all those present. On the appearance of the sacred effigy, the *Te Deum* was intoned in accordance with an ordinance of St Leo IV; the Pope then went up to the platform which had been erected for this purpose. He first kissed the feet of the Saviour and then laid the picture down on the altar itself.

In the afternoon all the higher clergy of the Lateran Patriarchate together with the Pontiff repaired to St Mary Major to celebrate vespers, after which they sat down to a frugal meal, which was the only refection allowed on that day of rigorous fasting. The abstemious repast ended at sunset and the palatine clergy retired to take a short rest in the rooms of the adjoining palace.

At cock-crow the Pope and his clergy were again up and about, and returned to the basilica, which had been magnificently illuminated and adorned with hangings, in order to celebrate the vigiliary Office in the presence of the immense concourse of people. This Office, according to the Roman custom on greater festivals, consisted in a double service of Matins followed by the usual laudatory psalms which were to be sung at daybreak. The holy Sacrifice brought this lengthy ceremony to an end.

In the eleventh century this rite had undergone some alterations. It was the Cardinals, then, who, as it grew dark on August 14, went to fetch the picture of the Saviour from the Chapel of St Lawrence in the *Sancta Sanctorum*, and escort it in triumph through the great square which in those days stretched away in front of the palace of the Lateran Patriarchate.

Twelve *ostiarii* carrying lighted candles accompanied the sacred effigy, the subdeacon of the *regio* followed with the stational cross; next came the clergy attached to the palace, the *Primicerius* with the *schola* of the choristers, the Prefect of the City with a deputation of twelve members of the municipal council, and finally an innumerable gathering of people, who, abandoning that night the streets of the City, flocked to the Lateran.

From there the procession moved towards the Basilica of Sta Maria *Nuova* near the Vià Sacra in the Forum, where the titular feast of the church was also being celebrated. It must indeed have been a sight worthy of the Eternal City, to see on that brilliant August morning as the rising sun was gilding the Alban Hills the triumphal procession of the Redeemer and his Church pass along the same road, under the same arches of victory, beside those porticos and ancient amphitheatres called after Titus, Domitian, and Vespasian, which recalled the memories of three centuries of persecution and of blood generously shed in the confessing of Christ.

The greatly valued picture of the divine Redeemer was temporarily placed under the portico of Sta Maria *Nuova*, where the clergy as an act of veneration sprinkled the feet of the Saviour with perfumes made from the herb sweet basil. Then the *schola* of the choristers entered the church and the morning Office began, whilst the faithful, instead of waiting inactively until the singing of the psalms was finished, took momentary possession of the sacred effigy and carried it off in their arms amid the singing of psalms and hymns of thanksgiving to the neighbouring Basilica of St Adrian. There the ceremony of bathing the feet of the Saviour with perfumes was repeated, until at the conclusion of Matins the procession was formed once more in order to go this time to the Basilica of St Mary Major, where the stational Mass of the Assumption of the Blessed Virgin Mary was celebrated.

In the tenth century the history of imperial Rome had been strangely distorted by popular fancy, and in all those majestic marble remains of ancient monuments which then encumbered the Capitol and the neighbourhood of the Forum of the Emperors, the imagination of the masses beheld only the fearful abodes of basilisks and dragons which once poisoned with their tainted breath alone those persons rash enough merely to pass by.

The lively faith of the Middle Ages therefore felt the necessity of asserting itself resolutely before those trophies which recalled the diabolical reign of the idolatry of imperial Rome, hence the Roman rituals of the eleventh and twelfth centuries prescribed that the procession should pass before the so-called arch of Latona and before the *domus Orphei*, the ancient fountain adorned with the statue of the Thracian poet, expressly so that the Roman people might be delivered from satanic molestations through the supplications of so many of the faithful and the intercession of the great Mother of God.

The procession having at length reached St Mary Major after a night full of such appealing emotions, the Pope celebrated the stational Mass and gave his blessing to the people who by this time were tired out with fasting and watching. This was the reason why, following the early Roman rite, the second vespers were not recited on the afternoon of solemn feasts with the exception of Easter, but were left exclusively to the devotion of the monks in their monasteries. It was only later on, when, that is, the night vigils had fallen into disuse, that the Roman rite eventually adopted the recitation

The Festival of the Assumption

of second vespers, and even then the Pope did not as a rule take part in them.

In order to complete this picture of the Assumption in medieval Rome, we give here a hymn dating from the early eleventh century, which describes the solemn vigil of the Romans in honour of the Assumption of the Blessed Virgin.

It is important because it supplies some details omitted by the *Ordines Romani* themselves. This text is taken from a miscellaneous collection at Monte Cassino of the same century.[1]

Incipit Carmen in Assumptione Sanctae Mariae.	Hymn for the Assumption of the Blessed Virgin Mary
In nocte, quando Tabula portatur.	In the night when the *ikon* is carried in triumph.
1.	**1.**
Sancta Maria quid est? si caeli climata scandis? *Esto benigna tuis. Sancta Maria quid est?*	O holy Mary, dost thou ascend to the highest heaven? Be gracious to thy children, O holy Mary!
2.	**2.**
Unde fremit populus? Vel (cur) vexilla coruscant? *Quid sibi vult strepitus? Unde fremit populus?*	Why do the people rejoice? Why do the banners wave? Why is this noise made? Why do the people rejoice?
3.	**3.**
Quare volant (f)aculae? Luce(nt)[2] per strata coronae. *Luminas columna? Quare volant faculae? e*	Why are these torches borne along? Why do these poles crowned with lights illuminate the streets? Why are these torches borne along?
4.	**4.**
Astra nitent radiis. Rutilant et tecta lanternis, *Cuncta rubent flammis. Astra nitent radiis.*	The brilliance of the lamps dispels the darkness of the sky. The roofs of the houses gleam with lanterns. Everything is reddened by the glow of the torches, the lamps dispel the darkness of the sky.
5.	**5.**
Edita consulibus, numerasti, Roma, triumphos, *Signa moves planctus, edita consulibus.*	O Rome, daughter of Consuls, thou hast numbered many triumphs, Now art thou about to weep, O Rome, daughter of Consuls.

[1] Cod. 451, folio 318.
[2] The additions in ( ) are written by a contemporary corrector.

<table>
<tr><td>

6.
Quae tibi causa mali ? felix, O gloria mundi.
Cur manant oculis ? Quae tibi causa mali ?

7.
Plaude, parens patria, r(or)antia lumina terge,
Spem retinens veniae. Plaude, parens patria.

8.
Martyrii praetio, cecidit si prima propago,
Stas renovata modo Martyrii praetio.

9.
Limina primus adit, silvis digressus arator,
Nunc tua Piscator limina primus adit.

10.
Pulvere multiplici crines foedaverat ille,
Hic te mundat aquis pulvere multiplici.

11.
Paulus ovile tuum pascens, educit aquatum
Atque refert stabulis Paulus ovile tuum.

Respondet Roma.

1.
Quid memoras titulos ? aut cur insignia prisca
Obicis in vultum ? Quid memoras titulos ?

2.
Enitui facie. Toto memorabilis orbe
Callida, sed vulpes. Enitui facie.

3.
In mediis opibus, meretrix nocturna cucullos
Indui prostituens, in mediis opibus.

</td><td>

6.
What is the cause of thy woe, radiant splendour of the world ?
Why do thine eyes shed tears, what is the cause of thy woe ?

7.
Rejoice, O Mother-City, and wipe the tears from thine eyes.
Thou mayest surely hope for thy sins' forgiveness, O Mother-City, rejoice.

8.
If by a martyrdom thy children were once taken from thee,
Thou dost arise again to new life through a martyrdom.

9.
Thy threshold was first crossed by the uncultured ploughman,
Now is the Fisherman the first to cross thy threshold.

10.
Low in the dust the former bowed thy head,
The latter with cleansing water bathes thee bowed low in the dust.

11.
Shepherded by Paul thy flock to the spring is led,
Then returning home to the fold, it still is shepherded by Paul.

Rome replies.

1.
Why recall my triumphs ? why cast in my face
My former glories ? why recall my triumphs ?

2.
I painted my face, I became famous throughout the world,
And like a cunning fox, I painted my face.

3.
In the midst of wealth I put on the cloak of the shameless[1]
And abandoned woman in the night, in the midst of wealth.

</td></tr>
</table>

---

[1] The *cucullum* of the ancients was an ample hood under which people of bad character could hide their identity, especially at night.

The Festival of the Assumption

4.
Nec metuens Dominum, proieci carmine vultum
Offendens nimium. Nec metuens Dominum.

4.
Without fear of the Lord, I was shameless in my songs,
Deeply I offended, nor did I fear the Lord.

5.
Semino nunc lacrimas (ut seram) gaudia messis,
Et post delicias, semino nunc lacrimas.

5.
Now do I sow in tears to reap hereafter in joy.
Leaving past delights, now do I sow in tears.

6.
Gaudia sustinui. Lucrum si prima recepi,
Lucrificante Deo. Gaudia sustinui.

6.
I have tasted pleasure, and if now I pay the price
It is God who imposes the penalty because I tasted pleasure.

7.
Nec procul est Opifex, gemmam carbone refingens
Et gremium pandens. Nec procul est opifex.

7.
But the Creator is near, who can shape from the coal
A gem. He opens his arms to me. The Creator is near.

8.
En ubi Vultus adest. Quaerens oracula Matris
Prae natis hominum, en ubi Vultus adest.

8.
Behold his image here,[1] moving to the shrine of his Mother,
Beautiful beyond the children of men, behold his image.

9.
Vultus adest Domini, cui totus sternitur orbis
Signo iudicii: Vultus adest Domini.

9.
Behold the face of the Lord before whom the earth bows.
Judgement is in his hands. Behold the face of the Lord.

10.
Ergo fremit populus, nec cessant tundere pectus
Matres cum senibus. Ergo fremit populus.

10.
Therefore the people tremble, Matrons and old men
Beat their breasts without ceasing and all the people tremble.

11.
Sistitur in solio Domini spectabile signum,
Theotocosque suo sistitur in solio.

11.
On a high throne is placed the venerable image
And that of his Mother too, on a high throne is placed.[2]

---

[1] This was the effigy which was usually preserved in the papal oratory of St Lawrence in the Lateran and which was carried in triumph about the City on occasions of great solemnity.

[2] Originally all the most venerated pictures in Rome were carried in the processions of Our Lady, but gradually the image of the Blessed Virgin at the Liberian Basilica on the Esquiline attracted all the attention and devotion of the people.

12.
Hinc thimiama dabunt, hinc balsama prima reponunt
    Thus mirraque ferunt. Hinc thimiama dabunt.

12.
Here incense is burnt, here precious balm is poured,[1]
    Myrrh and spices are brought, whilst incense is burnt.

13.
Dat schola graeca melos, et plebs romana susurros,
    Et variis modulis dat schola graeca melos.

13.
The Greek choir chants,[2] the Romans softly reply
    To the varying harmonies, which the Greek choir chants.

14.
Kyrie centum plicant, et pugnis pectora pulsant,
    Christe, faveto, tonant, Kyrie centuplicant.

14.
A hundred Kyries they chant, and striking their breasts
    Cry: Have mercy on us, O Christ! repeating a hundred Kyries.[3]

Invitatio ad orationem.

The Invitation to prayer.

1.
Sollicitemus ob hoc prece, carmine, lingua,
    Et Matrem Domini sollicitemus ob hoc prece.

1.
Let our prayers invoke the Mother of God, let our tongues
    Call upon her and our hymns, and let our prayers invoke her.

2.
Virgo Maria, tuos clementius aspice natos,
    Exaudi famulos, Virgo Maria, tuos.

2.
O Virgin Mother, look down in mercy on thy children,
    Listen to thy servants, in mercy look down, O Virgin Mother!

3.
Supplicibus lacrimis Tibi grex conspargitur Urbis,
    Alma Maria, fave supplicibus lacrimis.

3.
Their tears and prayers the whole people of Rome pour forth:
    Sweet Mary, be propitious to their tears and prayers.

---

[1] The liturgical custom of sprinkling holy images as well as crosses and relics of saints with balm and perfumes is most ancient, and is derived from the classic rite of pouring ointments and perfumes into the tombs of the departed on certain occasions.

[2] The origin of this school of music at Rome must date back at least to the fifth century. But the most remarkable feature is that it continued to exist in the City even when the Byzantine Empire had already long been a thing of the past. In studying the Gregorian Chant this school of Greek and Roman music at Rome should be compared with the celebrated school of the Monastery of St Gall, where in the ninth century we find numerous and very important elements of Byzantine music.

[3] The custom of repeating the Kyrie hundreds of times was very common in ancient Liturgies, and several Pontifical acts exist which at the founding of some church or monastery lay upon the clergy the obligation of reciting a hundred, two hundred, or three hundred Kyries daily for the repose of the soul of the founder.

4.
Turba gemit populi (modico discrimine laeti,
Sancta Maria Tibi turba gemit populi).

The people cry to thee, rejoicing at their escape from worse evils.
O holy Mary, behold, the people cry to thee.

5.
Sancta Dei Genetrix, romanam respice plebem,
Ottonemque fove, Sancta Dei Genetrix.

Holy Mother of God, look down on the people of Rome,
Protect our Emperor Otho, O holy Mother of God!

6.
Tertius Otto tuae nixus solamine palmae
Praesto sit veniae, tertius Otto tuae.

Protect Otho the Third, who trusts in the help of thine arm.
May he soon obtain pardon, do thou protect Otho the Third.

7.
Hic Tibi, si quid habet devoto pectore praestat
Spargere non dubitat hic Tibi, si quid habet.

All that he possesses with devout mind he offers to thee,
Ready to spend in thine honour all that he possesses.[1]

8.
Gaudeat omnis homo quia regnat tertius Otto,
Illius imperio gaudeat omnis homo.

Let the world rejoice, for the third Otho is our ruler;
Under his glorious sceptre let all the world rejoice.[2]

The dogmatic importance of the rites which we have summarily described here cannot fail to strike everyone. At a time when some ecclesiastical writers, as for instance the famous Ambrosius Autpert, Abbot of St Vincent at Volturnum (eighth century), confessed that some local churches had not yet reached complete agreement with regard to the doctrine of the corporal assumption of the Blessed Virgin into heaven, we find the Apostolic See counting the solemnity of August 15 amongst the most important of the liturgical Year.

The object of this feast is clearly expressed in the various Collects of the Gelasian and Gregorian Sacramentaries; it is always the bodily Assumption of our Lady, although some-

---

[1] After the gruesome period when medieval Rome had seen Popes and Antipopes stabbed to death, strangled in prison, poisoned, or dragged in mockery through the streets, the reigns of the three Othos who succeeded each other on the Imperial throne must have appeared like a golden age of peace and the restoration of the ancient universal "Imperium," the dream of all times. In the above lines the poet shares this hope and rejoices in the reign of the youthful Otho III.

[2] In spite of the stains which dimmed the glory of Otho III all historians agree as to his deep religious feeling and the wide protection which he granted to the Papacy, to churches and to monasteries. It is not rare to find in following his itineraries that he had retired to the Abbeys of Farfa, Subiaco, Ravenna, etc., where he sometimes spent the whole of Lent in fasting and penitential exercises.

times the Liturgy contemplates two distinct events, that of her death, and that of her being taken up into heaven. For instance, the Gelasian Sacramentary has the following beautiful Secret:

Accipe munera, Domine, quae in beatae Mariae iterata solemnitate deferimus, quia ad tua praeconia recurrit ad laudem, quod vel talis assumpta est. Per Dominum, etc.

"Receive, O Lord, the oblation which we offer to thee on this second solemnity of the Blessed Mary, for it redounds to the praise of thy glory that so noble a virgin should be assumed into heaven. Through our Lord."

To what does this "second solemnity" refer? Perhaps to the celebration of the Vigil in the preceding night, or, as seems more probable, to a feast kept a few days earlier, for instance that of August 5, the object of which was precisely the *Dormitio Sanctae Mariae*. The data which would enable us to decide this are wanting, but in any case it is important to note that in the Gelasian Sacramentary the *Assumptio* of the Mother of God was celebrated with a solemnity distinct from another feast which preceded it by a few days.

The Gregorian Sacramentary is still more explicit. As in the Greek rite, the object of the feast is the *dormitio*, repose, translation, or assumption of the Blessed Virgin Mary, but the Faith of the Roman Church concerning her resurrection and bodily assumption into heaven is so firm, undisputed and uncontroverted, that the miracle is generally implied rather than explicitly declared. It is a point of Catholic Faith, about which no doubt is entertained. Thus, for instance, we read in the first Collect of the Gregorian Sacramentary:

Veneranda nobis, Domine, huius est diei festivitas, in qua sancta Dei Genetrix mortem subiit temporalem, nec tamen mortis nexibus deprimi potuit, quae filium tuum Dominum nostrum de se genuit incarnatum. Qui tecum, etc.

"Truly venerable to us, O Lord, is this solemnity in which the holy Mother of God endured temporal death, but remained free from its fetters, having given birth to the incarnate Lord thy Son, who with thee . . . ."

In this Collect, belief in the triumph over death of the Blessed Virgin and, in consequence, belief in her bodily resurrection is clearly asserted; indeed (and we should make note of this) the same reason for it is given as that advanced by St John Damascene, i.e. the divine Maternity of Mary. *Quonam modo mors devoraret? Quomodo inferi susciperent? Quomodo corruptio invaderet corpus illud in quo vita suscepta est?*[1]

---

[1] *Orat. II de dormit. B. Mariae.*

The Festival of the Assumption

It should, however, be borne in mind that though the divine maternity of the Blessed Virgin Mary may be regarded as the immediate reason of her Assumption into heaven, yet the first and formal reason of this privilege is to be sought in her Immaculate Conception. It is true, indeed, that the dignity of the Mother of the Incarnate Word was the primary reason for which God preserved the Immaculate Conception of Mary from all stain of original sin—and in this sense the Gregorian Sacramentary rightly attributes the reason of the bodily resurrection of the Blessed Virgin to her prerogative as Mother of the Word—but in order to express this truth with perfect accuracy, it is necessary to say that the formal reason for the preservation of her body from corruption was precisely her immunity from all stain of original sin.

The consecrated formulas of the Roman Liturgy have not any difficulty in expressing and indeed in reconciling the fact of the death of the Blessed Virgin with her bodily resurrection, due to her exalted dignity.

The end of that transitory state in which the pilgrim soul finds itself on earth is called by us Death, but it does not necessarily imply any idea of pain or abasement in the case of the Immaculate Mother of God. This termination, or death, is a consequence of the formation of the human body, wherefore according to a Secret from the Gregorian Sacramentary which has passed into the present Roman Missal, the Blessed Virgin *pro conditione carnis migrasse cognoscimus*, but without the penalties of death. The state of separation of soul and body with all its consequences, such as bodily corruption, long and violent separation of form from matter, etc., had no power over the Mother of God. Therefore the Gregorian Sacramentary says: *Mortem subiit temporalem, nec tamen mortis nexibus deprimi potuit.*

The authority of the Roman Liturgy concerning the possibility of dogmatic definition of the Assumption of the Blessed Virgin is paramount, for it reflects the teaching and authority of the supreme Pontiff. Now that Catholic devotion anticipates the day when the infallible Teacher of Truth will place this last gem in the diadem which adorns Our Lady in heaven, theologians will be able to draw largely on that fount of Catholic tradition which is contained in the Liturgy, especially that of Rome. They will thus justify once more the words of Pope Celestine, when in writing to the Bishops of Gaul he declared: *Legem credendi lex statuat supplicandi.*

SANCTAE ROMANAE ECCLESIAE FERIALE

N.B.—The three columns of the Feriale show as follows :

The 1st, marked A, the primitive Feriale contained in the Philocalian Calendar and in the Sacramentaries.

The 2nd, marked B, gives the medieval feasts noted in the liturgical books of the eleventh century.

The 3rd, marked C, indicates the modern feasts inserted in the Roman Missal since the thirteenth century.

SANCTAE ROMANAE

Mense A

15 XVIII		15 Assumpt. B.M.V.
16 XVII		
17 XVI		
18 XV		
19 XIV		
20 XIII		
21 XII		
22 XI		22 S. Timothei M.
23 X		
24 IX		
25 VIII		
26 VII		
27 VI		
28 V		28 S. Hermetis M.
29 IV		
30 III		30 Felicis et Adaucti Mm.
31 Pridie Kalendas Sept		

Mense

1 Kalendis		
2 IV Nonas		2 Acontii in Portu, Nonni, Herculani et Taurini
3 III		
4 Pridie		
5 Nonis		
6 VIII Idus		
7 VII		
8 VI		8 S. Hadriani M.—Nativitas B. M. V.
9 V		9 S. Gorgonii M.
10 IV		
11 III		11 SS. Proti et Hyacinthi Mm.
12 Pridie		
13 Idibus		
14 XVIII Kal. Oct.		14 S. Cornelii et Cypriani—Exaltatio S. Crucis
15 XVII		15 S. Nicomedis M.
16 XVI		16 S. Caeciliae Virg. M.—S. Euphemiae M.
17 XV		
18 XIV		
19 XIII		
20 XII		
21 XI		
22 X		
23 IX		

ECCLESIAE FERIALE

Augusto

B	C
	16 S. Ioachim Patris B. M. V.
17 Octav. S. Laurentii M.	17 S. Hyacinthi Conf.
18 S. Agapiti M.	
	20 S. Bernardi Abb. Doct.
	21 S. Ioannae Fremiot De Chantal
22 SS. Hippolythi et Symphoriani Mm. Octav. Assumpt.	
23 Vigil. S. Bartholomaei	23 S. Philippi Benitii Conf.
24 S. Bartholomaei Ap.—S. Aureae	
	25 S. Ludovici IX Conf.
	26 S. Zephyrini Pap.
	27 S. Iosephi Calasanctii Conf.
28 S. Augustini Ep. Conf. Doct.	
29 S. Sabinae—Decoll. S. Ioh. Bapt.	
	30 S. Rosae Limanae Virg.
	31 S. Raymundi Nonnati Conf.

Septembri

B	C
1 S. Aegidii Abb.—SS. XII Fratrum Mart.	
	2 S. Stephani Regis Conf.
	5 S. Laurentii Iustiniani Ep. Conf.
	10 S. Nicolai a Tolentino Conf.
	12 SS. Nominis Mariae Virg.
16 SS. Luciae et Geminiani Mm.	16 SS. Cornelii et Cypriani Mm.
	17 Impress. SS. Stigmat. S. Francisci Conf.
	18 S. Iosephi a Cupertino Conf.
19 S. Ianuarii Ep. Mart.	
20 SS. Eustatii M.—Vigil. S. Matthaei Ap.	
21 S. Matthaei Ap. Evang.	
22 SS. Mauritii et Soc. Mm.	22 S. Thomae de Villanova Ep.
23 S. Theclae Virg. M.—S. Lini Pap.	

	Mense
	A
24 VIII	
25 VII	
26 VI	
27 V	27 SS. Cosmae et Damiani Mm.
28 IV	
29 III	29 Dedicatio S. Angeli via Salaria
30 Pridie Kal. Oct.	
	Mense
1 Kalendis	
2 VI Nonas	
3 V	
4 IV	
5 III	
6 Pridie	
7 Nonis	7 S. Marci Pap.
8 VIII Idus	
9 VII	
10 VI	
11 V	
12 IV	
13 III	
14 Pridie	14 S. Callisti Pap.
15 Idibus	
16 XVII Kal. Novembr.	
17 XVI	
18 XV	
19 XIV	
20 XIII	
21 XII	
22 XI	
23 X	
24 IX	
25 VIII	25 SS. Chrysanthi et Dariae Mm.
26 VII	
27 VI	
28 V	
29 IV	
30 III	
31 Pridie Kal. Nov.	
	Mense
1 Kalendis	
2 IV Nonas	
3 III	
4 Pridie	
5 Nonis	
6 VIII Idus	

Septembri (continued)

B

26 SS. Cypriani et Iustinae Mm.

30 S. Hieronymi Conf. Doct.

Octobri

1 S. Remigii Ep. Conf.

7 SS. Sergii et Bacchi—Marcelli et Apuleii Mm.

9 SS. Dionysii, Rustici et Eleutheri Mm.

18 S. Lucae Ev.

21 SS. Ursulae et Soc. Mm. (S. Hilarionis Abb.)

26 S. Evaristi Pap.
27 Vig. SS. Symonis et Iudae Ap.
28 SS. Symonis et Iudae Apost.

30 S. Germani Ep.
31 Vigil. Omn. Sanct.

Novembri

1 S. Caesarii Mart.—Omnium Sanctor.
2 Comm. Omn. Defunct.

4 SS. Vitalis et Agricolae Mm.

C

24 B. M. Virg. de Mercede

28 S. Wenceslai Ducis Conf.

2 SS. Angelorum Custodum

4 S. Francisci Conf.
5 SS. Placidi et Socior. Mm.
6 S. Brunonis Conf.
7 Sacr. Ros. B. M. Virg.

8 S. Birgittae Vid.

10 S. Francisci Borgia Conf.

13 S. Eduardi Reg. Conf.

15 S. Teresiae Virg.

17 S. Hedwigis Vid.

19 S. Petri de Alcantara Conf.
20 S. Ioannis Cantii Conf.

24 S. Raphaelis Archang.

(Dominica ultima Octobris—Fest. D. N. Iesu Christi Regis.)

4 S. Caroli Ep. Conf.

The Sacramentary

Mense

A

7 VII	
8 VI	8 SS. Quat. Coronat. Mart.
9 V	
10 IV	
11 III	11 S. Mennae M.
12 Pridie	
13 Idibus	
14 XVIII Kal. Decembr.	
15 XVII	
16 XVI	
17 XV	
18 XIV	
19 XIII	
20 XII	
21 XI	
22 X	22 S. Caeciliae Virg. M.
23 IX	23 S. Clementis Papae—Felicitatis M.
24 VIII	24 S. Chrysogoni M.
25 VII	
26 VI	
27 V	
28 IV	
29 III	29 S. Saturnini
30 Pridie Kal. Dec.	30 S. Andreae Ap.

Sanctae Romanae Ecclesiae Feriale

Novembri (*continued*)

B	C
8 Oct. Omn. Sanctorum	
9 S. Theodori—S. Salvatoris	
10 SS. Tryphonis et Soc. Mm.	10 S. Andreae Avell. Conf.
11 S. Martini Ep. Conf.	
12 S. Martini	
	13 S. Didaci Conf.
	14 S. Iosaphat Ep. Mart.
	15 S. Gertrudis Virg.
17 S. Gregorii Thaumat Ep. Conf.	
18 Dedic. SS. Petri et Pauli App.	
19 S. Pontiani Pap. M.	19 S. Elisabeth Vid.
	20 S. Felicis de Valois Conf.
	21 Praesent. B. M. Virg.
	24 S. Ioannis a Cruce Conf.
25 S. Catharinae Virg. M.	
26 S. Petri Alexandr. Ep. M.	26 S. Silvestri Abb.
29 Vig. S. Andreae Ap.	

THE FEASTS OF THE SAINTS FROM AUGUST 14 TO SEPTEMBER 29

FEASTS IN AUGUST

THE NIGHT OF AUGUST 14
VIGIL OF THE ASSUMPTION OF THE BLESSED VIRGIN MARY

Collecta at St Adrian, Station at St Mary Major.

AMONG the feasts of the Blessed Virgin that of the *dormitio* (κοίμησις) *sanctae Mariae*, or of her bodily assumption into heaven, was from very early times the most solemn and the most widely observed. We have already described elsewhere the ceremonies with which it was observed, so it is only necessary to speak here of the Mass at the Liberian Basilica which brought the long torchlight procession to an end.

The originator of this nocturnal procession of the clergy and people was Sergius I. Leo IV merely revived the custom. Towards the tenth century, however, the festival increased in importance, and the procession, instead of starting from the Church of St Adrian *ad Forum*, began at once at the papal palace of the Lateran, bearing the *ikons* of the Saviour and of the *Theotokos* surrounded by hundreds of lights.

Outside Rome, in very many parts of Italy, the touching ceremony observed in the Eternal City was copied for the Vigil of the Assumption, and still on the evening of this day in some of the villages of Latium two processions are formed, the one carrying the image of the Saviour, and the other that of his blessed Mother, which move simultaneously towards each other. When the two companies meet, the bearers of the two *ikons* exchange a kiss of peace; the celebrant then incenses the sacred images, and with that of Christ on the right and that of the Virgin on the left, the triumphal procession goes to some church dedicated to our Blessed Lady, where the feast of the Assumption is begun.

This ceremonial has, for instance, been observed for many centuries at Leprignano in the district attached to the Abbey of St Paul.

According to the *Ordo Romanus XI*, on the morning of August 14, the Pope and the Cardinals, fasting and barefooted, went to the Oratory of St Lawrence in the Lateran Patriarchate, where they made seven genuflections before the Byzantine *ikon* of the Saviour which is still kept there. Then the Pope opened the door of the shrine and while the Te Deum was being sung he laid the *ikon* upon the altar, so that when evening came it might be carried in procession by the Cardinal Deacons.

The Vespers and the vigiliary Office with its nine Lessons were sung at dusk at St Mary Major, after which the Pope and all the clergy returned to the Lateran in order to take part in the nocturnal procession.

On this night the Introit of the vigiliary Mass is that for March 25: *Vultum tuum deprecabuntur*.

All humanity turns with confidence to gaze upon the beautiful countenance of Mary, the face which was so often kissed by the divine Child, the face which expresses majesty, purity and grace, the face which is the most perfect image of that of Christ.

Collect: " O God, who didst vouchsafe to choose for thy dwelling the virginal womb of blessed Mary, grant, we beseech thee, that we who enjoy her intercession may assist with joy at her festival."

The Lesson is like that of July 16, while the Gradual *Benedicta* and the Gospel are those of August 5.

It is worthy of note that the Würzburg List of Gospels ignores the vigil of the Assumption. This is an indication that, as a matter of fact, Pope Sergius instituted only a simple procession and litany on this night to precede the celebration of the festival Mass at St Mary Major. It must have been Leo IV who instituted the Office and the vigiliary Mass.

The Offertory is as it were an echo of the Gospel Lesson in which a pious woman acclaimed Our Lady as blessed. " Blessed art thou, O Virgin Mary, who didst bear the Creator of all things: thou didst bring forth him who made thee and remainest a virgin for ever."

Secret: " Look with mercy upon our offerings, O Lord, through the prayer of the Mother of God, whom thou didst take up out of this present world that she might boldly plead before thy face for the forgiveness of our sins."

Mary still fulfils in heaven the office of advocate for us which Christ entrusted to her on Calvary, and she does so in order that the redemption may restore all things and be of far greater power than our ruin. Over against Adam and Eve, the source on earth of our original sin, God has placed in heaven Christ and Mary, the Redeemer and the Coredemptress of the human race.

The Communion is the same as for July 16.

Post-Communion: "Grant, O merciful God, protection to us in our weakness, so that we who are looking forward to the festival of the holy Mother of God may by the help of her intercession rise up from our sins."

In opposition to the Pelagian heresy, and also to some recent teachings which do not by any means sufficiently realize the inclination to evil of our corrupt nature, the Church insists, in her Liturgy, in establishing as the foundation of our spiritual life the truth, that is, a clear notion of the work of inner reconstruction which lies before us. We are like a splendid monument fallen into ruin, for the restoration of which our free will no less than divine grace is necessary.

AUGUST 15

THE ASSUMPTION OF THE BLESSED VIRGIN MARY

Station at St Mary Major.

The *Ordo Romanus XI* of Benedict the Canon decrees that on this morning the procession *ascendentes ad sanctam Mariam, dominus Pontifex praeparatus cantat Missam, benedicit populum fatigatum; omnes recedunt.*[1]

It was therefore a kind of *Dominica vacat*; the early Mass was said after the long procession which had taken place in the night, the Papal blessing was given, and then all went home to break their fast and to take the necessary rest.

It is quite possible that there was in the eighth century a second Mass for those who had not been able to attend the night Offices—*a missa maior*—as on August 10, after the vigil of St Lawrence, and this is perhaps why the Würzburg List gives two different Gospels for to-day; that already quoted for the vigiliary Mass, and the other containing the story of Martha and Mary.

The Introit is of Greek origin, and was first composed for the feast of St Agatha. We have already quoted it on July 16.

The angels rejoice at the Assumption of Mary, for their own Queen has at last come amongst them.

Collect: "Forgive, O Lord, we beseech thee, the sins of thy servants, that we who by our own deeds are unable to please thee, may be saved by the intercession of the Mother of thy Son our Lord: who liveth and reigneth."

The "Mother of thy Son," but our Mother too, precisely because she is the Mother of him who for our sake became

---

[1] *P.L.* LXXVIII, col. 1052.

her Son, who humbled himself and exalted her, who died for us on the cross and left her to be our Mother.

The Lesson is from Ecclesiasticus (xxiv, 11–13, 15–20). The Church applies to-day to the Blessed Virgin, in whose womb the Word became flesh, that which the Scriptures say in praise of Jerusalem where the worship of the true God and Eternal Wisdom was enthroned. By reason of the divine Motherhood the dignity of the Blessed Virgin is so great that it surpasses all the glory and honour which the human mind can conceive.

Gradual (Psalm xliv): " Because of truth, and meekness, and justice, and thy right hand shall conduct thee wonderfully. V. Hearken, O daughter, and see, and incline thine ear: for the King hath greatly desired thy beauty."

As a great artist puts his whole self into his masterpiece and delights in it, so the Lord takes delight in Mary:

> " *Termine fisso d'eterno consiglio.*"[1]

" Alleluia, alleluia. Mary is taken up into heaven: the host of angels rejoices. Alleluia."

Nor is it the angels alone who rejoice at the Assumption of Mary; we sinners, too, take part in this joy, for to-day Our Lady ascends into heaven, and henceforth will intercede for us with greater efficacy at the tribunal of God.

The Gospel (Luke x, 38–42) relates the episode of the visit of Jesus to Bethany in the house of Lazarus. The Liturgy applies to the Blessed Virgin Mary to-day the words which our Saviour spoke in praise of the sister of Martha who sat at his feet, silently listening to his words. Mary has chosen, not merely the better part, but the best of all, for as her purity and sanctity surpass that of any other creature, so her glory in heaven is only surpassed by that of God.

Dante expresses the devout thought that the sight of the radiant countenance of Mary prepares the elect for the Vision of the face of Christ.

> *Riguarda omai nella faccia, che a Cristo*
> *Più si somiglia, che la sua chiarezza*
> *Sola ti può disporre a veder Cristo.*[2]

The Antiphon for the Offertory is the following: " Mary is taken up into heaven: the angels rejoice, and join together in praising and blessing the Lord. Alleluia."

The Sacred Liturgy, soberly and with dignity, but at the same time without equivocation, professes the Catholic belief in the Assumption of Mary into heaven. The title of to-day's feast is the Assumption, and the Liturgy constantly

---

[1] Paradiso. Canto XXX.   [2] Paradiso. Canto XXXII.

repeats this word "assumption," nor can it mean by this the assumption of the spirit common to all the elect, but alludes evidently to a privilege accorded only to Mary, and this can but refer to her virginal body.

Secret: "May the prayer of the Mother of God help thy people, O Lord, and although we know that she passed away from this life to satisfy the conditions of her mortal flesh, may we nevertheless have her to plead for us before thy face in the glory of heaven. Through the same."

So high is the dignity of the Mother of God and so deeply rooted in the hearts of the faithful the belief in her bodily assumption into heaven, that the composer of to-day's Mass does not conceal the difficulty he experiences in explaining the fact of the death of Mary. How could she who had been conceived without sin, and had given birth to the Author of life Himself, undergo death? This is the theological difficulty.

It appears as though, in order to solve it, the composer of the Collect would distinguish between death as the penalty of sin and death *status termini*, to which *pro condicione carnis* every human being must submit. Mary was, indeed, exempt from the pain and humiliation of death, in so far as these are consequences of original sin, she who had given birth to the Redeemer in joy. But as a creature—*pro condicione carnis*—Mary, too, came under the universal law which puts an end to the pilgrimage of every mortal.

The Gregorian Sacramentary expresses itself in the same manner in another Collect which was perhaps intended for the vigil of the preceding night: *Sancta Dei Genitrix mortem subiit temporalem, nec tamen mortis nexibus deprimi potuit.* Mary's death was, then, an undoubted fact, in spite of the hesitation attributed to St Epiphanius[1]: "I do not state that she was immortal but I am not certain either of her death." Her triumph over death is twofold: she gave up her soul in its original sanctity and holiness into the hands of her Son, and further *nec mortis nexibus deprimi potuit*, she was taken up bodily into heaven.

The Collect to-day in the Gelasian Sacramentary is interesting: *Accipe munera, Domine, quae in beatae Mariae iterata solemnitate deferimus;—iterata* perhaps with reference to the preceding synaxis of the vigil—*quia ad tua praeconia recurrit, ad laudem, quod vel talis assumpta est.*

The Preface which the Sacramentaries generally assign to to-day's feast, except for slight additions, is the same which is prescribed in the Missal for all feasts of the Blessed Virgin Mary.

[1] *Haeres.* XIX, ch. ii.

We will quote instead, in praise of Mary, one of the magnificent Leonine Prefaces for Christmas Day: *Vere dignum*, etc. *In die solemnitatis hodiernae, quo licet ineffabile, tamen utrumque conveniens editur sacramentum. Quia et Mater Virgo non posset nisi sobolem proferre divinam, et Deus homo nasci dignatus, congruentius non deberet nisi Virgine Matre generari. Propterea*, etc.

The Antiphon for the Communion of the faithful repeats to-day the words of Jesus in the Gospel (Luke X), "Mary hath chosen for herself the best part: which shall not be taken from her for ever." This best part is the Word of God, to whom the Blessed Virgin not only gave birth, but on whom she nourished herself spiritually, being entirely absorbed, as the Gospel shows her to us, in meditating in her heart upon the words of Christ.

Post-Communion: "We who have partaken of thy heavenly banquet, implore thy mercy, O Lord our God, so that we who pay honour to the Assumption of the Mother of God, may, through her intercession, be freed from all the evils which threaten us. Through the same."

The most favourable moment at which to obtain graces from Mary is that of Holy Communion, for when she sees us so intimately united with the Body and Blood of her Son, she feels herself on account of this participation, to be more than ever the Mother both of Jesus and of men.

AUGUST 15

St Tarcisius, Acolyte and Martyr*[1]

At the Cemetery of Callixtus.

On this day we find in the more modern Martyrologies the commemoration of Tarcisius the Roman acolyte, who was martyred by the pagans because he would not yield up to them the Blessed Sacrament which he carried hidden on his breast.

The Martyrology of St Jerome does not mention this saint, but the *Notitia Nataliciorum* of St Sylvester *in Capite* keeps his feast on July 26, together with that of Pope Zephyrinus. This latter day has an historical connection because, as a mark of special honour, the bones of the acolyte, who was actually compared by Pope Damasus to St Stephen,

---

[1] The feasts marked with an asterisk (*) do not belong in any way to the original collection in the Roman Sacramentaries, which contained at first only local feasts. They are, however, given here as they now form part of the universal calendar of the Church, and are included in the Roman Missal.

were laid in the same tomb as those of Pope Zephyrinus, the founder of the necropolis of Callixtus: *Sanctus Tarcisius et sanctus Zepherinus in uno tumulo iacent.* So the *De locis Sanctorum Martyrum* tells us.

This is the inscription by Damasus in honour of Tarcisius:

PAR · MERITVM · QVICVMQUE · LEGIS · COGNOSCE · DVORVM
QVIS · DAMASVS · RECTOR · TITVLOS · POST · PRAEMIA · REDDIT
IVDAICVS · POPVLVS · STEPHANVM · MELIORA · MONENTEM
PERCVLERAT · SAXIS · TVLERAT · QVI · EX · HOSTE · TROPAEVM
MARTYRIVM · PRIMVS · RAPVIT · LEVITA · FIDELIS
TARSICIVM · SANCTVM · CHRISTI · SACRAMENTA · GERENTEM
CVM · MALE · SANA · MANVS · PETERET · VVLGARE · PROFANIS
IPSE · ANIMAM · POTIVS · VOLVIT · DIMITTERE · CAESVS
PRODERE · QVAM · CANIBVS · RABIDIS · CAELESTIA · MEMBRA

"O Reader, whosoever thou art who dost read this, know that both those to whom, after their reward, Damasus dedicates these lines, were equal in merit. The Jews crushed Stephen under a rain of stones when he would have taught them the better way. The faithful Levite triumphed over his enemies, snatching from them the palm of martyrdom.

"Whilst he carried the holy Sacrament of Christ, an impious man stretched out his hand to take it from him and to expose it to the scorn of unbelievers. Tarcisius preferred to be struck down and to give up his spirit, rather than deliver to mad dogs the Body of Christ."

AUGUST 16

St Joachim, Father of the Blessed Virgin Mary*

The liturgical honours paid in the East to the happy parents of the most blessed Virgin date back to very early times. In the Menology of Constantinople their commemoration occurs on the day following the feast of the Nativity of the Mother of God, whilst amongst the Syrians it was kept on July 25. Their names and the events of their lives have been handed down to us by the Apocryphal *Protevangelium Jacobi;* but even apart from these narratives the great merit of the two saints Joachim and Anna was manifested and confirmed by God himself when he granted to them the honour of being the parents of the Blessed Virgin and grandparents of the Saviour.

The excellence of a fruit is always a sign of the quality of the tree which bore it. In the case of St Joachim, the Immaculate Conception of Mary reflects a splendid glory on the chaste union of her parents.

The Gospels speak of a sister of Our Lady who accompanied her even to the foot of the cross. According to some authorities she too was a daughter of Anna and of Joachim.

The feast of St Joachim was first introduced into the Breviary by Julius II, who fixed the date of March 20 in connection with that of St Joseph and of the Annunciation. Clement XII, however, transferred it to the Sunday after the Assumption, until, in the reform of the Breviary carried out by Pius X, August 16 was the date fixed.

The Introit is taken from the Mass of the Vigil of St Lawrence.

Collect: "O God, who of all thy saints wouldst choose blessed Joachim to be father to the Mother of thy Son, grant, we beseech thee, that we may evermore have for our advocate him to whose festival we pay honour."

The predominant idea in this Collect is expressed thus by St John Damascene: *De fructu ventris vestri cognoscimini. Pie enim et sancte in humana natura vitam agentes, Filiam angelis superiorem et nunc Angelorum Dominam edidistis.*[1]

The Lesson is the same as that for St Raymund on January 23, followed by the Gradual which is also assigned to the vigil of St Lawrence.

The alleluiatic verse is proper to the feast: "Alleluia, alleluia. O Joachim, holy spouse of Anne, father of the glorious Virgin, win for thy servants the grace of salvation. Alleluia."

The parents of the Mother of God and grandparents of Jesus are like the penultimate link in that chain of graces and blessings which through the patriarchs connects Adam with Christ. For this reason the genealogy of the Saviour according to St Matthew is read to-day as in the vigiliary Mass of December 7.

The Offertory, *Gloria et honore*, is the same as for St Canute on January 19.

Secret: "Receive, most merciful God, this sacrifice which we offer up to thy majesty in honour of the holy patriarch Joachim, the father of the Virgin Mary, that through his intercession, with that of his spouse and his most blessed child, we may become worthy to have our sins wholly forgiven, and to win everlasting glory."

The Antiphon for the Communion, *Fidelis servus*, is common to the Mass of St Sabba, on December 5.

Post-Communion: "We beseech thee, almighty God,

[1] *Orat. I de Virg. Nativ.*

that by these mysteries which we have received, and by the merits and prayers of blessed Joachim, father of the Mother of thy beloved Son, our Lord Jesus Christ, which plead for us, we may become worthy to receive thy grace in this life and everlasting glory in the world to come."

The close relationship which existed between the Saviour and St Joachim confers on the latter a great dignity, raising him above other saints, so that the honour paid to him is reflected upon Christ himself in a special manner and upon his Immaculate Mother. They loved him and honoured him in this world above all others. Their love is like a precious gem which adorns the crown of the holy Patriarch in heaven.

AUGUST 17

OCTAVE DAY OF ST LAWRENCE

In the Leonine Sacramentary there are among the Collects of the feast of St Lawrence a few which speak of a *solemnitas repetita*. These may refer to the commemoration of the Octave. It is, however, undoubtedly contained in the Gelasian and Gregorian Sacramentaries. The celebration of an octave was originally the prerogative of the paschal solemnity alone, but from the fifth century it gradually became the custom to commemorate the eighth day after the Nativity, SS Peter and Paul, etc. The Gospel List of Würzburg does not mention the Octave of St Lawrence.

The Introit derives its Antiphon from Psalm xvi. "Thou hast proved my heart, O Lord, and visited it by night: thou hast tried me by fire, and iniquity hath not been found in me." For this reason God sends us temptation, which to Christian virtue is like the atmosphere in which it lives. What does he know, who has never been tempted? What has he to gain? Instead of pitying those who are exposed to temptation, St James goes as far as to call them blessed because the trial is a proof of greater graces and wins for them a brighter crown.

The following Collect is to be found in the Leonine Sacramentary: "Stir up within thy church, O Lord, the Spirit which blessed Lawrence thy deacon obeyed, so that we too may be filled therewith, and may strive to love what he loved and to practise what he taught. Through our Lord . . . in the unity of the same."

The Paraclete stirs and directs the soul which moves as he inspires it. Wherefore the apostle says: *Qui Spiritu Dei aguntur, hi sunt filii Dei.*

August 17

The two Lessons and the alleluiatic verse are the same as for the feast of St Lawrence.

The Gradual, *Gloria*, etc., is taken from the Mass of St Eusebius on December 16, and the Offertory from that of St Sabba on December 5.

Secret: " Let the prayers of blessed Lawrence recommend our sacrifice to thee, O Lord, we beseech thee, so that it may be received by thee through the merits of him in whose honour it is solemnly offered up."

The following is the prayer from the Gelasian Sacramentary: *Beati Laurentii martyris honorabilem passionem muneribus, Domine, geminatis exsequimur, quae licet propriis sit memoranda principiis, indesinenter tamen permanet gloriosa."*

We should note the solemn and social character which always distinguishes these ancient stational formulas. In those days the entire populace joined in the liturgical Action, which in the early centuries of the Church was the only one which took place in the whole City and which was generally celebrated by the Bishop.

The Gelasian Sacramentary has this Preface for to-day: " *Vere dignum . . . Quoniam tanto iucunda sunt, Domine, beati Laurentii crebrius repetita solemnia, quanto nobis eius sine cessatione praedicanda sunt merita. Et ideo cum angelis,* etc.

The Antiphon for the Communion is the same as on the vigil of the feast of the Saint.

Post-Communion: " We humbly beseech thee, almighty God, through the intercession of blessed Lawrence thy martyr, to keep under thy protection for evermore those whom thou hast fed with these gifts from heaven. Through our Lord." The Holy Eucharist, whilst being a gift—indeed the " good gift "—is also a pledge of future glory, and includes the promise of all the graces which prepare us for it. For this reason, in the language of the Liturgy, Holy Communion becomes, too, a motive for intercession.

AUGUST 18

St Agapitus, Martyr

We commemorate to-day a martyr of Praeneste, noted in the Martyrology of St Jerome: *In civitate Prenestina, milliario XXXIII, Agapiti.* Felix III built a sanctuary in his honour near the Basilica of St Lawrence, so that his *natalis* has also been included in the Leonine Sacramentary. He was likewise the object of a very ancient and well-known devotion in the Eternal City.

The Basilica over the martyr's tomb—his death is usually

supposed to have taken place under Aurelian—stood *in agro*, a short distance outside Praeneste, and its interesting remains have been discovered. There are many sepulchral inscriptions invoking the intercession of Agapitus, amongst which the following is very important:

    . . . ILLVM · (that is, the deceased) ACCEPTVM · HABEAS · SANCTE · ROGAMVS
    EN · PVERVM · PLACIDIANVM · MERENTER · VERSIBVS · DIXI

and a beautiful invocation contained in another inscription, dating from 542 to 565:

    DOMINE · AGAPITE · ORA · PRO · ME

The body of St Agapitus was transferred to Corneto in 1437.

The Mass *Laetabitur* is as for St Saturninus on November 29.
The Gospel is taken from the Mass of St Lawrence.
The Collect is as follows: "Let thy church, O God, be gladdened by the intercession of blessed Agapitus, in which she puts her trust; through his glorious prayers may she ever keep devoted unto thee, and ever abide in peace and safety."
The Martyrs having won a decisive victory over the enemy of mankind, enjoy a special power in heaven to protect their votaries against the wiles of the devil.
The Index of Würzburg assigns for the Gospel the passage *Sint lumbi vestri*, etc., as for St Raymund on January 23.
Secret: "Receive, O Lord, the gifts which we offer up to thee on the festival of him by whose intercession we hope to be delivered."
The prayer for the Communion is the same as for December 13.
The following beautiful Collect is from the Gelasian Sacramentary: *Munera tibi, Domine, pro sancti Martyris Agapiti passione deferimus, qui dum finitur in terris, factus est caelesti fide perpetuus.*

AUGUST 19

St Magnus, Martyr

This Saint is seldom mentioned in the Gelasian Sacramentary, but his name appears in the Martyrology of St Jerome: *In Fabriteria, Magni.* This village of Fabriteria was in the neighbourhood of Ceccano, and devotion to St Magnus spread throughout the provinces of Campania and Lazio.

August 19

At Amelia an ancient convent of Benedictine nuns is dedicated to St Manno or Magno.

In Rome, too, there exists near St Peter's a most ancient little basilica of the time of Leo III dedicated to the Archangel Michael and St Magnus. For this reason, perhaps, the name of the martyr of Fabriteria is to be found in the Sacramentary.

The Secret in the Gelasian Sacramentary is simple and graceful: *Grata tibi sint munera nostra, Domine, quae et tuis sunt instituta praeceptis, et beati Magni festivitas gloriosa commendet.*

AUGUST 20

ST BERNARD, ABBOT, CONFESSOR AND DOCTOR*

In the lunette above the tomb of Pope Innocent II at the Basilica of St Mary *in Trastevere*, appears the white figure of a monk who leads the Pope back to Rome, and seats him in triumph upon the throne of St Peter. That monk is Bernard, Abbot of Clairvaux.

A truly heroic figure, Bernard was at once a reformer of monastic life, a preacher of the Crusade, a Doctor of the Universal Church, a worker of miracles, a peace-maker between kings, princes and peoples, the oracle of Popes, and the champion of the Roman See against schisms and heresies. The mortal frame of the saint, consumed by penance and by sickness, could scarcely contain his soul on fire for the glory of God. This fire communicated itself to those around him; his secretaries had difficulty in recording the numerous miraculous cures which he worked by the touch of his hand, or simply by a blessing.

The necessities of the Church drew Bernard to Italy, and he journeyed several times to Rome. To him was due the renewal of the Abbey *ad aquas Salvias* on the Via Laurentina, where he installed as first Abbot Bernardo Pisano, who was afterwards known as Eugenius III.

The subsequent relations between the Master and his disciple are noteworthy. Bernard cannot forget that he is still in a manner the spiritual father of the Pope, and in order to help him to meditate, he dedicates to him the work *De Consideratione* which, together with the *Pastorale* of St Gregory the Great, was, until the sixteenth century, always found in the pontifical palace.

The Mass is the Common of Doctors as on April 4, but the Lesson is the same as on April 11.

St Bernard indeed several times refused the proffered episcopal dignity. His work as a Doctor was carried out largely within the enclosure of his own Abbey, where he constantly preached to the monks, commentating on the Scriptures. This aspect of Bernard's activity is entirely in keeping with the Rule of St Benedict, in which the monastery is regarded as a *Dominici schola servitii*, in which the Abbot should ever be active in imparting spiritual knowledge to his monks.

St Bernard had many distinguished disciples, noted for their great holiness. Amongst these were his own parents and his brothers who followed him into the cloister. It is said that when St Bernard, accompanied by his brothers and relatives, about thirty in number, who had been attracted by his words to the religious life, was about to leave his father's castle, he said to his little brother Nivard, whom he saw playing in the courtyard: " Farewell, Nivard, we leave all this to you henceforth." The child, however, answered with a wisdom beyond his years: " This division is not just. What! do you leave earthly goods to me and keep heavenly treasures for yourself?" And he begged to be allowed to follow them, but was restrained from so doing until he had reached years of discretion.

We may quote here an expressive phrase of St Bernard on the call for sanctity in a minister of God: *Si non placet, non placat.*

AUGUST 21

ST JANE FRANCES FREMIOT DE CHANTAL, WIDOW*

This disciple of St Francis de Sales did great credit to her Master, and proved that without following the extraordinary methods of sanctity practised by the Fathers of the desert, it is quite possible to reach a high degree of Christian perfection, by loving God ardently and by fulfilling the duties of a wife, mother, widow, and religious, which were successively the lot of St Jane Frances. Clement XIV introduced this saint's feast into the Missal with the rank of a double.

The Mass is that of March 10, but the Collects are proper to the feast.

Collect: " Almighty and merciful God, who didst endow blessed Jane Frances, ever burning with love for thee, with marvellous spiritual strength in keeping the perfect way through every path of life, grant through her merits and prayers that we, who know how weak we are and trust only in thy might, may be helped by grace from heaven and may overcome all things that withstand us."

The composer has tried to introduce too many subjects

into this prayer, and has therefore given us a Collect without a *cursus* and devoid of a really dominant idea.

Secret: "May this victim of salvation, O Lord, make us burn with that selfsame love which it enkindled fiercely in the heart of blessed Jane Frances, consuming it in the flames of everlasting charity."

This is indeed one of the objects of Holy Communion according to the words of the Gospel: *ignem veni mittere in terram, et quid volo nisi ut accendatur?*

We must, however, note that the symbol of the fire of the Holy Ghost recurs several times in the Missal, and each time in the prayer over the oblations. But in the liturgical conceptions of the ancients, the fire of the Paraclete was called down upon the altar in order that it might consecrate and consume the sacrifice like that of Elias:—*Sacrificia, Domine, tuis oblata conspectibus, ignis ille divinus absumat*, we read on the Friday before Pentecost,—whilst in to-day's Collect the modern composer changes the idea somewhat, and instead of an *oratio super oblata*, he anticipates a Post-Communion, and asks for the sacred fire of Charity which is indeed the result and fruit of Holy Communion.

Post-Communion: "Pour forth upon us, O Lord, the spirit of thy love, so that those whom thou hast fed and strengthened by this food from heaven may have grace to despise the things of this world, and with clean hearts to seek after thee, the only God."

In the school of the Bishop of Geneva piety becomes attractive without any trace of that dulness and weariness which novices in the devout life sometimes succeed in inspiring amongst those who surround them.

With regard to this, members of the household of Madame de Chantal used to say at the time when she first placed herself under the direction of St Francis de Sales: "Under her former confessors, Madame prayed for only a few hours a day, and the whole house was disturbed. Now, Monsieur de Genève teaches her to make her whole day a prayer and it does not trouble any one."

AUGUST 22

St Timothy, Priest and Martyr

Station on the Via Ostiensis, in hortis Theonae.

To-day the *Natalitia Martyrum* of the Philocalian Calendar notes *XI Kal. Septembres. Timothei, Ostense.*

This is a martyr who came from Antioch, and who suffered in the last persecution. He was buried in a special grave in the gardens of Theona, which were above the cemetery of St Paul, at that time closed, perhaps on account of the confiscation of property. The motive of the saint's interment here is explained thus: *ut Paulo Apostolo, ut Timotheus quondam, adhaereret.*

The burial-place of Timothy is very small, for it consists of a long steep staircase, on one side of which is a crypt containing the tomb of the martyr. The place is devoid of any inscription or painting. De Rossi, however, found there many writings and signatures of pilgrims, mostly those of natives of Antioch.

The body of Timothy was transferred afterwards to the neighbouring basilica, where it rests under the altar in the same vault *ad corpus* of the Apostle of the Gentiles. Therefore, even now, the new Timothy is not parted from Paul.

The greater number of the early Sacramentaries only notice on this day the station on the Ostian Way at the tomb of St Timothy.

The Collects are the following:

Collect: " Be appeased, O Lord, we beseech thee, and lend us thy help, and through the intercession of thy blessed martyr Timothy, stretch forth the hand of thy mercy upon us."

In the mosaic of the *titulus* of Pudens this gesture of protection is beautifully expressed. Christ is seated in majesty on his throne and extends his right arm as a mark of protection over the *domus pudentiana*, whilst with the left hand he holds the scroll on which is written:

DOMINVS · CONSERVATOR · ECCLESIAE · PVDENTIANAE

According to the Würzburg List, the Gospel Lesson to-day was from Luke xiv, 26–35, as on June 14.

Secret: " May the offering which thy holy people make to thee, O Lord, be received by thee in honour of thy saints, through whose merits they know that they have had help in trouble."

We may note here the sacred character of the Christian people, the holy race and royal priesthood, as it is often described in liturgical prayers. To-day in the Secret, the faithful are called *Sacrata plebs*, as, in the solemn prayers on Good Friday, they are spoken of as *populus sanctus Dei*. This was the title given to the faithful at Rome by the Popes in their dedicatory inscriptions:

HILARVS · EPISCOPVS · SANCTAE · PLEBI · DEI

As the manna no longer fell when Israel reached the

promised land, so the Sacraments accompany us only to the threshold of Eternity. Communion with God, however, continues, for the Sacraments are succeeded by that which was hidden under the appearances of the *sacrum signum* and which they both contained and promised. The appearances fall away and the Pearl of the Gospel is seen in its brilliancy, purchased by the soul which has given all to possess Christ.

AUGUST 22

St Hippolytus " Qui et Nonnus "

Station in portu urbis Romae, on the Isola Sacra.

Besides St Timothy, the Martyrology of St Jerome notes to-day : *In portu urbis Romae, Ypoliti, qui dicitur Nonnus.* This Hippolytus, a completely different person from the celebrated Doctor and rival of Pope Callixtus, was a local martyr, whose history is however wrapt in obscurity. The Philocalian Calendar joins with the name of Nonnus, those of the martyrs Taurinus and Herculanus, but gives September 5 as the date of their *natalis*.

The Basilica of Hippolytus stood on the Isola Sacra, also called *Insula Portuensis*. It was destroyed in 455, but it was restored by Peter the Bishop, who placed this inscription there to commemorate the event :

✠VANDALICA · RABIES · HANC · VSSIT · MARTYRIS · AVLAM
QVAM · PETRVS · ANTISTES · CVLTV · MELIORE · NOVAVIT

The martyrs of the *Insula Portuensis*, Taurinus and Herculanus, are also commemorated in another epigraph in the Abbey of St Paul :

> DEO · PATRI · OMNIPOTEN
> TI · ET · XPO · EIVS · ET · SANCTIS
> MARTYRIBVS · TAVRINO
> ET · HERCVLANO · OMNI
> ORA · GRATIAS · (agi)MVS
> NEVIVS · LARI(stus-e)T
> CONSTANT(ia . . . V
> RIA · SIBI · FEC(erunt)

When in the ninth century Porto was ravaged by the Saracens, Pope Formosus, Bishop of the City, saved the relics of the saints and placed them on another island in the Tiber, that is the *Insula Lycaonia*, in the church which was afterwards known as *Sancti Johannis de Insula*.

The following inscription testifies to the fact:

✠HIC · REQVIESCVNT · CORPORA · SCŌR
MARTYRVM · YPPOLITI · TAVRINI · ET · HERCVLANI
ATQVE · JOHANNIS · CALIBITIS · FORMOSVS
EPS · CONDIDIT

AUGUST 22

St Symphorian, Martyr

This celebrated martyr of Autun, whose praises were sung by Venantius Fortunatus, is named in the Bernese version of the Martyrology of St Jerome, and is honoured with a vigil. His *Acta* seem genuine, and impress us very favourably.

The sepulchral basilica of the martyr was built towards the end of the fifth century by the priest Euphronius, who afterwards became Bishop of Autun. Its dedication is recorded in the copies of the Martyrology of Berne and of Wissemberg on July 31: *Agustiduno dedicatio ecclesiae Maioris (et sancti Nazarii) et translatio multorum sanctorum Martyrum (in ipsa Ecclesia).*

We know from St Gregory of Tours that, in the sixth century, the feast of St Symphorian (August 22) was celebrated at the sepulchral Basilica of St Martin.

The festival of the martyr of Autun was introduced into the Roman Calendar by the influence of the Frankish Sacramentaries. Our present Missal assigns to the martyrs Timothy, Hippolytus, and Symphorian, who originally were distinguished with three separate Masses, a Common Mass, that of February 15: *Salus autem.* The Collects are those of the feast of St Timothy, with the addition of the names of the other two saints.

We read in the *Acta* of St Symphorian a beautiful incident which is worthy of record. When he was being led to martyrdom it is said that his pious Mother called to him: " My son, my son, look up to heaven and behold him who reigns there. You are not being led to death, but to a better life."

AUGUST 22

Octave Day of the Assumption of the Blessed Virgin Mary

Station at St Lawrence.

This station was instituted by St Leo IV. The choice of the basilica was suggested by the fact that the *aula Maior* of Sixtus III, near the sepulchre of St Lawrence, whose octave had been celebrated six days previously, was indeed dedicated to the Blessed Virgin.

Further, to-day is the feast of St Hippolytus of Porto. As, however, this saint was confused with the Doctor Hippolytus, venerated on the Via Tiburtina, so probably, it was intended by this station at the *basilica maior* to honour the memory of Hippolytus at the same time as that of the Blessed Virgin, because he was buried in that church and commemorated in the medieval inscription of the list of saints venerated at St Lawrence :

POST · HOS · IPOLITVS · COLLIS · RELIGATVS · EQVORVM
CVM · NVTRICE · SVA · CVM · CVNCTA · PLEBE · SVORVM

The Mass is the same as on August 15, and this is out of respect for St Gregory, whose Sacramentary was regarded in the Middle Ages as inspired, and therefore unalterable. No person then would have dared to compose new parts and add them to the Liturgy.

In order to atone for this lack and to honour the Blessed Virgin whose Assumption into heaven we contemplated eight days ago, we may select the following Collect from the Gelasian Sacramentary : *Oblationes nostras, quaesumus Domine, propitiatus intende ; quas in honore beatae et gloriosae semper virginis Dei Genitricis Mariae annua solemnitate deferimus ; et coaeternus Spiritus Sanctus tuus, qui illius viscera splendore suae gratiae veritatis replevit, nos ab omni facinore delictorum emundet benignus.*

Mary is the Creator's finest work. When, in Holy Scripture, we read the praises of the Spouse of the Canticles, of sacred wisdom, and of the Church, these praises must be applied to Mary first and foremost, because she embodies in the highest degree the holiness and perfection which is attributed to the mystical Spouse of Christ—the Church.

AUGUST 23

SS Abundius and Irenaeus, Martyrs

Station at St Lawrence.

The Martyrology of St Jerome sends us back to the Via Tiburtina to-day : *In cimiterio sancti Laurentii, Habundi et Herenaei.* The Itineraries also mention these martyrs, adding the information that the stone which was hung about the neck of Abundius when he was thrown into a well, was preserved in the portico of the basilica. *Ibi quoque sub eodem altare Abundus est depositus, et foris in portico lapis est, qui aliquando in collo eiusdem Abundi pendebat, in puteum missi.* This is quoted from the Epitome *De Locis Sanctis*, whilst the Itinerary of Salzburg remarks: *Ibi pausat sanctus Abundius et Herenius martyr via Tiburtina ; et ibi est ille lapis quem tollent digito multi homines, nescientes quid faciunt.*

The bodies of the two martyrs were buried originally, not in the Basilica of St Lawrence, but in a neighbouring oratory: *parvum cubiculum extra ecclesiam*, precisely as is asserted in the Itinerary of Salzburg. It was only in later days that they were laid beside St Lawrence.

The ancient list of the relics preserved at the *Agro Verano*, thus mentions our two martyrs:

MARTYR · IRENEVS · QVI · TECVM · MARTYR · ABVNDI
DECEDENS · SPREVIT · FALLACIS · GAVDIA · MVNDI

It is probable that the two saints were also mentioned in an inscription composed by Damasus in honour of several martyrs, and of which only a few fragments have been recovered:

MARMORIBVS · VESTITA · (novis veneranda sepulchra)
QVAE · INTEMERATA · FIDES · (decorat Christique corona)
HIC · ETIAM · PARIES · IVSTO (rum nomina pandit ?)
OMNIA · PLENA · VIDES · (divino lumine caeli).

AUGUST 23

St Philip Benizi, Confessor*

It was Pope Innocent XII who included the feast of St Philip Benizi in the Missal with the rank of a double. This saint (who died in 1285) was a zealous apostle, and may indeed be regarded as a second founder of the Order of the Servants of Mary. Had he consented, he would have been elected to the Pontifical See.

It is said that when he was dying, he repeatedly asked for his book, and when the infirmarian did not understand his meaning the saint made signs that he wanted his crucifix, which was the book in which he was accustomed to meditate.

The Mass *Justus* is the same as on January 21.

In the first Collect we find an allusion to the saint's humility, which caused him to fly from the honours of the Papacy.

" O God, who in blessed Philip thy confessor didst give us a noble pattern of meekness, grant that thy servants may follow his example by despising earthly welfare, and by seeking after heavenly things."

The world is like grass or the flowers of the field: to-day it is fresh and blooming, and to-morrow it will be dry and withered. We should not place our trust in it.

The other two Collects are the same as on July 19.

AUGUST 23

VIGIL OF ST BARTHOLOMEW, APOSTLE

Like the other Apostles, the holy Nathanael or Bartholomew, a true Israelite, sincere and without guile, as our Saviour himself testified, was honoured with a vigil which was already noted in the Martyrology of St Jerome.

The Mass is that of December 20, but at Rome the Office of to-day was not introduced until much later.

AUGUST 24

ST BARTHOLOMEW, APOSTLE

One of the many translations of the body of St Bartholomew is commemorated to-day, and this feast is kept by the Greeks under the following title: Ἡ ἐπάναδος τοῦ λειψάνου τοῦ ἁγίου Ἀποστόλου Βαρθολομαίου.

Theodore the Doctor relates that the Emperor Anastasius first caused the body of the Apostle to be carried to Dara in Mesopotamia[1] where Justinian built a basilica over it.[2] Gregory of Tours next asserts that in his day the relics of St Bartholomew were venerated in the Island of Lipari, whence they were finally transferred, towards the ninth century, to Benevento. They are still preserved there.

For many centuries the Romans and the people of Benevento bitterly disputed whether the latter had really granted to Otho III a portion of that precious relic, or whether they had deceived him by substituting the bones of St Paulinus of Nola for those of the Apostle.

In the Eternal City the monastery which Pope Honorius built in his family palace near the Lateran, was dedicated to the Apostles Andrew and Bartholomew, and is therefore described in the *Liber Pontificalis* as *monasterium . . . quod appellatur Honorii*. The little church with its mosaic pavement still exists, and stands between the buildings of the ancient hospital of St Michael the Archangel, and those constructed by Everso dell' Anguillara. Many Popes, amongst whom are Adrian I and Leo III, have restored and enriched it with gifts.

[1] *P.G.*, LXXXVI. 212.   [2] *Procopius, De aedif.* II, 2, 3.

After the tenth century another sanctuary in honour of St Bartholomew arose on the Isola Tiburtina, where the church dedicated by Otho III to his former friend St Adalbert of Prague in time changed its title to that of St Bartholomew.

There were other medieval churches in Rome also dedicated to this saint: St Bartholomew *in Cancellis*, St Bartholomew *de capite Merulanae*, St Bartholomew *de Vaccinariis*, etc.

The *Acta* of St Bartholomew do not inspire much confidence, whereas the Armenian tradition which asserts that he preached the Faith at Areobanus, not far from Albak, seems more reliable. Here he converted to the Christian religion the sister of the king, and the latter, seized with anger, caused him to be beaten so cruelly that he died three hours later.

The Armenians rightfully regard St Bartholomew as the Apostle of their nation.

The Introit is that of the Apostles on November 30.

Collect: " Almighty and everlasting God, who hast given us a reverent and holy joy in this day's festival of thy blessed apostle Bartholomew, grant, we beseech thee, that thy church may love what he believed and preach what he taught."

The Church is called Catholic and Apostolic in the Creed because that which we now believe was taught by the apostles, who confirmed their good tidings by martyrdom. This common Faith which links us with the martyrs and the apostles, and through them with Christ, kindles in our heart the flame of love, and is also the cause of the joyousness which distinguishes the spirit of the Catholic Church from the gloomy outlook of heretical sects.

The Lesson is taken from the First Epistle to the Corinthians (xii, 27-31), in which the Apostle St Paul shows that precisely because the Church is a living organism there must be in her unity of spirit, but multiplicity of offices and organs. Thus, all will not be empowered to act as apostles, prophets, and teachers, some will carry out one work, some another; but everyone must desire charity, that is the spirit which pervades the mystical body of Christ and unites us with him and with our neighbour, in which twofold love *universa lex pendet et prophetae*.

The Gradual *Constitues* is like that of November 30, while the alleluiatic verse is taken from the famous triumphal hymn of Nicetas of Remesiana. " The glorious choir of the apostles praise thee, O Lord."

The Gospel is taken from St Luke (vi, 12-19) and refers to the vocation of the apostles. Before making this choice, Jesus spent the whole night in prayer on a mountain-top, in order to teach us that the vocation of an apostle is divine and

August 24

needs much prayer and interior illumination. It is Jesus who chooses and calls the minister of the altar, for none can presume to co-operate with God in his most divine work, the salvation of souls, unless God himself has first marked him as his fellow-labourer. The Redeemer chose all the apostles at once, and formed them from the beginning into a hierarchical group with St Peter at their head, in order to show us that the rightful priesthood instituted by Christ is that which is derived in unbroken succession from the twelve Apostles chosen by our Saviour, and being in communion with the See of Peter, is also in communion with the entire Catholic Episcopate.

The Offertory is the same as on November 30.

Secret : " We who keep the solemn festival of thy blessed apostle Bartholomew, beseech thee, O Lord, that we may receive blessings from thee by means of him in whose honour we offer up to thee this victim of praise." Such is Catholic prayer, humble and sincere. The Church knows that our human nature has been deeply wounded by original sin, therefore she prays God to stretch out his hand, that we may be raised and made whole.

Some Sacramentaries give the following Preface for to-day, which, however, differs very little from that which is common to all the apostles. *Vere . . . Qui ecclesiam tuam sempiterna pietate non deseris, sed per beatos Apostolos tuos iugiter erudis et sine fine custodis. Per . . .*

The Communion is like that of St Matthew on February 24.

Post-Communion : " May the pledge of eternal life, which we have received, O Lord, we beseech thee, through the intercession of blessed Bartholomew thine apostle, bring us help both for this present life and for that which is to come." The holy Eucharist is called here the pledge of eternal redemption, because in it God gives himself to us. He desires to be our reward and our beatitude. But as this happiness is reserved to a time unknown to us, Jesus gives us a foretaste of it here, and this token is nothing less than the reward itself in all its fulness—our God.

AUGUST 25

St Genesius, Martyr

Synaxis at the Agro Verano.

To-day we again keep a feast near St Lawrence, *Romae Genesii Martyris*, as the Martyrology of St Jerome announces.

It is not, however, certain whether St Genesius whose small basilica stood near the Agro Verano, was the same St Genesius the martyr of Arles, devotion to whom was widespread in the early Middle Ages. The Roman Itineraries constantly refer to St Genesius, together with the local saints of the cemeteries of Cyriacus and Hippolytus.

We know, too, from the *Liber Pontificalis* that Gregory III repaired the roof of the *ecclesia beati Genesii Martyris*.

Many Roman documents mention the feast of the martyr Genesius on this day.

AUGUST 25

St Louis, King and Confessor

To-day we commemorate a king who was a faithful disciple of Christ Crucified, and whose life bears witness to the truth that virtue is not always rewarded in this world. Louis was inspired by his zeal for the Faith to attempt the reconquest of the Holy Places sanctified by the blood of the Redeemer, but instead of triumph and victory, he only met with defeat and captivity, and when he was at last ransomed by his people, he brought back to Paris as a symbolic trophy of his campaigns the Crown of Thorns once worn by our Saviour.

He died of plague under the walls of Tunis, to which city he was about to lay siege, on August 25, 1270. Christian Rome dedicated a celebrated church to him, not far from the *Stadium Domitiani*.

* * * * *

The Mass is that of January 23, the feast of St Raymund. The Lesson is taken from the Mass of a Martyr, as on the feast of St Canute on January 19, and alludes to the cruel imprisonment which the saintly king suffered because of his zeal in fighting for the Holy Places.

The wisdom of God, which always guides his servants, did not desert Louis in his bonds, and though it led him to bitter warfare in this life, it was in order that he might win a more glorious palm in heaven.

On the festival of this monarch, who in France during many centuries seemed to personify " the most Christian kingdom of the eldest daughter of the Church," the Gospel is the parable of the king who distributes his wealth among his servants in order that they may traffic with it until his return (Luke xix, 12–26). The meaning is almost the same as that of the parable of the master who gave his capital to his servants in order that they should put it out at interest (Matt. xxv, 14–23). In to-day's passage, however, we are struck by one phrase. The indolent servant tells his lord

August 25

that he is *homo austerus*, and the lord accepts it and repeats the word.

God shows himself to us, as we are to him. To those who truly love him he is the Father of mercies and of love; but those who refuse these graces and withdraw from his embrace, he governs with the sceptre of his unapproachable sanctity and justice.

The three Collects are proper to the feast.

Collect: " O God, who didst remove blessed Louis, thy confessor, from an earthly throne to the glory of the heavenly kingdom, grant, we beseech thee, through his merits and prayers that we may have fellowship with the King of kings, Jesus Christ, thy Son."

In this Collect, the Church recalls the faithful to a sense of the royal dignity to which, by reason of our incorporation with Christ, king and priest, we have been raised in Baptism. If all Christians belong to this sacred dynasty founded by Christ—*regale sacerdotium*—it is right that they should truly rule over themselves and subdue their passions.

A fine phrase referring to this royal liberty, which a Christian should never permit to be infringed, is attributed to St Columbanus. This holy Abbot said one day to a tyrannical king: *Si aufers libertatem, aufers dignitatem*.

Secret: " Grant, we beseech thee, almighty God, that even as blessed Louis, thy Confessor, spurning the blandishments of the world, sought to become well-pleasing unto Christ his King alone, so may his prayers make us acceptable unto thee."

There is nothing more cowardly than to stifle one's own conscience for fear of displeasing others. With the best intentions, in spite of the greatest tact and prudence, it is impossible to please all. St Paul endeavoured to do so, but he himself wrote: *Si adhuc hominibus placerem, Christi servus non essem*.

The Psalmist has a yet sterner word about these cowardly victims of human respect: *disperdet ossa eorum qui hominibus placent, quoniam Deus sprevit eos*.

Post-Communion: " O God, who didst give thy blessed Confessor Louis renown on earth and glory in heaven, appoint him, we beseech thee, the defender of thy Church."

What living man remembers with any enthusiasm the names of the ancient Frankish dynasties? And yet the name of Louis IX still stands out in the eyes of the whole French nation as a type of faith, purity, valour and chivalry, which raises the lilies of France far above the dust to which rival factions destructive of the spirit of their country have descended.

AUGUST 26

St Zephyrinus, Pope*

The *Liber Pontificalis* notes the death of Zephyrinus to-day, but in this it is not in agreement with the Martyrology of St Jerome in which we find it on December 20, 217.

The reign of the aged Pontiff was lengthy, and is memorable because the Roman Church developed considerably at that period and organized its resistance against the heretics, especially by means of the labours of the learned Archdeacon Callixtus. We know from the writings of Optatus of Milevis, that the Pope himself confuted them in his writings and left a work exposing their errors. It was under Zephyrinus, too, that the priest Caius wrote his dialogue against the Montanist Proclus; at the same time Callixtus opposed the doctrines of Hippolytus, who appeared to separate the Blessed Trinity almost to the point of making of the three Persons three Gods.

It is to Zephyrinus, too, that the honour is due of having enlarged the cemetery on the Via Appia, which later on was known by the name of Callixtus, after the Archdeacon to whom its administration was entrusted. At this time the custom of burying the Popes at the Vatican, near St Peter's, fell into disuse, and the foundations of the Papal Crypt on the Via Appia were laid.

Zephyrinus, however, did not wish to be laid in the vault, but was interred under the pavement of the building still existing in the cemetery of Callixtus, towards the Via Ardeatina, which De Rossi erroneously called St Soter. Later, perhaps on account of the destruction which the cemeteries suffered at the hands of the Goths, the bones of St Tarcisius were placed in the same tomb as those of Zephyrinus, and were thus the object of equal veneration. *Ibi sanctus Tarcisius et sanctus Zeferinus in uno tumulo iacent*, says the Epitome of the *Locis Sanctis*. In the ninth century the relics were translated to the new Church of San Silvestro in Campo Marzio, where indeed they are recorded on the marble *Notitia Nataliciorum* existing there.

MENSE · IVLIO · DIE · XXVI · N͡AT · SCORV͡M · ZEFIRINI · PAPAE
ET · TARSICII · MARTYRIS

The Mass is the same as that of St Eusebius of Vercelli, on December 16.

The Collect, however, is the following: " Grant, we beseech thee, almighty God, that we who rejoice in the merits of blessed Zephyrinus, thy bishop and martyr, may be taught by the example of his life."

St Zephyrinus did not die a violent death. If he has sometimes been given the title of martyr by writers of a later date, it must be accepted in a general sense, as signifying that he lived during the time of persecution.

AUGUST 27

St Joseph Calasanctius, Confessor*

This Saint was ever a devout pilgrim at the shrines of the martyrs, and daily visited the seven Churches of Rome. St Joseph, whose patience God was pleased to try, as he tried that of Job, has a right to be considered a Roman citizen, for he lived for more than fifty years on the banks of the Tiber. After having founded the Congregation of the " Scuole Pie," after having refused the Cardinal's hat, in order that nothing should be wanting to the trial of his virtue, he was dragged through the streets of Rome when nearly eighty years of age, and brought before the tribunal of the Inquisition as a malefactor. Deposed from the office of General of his Order, despised even by his disciples, as though his great age had dulled his wits, St Joseph endured all with perfect serenity.

When he died on August 25, 1648, at ninety-two years of age, the Congregation of the " Scuole Pie " was almost extinct, but man cannot destroy the work of God, and in his last moments the saint predicted its revival. This prophecy was fulfilled.

The Mass is in keeping with the spirit and the special vocation of the members of the Congregation of the " Scuole Pie."

* * * * *

The Introit takes its Antiphon from Psalm xxxiii : " Come, ye children, hearken to me : I will teach you the fear of the Lord." The first part of the same Psalm follows : " I will bless the Lord at all times : his praise shall be ever in my mouth."

Not many people bless the Lord in the midst of tribulation, but still fewer receive the good things of this life as coming from his hands ; therefore, if temptation is dangerous for those whose virtue is not solidly established, prosperity is even more harmful to the majority, and is very rarely conducive to sanctity. The wise man was satisfied with a modest sufficiency and prayed the Lord: *Divitias et paupertatem ne dederis mihi, sed tantum victui meo tribue necessaria.*

Collect: "O God, who by means of holy Joseph, thy Confessor, didst provide thy Church with new helpers for training the young in the spirit of understanding and piety; grant, we beseech thee, that through his example and teaching we may so work and so teach as to win everlasting rewards."

Jesus said to his Apostles, *Euntes docete omnes gentes, baptizantes eos.* Therefore, even before the administration of the Sacraments, the Church received from God the authority to teach, to open schools, to raise pulpits whence the words of truth might be taught, nor can any human authority forbid her to do so. Faithful to this mission of education, we find the Church even in the Middle Ages erecting schools besides presbyteries and cathedrals, in which the lamp of classical learning was kept alight. And when after the seventeenth century, before the altered conditions of European life had allowed the people to gain a wider influence in public affairs, learning was still the monopoly of the rich, it was the Church which, with great foresight, opened free, popular schools through the agency of St Joseph Calasanctius, St John Baptist de la Salle, Blessed Don Bosco and others.

The Lesson is like that of St Zephyrinus, and contains allusions to the persecutions endured by the saint, and his arrest by the officials of the Inquisition.

The Gradual is the same as on January 31, whilst the alleluiatic verse, which harmonizes with the thought of the prolonged martyrdom of St Joseph Calasanctius, is that of the Mass of St Raymund on January 23.

The Gospel is that of St John the Baptist de la Salle on May 15. Little children are set before us as examples of Christian perfection, because the qualities which they naturally possess, of purity, humility and disinterested affection, are to be acquired by us by means of grace. At the foundation of the whole spiritual structure there is one virtue which outweighs all the others. The Lord says: *Quicumque humiliaverit se, sicut parvulus* . . . Humility, then, is the essential condition which helps us to return to this blessed childhood of the soul, and far from being an easy matter, requires the most heroic self-effacement on the part of those who practise it.

The Antiphon for the Offertory is taken from Psalm ix: "The Lord hath heard the desire of the poor: thy ear hath heard the preparation of their heart."

We must distinguish between two kinds of poverty. That which is praised in the Bible is the poverty of spirit which is practised interiorly, and is one and the same thing as humility.

Secret: "We lay our offerings upon thine altar, O Lord, that they may win mercy for us through the prayers of him whom thou hast given us for our advocate and helper."

The prayer is inspired by the language of the Sacramentaries, but is too archaic in tone. Originally the faithful did, indeed, heap up their gifts upon the altar, but nowadays the words *altare muneribus cumulamus* have no meaning because they no longer correspond with the liturgical practices of the time.

The Antiphon for the Communion is in keeping with the scene described in to-day's Gospel, but it is taken from St Mark (x, 14). "Suffer the little children to come to me, and forbid them not: for of such is the kingdom of God." Purity and humility have an irresistible power over the heart of the Lamb of God.

Post-Communion: "We who have been sanctified by this mystery of salvation, beseech thee, O Lord, that by the intercession of holy Joseph thy Confessor we may ever become more and more devout."

Devotion is the direction of our mind and heart to God. It helps us in every undertaking, for, as St Paul wrote to Timothy, it is a general virtue which gives a supernatural meaning to all our actions.

AUGUST 28

St Hermes, Martyr

Station at the Cemetery of Basilla on the Via Salaria Vecchia.

The Philocalian Calendar contains this notice to-day: *V. Kal. Sept. Hermetis in Basillae Salaria vetere.*

Hermes, according to his *Acta*, was a prefect of Rome, but his name does not appear in the *fasti*. He may, however have been connected with that office as an *adlectus*.

The primitive crypt of the martyr was transformed when the persecutions had ceased into a spacious subterranean basilica, which was decorated by Pope Damasus. The only words left of the marble inscription upon the altar are: HERME . . . INHERENS.

The body of St Hermes was translated by Gregory IV to the *titulus Marci*, at the Pallacine, where his image is to be seen in the crypt under the apse of the church.

* * * * *

The Mass *Laetabitur* is the same as for St Saturninus on November 29. The Collects are the following: "O God, who didst endow blessed Hermes, thy martyr, in his passion with the virtue of constancy; by thy grace may we so follow his example as to despise for thy love's sake all worldly prosperity, and fear no temporal harm."

The spirit of the world is sharp and subtle; it soon discovers whether we are in agreement with it or whether we follow the spirit of Christ. These two spirits are irreconcilable and there can be no compromise between them. He who desires to follow Christ, or as St Paul says: *omnes qui pie volunt vivere in Christo Jesu, persecutionem patientur*, must be resigned to suffer at the hands of the world—nay, he should rejoice and thank God with St Jerome: *Gratias ago . . . quod dignus sim quem mundus oderit*.

In the Codex of Würzburg the Gospel to-day is like that of the feast of St Sebastian on January 20.

Secret: "We offer up to thee, O Lord, the sacrifice of praise in memory of thy saints; grant, we beseech thee, that what won for them their glory may avail us unto salvation."

How far preferable to the style adopted by modern composers of the new Collects in the Missal which are founded on allusions to the events in the life of a saint, is the golden *concinnitas* of the early writers, who, without dwelling on details, expressed in a single thought the special character of a particular festival.

There was a Preface proper to this feast: "*Vere dignum . . . aeterne Deus: quoniam fiducialiter laudis tibi immolamus Hostias, quas sancti Hermetis martyris tui precibus, tibi esse petimus acceptas. Per . . .*"

Post-Communion: "We who have been filled with heavenly blessings, beseech thy clemency, O Lord, that by the intercession of blessed Hermes, thy martyr, we may enjoy the benefit of that which we humbly celebrate."

The Church is careful to teach us with what humility we should draw near to minister at the altar of God. If it is an honour for us to do so, it is an immense condescension on the part of the Lord to accept our gifts. Therefore Daniel, when he was far from the Temple, prayed thus at Babylon: May the humility and contrition of our hearts, O Lord, be as the sacrifice of thousands of lambs which we can no longer offer to thee, as thy Temple is a heap of smoking ruins.

AUGUST 28

St Augustine, Bishop, Confessor and Doctor

To St Augustine belongs the glory of being the first Doctor of the Church and of having achieved for Catholic theology in the fourth century what St Thomas Aquinas accomplished

August 28

for Scholasticism eight centuries later. All the Doctors of the early Middle Ages follow in word and in thought the great Bishop of Hippo, whose personality reminds us in some ways of another convert, St Paul, who from being a fierce enemy of Christ became the herald of the Gospel throughout the earth.

The body of St Augustine, which was saved by African bishops from the profanation of the Vandals, was first taken to Sardinia, and then to Pavia, by the agency of Luitprand, where it is still preserved in Ciel d'Oro.

At Rome in the fifteenth century, on the spot where once there stood a chapel dedicated to St Augustine near San Trifone, Cardinal d'Estouteville caused a splendid church to be built in honour of St Augustine, which is one of the most popular sanctuaries in the Eternal City.

* * * * *

The Mass, which is not ancient, has been gathered from various parts of the Sacramentary.

Thus the Introit and the two Lessons are from January 29; the Collect is identical with the *oratio super populum* on Monday in the second week in Lent. The remainder is from the Common of Doctors (January 29), except the alleluiatic verse, which is from the Mass of St Sylvester I.

In the Sacramentaries of the late Middle Ages we find the following Preface: "... *aeterne Deus. Qui beatum Augustinum confessorem tuum, et scientiae documentis replesti, et virtutum ornamentis ditasti; quem ita multimodo genere pietatis imbuisti, ut ipse tibi et ara, et sacrificium, et sacerdos esset et templum. Per* ..."

We may remember to-day, for our spiritual edification, three famous sentences of the great Doctor of Hippo: " Thou hast made our hearts for thyself, O Lord, and they cannot find peace except in thee alone." " Lord, teach me to know thee and to know myself." " Too late have I loved thee, O Eternal Beauty."

St Augustine is one of the few saints who was appreciated even during his lifetime, before the light of eternity had set his greatness apart from that of other mortals. Even his contemporaries felt it, and no council was held at that time in Africa of which the Bishop of the small city of Hippo was not the leading spirit. The Consul Bassus mingled the praises of the son with those of the mother when he placed on the tomb of St Monica at Ostia the words:

GLORIA · VOS · MAIOR · GESTORVM · LAVDE · CORONAT
VIRTVTVM · MATER · FELICIOR · SVBOLIS

AUGUST 29

St Sabina, Martyr

Station at the Titulus Sabinae.

To-day's station on the Aventine is already recorded at the end of the sixth century by the *Registrum* of St Gregory the Great : *Facta sunt haec in basilica sanctae Sabinae sub die IIII Kal. Sept. Indict. VI*[1].

Even the earliest *Comes* of Rome contained in the Codex of Würzburg[2] notes this feast, but like others which do not actually belong to Rome and were introduced at a later date, it is excluded from the catalogue of the various *Comuni*.

Sabina and Serapia, who are said by their *Acta* to have been buried *in oppido Vendinensium ad arcum Faustini, iuxta aream Vindiciani*, appear to have been Umbrian martyrs. Indeed De Rossi has shown that there existed at a short distance from *Interamna* (Terni), the village of Vindena, from whence the relics of the two saints were brought to the *Titulus Sabinae* on the Aventine.

The Mass is the same as that on March 6 for the famous martyrs of Carthage, Perpetua and Felicitas. The first Collect, omitting the title of virgin, is the same as for St Agatha on February 5 ; the other two are those of St Emerentiana on January 23.

The alleluiatic verse is taken from Psalm xliv : " With thy comeliness and thy beauty, set out, proceed prosperously, and reign." The glory and triumph of Christ are reserved for us, says St Paul, in the same measure as we shall have shared, like the martyrs, in the ignominy of his Passion. This is why the Liturgy of the Church, which is a reflection of that of heaven, gives the highest honours to the holy martyrs.

According to the *Comes* of Würzburg the Lesson to-day was that which is read on July 10, praising the valiant woman, which is taken from Proverbs xxxi, 10–31. In order to deserve this praise it is not necessary, as St Philip said, to do extraordinary things. The Holy Ghost praises the housewife who weaves flax and wool and holds the distaff and spindle. In the life of a Christian even the most common actions performed in discharging the duties of her state become sublime, and worthy of eternal life when performed in a state of grace. Humble and faithful attention to duty marks a life that is already heroic, and which, if God wills it, may be a sufficient preparation for the grace of martyrdom.

[1] *Reg. Lib.* XI, n. 2. Edit. Hartmann, II, 367.   [2] Mp. th. fol. 62.

August 29

At what date was the *Titulus Sabinae* dedicated to the martyr of Vindena who bore the same name ? This is a problem which cannot be easily solved, since from the mosaic inscription still existing above the door of that basilica we find, indeed, that its founder was the priest Peter Illyricus at the time of Constantine I, but St Sabina is not mentioned in it. Who then was this matron Sabina, from whom the church took its name ? Should we connect, in some way, the Umbrian martyr with the former owner of the *domus* on the Aventine, afterwards enlarged by Peter Illyricus and turned into a vast basilica ? Or did a second Sabina at Rome complete the building left unfinished by the Illyrian priest, and give her name to it ? These are questions to which at present we can furnish no answer.

In the cloister of the Basilica of St Paul there is preserved the epigraph of a priest of the *Titulus Sabinae* when the church had not yet been dedicated to the martyr of Vindena :

LOCVS · PRESBYTERI · BASILI · ·TITVLI · SABINE Ɔ

AUGUST 29

The Beheading of St John the Baptist

It would appear in the Codex of Würzburg that this feast was postponed to the following day, perhaps on account of the stational festivity at Santa Sabina.

However, the Beheading of St John the Baptist has been commemorated on August 29, ever since the fourth century, in Africa, in the East, in Syria, and in many places all over the world. It is omitted from the Leonine, but appears in the Gelasian Sacramentary.

The fate of the relics of the Precursor of Christ is well known. At first they were interred in Samaria, but in 362 the pagans violated the tomb and burned the holy remains. A small portion of them was, however, saved by some monks, who took it to St Athanasius at Alexandria.

The Emperor Theodosius caused the reputed head of St John the Baptist, which had been preserved at Jerusalem by certain monks, to be placed at Hebdomon, near Constantinople. Another tradition, however, relates that the holy relic was brought from Jerusalem to Emesa, where Bishop Uranius in 452 recognized the authenticity of the skull.

It is not known that the head of St John the Baptist was ever brought to Rome ; the head which is venerated at San Silvestro *in Capite* is not that of the Precursor, but that of the famous priest and martyr John, whose sanctuary was visited by pilgrims in the early Middle Ages on the Via Salaria Vecchia, at the cemetery which was called *ad septem palumbas ad Caput Sancti Johannis*. This is how it is described in the *De Locis SS Martyrum*:

Inde, non longe in Occidente, ecclesia sancti Johannis martyris, ubi caput eius in alio loco sub altari ponitur, in alio corpus.

His name probably appeared in the Martyrology of St Jerome on June 24, together with that of Festus, but it was, no doubt, superseded by that of the Baptist.

A small church was specially dedicated to this St John of the Via Salaria, near the church of St Sylvester, and it took the title *in Capite* from the holy relic preserved there.

Originally the chants of to-day's feast were thus described in the Antiphonary: ANT. *In virtute tua.* PSALM. *Vitam petiit.* RESP. *Domine, praevenisti.* VERS. *Vitam petiit.* ALLEL. *Beatus vir.* OFF. *Iustus ut palma.* AD COMMUN. *Magna est gloria.*

Now, however, the primitive order has been modified in the Missal. The Antiphon for the Introit is taken from Psalm cxviii, as for the feast of St Praxedes on July 20, and this has been done in order to commemorate the fearless attitude of the Precursor in the presence of King Herod. We must fear God in order not to fear man.

The Psalm which follows the Antiphon, showing it to be the work of a modern compiler, is Psalm xci, as on the Nativity of St John the Baptist. " It is good to give praise to the Lord: and to sing to thy name, O most High."

This is the Collect: " O Lord, we beseech thee that the holy festival of thy forerunner and martyr, St John the Baptist, may win for us help unto salvation."

In these Collects of the Church we constantly pray for divine grace, and in doing so we show our belief in a most important truth which was violently opposed by Pelagius in the fourth century. In order to work out our eternal salvation we all need the grace of God, to whose merciful help we must therefore attribute all the good which we accomplish. On this account St Paul himself said: *Gratia autem Dei sum id quod sum.*

The Lesson is taken from Jeremias (i, 17-19), and is the continuation of the passage read on June 24. The Lord warns his Prophet not to give way to vain fear of earthly powers. These may indeed rise up against the messenger of Jehovah, but cannot overcome him, for the power of God is greater than that of man, and the latter will always be worsted in the struggle. It is wiser, then, to surrender at once, as Saul surrendered on the way to Damascus.

The Gradual is the same as on December 3, for the feast

August 29

of St Francis Xavier. We may ask now: how can we say of the martyr that he will flourish like the palm, whereas his head was struck off by the sword? But the answer is clear. As Christ on one day died upon a cross, and on the next was adored in Limbo, and on the third day rose again, so his disciples too will receive the reward of their sufferings after death, and at last will rise once more in glory from their tombs and will be all the more like to Christ in brightness, the more their bodies have suffered for his sake the ignominy of the Cross.

Tertullian holds that the rapid spread of Christianity through the world in the first three centuries was an early blossoming of the seed sown by the blood of the martyrs.

The alleluiatic verse in which the just man is compared to a flourishing lily is the same as on January 15 for St Paul the Hermit.

The Gospel for to-day is taken from St Mark (vi, 17-29) and is given also in the Codex of Würzburg. The greatest amongst those born of woman falls a victim to the shameful intrigue of an adulterous pair. According to human judgement there is nothing glorious or dramatic in the death of John, who was slain in secret in the silence of the prison at Machaerus. How different are God's views: John had desired that his influence and his renown should fade in order that Jesus alone should be glorified. His prayer was heard. He died because his sanctity as precursor of Christ was intolerable to the immoral Herodias. He anticipated in his death the humiliations of Calvary, but he was rewarded by having his praises spoken by the Saviour himself, even if Jesus and his disciples did not actually assist at his funeral, as some legends maintain. What other saint has been honoured as John was honoured?

The Antiphon for the Offertory is the same as for St Paul the Hermit.

Secret: "We beseech thee, O Lord, that the offerings which we bring to thee in honour of the suffering of thy holy martyr John the Baptist may by his intercession be profitable for our salvation."

Some Sacramentaries give the following Preface for to-day: *Vere dignum . . . aeterne Deus. Qui Praecursorem Filii tui tanto munere ditasti, ut pro veritatis praeconio capite plecteretur, et qui Christum aqua baptizaverat, ab ipso in Spiritu baptizatus, pro eodem proprio sanguine tingeretur. Praeco quippe veritatis, quae Christus est, Herodem a fraternis thalamis prohibendo, carceris obscuritate detruditur, ubi solius divinitatis tuae lumine frueretur. Deinde capitalem sententiam subiit, et ad inferna Dominum praecursurus descendit. Et quem in mundo digito demonstravit, ad inferos pretiosa morte praecessit. Et ideo . . .*"

The Antiphon for the Communion is the same as on January 26.

The sword of the executioner struck off the head of St John, but God had already placed upon his brow the triple crown of the prophet, the martyr, and the virgin, as St Paul the Deacon sings in the hymn for June 24 :

> *Serta ter denis alios coronant*
> *Aucta crementis, duplicata quosdam ;*
> *Trina centeno cumulata fructu*
> *Te sacer ornant.*

Post-Communion : " May the festival of St John the Baptist bring us grace, O Lord, both to venerate what is signified by the splendid sacraments which we have received and to rejoice at what they have wrought within us."

Several churches and confraternities for the assistance of those condemned to death arose in the late Middle Ages under the title of the Beheading of St John the Baptist. They accomplished a great deal of good and it was thanks to them that the execution of human justice, being carried out in a spirit of love and compassion, became almost an act of religion. Therefore these unhappy men, assisted by the " Confortatori " and clasping the crucifix, ascended the scaffold with resignation, rejoicing that they were about to give satisfaction to God and the world for the crimes they had committed. Thus Blessed John Cafasso, one of the most zealous " comforters " of those condemned to death, used to say that out of a hundred who were executed, a hundred were saved.

There were two churches at Rome dedicated to the Decollation of St John the Baptist. The first was near the prisons of Tor di Nona opposite the Castello ; the other still exists not far from the Velabro, and amongst the many privileges enjoyed by the confraternity which bore its name, was the permission to restore a condemned criminal to freedom every Lent.

AUGUST 30

SS Felix and Adauctus, Martyrs

Station at the Cemetery of Commodilla on the Ostian Way.

The Martyrology of St Jerome invites us to go to-day to the second milestone on the Ostian Way, not very far from the tomb of the Apostle St Paul : *Via Ostense, in cimiterio Commodillae, Felicis et Adaucti.*

Adauctus is not an unusual name in Roman inscriptions, and the Christians, according to the acts of the martyrs, gave it to the anonymous Levite who mingled his blood with that of the martyr priest Felix.

A small sepulchral basilica in their honour was excavated in the Cemetery of Commodilla, which was of an irregular shape and had a deep niche at the end, in which the bodies of Felix and Adauctus reposed. On this sepulchre Pope Damasus caused the following inscription to be placed:

O · SEMEL · ATQVE · ITERVM · VERE · DE · NOMINE · FELIX
QVI · INTEMERATA · FIDE · CONTEMPTO · PRINCIPE · MVNDI
CONFESSVS · CHRISTVM · COELESTIA · REGNA · PETISTI
O · VERE · PRAETIOSA · FIDES · COGNOSCITE · FRATRES
QVA · AD · CAELVM · VICTOR · PARITER · PROPERAVIT · ADAVCTVS
PRESBYTER · HIS · VERVS · DAMASO · RECTORE · IVBENTE
COMPOSVIT · TVMVLVM · SANCTORVM · LIMINA · ADORNANS

O happy in truth as well as in name, Felix !
Thou who didst with fearless faith despise the prince of the world,
And confessing Christ, didst ascend to the heavenly kingdom.
Know, O brethren, how precious was the faith by whose merits Adauctus too hastened to heaven together with Felix.
The priest Verus, at the command of the Pontiff Damasus,
Constructed and adorned this tomb of the saints.

The memory of the two martyrs pervades the whole cemetery of Commodilla. Several inscriptions and carvings implore their intercession in favour of the dead, whilst their images appear in more than one place in the sepulchral crypt.

A beautiful painting of the sixth century on the tomb of a certain Turtura represents the deceased led before the supreme judge by the two saints Felix and Adauctus, her protectors. The peculiarity of the picture consists in the circumstance that Christ the Judge is depicted as an infant upon the lap of the most Blessed Virgin, who is seated on a throne, and is robed like a Byzantine Empress (*Maria Regina*). As an emblem of her royal power she holds the consular *Mappula* in her hand, and her feet rest upon a footstool. To the right and left of the throne stand Adauctus and Felix, both with the priestly tonsure. Felix is an old man, but Adauctus stands on the right-hand side, although he is young and beardless. Indeed he is the first to fulfil his office as advocate, for he places his hand on the shoulder of Turtura, as a sign that he has taken her under his protection.

* * * * *

The Introit from the Mass *Sapientiam* is the same as for the martyrs of Nomentum on June 9.

Collect: "We humbly beseech thy majesty, O Lord, that even as thou dost continually gladden us by the memory of thy saints, so thou wouldst evermore defend us by their prayers."

The saints in heaven imitate Christ, who is, as St Paul says, our advocate, *semper vivens ad interpellandum pro nobis*. He prays for us, and the angels and saints all unite their prayers to his.

The Lesson is like that of July 28 for the martyrs Nazarius, Celsus, etc. The Lord treats his elect as he treated the people of Israel long ago. In order to establish them in the land promised to the Patriarchs, he first led them out of the land of Egypt, across the Red Sea, through the desert, in the midst of perils and sufferings of every kind. But God fought on the side of Israel, and the Jewish people, tried and purified by tribulation, conquered the enemy, and was at length established in the fruitful land which was promised to the Patriarchs.

The responsory intended to be sung on the steps of the ambo, is the same as on January 17, for the martyrs Marius, Martha, etc. The alleluiatic verse is taken from the Book of Wisdom (iii, 3), and is the continuation of the Gradual text: "The just shall shine and shall run to and fro like sparks among the reeds."

The gain is great indeed—a brief hour of shame when the names of the servants of God are inscribed by the wicked amongst those whom they cast out from their cities, and after that an eternity of glory in heaven.

The Gospel is the same as for St Vitus on June 15. By this we see how popular was the devotion to the two martyrs Felix and Adauctus in early times, and how many miracles were worked at their tomb.

The Antiphon for the Offertory is that used for many martyrs at Eastertide, omitting the Alleluia: "Be glad in the Lord, and rejoice, ye just, and glory all ye right of heart, alleluia, alleluia."

He is called "right of heart" whose heart is conformed to that of God, and who loves, desires, and works those things which God loves, desires and works in him.

Secret: "Look down, O Lord, upon the sacrifice which thy people offer to thee, and while they celebrate it in honour of thy saints, may they know that it avails to their own salvation."

The phrase which constantly recurs in these ancient Secrets should be noted: "the sacrifice which thy people offer." In early times the Mass represented more strikingly the common sacrifice of the Christian community, because

August 30

all the faithful contributed to it, bringing their own gifts to the altar during the Offertory.

The Antiphon for the Communion, in defiance of the general rule, for it does not correspond with to-day's Gospel, is the same as on February 15.

Jesus announced the Gospel, as it were, in the dark, because he preached only in the small province of Judea and amidst persecution and opposition. His Church, however, receives from him the mission and the command to teach the Law of God in the full light of day, for she is to instruct all the nations of the earth.

Post-Communion : " We who are filled with gifts from heaven, beseech thee, O Lord, that through the intercession of thy saints we may never cease to offer thanks to thee."

In the Book of Wisdom the Holy Ghost compares the heart of an ungrateful man to the earth when it is covered with ice. In order that grace may bear fruit, it is necessary that gratitude should warm the heart and cause it to appreciate the gift which it has received and bring forth fruit in honour of the donor. St Teresa was wont to say that the moment of thanksgiving after Holy Communion is very important and decisive for our spiritual progress. Our thanksgiving after one Communion will serve as preparation for the next, and grace will not find us unready. Thus the sudden call to martyrdom did not find the young Adauctus unprepared, for when he met Felix being led forth to die, instead of returning to his family he resolved on the spot to follow the martyr on the road to heaven :

. . . *Qua ad caelum victor pariter properavit Adauctus.*

* * * * *

The Martyrology of St Jerome makes no mention of the martyr Nemesius, whose tomb is, however, noticed by all the ancient itineraries in the cemetery of Commodilla. *Ibidemque . . . sunt martyres Felix, Adauctus et Nemesius*, as, amongst others, and indeed last of all, William of Malmesbury notes.

From the hymn, written after the manner of St Damasus, which was placed on that ancient tomb, we learn the probable cause of this absence from the hagiographical lists ; it was because for some time the authenticity of the martyrdom of Nemesius was considered doubtful. When, however, further investigations had been made, the tomb was adorned as befitted that of an authentic *martyr vindicatus* and public veneration was permitted.

MARTYRIS · HAEC · NEMESI · SEDES · PER · SAECVLA · FLORET
SERIOR · ORNATV · NOBILIOR · MERITO
INCVLTAM · PRIDEM · DVBITATIO · LONGA · RELIQVIT
SED · TENVIT · VIRTVS · ADSERVITQVE · FIDEM

"This is the tomb of the martyr Nemesius; may it be glorious throughout the ages. Although the last to be adorned, it is the greatest by the merits of the martyr. A long enduring doubt had caused it to remain neglected, but the proof of the martyr's virtue triumphed and showed his faith."

Some archeologists have identified the tomb of this martyr Nemesius with that which is to be found beside the entrance to the Basilica of SS Felix and Adauctus, near which is a fresco representing the Saviour with St Peter, St Paul, St Stephen, St Merita and the two saints Felix and Adauctus. This sixth-century painting covers a more ancient one, having an inscription of which only the following words remain:

SANCTO · MARTYRI · VENERABILI

AUGUST 30

St Rose of Lima, Virgin*

It was the rare privilege of this virgin saint of Peru, that her Office was composed by the learned and devout liturgist Cardinal Bona. The feast of St Rose was raised by Benedict XIII to the rank of a double, and it has therefore practically superseded that of the two martyrs of the Cemetery of Commodilla.

Like St Catherine of Siena, St Rose belonged to the Third Order of St Dominic, and for this reason the crucifix before which she prayed is venerated in the Basilica of Santa Maria *sopra Minerva* in Rome, near the tomb of the Sienese Virgin.

Before raising this holy Peruvian maiden to the mystical marriage, God was pleased to make her pass through a fiery trial. He purified her by severe corporal penances, and by those spiritual sufferings which the soul endures, before it becomes accustomed to contact with the Godhead, who as the Apostle tells us is always *ignis consumens*.

* * * * *

The Mass is the same as for February 18, but the Collect is proper to the feast.

Collect: "Almighty God, the giver of all good gifts, who didst will that blessed Rose, being watered by the heavenly

August 30

dew of thy prevenient grace, should bloom in the Indies in the beauty of virginity and patience; grant that we thy servants may run in the odour of her sweetness and be found worthy to become a sweet savour to Christ."

This prayer sets before us a beautiful ideal of the spiritual life. Each of us should show forth Christ in his life, in his thoughts, in his words, carefully keeping the practice of religion free from any sharpness or rigidity which want of mortification might give it, in order that our devotion may appear as sweet and amiable to others as did that of our Divine Master.

AUGUST 31

St Raymund Nonnatus, Cardinal and Confessor*

The feast of this heroic son of the Order of Our Lady of Mercy, who died about 1240, was introduced into the Breviary by order of Clement IX and Innocent XI. He is worthy of the title of Confessor in the sense in which it was used by the ancients, on account of the long and cruel torments endured by him in Africa in defence of the Faith.

The Mass is the same as for his namesake St Raymund of Pennafort, on January 23, except the Collect which is proper to the feast.

Collect: " O God, by whose grace blessed Raymund thy Confessor wrought wonders in redeeming thy faithful people from the hands of wicked men; grant, we beseech thee, that, being loosed from the bondage of our sins, we may with free minds always do what is well-pleasing unto thee."

Freedom is the great gift which God bestowed upon humanity, and which Christ restored. Therefore, St Columban once said to a royal tyrant: *si aufers libertatem, aufers dignitatem.* We should jealously guard this prerogative derived from our dignity as sons of God, and never become slaves of the degrading tyranny of our passions. Freedom means order and harmony, and to enjoy the fruits of true freedom it is necessary to conquer ourselves and to submit willingly to the sweet yoke of the law of Christ.

FEASTS IN SEPTEMBER

SEPTEMBER 1

The Twelve Holy Martyrs of Beneventum*

We have here a group of twelve martyrs whose bodies were brought from various places in the Province of Lucania, in the Middle Ages, and placed in the Basilica of St Sophia at Beneventum, by order of the Duke Arichis.

They belong to the same category as Felix and Arontius, Sabinianus and Honoratus, who are mentioned in the Martyrology of St Jerome *in Lucania, civitate Potentiae* on August 26. Septimius, Januarius, and Felix are connected with Venosa and were slain on August 28, whilst three others, Vitalis, Sator, and Repositus, have their *natalis* on the following day. The two last martyrs of the group, Felix and Donatus, are recorded in the Martyrology of St Jerome on September 1 : *In Apulia Felicis, Donati.*

The translation of the holy bodies to Beneventum took place about 760, and on their tomb the following inscription could be read :

BIS · SENOS · TEGIT · VRNA · FRATRES · QVOS · VNA · CREAVIT
THECLA · DEO · FORTES · INNOCVOSQVE · DVCES
PAR · PIETAS · FVERAT · PAR · MORS · PAR · VITAQVE · ARECHVS
PRINCEPS · TRANSLATOS · ORNAT · HONORE · PARI

"This sepulchre contains the bones of twelve brothers, whom Thecla, their mother, bore to the glory of God. They were innocent and brave. They were all alike in piety and were united in their life as also in their death. Prince Arichis, who brought their bodies here, surrounds them all with equal veneration."

The feast of the martyrs interred by Arichis at Beneventum was placed in the Roman Calendar in the early Middle Ages, and through the *Brevarium Curiae* which was adopted by the Franciscans in the thirteenth century, it came to be universally observed.

* * * * *

The Mass is like that of St Symphorosa, with the exception of the Collects which are proper to the feast.

Collect : "May the brothers' crown of martyrdom gladden us, O Lord ; may it give greater steadfastness to our faith, and strengthen us by the intercession of so many saints."

Secret : "May we devoutly celebrate thy mysteries, O Lord, in memory of thy holy martyrs, and may they bring us both surer protection and greater joy."

Post-Communion : "Grant, we beseech thee, almighty God, that we who keep the memory of thy saints by receiving thy holy sacrament, may ever follow with greater steadfastness the example of their faith."

Such is the true meaning of the Eucharistic Sacrifice and of Holy Communion. Christ immolates himself to the glory of his Heavenly Father ; he now associates his whole Church with him in this tremendous Sacrifice, in which is centred the entire, true, and perfect worship which the New and the Old Testament pay to God throughout the centuries. *Una enim oblatione consummavit in aeternum sanctificatos.*

SEPTEMBER 1

ST GILES, ABBOT

The *cultus* of this celebrated saint was introduced into Italy towards the tenth century, and soon obtained great popularity, so that there are many churches dedicated to him throughout the Peninsula. At Rome, too, there is one close to the Vatican, and Boniface VIII joined it to the chapter of St Peter's. This feast was kept there with great solemnity, with fireworks, music, races through the streets, etc. It was also the meeting-place of an important confraternity.

A second church dedicated to St Giles still exists in Trastevere, and occupies the site of the ancient Church of St Lawrence *in Janicolo*. It was built by the Princess of Venafro at the beginning of the seventeenth century, and was given to the Carmelite nuns of St Teresa's reform.

The *Acta* of St Giles are not very trustworthy. He lived, probably, in the second half of the seventh century, and founded in the diocese of Nîmes a celebrated monastery in honour of the holy Apostles Peter and Paul, in which, at his death, he received honourable burial. St Urban made his feast common to the universal Church.

The Mass is the Common of Abbots, throughout, as for St Sabbas on December 5.

SEPTEMBER 2

ST STEPHEN, KING OF HUNGARY, CONFESSOR

To-day we greet a holy and glorious king, who advances preceded by the cross, like an Archbishop, having received this great privilege from Sylvester II on account of the apostolate exercised by him in the conversion of the Hungarians to the Faith.

When we have described St Stephen as the apostle of Hungary, we have summed up his praises. All that a fervent apostle can do, this king accomplished. By his example and his influence he induced the nobles and the people to embrace the Catholic Faith ; he gave Christian legislation to the kingdom; he founded and endowed episcopal Sees, he built monasteries and established charitable institutions, not only in Hungary but even in Constantinople, Jerusalem, Ravenna and Rome.

The ancient monastery of St Stephen *Kata Barbara Patricia* was in later times called after the Hungarian nation, when the holy king had restored the church and had added to the building a hostel. There pilgrims from his kingdom who came to visit the tombs of the Apostles at Rome were lodged. This hostel stood on the spot now partially occupied by the modern sacristy. The church was a parish church, and on its façade ran the following inscription:

ECCLA̰ · HOSPITALIS · SC̃I · STEPHANI · REGIS · HVNGAR

St Stephen, seven years before his death, saw his young and most innocent son Emerich, an angel of purity and holiness whom God glorified by many miracles, precede him on the way to heaven. He followed him to the tomb on August 15, 1034, but Innocent XI appointed his feast to be kept on September 2, in memory of the victory which the Christian army won over the Turks at Budapest on this day.

* * * * *

The Mass is the same as for St Louis IX on August 25, with the exception of the Collects.

Collect: "Grant, we beseech thee, almighty God, that even as the faith of thy church was spread abroad by blessed Stephen, thy confessor, while he reigned upon earth, so she may be deemed worthy to have him also for a glorious champion in heaven."

We should note the special characteristic which the Liturgy brings forward to-day in the Office of St Stephen. Besides being a king he was also an apostle, so that he may claim a right to the glorious title which the Byzantine Liturgy gives to Constantine the Great for the same reason: ἰσαπόστολος.

Secret: "Look, O God almighty, upon the victims which we offer up; so that we who celebrate the mysteries of our Lord's passion may live according to the pattern which is set before us therein."

This prayer is inspired by a phrase in the Roman Pontifical for the ordination of priests: *agnoscite quod agitis; imitamini quod tractatis*. This special allusion to the passion of our Saviour in the Mass for St Stephen reminds us of his devotion to the Holy Places of Jerusalem consecrated by the blood of our Redeemer. The monastery of St George built by the King of Hungary in the Holy City, and having a hostel for the Hungarian pilgrims attached to it, may be regarded as a monument of his special devotion.

Post-Communion: " Grant, we beseech thee, almighty God, that we may follow with true devotion the faith of blessed Stephen thy confessor, who, by spreading the same faith, became worthy to pass from an earthly realm to glory in the heavenly kingdom."

It is not enough, then, that we should ourselves enjoy so great a treasure as our Catholic faith. In order that our talents should increase, it is necessary to trade with them.

By becoming apostles we shall ensure our eternal salvation and acquire great merit, according to the saying attributed to St Augustine: *animam salvasti, tuam praedestinasti*.

SEPTEMBER 3

The Martyrology here commemorates Serapia, a martyr (who does not belong to Rome, however, but to Umbria), at the *oppidum Vendinensium, ad arcum Faustini iuxta aream Vindiciani*, as the Acts of St Sabina describe it. Her *cultus* is connected with that of the latter martyr whose memory was supreme at the *titulus Sabinae* on the Aventine ever since the seventh century.

SEPTEMBER 4

The Martyrology of St Jerome notes to-day: *Romae in cimiterio Maximi, Via Salaria, ad sanctam Felicitatem, Bonifacii episcopi*. We have already mentioned, on another occasion, that Boniface I took refuge beside the cemetery of Maximus during the schism which was brought about by Eulalius. The Pope was not satisfied with having shown his gratitude to the martyr St Felicitas by adorning her tomb, but desired also to be buried near her: *Venies ad sanctam Felicitatem altera via, quae similiter Salaria dicitur: ibi illa pausat in ecclesia sursum, et Bonifacius papa et martyr in altero loco*. So says the Itinerary of Salzburg.

In honour of Pope Boniface I, the date of whose death as given in the *Liber Pontificalis* is, however, erroneous, we may record here the ancient inscription copied by early collectors, which is to be seen in the Vatican Baptistery.

SACRI · FONTIS · HONOR · LABOR · EST · MERITVMQVE · DVORVM
PONTIFICVM · PER · QVOS · CONTVLIT · ISTA · DEVS
NAM · QVAE · MAGNIFICIS · COEPTIS · BONIFATIVS · AVXIT
HAEC · CAELESTINVS · COMPSIT · AD · OMNE · DECVS

"The honour, the labour, and the merit of having adorned the holy font are due to two Pontiffs whom God made use of for this work, since that which Boniface had commenced on a noble design, was finally finished and perfected by Pope Celestine."

SEPTEMBER 5

SS ACONTIUS, NONNUS, HERCULANUS AND TAURINUS, MARTYRS

Station at Porto in the Basilica of St Acontius.

To-day we find in the Martyrology of St Jerome: *In Portu Romano, Taurini, Herculani, Aristonis.* Whereas the Philocalian Calendar notes: *Nonis Septembris, Aconti in Porti, et Nonni et Herculani et Taurini.* We have here, therefore, a group of martyrs of Porto who, apparently, did not all die on this day. Indeed, in the Martyrology of St Jerome, Acontius, whose sepulchral basilica is mentioned by Auxilius, *ad ripam prope titulum sancti Acontii*[1] is recorded on July 15; the Philocalian Calendar, on the other hand, mentions Aristonus on December 22, whilst the St Nonnus of September 5 is identified with Hippolytus of August 22.

The martyrs Taurinus and Herculanus are also mentioned on the tablet of a sarcophagus, now in the Museum of the Abbey of St Paul at Rome:

> Deo · Patri · Omnipoten
> ti · et · χρο · eius · et · Sanctis
> Martyribus · Taurino
> Et · Herculano · omni
> Ora · gratias · AGIMVS
> NEVIVS · LARI . . . T
> CONSTANT   V
> RIA · SIBI · FEC

The fact that to-day's liturgical station is mentioned in the Philocalian Calendar of the Roman synaxes proves the popularity of the *cultus* of these martyrs, whose Basilica was probably dedicated on this very day.

The bodies of the martyrs Hippolytus, Taurinus and Herculanus were placed in safety on the Isola Tiberina, by Bishop Formosus, after the devastation of Porto by the Saracens. The inscription taken from their sarcophagus is now in the Lateran Museum.

> ✠Hic · Requiescunt · corpora · Scōr
> Martyrum · Yppoliti · Taurini · Herculani
> Atque · Johannis · Calibitis · Formosus
> Eps̄ · Condidit

[1] Cf. Dummler, *Auxilius und Vulgarius*, p. 72. Leipzig, 1866.

SEPTEMBER 5

ST LAWRENCE JUSTINIAN, PATRIARCH OF VENICE

This saintly bishop, who was a remarkable model of humility and pastoral zeal, died on January 8, 1455, but as his feast would have occurred within the Octave of the Epiphany, Innocent XII transferred it to this day, which was the anniversary of his episcopal consecration.

St Lawrence Justinian may be regarded in a manner as one of the precursors of the ecclesiastical reform which was carried out later by the Council of Trent and by St Charles Borromeo. Like St Antoninus, Bishop of Florence, whose contemporary he was, he firmly resisted the glamour of the Renaissance, and practised the virtues of a monk in the Patriarchal Palace. He belonged to the new congregation of the Canons of St George in Alga. Of great simplicity of manner and austerity towards himself, he was a true victim for the sake of the flock entrusted to him. All his revenues were spent on the poor and on building new monasteries. The most serene Republic was then at the apex of her glory and power; but it pleased God to make it known that the safety of the Venetian state was due, not to the diplomatic skill of her doges or to her formidable galleys, but to the holiness and merits of her bishop.

* * * * *

The Mass is that of February 4, for St Andrew Corsini.

The Collect is as follows: " Grant, we beseech thee, almighty God, that the holy festival of blessed Lawrence, thy confessor and bishop, may both increase our devotion and advance our salvation."

We must remember the ancient meaning of the Latin word *devotio*. It represents not so much an act of worship as a complete and lasting consecration of the Christian man to God, a kind of religious profession of which that made by a monk is only a development. This vow or consecration of the soul to God is sealed by an irrevocable Sacrament: the sacrament of Baptism.

SEPTEMBER 6

The martyr Eleutherius mentioned to-day by the Martyrology of St Jerome: *Romae, Via Salaria, natalis Eleutheri episcopi*, is not, as later Martyrologies would suggest, the holy Abbot of this name who was a companion of St Gregory the Great, but the Bishop Eleutherius of Rieti, of whom the same St Gregory speaks. In his Dialogues the saintly Pope relates how the martyrs Eleutherius and Juvenal of Narni appeared to Bishop Probus of Rieti to console him at the hour of death ; *ad me sanctus Juvenalis et sanctus Eleutherius martyres venerunt.*[1]

SEPTEMBER 7

THE VIGIL OF THE NATIVITY OF THE BLESSED VIRGIN MARY

Collecta at St Adrian.

According to the *Ordines Romani* of the fifteenth century, the Pope to-day presided at the first Vespers of the Birthday of the Blessed Virgin *cum pluviali rubeo et mitra consistoriali aurifrigiata, et cardinales veniunt cum pluvialibus albis* . . . Matins of the following day were sung in the evening in the presence of the Pope, who celebrated High Mass the next morning assisted by the first of the Cardinal Bishops.[2]

In accordance with the decree of Pope Sergius I, which we have already mentioned several times, the solemn morning procession in honour of the Mother of God, which started from St Adrian and generally went to the Liberian Basilica, took place on the four great feasts of the Blessed Virgin Mary : the Purification, the Annunciation, the Assumption, and the Birthday of the Blessed Virgin. This custom continued until the Papal Court was transferred to Avignon.

The clergy and people first assembled in the Basilica of St Adrian at the Forum, where the procession was formed. Blessed candles were distributed amongst the clergy ; eighteen deacons carried as many ikons of the Blessed Virgin and the Saviour chosen from the most celebrated of the city, and the subdeacons of the *Regio* bore the stational cross. The Pope and the clergy walked bare-footed as was the custom in all penitential processions.

SEPTEMBER 8

THE DEDICATION OF ST ADRIAN, MARTYR

Station at St Adrian in the Forum.

The Gospel List of Würzburg on this day refers only to the feast of St Adrian in whose honour Honorius I converted the ancient *Curia Senatus* into a Christian basilica. St Adrian

---

[1] Dialog. IV, 12. *P.L.* LXXVII, col. 340.
[2] *P.L.* LXXVIII, col. 1344–5.

is the object of a widely spread *cultus* in the East, where his name is found in almost all calendars, but it does not appear in any of the ancient hagiographical documents.

In spite of this obscurity concerning his identity, devotion to the martyr existed at Rome from the seventh century, and attained some notoriety, for besides the Basilica in the Forum, there was an oratory dedicated to him at the Vatican, and another church with a monastery called after St Adrian rose on the Esquiline near the Liberian Basilica. It had various names: *Sancti Hadriani in Massa Iuliana, Sancti Hadriani ad duo furna, Sancti Hadriani et Laurentii*, and was indeed one of the religious houses whose monks were entrusted with chanting the Divine Office at St Mary Major.

* * * * *

The Mass is the same as for St Valentine on February 14.

Collect: "Grant, we beseech thee, almighty God, that we who are keeping the festival of blessed Adrian thy martyr, may through his intercession be strengthened in the love of thy name."

This is true virtue, and as St Paul calls it: *vinculum perfectionis*. The holiest man is not he who spends most time in prayer, nor he who mortifies his body with the greatest severity, but he who loves God most intensely, and who lives and labours in this love.

The other two prayers are the same as on the feast of St Canute.

In spite of the different arrangement of the Missal, the Codex of Würzburg assigned the following Gospel to be read to-day: *Ego sum vitis—gaudium vestrum impleatur* (John xv, 1-11), as for several martyrs at Eastertide.

SEPTEMBER 8

THE BIRTHDAY OF THE BLESSED VIRGIN MARY

Station at St Mary Major.

As Eve, our first Mother, arose from the side of Adam, dazzling with life and innocence, so Mary came forth, bright and immaculate from the heart of the eternal Word, who, by the co-operation of the Holy Spirit, as the Liturgy teaches us, was pleased to form that body and soul which were to be, one day, his Tabernacle and altar. This is the sublime meaning of the feast of the Birthday of the Blessed Virgin Mary. It is the dawn foretelling the day which already breaks behind the eternal hills, the mystic rod which rises from the venerable root of Jesse; the stream which springs from Paradise; it is the symbolical fleece which is stretched on our dry earth to catch the miraculous dew. This is the new Eve, that is to say the life and the Mother of all the living, who is born to-day for those to whom the first Eve became the Mother of sin and death.

The origin of this festival must be sought in the East, where we find it mentioned in the homilies of Andrew of Crete (died 720). At Rome, on the other hand, the feast of the dedication of St Adrian was kept on this day from the time of Pope Honorius I; thus the festival of the Nativity was not observed before the reign of Sergius I. It is, therefore, only to be found in the Martyrology of St Jerome, in the so-called Gelasian Calendar and in other Gallican Calendars of later date. The *Capitulare Evangeliorum* of Würzburg ignores it.

Collecta at St Adrian.

The clergy and people having assembled in what was once the Curia of the Senate, the Introit *Exsurge, Domine*, followed by the Doxology, was sung before the procession started, as on February 2. In conclusion the Pope recited the following Collect: *Supplicationem servorum tuorum, Deus miserator, exaudi; ut qui in Nativitate Dei Genitricis et Virginis congregamur, eius intercessionibus a te de instantibus periculis eruamur. Per eumdem.*

Then, bare-footed, the procession moved on to the Esquiline Hill, passing by the *Carine*, the Forum of Nerva, the Forum and baths of Trajan, by the titles of Eudoxia and Praxedes. When it drew near to the Liberian Basilica, the Litany, which on this day took the place of the Introit and the *Kyrie*, was intoned.

Station at St Mary Major.

The early Antiphonaries generally assign to the station of to-day the same chants which were used on August 15, whereas the present Missal now repeats the Mass which is given on July 2 for the feast of the Visitation. Only the two Lessons are different. The first is the same as for December 8, in which the words of Scripture concerning the eternal origin of the uncreated Wisdom are applied to the Mother of the Word.

The Gospel with the genealogy of the Saviour is the same that is read on the eve of the Immaculate Conception, a feast resembling that of to-day, for it, too, is concerned with the mystery of grace and redemption which surrounded the first moments of Mary's existence.

September 8

The Sacramentaries assign a special Preface to this feast: *Vere dignum . . . aeterne Deus, et praecipue pro meritis beatae Dei Genitricis et perpetuae Virginis Mariae, gratia plenae, tuam omnipotentiam laudare, benedicere et praedicare. Per quem*, etc.

There was also a final blessing *super populum*.

Ad complendum. Adiuvet nos, quaesumus Domine, sanctae Mariae intercessio veneranda, cuius etiam diem quo felix eius est inchoata nativitas celebramus. Per . . .

According to Cencio Camerario, in the thirteenth century, the eighteen images of Our Lady belonging to eighteen Diaconal churches were carried in procession on this day. The Pope took off his shoes at the Church of St Adrian, but wore slippers on his feet during the procession—*reaccipit planellas*[1]—which, however, he removed at the threshold of St Mary Major. As soon as the assembly had entered the church, the *Te Deum* was intoned and the *schola* of *mappulari* and *cubicolari* washed the Pontiff's feet with warm water, after which he prepared to celebrate the solemn Sacrifice.

Mary became the Mother of the Divine Word Incarnate for the sake of sinful man. Will she not be to us also a loving Mother?

SEPTEMBER 9

St Gorgonius, Martyr

Station at the Cemetery " ad duas lauros " on the Via Labicana.

To-day the Martyrology of St Jerome and the Philocalian Calendar note: *Gorgonii in Lavicana*. This martyr, sometimes mistaken for the Gorgonius of Nicomedia who suffered under Diocletian, was, as we know, interred in the Cemetery *ad duas lauros* on the Via Labicana, and Pope Damasus adorned his tomb with the following inscription:

MARTYRIS · HIC · TVMVLVS · MAGNO · SVB · VERTICE · MONTIS
GORGONIVM · RETINET · SERVAT · QVI · ALTARIA · CHRISTI
HIC · QVICVMQVE · VENIT · SANCTORVM · LIMINA · QVAERAT
INVENIET · VICINA · IN · SEDE · HABITARE · BEATOS
AD · CAELVM · PARITER · PIETAS · QVOS · VEXIT · EVNTES

"This sepulchre hollowed out of the hill-side contains the body of the martyr Gorgonius, who thus watches before the altar of Christ. Whosoever comes to seek the tombs of the saints in this place will find that other blessed ones rest here, who were led to heaven by the same faith."

[1] *Ord. Rom.* XI. *P.L.* LXXVIII, col. 1068.

The martyrs who surrounded Gorgonius and to whom Damasus alludes, were Peter and Marcellinus, Tiburtius and the four Holy Crowned Martyrs, i.e. Clement, Sympronianus, Claudius, and Nicostratus. Subsequently the relics of St Gorgonius were translated to St Peter's.

* * * * *

The Mass is the same as for St Saturninus on November 29, but the Collects are proper to the feast.

Collect: "May thy holy Gorgonius, O Lord, gladden us by his intercession, and fill us with joy at this his holy festival."

Secret: "May the sacrifice which we thy servants offer up to thee, O Lord, be well-pleasing in thy sight through the intercession of the holy martyr Gorgonius."

The phrase *oblatio servitutis nostrae* occurs also in the Canon, and in its original significance it expressed, as we have elsewhere explained, the sacrifice which the body of the priesthood offered to God in thanksgiving for their own office and dignity.

Post-Communion: "May eternal sweetness descend upon and strengthen thy servants, O God; and may they be ever refreshed with the good odour of Christ thy Son in thy martyr Gorgonius."

By the perfume here spoken of, we do not mean merely the miracles worked at the martyr's tomb, but we refer also, and with even more truth, to the attraction exercised by his gallant example. Good deeds have a stronger influence than any book or sermon, for it is easy enough to preach, but only a good example can lend persuasive force to our words. Thus St Luke tells us in speaking of Christ: *coepit facere et docere.*

SEPTEMBER 9

St Hyacinth, Deacon and Martyr

The Martyrology of St Jerome announces a second feast to-day, which was kept at Sabina, thirty miles from Rome: *In Sabinis, Iacinti.* His sepulchral basilica on the Via Salaria was given by Duke Lupo of Spoleto to the Abbey of Farfa in the seventh century, and Leo III enriched it with valuable vestments: *Fecit autem et in basilica beati Iacinthi, sita in Sabinis, ubi et corpus eius requiescit, vestem de stauraci pulcherrimam.*[1]

Later, in order to save the holy relics from profanation at the hands of the Saracens, it was translated to the fortified enclosure of the famous Abbey of Farfa, where St Hyacinth's

[1] *Lib. Pontif.* Edit. Duchesne, II, 13, 42.

September 9

feast is celebrated to this day. The names of Alexander and Tiburtius who are mentioned in the Acts as companions of Hyacinth the martyr do not appear in the earliest documents, and are also unknown to the liturgical tradition of Farfa. In the tenth century a portion of the body of St Hyacinth was given by the Abbot John III to Theodoric, Bishop of Metz.

SEPTEMBER 10

St Nicholas of Tolentino, Confessor

This feast dates from the time of Sixtus V, who raised it to the rank of a double. Clement VIII reduced it once more to a semidouble, but Clement IX restored it to its former rank.

St Nicholas of Tolentino is one of the chief glories of the congregation known as the Hermits of St Augustine, which in his day had been recently founded, and his life is remarkable because of the great devotion which he showed to the mystery of the Cross. Before he attained to the enjoyment of the celestial favours mentioned in the Breviary, St Nicholas had passed through the sharp martyrdom of daily austerities by which he impressed upon his body the stigmata of Christ.

The Discalced Augustinians dedicated to this saint a church in the *alta semita*, near the title of St Susanna, where, however, the Armenian Pontifical College is now established, which keeps his feast according to the national Armenian rite.

* * * * *

The Mass *Justus* is the same as for St Peter Nolasco on January 31. The Collect is the following: " Give ear, O Lord, to our humble prayers, which we present to thee on the festival of blessed Nicholas thy confessor; and may we who trust not in our own righteousness, be helped by the prayers of him who was well-pleasing to thee."

This should be the spirit of Christian prayer: humble like that of the publican in the Gospel, but animated at the same time by confidence in the merits of Christ and the Communion of the Saints.

SEPTEMBER 11

SS Protus and Hyacinth, Martyrs

Station on the Via Salaria Vecchia in the Cemetery of Basilla.

To-day the Philocalian Calendar notes in accordance with the Martyrology of St Jerome: *III idus septembris, Proti et Iacinti in Basillae.*

Protus and Hyacinth were commemorated by Pope Damasus in the following epigram:

EXTREMO · TVMVLVS · LATVI｜t sub aggere montis
HVNC · DAMASVS · MONSTRAT｜servat quod membra piorum
TE · PROTVM · RETINET · ME｜lior sibi regia caeli
SANGVINE · PVRPVREO · SE｜queris Hyacinthe probatus
GERMANI · FRATRES · ANIM｜is ingentibus ambo
HIC · VICTOR · MERVIT · PAL｜mam prior ille coronam.

"The sepulchre was hidden under the fall of the hill-side when Damasus undertook to recover the remains of the blessed. The kingdom of heaven holds thee, O Protus, and thither dost thou follow him, O valiant Hyacinth, robed in the purple of thy blood. They were brothers and were unconquered in spirit. Protus first won his crown, but Hyacinth equally deserved the palm."

The following verses are concerned with the same works executed by Damasus:

ASPICE · DESCENSVM · CERNES · MIRABILE · FACTVM
SANCTORVM · MONVMENTA · VIDES · PATEFACTA · SEPVLCHRIS
MARTYRIS · HIC · PROTI · TVMVLVS · IACET · ATQVE · YACINTHI
QVEM · CVM · IAM · DVDVM · TEGERET · MONS · TERRA · CALIGO
HOC · THEODORVS · OPVS · CONSTRVXIT · PRESBYTER · INSTANS
VT · DOMINI · PLEBEM · OPERA · MAIORA · TENERENT

"Observe the stair and the other remarkable work carried out in order to bring to light the sepulchre of the saints. Here is the tomb of Protus and Hyacinth, which lay once in the darkness covered by the earth fallen from the hill. This work was executed by the zealous priest Theodore, who desired thus to encourage the people of God to greater devotion."

It seems probable that Pope Symmachus had a special devotion to these two martyred brothers. After having dedicated an altar to them in the *rotonda* of St Andrew in the Vatican, he also restored their sepulchre in the Cemetery of Basilla. This is proved by the following inscription, which, however, has been erroneously connected with the Basilica of St Peter:

MARTYRIBVS · SANCTIS · PROTO · ATQVE · HIACYNTHO
SIMACHVS · HOC · PARVO · VENERATVS · HONORE · PATRONOS
EXORNAVIT · OPVS · SVB · QVO · PIA · CORPORA · RVRSVS
CONDIDIT · HIS · AEVO · LAVS · SIT · PERENNIS · IN · OMNI

September 11

"In honour of the holy martyrs Protus and Hyacinth, Symmachus, after having shown his devotion to his great patrons by the decoration of their sepulchre, replaced their holy bodies within it. May eternal praise be given to them."

The history of this work is completed by another inscription, of the year 400, which was found in the Cemetery of Basilla, near the tomb of the saints.

```
FELIX · DIGNA · TVLIT · PARVM · SENES · MVNERA · CHRISTI
ET · SVO · CONTENTVS · HABVIT · PER · SAECVLA · NOMEN
LAETIFICVM · RENOVANS · PRIMA · AB · ORIGINE · TEMPLVM
INFANDAQVE · FVGIENS · ISTIVS · IVRGIA · VITAE
CERTVM · EST · IN · REGNO · CAELESTI · PERQVE · AMOENA ·
   VIRETA
ISTVM · CVM · ELECTIS · ERIT · HABITATVRVS · IN · AEVVM
SEMPER · ET · ASSIDVAE · BENEDICET · MVNERA · CHRISTI
QVI · VIXIT · ANN · LXIIII · M · VIII · D · XXIII
FL · STILICONE · CONS
```

"The venerable Felix met an undeserved fate which he received as a gift of Christ, and contented with his lot, he left behind him an undying name. He restored the foundations of this church and retired from the unworthy dissensions of the world. It is certain that he will live for ever in the heavenly kingdom amongst pleasant fields, with the elect, and will ever bless the grace which he received from Christ. He lived sixty-four years, eight months, twenty-three days; he died during the consulate of Flavius Stilicho."

It was formerly believed that in the ninth century during the period of the great translations, the bodies of the martyrs Protus and Hyacinth had been brought into the City. They were venerated during the Middle Ages at the little Church *Sancti Salvatoris de pede pontis*, that is to say at the foot of the Bridge of the Senate. In 1845, however, the tomb of Hyacinth was discovered, and found to be intact in the Cemetery of Basilla. A workman happened to strike the wall of a crypt with his pickaxe, and under the coating of plaster the following inscription appeared:

```
        DP III IDVS Septembr.
    YACINTHVS
    MARTYR
```

The tablet being removed, instead of a tomb of ordinary dimensions there appeared a small niche containing charred bones wrapped in a cloth to which the odour of perfumes still clung.

Apparently the pagans had either condemned the martyr to death at the stake, or had burnt his dead body.

The sepulchre of Protus must have been close by, as was proved by the discovery of a fragment of an architrave with the words:

SEPVLCRVM PROTI M(artyris).

Pius IX desired that the newly-found relics of Hyacinth should be magnificently interred in the patriarchal Basilica of St Paul, which was then being rebuilt with great splendour. He therefore deposited them temporarily in the College of Propaganda, intending to convey the martyr's body in solemn procession from the City to the Ostian Basilica. Fully nine years passed by, however, before the Pope was able to celebrate the desired dedication of the new Church of St Paul, so for a time the body of St Hyacinth and the intended procession were forgotten. Thus the holy relics remained during more than half a century in the chapel of the Propaganda, until they were at last placed in a worthy tomb in the Oratory of that venerable house, the School of future Apostles.

The Mass is the same as on February 15, for the martyrs Faustinus and Jovita.

The Collects are the following: "Lord, let the glorious martyrdom of thy blessed martyrs Protus and Hyacinth strengthen us, and let their loving intercession continually shield us."

The Lectionary of Würzburg gives for to-day's Gospel, the passage which was read on May 2 for St Athanasius: *Cum persequentur vos in civitate ista.*

Secret: "We present to thee, O Lord, the offerings which we owe to thee in memory of thy holy martyrs Protus and Hyacinth; grant, we beseech thee, that they may work within us healing and salvation for evermore."

Post-Communion: "May thy holy gifts which we have received, cleanse us, O Lord, we beseech thee, through the prayers of thy blessed martyrs, Protus and Hyacinth."

This prayer suggests a slight theological difficulty. The Eucharist is a Sacrament of the living and the soul must, therefore, be in a state of grace to receive it; why then do we speak of purification at this moment? The answer is as follows: the Collect speaks of the cleansing of the heart from disordinate affection to venial sin, or any imperfection, however slight. The holy Eucharist kindles in our heart the fire of charity which consumes these, as flames consume straw and chaff.

Further, the value of the holy Sacrifice as satisfaction for our sins is so great, that, according to the teaching of the Council of Trent, on account thereof the Lord often condones the punishment due even to grave faults.

SEPTEMBER 12

FEAST OF THE HOLY NAME OF MARY

On September 11 and 12 the Martyrology of St Jerome commemorates once more the martyr Hippolytus of Porto, whose feast we kept a few days ago. But in the last great reform of the Roman Breviary under Pius X, the feast of the Holy Name of Mary, originally instituted by Innocent XI, in memory of the great victory won over the Turks before the walls of Vienna (September 13, 1683), was fixed for this day. Previous to this Innocent XII had ordained that it should be kept on the Sunday within the Octave of the Nativity of Our Lady.

Whatever interpretation of the name of Mary we may accept, whether it means *bitterness*, the *lady of the sea*, or *beloved of God*, it is still the name of our Mother in heaven, the name which was first on the lips of the divine Child, the name which after that of Jesus holds all our hope of salvation. Many saints, especially St Bernard and St Gabriele dell' Addolorata, recognize in the most sweet name of Mary the virtues and prerogatives which the Doctors of the Church find in the name of the Saviour, such as light, strength, sweetness and protection. Therefore the devout Christian desires above all things to pronounce the holy names of Jesus and Mary with his last breath before going forth to behold their countenances.

Pius X granted great indulgences to those who should make use of this pious invocation.

* * * * *

The Introit is the same as on March 25.

Collect: "Grant, we beseech thee, almighty God, that thy faithful people, who rejoice in the name of the most holy Virgin Mary, and enjoy her protection, may, by her loving intercession, be delivered from all evils here on earth, and be found worthy to attain to everlasting joys in heaven."

The Lesson and the Gradual are those of July 16; the Gospel is that of March 25; the alleluiatic verse and the remainder are the same as for August 5.

St Bernard was one of the most eloquent panegyrists of the holy name of Mary. Each year, on Wednesday of Ember week in December, he was in the habit of preaching to his monks at Clairvaux on the Gospel of the day, and on this occasion he would utter magnificent words of praise concerning her whose name has never been worthily pronounced except by her own Divine Son. Some of the holy Abbot's praises have been preserved in the Breviary on this day.

Christian Rome possesses a fine church dedicated to the holy name of Mary, near the Ulpian Basilica, in the Forum of Trajan. Here is kept an ancient ikon of the Mother of God which came from the Oratory of St Lawrence in the Lateran.

SEPTEMBER 14

SS Cornelius, Pope, and Cyprian, Martyrs

Station at the Cemetery of Callixtus.

The Martyrology of St Jerome notes to-day: *Romae in cimiterio Callisti, Cornili episcopi;* an indication which is derived from the Philocalian Calendar, where we find: *XVIII Kal. Oct. Cypriani Africae, Romae celebratur in Calisti.* Pope Cornelius died in exile at Civitavecchia on September 14, 253, after a Pontificate of two years' duration, which had been greatly troubled by the schism of Novatian. His body was brought to Rome and interred at the Cemetery of Callixtus in the crypt of Lucina, where his family burial place may once have been.

We still possess his sepulchral inscription:

```
CORNELIUS   ☧   MARTYR
         EP
```

Pope Damasus caused the crypt of the martyr to be decorated, and composed an epigraph in his honour, of which, however, only some fragments remain.

(Aspice descensu extruc) TO · TENEB(ri)SQ(ue fu)GATIS
(Corneli monumenta vides t)VMVLV(mque) · SACRATVM
(Hoc opus egroti Damasi)PR(aes)TANTIA · FECIT
(Esset ut accessus meli)OR · POPVLISQVE · PARATVM
(Auxilium Sancti et v)ALEAS · SI · FVNDERE · PVRO
(Corde preces, Damasus)MELIOR · CONSVRGERE · POSSET
(Quem non lucis amor te)NVIT · MAGE · CVRA · LABORIS

" Behold here is the stair, behold, the darkness has been banished, and the crypt of Cornelius appears with the sacred tomb. This is the work which the infirm Pope Damasus zealously accomplished in order that the faithful might have easier access. Implore the help of the saints that Damasus may arise restored to health, he who loves labour more than life itself."

St Cyprian was decapitated in the neighbourhood of Carthage on September 14, 258. He was the impersonification of the early African Church, and was, above all, as St Augustine called him : *Catholicum episcopum, catholicum martyrem*. He still lives and moves in the spirit of the unity of the Church for which he lived, laboured, and died. Even his temporary disagreement with Pope Stephen on the question of the validity of baptism conferred by heretics, arose from an exaggerated application of this principle of Catholic unity, but God permitted that the separation of the Church of Africa from Rome should be prevented by the death of the Pope, and that Cyprian, who was in perfect good faith, should be spared the terrible responsibility of having led his nation into the way of schism.

Carthage raised three basilicas to her great Bishop. Of these one was near the port ; another stood on the place of his execution, where the altar was simply called *mensa Cypriani ;* and, lastly, a third at Mappalia was erected over his tomb.

The festival of St Cyprian on September 14, the Κυπριανά, became so popular, that in the fourth century it was celebrated at Rome, at Constantinople, and in Spain, where Prudentius composed a hymn in honour of the martyr.

In the Eternal City the *cultus* of St Cyprian was associated from the first with that of Cornelius, and therefore his picture, which was painted beside that of the Pope in the crypt of Cornelius, misled the author of the *Itinerarium de Locis Sanctis*, who boldly writes : *haud procul in coemeterio Calisti Cornelius et Cyprianus in Ecclesia dormiunt.*

The body of Cornelius, or at least, a portion of it, is preserved in the Basilica of St Mary in Trastevere ; that of St Cyprian is said to have been taken to Lyons.

In the Gospel List of Würzburg a strange anomaly occurs : the Mass of September 14 is named after St Cornelius only, with the same Gospel as the feast of SS Marcus and Marcellinus on June 18 : *Vae vobis qui aedificatis monumenta*, etc. Whereas the following Sundays are, according to custom, named after the Bishop of Carthage only ; thus : *hebdomada I, II, etc., post natale sancti Cypriani*, etc.

● ● ● ● ●

The Mass is the same as on January 22, but the Collects

are taken from the Mass of the Popes Soter and Caius on April 22, whose names are replaced, of course, by the names of the Saints of to-day.

The Leonine Sacramentary has a proper Preface: *Vere dignum . . . tuamque in sanctis martyribus Cornelio simul etiam Cypriano praedicare virtutem ; quos discretis terrarum partibus greges sacros divino pane pascentes, una fide eademque die, diversis licet temporibus, consonante, parique nominis tui confessione coronasti. Per . . .*

We learn from a letter of Pope Cornelius to Bishop Fabius of Antioch that, at the time when Novatian attempted to supersede him in the Pontificate, the Roman hierarchy included forty-six priests, seven deacons, as many subdeacons, forty-two acolytes and fifty-two clerks, while more than five hundred widows were maintained by the alms of the Church.

We read of another interesting particular concerning the Eucharistic Celebration. When he administered Communion to his followers, instead of the usual formula, Novatian made them take the following oath upon the Body of the Lord: " I will never return to Cornelius."

The liturgical tradition that the faithful should kiss the hand of the bishop when he administers Holy Communion, as a sign of union with him in the Catholic Faith, dates from these early times.

SEPTEMBER 14

THE EXALTATION OF THE CROSS AND THE DEDICATION OF THE " MARTYRIUM " ON CALVARY

Station at St John Lateran.

To-day occurs the anniversary of the Finding of the holy Cross (September 14, 320), and the Dedication of the Constantinian Basilica the *Martyrium*, on the spot where our Lord was crucified. Owing to the religious importance of the holy City the observance of this feast spread rapidly throughout the Christian world, especially in the East; the more so because particles of the true Cross were brought from Jerusalem to many other churches in the East and West from the fourth century onwards. Therefore, the principal cities sought to imitate the solemn ceremonies in use at Jerusalem in order to do homage to the holy Cross, the triumphant standard of our salvation.

The festival was preceded at Jerusalem by four days of preparation. An immense stream of pilgrims made their way to Calvary at that time from Egypt, Mesopotamia, and

September 14

Persia, and the sacred sign of redemption was shown to them, for which reason the feast was also known as Ὕψωσις τοῦ τιμίου καὶ ζωοποιοῦ Σταυροῦ. It was on one of these occasions that Mary of Egypt the sinner, having also visited the holy City, was converted and began to lead a new life.

In course of time the Latins confused this festival with the other one kept in memory of the restitution of the holy Cross to Heraclius by the Persians. The *Basileus* himself carried the relic from Tiberias to Jerusalem on this occasion, and delivered it into the hands of the Patriarch Zachary, on May 3, 630.

The recovery of the Cross from the infidels was greeted by the Latins especially with great enthusiasm. Thus, whilst the Easterns continued to celebrate the feast of the *Martyrium* with magnificent rites on September 14, that of May 3 was more popular in the West, where it changed its title and significance and became simply the *dies sanctae Crucis* or *inventio sanctae Crucis*.

The feast of September 14 is, however, to be found in the Weissenburg Codex of the Martyrology of St Jerome and in the Gregorian Sacramentary. Because of this it was preserved in the Codices, but in liturgical practice it was only very gradually accepted in the Western countries, as September 14 was already dedicated to the feast of the martyrs Cornelius and Cyprian.

In the late *Ordo Romanus* of Cencio Camerario it is prescribed that on the morning of this day the Pope and the Cardinals should go to the Oratory of St Lawrence in the Lateran palace, whence they would take the relic of the true Cross.

Singing the *Te Deum*, the procession first made its way to the Oratory of San Silvestro, where the *primicerius* of the *Schola* and his cantors had already preceded it. Here the solemn adoration of the Cross took place, which is now only in use on Good Friday. It had, however, been practised on this day of the Ὕψωσις, both at Jerusalem and Constantinople, since the fourth century. During this ceremony the antiphons and psalms of the Morning Office were sung.

The holy rite being ended, after all the clergy had made their genuflection before the sacred Relic, the procession finally moved towards the great Lateran Basilica of the Saviour, where, at the end of Terce, the Pope celebrated the holy Sacrifice.

* * * * *

The Mass is the same as on May 3, except the following portions.

Collect: "O God, who year by year dost gladden us by the festival of the exaltation of Christ's holy cross; grant, we beseech thee, that we who while living upon earth acknowledge the mystery of Redemption, may be found worthy to receive in heaven the rewards he has purchased for us."

The Gradual is that of Holy Thursday. The glory of Christ triumphing over death and sin, has its root in the humiliation of the cross, which, from having been an instrument of shame, became through the death of Jesus *virga virtutis suae quam emittet Dominus ex Sion*, the mystical rod of which the Psalmist sings.

The alleluiatic verse is like that of May 3, and was suggested by the celebrated hymn of Venantius Fortunatus.

The Gospel (John xii, 31–36) is included in the Lesson read on the Saturday before Palm Sunday. The throne on which the Redeemer is raised in order to triumph over pride, disobedience, and sensuality, is the Cross, which for Christ is a seat of shame, but for us a seat of mercy. He was raised upon it first by the malice of the Jews; he is raised upon it now by the ardent faith of all Christians, who adore the crucified victim of Calvary as their God and their Redeemer.

The choice of this passage has been made chiefly in connection with the title of the feast: *Exaltatio Sanctae Crucis*. For this Gospel treats of the reason why it was necessary *exaltari Filius hominis*.

The Antiphon for the Offertory is merely a devout prayer, and this fact betrays that it belongs to a later period, when the true liturgical Office of this chant was no longer understood.

Secret: "We are about to feed on the body and blood of our Lord Jesus Christ, who made of the cross a holy sign; we beseech thee, O Lord our God, that even as we have been deemed worthy to honour the cross, so we may enjoy for evermore the salvation which has been won for us by its triumph."

In some codices this prayer is given as a Post-Communion, and the following is prescribed for the Secret: *Devotas, Domine, humilitatis nostrae preces et hostias misericordiae tuae praecedat auxilium, et salutem quam per Adam in paradisi ligno clauserat temerata praesumptio, Ligni rursus fides aperiat.*

Post-Communion: "Be nigh to us, O Lord our God; and even as thou lettest us rejoice in honour of the cross, so may it be a safeguard to us for evermore."

Pius IX found in a tomb in the Cemetery of Ciriaca an ancient cross of gold on which was engraved the following inscription:

CRVX · EST · VITA · MIHI
MORS · INIMICE · TIBI

This precious ornament is now preserved in the Vatican Library.

The inscription on what is known as the Medal of St Benedict, which is enriched with many indulgences, and which has great efficacy against evil spirits, is very similar to that on the above-mentioned medal. The Medal of St Benedict is to be found everywhere, especially in the missions of Africa and Asia, where it is used as a protection against witchcraft and magic, so common in those heathen countries.

It consists of a short form of exorcism inscribed upon a medal having on one side the sacred sign of Redemption, and on the other the image of the holy Patriarch St Benedict holding up the cross to drive away devils. The blessing of this indulgenced medal is reserved to monks of the Benedictine Order.

The following is the form of exorcism engraved on the cross:

Crux sancta sit mihi lux
Numquam daemon sit mihi dux.

Around the cross runs the following inscription: *Vade retro Satana; numquam suade mihi vana; sunt mala quae libas; ipse venena bibas.*

In ancient times the power of the triumphant symbol of our Redemption was concisely expressed by this anagram:

$$\begin{array}{c} \Phi \\ Z \; \Omega \; H \\ C \end{array}$$

The Cross is Light and Life.

SEPTEMBER 15

St Nicomedes, Martyr

Station at the Cemetery of Nicomedes.

This feast is omitted in the earliest copies of the Martyrology of St Jerome, but it is to be found in others of the early Middle Ages, and as it is noted both in the Gregorian Sacramentary and in the Gospel List of Würzburg, we must conclude that it belongs to the Liturgy of Rome in the period of its finest classical development.

The Martyrology of St Jerome, indeed, notes another feast of St Nicomedes of June 1, as we have remarked elsewhere, but this was connected with the dedication of his *titulus* in the city and had no reference to the *natalis* of the martyr.

The Cemetery of Nicomedes, where the station was celebrated on this day, is on the Via Nomentana, at a short distance from the walls of the town: *in orto iuxta muros*, as the Acts say. Boniface I (619–625) built a small basilica over the tomb of the Saint, and it was subsequently restored by Adrian I. The body of St Nicomedes, from whom the Via Nomentana had at one time taken its name, was removed at a later date by Paschal I to St Praxedes, the cemetery having fallen into neglect.

* * * * *

The Mass is the same as for St Valentine on February 14, but the Collects are proper to the feast.

Collect: " Be nigh, O Lord, to thy people, that they may profit by the glorious merits of blessed Nicomedes thy martyr, and may ever be helped by his prayers to win thy mercy."

In the Würzburg List the Gospel is taken from Matthew xvi, 24–28.

Secret: " Graciously receive, O Lord, the gifts which we offer up; and may the prayer of blessed Nicomedes the martyr make them acceptable to thy majesty."

Like the unhappy sinners who, in the third century, had recourse to the Confessors lying in prison for the faith in order to obtain from them recommendations to the Bishop, that they might be readmitted to Communion with the Church, so we too implore the martyrs' intercession with God, that by the merits of their blood he may give us peace and pardon.

When the holy Sacrifice was offered in the catacombs over the body of a martyr, it was as if the saint joined his prayer to those of the faithful in order to invoke the mercy of God upon them.

Post-Communion: " May the sacraments which we have received cleanse us, O Lord, and through the intercession of blessed Nicomedes thy martyr, loose us from all sin."

In order to understand the full meaning of these words we must remember what the Gospel says about the servitude into which the sinner has voluntarily fallen: *Omnis qui facit peccatum, servus est peccati.* (John viii, 34.)

According to his *Acta* the *presbyter* St Nicomedes, found guilty of having given sepulture to the relics of St Felicula, was first scourged, and then thrown into the Tiber.

The site of the *Titulus Nicomedis* mentioned in the Acts of the Roman Council held under Symmachus, as well as in the epigraph of a certain priest called Victor *presb. tituli Nico-*

medis, is not known. As this martyr was so celebrated, it is not improbable that his portrait adorned the mosaic of Sixtus III in St Mary Major, the dedicatory inscription of which mentions, indeed, a martyr who had been drowned in the river:

Ferrum, flamma, ferae, fluvius, saevumque venenum.

SEPTEMBER 16

St Euphemia, Virgin and Martyr

Station at the Monastery Sanctorum Euphemiae et Archangeli, quod ponitur intra titulum Pudentis.

St Euphemia is the celebrated martyr in whose sepulchral church, described by Asterius of Amasea, the Council of Chalcedon was held. This circumstance contributed greatly to the spread of her *cultus*, and her praises are sung by Paulinus of Nola, St Peter Chrysologus, Venantius Fortunatus, and Ennodius of Pavia. In the Leonine Sacramentary there are no less than four Masses in her honour.

At Rome a church was dedicated to St Euphemia on the Viminal near the *titulus Pastoris*, where, therefore, to-day's festive station was held. St Gregory the Great mentions this church on the occasion of his *litania septiformis*, since it was thence that the procession of widows accompanied by priests of the Fifth *Regio* set out.

Pope Donus (676–678) dedicated another church to the martyr on the Appian Way, near Boville, as Gelasius I (492–496) had also done, when he built a sanctuary in her honour on the Via Tiburtina.

Leo III bestowed vessels of silver on the Church of St Euphemia in the *vicus Patricius*, and Sergius I restored it later from the very foundations. Until the time of Sixtus V, who caused this sanctuary to be demolished, there could be seen in the mosaic of the apse the image of the martyr, robed and loaded with jewels after the Byzantine custom, standing between two serpents.

The venerable *cultus* of the Martyr of Chalcedon appears to be assured in Rome to-day, chiefly because of another Church of St Euphemia which stands by the Forum of Trajan. An ancient chapel in her honour existed in 1461, near the column of Trajan, but later it was destroyed, and was rebuilt a little way off.

The following is one of the beautiful Prefaces in honour of St Euphemia, contained in the Leonine Sacramentary: *Vere dignum . . . in hac celebritate gaudentes, qua sancti Spiritus fervore praeclarus beatae martyris Euphemiae sexus fragilitate pretiosior sanguis effloruit, et virtute foeminea rabiem diabolicas persecutionis elidens, geminatae gloriae triumphum virginitas implevit et passio. Per Christum.*

SEPTEMBER 16

SS LUCY AND GEMINIANUS

Two separate Masses are noted in the Gregorian Sacramentary to-day, one in honour of St Euphemia, and the other for St Lucy and St Geminianus.

This St Lucy is commemorated in various examples of the Martyrology of St Jerome and even in the Gospel List of Würzburg. The latter manuscript, however, in agreement with many Sacramentaries, couples Lucy with Euphemia, but makes no mention of Geminianus.

Morin holds that the diaconia of St Lucy *in silice* on the Esquiline, which was restored by Honorius I, was dedicated to the same St Lucy whose feast we keep to-day. We, however, find it hard to believe that the churches founded at Rome by Symmachus and Honorius to the memory of St Lucy were not built in honour of the celebrated Sicilian martyr, whose name was even included in the Roman Canon.

The Martyrology of St Jerome records, it is true, on June 24 in the *cimiterio ad clivum Cucumeris*, a *Lucia cum aliis XXII;* but it may be merely a case of a confusion of names, for all the other documents mention a certain *Longinus* or *Longina*, on the Via Salaria, who is sometimes even referred to as the mother of the martyr John the priest.

However this may be, Rome, whether in ancient times or in the Middle Ages, knew no other St Lucy but the martyr of Syracuse; so, unless it be the feast of the dedication of one of the many Roman churches named after her, we cannot point out another saint of this name whose festival occurred at Rome to-day.

Again, the Martyrology of St Jerome is unusually full of local feasts on this very day. On the Via Nomentana in the *coemeterium maius*, there was kept, indeed, a kind of collective solemnity of the local Saints: Emerentiana, Papia, Felix, Victor and Alexander. On the Appian Way the feast of St Cecilia was also celebrated. It is no wonder then that St Lucy, whose name occurs twice in the same Martyrology on December 13 and February 7, should have been commemorated on this day, too, if it were the anniversary of the *encaenia* of one of the Roman churches dedicated to her, that for instance

September 16

of the monastery of St Andrew and St Lucy, which dates from the sixth century, or the other *in silice* on the Esquiline.

We may go further still. The *Acta* of the martyrs Lucy and Geminianus are so legendary as to deserve no credit, and the Bollandists have not even included them. The *cultus* of the two saints is relatively ancient, for it has passed into all the medieval martyrologies and even into the Greek Menologies; but this does not prove the authenticity of their history.

We know, on the testimony of Cencio Camerario, that a church dedicated to St Geminianus existed on the Aventine, to whose clergy six *denari* of *presbyterium* were due on the occasion of the solemn Papal festivals. Baronius mentions the little church, but after his time it disappeared and no trace of its exact site can be found.

Taking into account the uncertainty which surrounds the history of St Lucy and St Geminianus, we are inclined to entertain the hypothesis that we have here two martyrs from the extra-mural cemeteries, whose bodies were brought into Rome, like that of St Martina, by Honorius I. It is curious, however, that the devotions promoted by this Pope to St Martin, St Adrian, St Lucy, and St Geminianus should all be lacking in historical confirmation.

* * * * *

In the Roman Missal to-day the Mass common to the three saints, Euphemia, Lucy, and Geminianus, is the same as on January 22. The Collects are proper to the feast.

Collect: "Grant a joyful issue to our prayers, O Lord, so that we who year by year devoutly keep the day on which thy holy martyrs Euphemia, Lucy and Geminianus suffered, may also follow them in the steadfastness of their faith."

This prayer recalls the famous saying of St John Chrysostom concerning the saints: *Imitari non pigeat quos celebrare delectat;* and also those words from the Epistle to the Hebrews: *Quorum intuentes exitum conversationis, imitamini fidem.*

The Gospel according to the Index of Würzburg should be that appointed to be read on the feast of St Lucy, on December 13.

Our present Missal, however, prescribes the passage which has already been referred to on June 19, for the feast of the Milanese martyrs Gervase and Protase.

Secret: "Mercifully consider the sacrifice of thy people, O Lord, we beseech thee; and may we enjoy the intercession of those whose festival we are keeping by thy grace."

When we are present at the celebration of the holy Sacrifice, we should, therefore, do more than merely assist at it. We should participate in it actively by uniting ourselves with the priest in making the oblation, and by placing on the paten, together with the Host, our desires and our aspirations, which he will then offer up to God.

Post-Communion : " Graciously hear our prayers, O Lord, and let us never cease to enjoy the help of thy holy martyrs Euphemia, Lucy, and Geminianus, whose feast we are solemnly keeping."

We should note here the last words of this prayer : *solemniter celebramus*, which show the traditional spirit of Catholic Liturgy with regard to the *cultus* of the saints and especially of the martyrs. We do not think that those enter entirely into the mind of the Church, who attribute so little importance to the great solemnities of the Roman Missal that, in order to save time, they habitually substitute the votive Mass for the Dead instead of offering the holy Sacrifice (*solemniter celebramus*) in memory of the saints named in the Sacramentaries.

SEPTEMBER 16

SS ABUNDIUS, PRIEST, AND ABUNDANTIUS, DEACON, MARTYRS

The later Martyrologies also commemorate these two martyrs, who, however, belong to the district outside Rome, as they were buried in the *coemeterium Theodorae* which is at the twenty-eighth milestone on the Flaminian Way near Rignano. Two other local martyrs, Marcian and John, shared their crown with them.

The original epitaph of the priest Abundius is still preserved in the Lateran Museum.

ABVNDIO · PRB
MARTYRI · SANCT
DEP · VII · IDVS · DEC

Therefore his feast should be kept, not on this day, but on December 7.

The bodies of the martyrs Abundius and Abundantius were first brought by Otho III to the Basilica of SS Adalbert and Bartholomew on the Isola Tiberina. At a later date—it is not known how or when—it became necessary to transfer the relics, or at least a portion of them, to the diaconia of SS Cosmas and Damian on the *Via Sacra*, whence they were carried in 1583 to the Farnese Basilica of the Society of Jesus.

SEPTEMBER 16

St Martin, Pope and Martyr

To-day is also the anniversary of the death of this holy Pope, who, because he defended the orthodox faith against the heretical *Basileus* of Byzantium, ended his life in exile in the Chersonesus. He died on the feast of St Euphemia in 655. *Obiit autem idem sanctissimus Martinus papa, recens revera confessor et martyr Christi . . . mense septembri, die sextadecima, in qua felicissimae martyris et Fidem custodientis orthodoxam Euphemiae celebratur memoria . . . Positus est autem in tumulis Sanctorum extra muros Chersonitarum civitatis . . . in templo sanctissimae Dei genitricis.*[1]

The *Liber Pontificalis* already alludes to the wonders which took place at Chersona at the tomb of the exiled Pope.

Many miracles were still being worked there in 730, and they are mentioned by Gregory II in a letter to Leo I the Isaurian.[2]

It is not known whether the body of St Martin was ever brought to Rome; therefore, the feast dedicated to him, on November 12, in the present Missal, seems to be only the Roman celebration in honour of St Martin of Tours, which was postponed to the following day, as the feast of St Mennas occurred on November 11.

Pope Martin was still living when, owing to pressure exerted by the Emperor, Eugenius I was chosen to succeed him. The holy Pope yielded therefore to force, and out of zeal for the peace of the Church ended by approving this election. In a letter of September 655, St Martin described to a friend the extreme poverty which he suffered in exile, but added that he never ceased to pray for the Church of Rome and for his own successor in the Apostolic See.

Amongst the Greeks the memory of Μαρτίνου πάπα Ῥώμης τοῦ ὁμολογητοῦ is kept several times in the year, on April 13, 15, and September 20, together with that of St Maximus the Confessor.

The Slavs keep his feast on April 20.

SEPTEMBER 17

The Imprinting of the Holy Stigmata on St Francis, Confessor*

This festival was introduced into the Martyrology of Baronius through the influence of Cardinal di Montalto, afterwards Sixtus V. On his accession to the Papacy he

[1] Cf. *Commemoratio*, P.L. LXXXVII, 120.   [2] Jaffe, 2181.

desired that the feast of his holy founder should be observed by the whole Church. Clement VIII, however, suppressed the feast of the Stigmata, as the Church only dedicates special solemnities to the mysteries of our redemption, which she recognizes as the founts of divine and life-giving grace, whereas the particular favours granted to the saints by God directly concern their individual sanctification, and are all commemorated in a glorious synthesis when the life of each saint is read in the Breviary on the day of his feast.

But Paul V restored, in a great measure, the solemnity of the Stigmata by giving to it the rank of semidouble *ad libitum*. Clement IX again made the festival obligatory, and lastly another son of St Francis, Clement XIV, raised it once more to the rank of a double. The commission for the reform of the Breviary under Benedict XIV suggested the suppression of the feast of the Stigmata, but the proposals made by that assembly never came into effect.

We can see clearly from the diversity of views held at different times by the supreme authority of the Church concerning the continuance of this solemnity, that the concession made in its favour is one which oversteps the ordinary rules of the Liturgy, and is a special privilege in honour of St Francis, to be regarded not only as rare, but almost unique.

And, indeed, the sacred Stigmata impressed upon the body of St Francis by the crucified Saviour constituted in themselves a unique privilege. The fire of charity had cooled throughout the world when it pleased God to kindle it anew by the preaching of the Seraph of Assisi. St Francis came to show forth once more in his life and in his words the life and the words of Christ who, being himself poor, announced the beatitudes to the poor and lowly, and founded the Church and the religious state on evangelical poverty.

It was, however, necessary that the new apostle, the Herald of the Great King, as he called himself, should be able to show his credentials to the world, and therefore Christ was pleased to imprint upon him the " final seal," changing him to his own image and likeness and uniting him to himself on the rood of the Cross.

* * * * *

The Antiphon for the Introit is like that for St Ignatius of Antioch on February 1. It is followed, however, by Psalm cxli, which was recited by St Francis as he went to meet

sora nostra morte corporale.[1]

---

[1] *Laudes creaturarum* or Canticle of Brother Sun.

September 17

Psalm: "I cried to the Lord with my voice: with my voice I made supplication to the Lord."

The Collect sets forth the reason why the Stigmata of St Francis had an influence over the whole life of the Church.

Collect: "O Lord Jesus Christ, who, when the world was growing cold, didst renew the sacred marks of thy passion on the body of blessed Francis, so as to kindle in our hearts the fire of thy love; grant, in thy mercy, that with the help of his merits and prayers we may ever carry our cross and bring forth worthy fruits of penance."

The Lesson is taken from the Epistle to the Galatians (vi, 14–18). The opponents of St Paul had sown discord amongst the early Christian Communities by upholding the necessity for circumcision and Jewish ritualism. The Apostle declares in reply that he glories only in the cross of the Lord Jesus, to whom circumcision and uncircumcision are alike. However, if any desire that he should bear the mark of circumcision, he can show them the scars of the scourges and the chains endured for Christ, upon his body. These are the glorious wounds of Christ which he bears imprinted on his flesh.

The Gradual is like that of January 29, for St Francis de Sales.

The alleluiatic verse is inspired by an ancient Antiphon in honour of St Martin of Tours.

"Alleluia, alleluia. Francis, poor and humble, enters rich into heaven, and is honoured with celestial hymns."

How insignificant are these two qualities typical of St Francis! *Pauper et humilis!* Innocent III, in a dream, saw this poor and humble man support the falling Lateran Basilica upon his shoulders.

The Church was founded on poverty and humility, and therefore at the most decisive moments of the history of Catholicism, it has always pleased God to send saints, who, chiefly through their humility and detachment from earthly things, reformed Christian society and led it back to the ideals of the Gospel.

The Gospel for this new martyr of Christ crucified is taken from the Common of Martyrs, as on December 16, for St Eusebius of Vercelli.

The Antiphon for the Offertory is the same as that of December 3, for St Francis Xavier; the Communion is that of December 5, for St Sabbas.

Secret: "Hallow these gifts which we offer up to thee, O Lord, and by the intercession of blessed Francis cleanse us from all stain of sin."

When we make use of the word *sanctify* to-day, we pray

that the Holy Eucharist, which is always holy in itself—the ancients called it the *Sanctum*—may also be celebrated and offered up by us in a holy manner.

Post-Communion : " O God, who in divers ways didst show in blessed Francis thy confessor the wonderful mysteries of thy cross, grant, we beseech thee, that we may ever follow the example of his devotion, and be strengthened by constant meditation on that cross."

When the catechumen is brought to the church, the priest at once makes the sign of the Cross on his forehead and heart, in order to teach us that the mystery of the Cross which was fulfilled in the Head must also be fulfilled in the members of his mystical body.

SEPTEMBER 18

St Joseph of Cupertino, Confessor

To-day we commemorate a glorious Son of the Seraph of Assisi, whose feast was made universal throughout the Church by a Pope of the same Order, Clement XIV. St Joseph of Cupertino is as famous for his evangelical simplicity as for his ecstasies, and the whole of the following Mass is designed to bring out this mystical side of his sanctity.

✳ ✳ ✳ ✳ ✳

The Introit takes its Antiphon from Ecclesiasticus (i, 14–15) : " The love of God is honourable wisdom : and they to whom she shall show herself, love her by the sight and by the knowledge of her great works."

This is followed by Psalm lxxxiii : " How lovely are thy tabernacles, O Lord of hosts ! my soul longeth and fainteth for the courts of the Lord."

Although he was a priest, St Joseph of Cupertino was not distinguished by a high degree of learning, but on account of his sanctity he received from God the science of heavenly things, that which is called in holy Scripture *scientia Sanctorum*.

The Collect contains a veiled allusion to the ecstasies of the saint in which he was lifted up to kiss the picture of Christ or the Blessed Virgin.

Collect : " O God, who didst ordain that thine only-begotten Son should be lifted up above the earth and draw all things to himself ; in thy mercy bring it to pass that through the merits and example of thy seraphic confessor Joseph we may be lifted up above all earthly lusts and may be found worthy to come unto him."

The Lesson, which speaks of the quality and beauty of charity (1 Cor. xiii, 1–8), is contained in that which is read on

September 18

Quinquagesima Sunday. The compiler of the Mass ends it at verse 8, in which St Paul declares that charity can even dispense with knowledge. He had perhaps in mind the seraphic simplicity of the saint of to-day, who was so rich in the science of God although he had not won a name amongst scholars.

The Gradual is the same as for St Sabbas on December 5. Alleluia, alleluia. (Ecclus. xi, 13): "The eye of God hath looked upon him for good, and hath lifted him up from his low estate, and hath exalted his head. Alleluia."

In order to test the mystical graces which St Joseph received, his superiors subjected him to long and severe trials, and to frequent humiliations, sending him to monasteries in solitary places, lest the enthusiasm of the people, aroused by the miracles worked by him, should lead to any disorder.

The Gospel (Matt. xxii, 1–14) contains the parable of the wedding feast, to which the beggars from the highways were invited, and is also read on the Nineteenth Sunday after Pentecost.

Whereas many learned men have not profited by the graces given to them by God, and have not followed the divine call, this saint who was truly "poor in spirit" responded to the Lord's invitation in simplicity of heart and was admitted to the wedding feast.

The Offertory (Ps. xxxiv) refers to the terrible penances which St Joseph inflicted upon himself, and to his meekness with those who persecuted him. "But as for me, when they were troublesome to me, I was clothed with hair-cloth. I humbled my soul with fasting; and my prayer shall be turned into my bosom."

The Secret and the Post-Communion are from the Common of a Confessor not a Bishop, as on February 8.

The following is the Communion (Ps. lxviii): "I am poor and sorrowful: thy salvation, O God, hath set me up. I will praise the name of God with a song; and I will magnify him with praise."

This was the price which St Joseph of Cupertino paid for the wonderful graces he had received: *Ego sum pauper et dolens*. He became poor, that is to say humble, obedient, and lowly in his own estimation, and *dolens*, for he bore, imprinted on his flesh by his severe mortification, the Stigmata of the Passion.

It is told of St Joseph that he was once sent by his superior to exorcise a man who was possessed by the devil. When the saint reached the spot he merely showed the evil spirit the letter in which his superior had commanded him to drive the devil out of the unhappy man, and declared at the same time that it was in the name of obedience and not by his own power that he ordered him to release his victim. The devil was unable to withstand such humility and immediately went out of the possessed man.

SEPTEMBER 19

St Januarius, Bishop, and his Companions, Martyrs

We find a valuable reference to St Januarius in the account given by Uranius of the death of St Paulinus of Nola. This Saint, in his last agony, believed that St Martin and St Januarius stood at his side. Uranius adds: *Januarius episcopus simul et Martyr Neapolitanae urbis illustrat ecclesiam.*[1]

The government of the Church of Beneventum is not mentioned in any early document. Although he was decapitated at Pozzuoli, the remains of Januarius have rested since the fourth century in the cemetery at Naples which bears his name, and his earliest successors were all buried round his grave, which was regarded as the foundation stone of the Neapolitan hierarchy.

Januarius is mentioned to-day in the Martyrology of St Jerome and in the Calendar of Carthage. Amongst those who were his companions in martyrdom, or at least in captivity, should be numbered Sosius, who is commemorated on September 23, Festus and Desiderius on September 7, and Eutyches on October 18.

St Januarius is celebrated chiefly on account of the miraculous liquefaction of his blood, which takes place on the three feasts kept annually in his honour, at Naples.

The ampulla containing his blood is exposed before the people, together with the reliquary in which the head of the martyr is preserved, and after an interval during which prayers are said, the blood begins to liquefy, increasing in volume, as though it were bubbling up. The writer has been able to verify this miracle, which he has observed closely, and, like others who have studied it, he is obliged to confess that there seems to be no possible natural explanation of this phenomenon. It may be that, in this manner, God is pleased to show to the people of Naples that the blood of their great Patron—*aeterno flori* as the ancient sepulchral inscription calls it—is still active and powerful in the sight of the Lord, for with God there is no past, but all is present and living in his sight. The martyrdom of the glorious Bishop Januarius still protects the beautiful city of Naples, which is as famous

[1] *P.L.* LIII, col. 861.

September 19

for the genius of her sons as for the holiness of her many saints.

* * * * *

The Mass is the same as on July 12 for SS Nabor and Felix, but the Collects are those of June 19, for SS Gervase and Protase, and the Gospel is that of the feast of the Martyrs Marius, Martha, etc., on January 19.

Long before the time of St Gregory the Great a church was built in honour of St Januarius at Rome, near the Porta Tiburtina, and was afterwards restored by Adrian I. All traces of it have, however, disappeared.

Pope Symmachus also built an oratory in honour of St Sosius at the Vatican, which existed until the fifteenth century. The dedicatory inscription of this chapel is given below, in which the praises of the Bishop Januarius are blended with those of the Deacon. It is valuable on account of the historical information which it contains.

PONTIFICIS · VENERANDA · SEQVENS · VESTIGIA · SOSIVS
AEQVAVIT · MERITI · NOBILITATE · GRADVM
MARTYRIO · CONIVNCTVS · ORAT · VERVSQVE · MINISTER
REDDIDIT · OFFICII · DEBITA · IVRA · SVI
ILLE · SACERDOTEM · CVPIENS · SVBDYCERE · MORTI
CONTIGIT · OPTATAM · SVB · PIETATE · NECEM
O · LAETA · ET · IVCVNDA · QVIES ! · O · VITA · DVORVM
FVNERE · SVB · GEMINO · QVOS · TENET · VNA · SALVS
ITE · SIMVL · SEMPER · CAELESTIA · SVMITE · DONA
PAR · PRETIVM · POSCIT · GLORIA · PAR · FIDEI
SYMMACHVS · ANTISTES · TANTI · SACRATOR · HONORIS
HAEC · FECIT · TITVLIS · COMMEMORANDA · SVIS

"Sosius, following in the steps of his Bishop, equalled him by the sublimity of his merits.

United to him in his martyrdom he raised his voice in prayer, fulfilling thus the true office of a deacon.

His desire to save the Bishop from death was the cause of his receiving the longed-for grace of martyrdom.

O happy and joyful rest! O life found by two in a double death, which holds salvation for both!

Remain united for ever and rejoice in the heavenly reward, for the same Faith deserves the same recompense.

Symmachus the Bishop dedicated this memorial to them and placed upon it this commemorative inscription."

* * * * *

These records of the saints which are contained in the Liturgy through the intervention of the early Popes have a claim to our special veneration. The devotion to the martyrs Januarius and Sosius was especially important, because the fact that a sanctuary was dedicated to them at Rome in close proximity to the Vatican Basilica proves how popular the *cultus* of those saints had become.

SEPTEMBER 20

St Eustace, Bishop and Martyr

Station at the Diaconia of St Eustace in Platana.

Strange legends have grown up around the story of this celebrated Bishop of Antioch, whose praises were already sung by St John Chrysostom and by Severus, and whose *cultus*, according to Prudentius, was extremely popular even in the West during the fourth century.

St Eustace died in exile at Trajanopolis in Thrace; but Calandionus the Bishop caused his bones to be brought back to Antioch in 484, a century after his death. On this occasion the whole population went out to a distance of about eighteen miles from the city to welcome their former pastor.

We must, however, distinguish this St Eustace from another martyr bearing the same name, who is recorded in the Martyrology of St Jerome on July 16, and lastly from a third Eustace or Eustracius, one of the forty martyrs of Sebaste, who are venerated at Rome on December 13. Much confusion has arisen concerning these various martyrs, and the great Bishop of Antioch has been transformed by legends, first into a valiant captain living in the second century, and then into the saintly father of a family, who, with his wife and children, suffered martyrdom in a brazen bull.

The earliest mention made of the church of St Eustace or Eustachius at Rome dates from the time of Leo III, who bestowed gifts upon it. The sanctuary was, however, rebuilt under Celestine III, and was throughout the Middle Ages one of the most famous deaconries in Rome.

The following interesting distich could formerly be seen above the door:

VT · MIHI · CAELESTIS · RESERETVR · PORTA · IOHANNI
HAS · SACRAS · EVSTATHI · POSTES · ET · LIMINA · STRVXI

* * * * *

The Introit, taken from the Mass *Sapientiam*, is the same as on June 9. The Collects are like those of the feast of St Symphorosa on July 18; whilst the Lesson is taken from the Mass of SS Primus and Felician on June 9.

The Gradual *Anima nostra* follows, as on the feast of the Holy Innocents, and the alleluiatic verse is added to it. " Alleluia, alleluia." (Ps. lxvii) : " Let the just feast and rejoice before God, and be delighted with gladness. Alleluia."

The Gospel is the same as on January 20 ; the Antiphon for the Offertory is taken from the Mass of St Basilides and his companions on June 12 ; lastly, the Communion is that of the Mass of the Machabees on August 1.

St Eustace died in exile because he had defended the Faith of Nicea. Not infrequently, persecution, imprisonment and exile have been the lot of those who held the office and fulfilled the duties of a Bishop.

SEPTEMBER 20

THE HOLY VIGIL OF ST MATTHEW, APOSTLE AND EVANGELIST

The Vigil of to-day is recorded in the Bernese *Laterculus* of the Martyrology of St Jerome : *Vigilia Mathei apostoli*.

The Mass is the same as that of the vigil of St Thomas, with the exception of the Gospel, which is taken from Luke v, 27–32. Jesus called Matthew from the receipt of custom, and in answer to the murmurings of the Pharisees, who were scandalized that Christ should consent to be present at the feast of the converted publican, he replied that he had not come to call the just but sinners to penance.

This scene from the Gospel illustrates the condescension of the Sacred Heart of our Saviour. St Matthew wished to show his gratitude for the grace he had received when Christ called him, and Jesus, seeing in his invitation an opportunity of approaching sinners and of saving souls, accepted it. He acts as a man amongst men, and consents even to sit at table with Matthew and his former companions, the receivers of custom, thus giving an example of the principle which St Paul was later to declare in his Epistles, that it is necessary for an Apostle to be all things to all men in order to gain all for God.

SEPTEMBER 21

ST MATTHEW, APOSTLE AND EVANGELIST

Station at St Matthew in Merulana.

This extremely ancient title, which has now disappeared completely, is mentioned in the Council of Rome, held in 499, under Symmachus, in which one of the signatories wrote his name as follows: *Andreas presbyter tituli sancti Mathaei subscripsi.*

An endeavour seems to have been made in ancient times to assemble the memorials to the Apostles in that district of Rome which lies around the Lateran *Episcopium* and the Merulana, for here were the Oratory of St John the Evangelist, of St Bartholomew *in Capite Merulanae*, of St Matthew, of St Andrew, and of St Thomas, at the Lateran.

There was another oratory also in honour of St Matthew, which stood in the vicinity of the deaconry of Sta Maria *in Xenodochio*.

To-day's festival of St Matthew already exists in the Martyrology of St Jerome, but is especially celebrated by the Greeks on November 16. The *Acta* of the Apostle are apocryphal and little is known of his life.

The Fathers in general, as, for example, St Ambrose, held that his death occurred in Persia,[1] whereas St Paulinus of Nola asserts that he died amongst the Parthians.[2]

Venantius Fortunatus writes:

> *Matthaeus Aethiopes attemperat ore vapores*
> *Vivaque in exusto flumina fudit agro . . .*
>
> * * * * *
>
> *Inde triumphantem fert India Bartholomaeum*
> *Matthaeum eximium Naddaver alta virum*
> *Hinc Simonem ac Iudam lumen Persida gemellum*
> *Laeta relaxato mittit ad astra sinu.*[3]

St Matthew added the glory of an Evangelist to that of an Apostle. He wrote his Gospel in Aramaic, and it was afterwards translated into Greek. The Aramaic text no longer exists, but it is supposed to have been very similar to the *Evangelium secundum Hebraeos* which St Jerome translated into Greek and Latin. In any case the Greek version of St Matthew, which is in the eyes of the Church the canonical text of the first Gospel, must be regarded by us as a divinely inspired work.

The relics of St Matthew were discovered, it is said, in the year 954 at Velia, near the Bay of Policastro, and were translated to the Cathedral of Salerno. In 1084 Pope Gregory VII journeyed to Salerno, from Monte Cassino, in order to perform the ceremony of consecration. Death, however, overtook him in the capital of the Norman Duchy, and he was buried near the tomb of St Matthew. He was a courageous and high-minded Pontiff whose last words were: *Dilexi iustitiam et odivi iniquitatem; propterea morior in exilio!*

---

[1] *In Psalm.* xlv.   [2] *Carm.* XXVI.
[3] Lib. III, c. ii. Lib. VIII, c. iv.

September 21

In the little old church at Velia, which is dedicated to St Matthew—*Sancti Matthaei ad duo flumina*—the ancient sarcophagus is still preserved in which the bones of the great Evangelist once rested.

* * * * *

The Introit of the Mass *Os justi* refers to the inspired wisdom of the Evangelist, and is the same as on December 3. The Collect for St Matthew was adapted later to the feast of St Joseph.

"Grant, O Lord, that we may be helped by the prayers of thy blessed apostle and evangelist, Matthew; so that what we may not obtain of ourselves may be given to us through his intercession."

It is not possible for us to accomplish those actions which belong to the supernatural order by our natural strength alone. Therefore we always need the grace of God in order to perform meritorious works, worthy of eternal life. This is the true and safe foundation of Christian humility: practical knowledge of our own incapacity, and recognition of the need for the grace of God.

The Lesson describes Ezechiel's vision of the four symbolical animals, and is the same as on April 25. The animals which the prophet beheld in the heavens were surrounded by fire, lightning, and flames, because the word of God is always full of power, and the holy Gospel which is read and preached by the priests of the Church to-day, still produces in minds which are well disposed the same salutary effects which it produced nineteen centuries ago, when Jesus first preached to the crowds in Palestine. It is of supreme importance that the Gospel should be announced, and announced with faith and authority.

The Gradual *Beatus vir* is the same as on February 4 for St Andrew Corsini. The alleluiatic verse follows, and is taken from the celebrated hymn of Nicetas of Remesiana, *Te Deum*: "Alleluia. The glorious choir of the Apostles praise thee, O Lord."

In the Gospel, St Matthew himself humbly relates the story of his own conversion. (Matt. ix, 9–13.) Jesus called him from the receipt of custom, and Matthew, arising immediately, followed him and became an apostle. Here we see the importance of corresponding at once to God's call and of fulfilling the vocation revealed to us. Jesus may call some souls at the eleventh hour, but, as a rule, he calls the young, as he did in the case of the Apostles, because the evangelical life—especially life in a community, which resembles most nearly that of the Lord and his first disciples—requires the strength and energy of youth.

The Antiphon for the Offertory is like that for St Romanus on August 9.

Secret: "May the offerings of thy church be made acceptable to thee, O Lord, we beseech thee, by the prayers of the blessed Matthew, thine apostle and evangelist, by whose glorious tidings she is enlightened."

The Sacramentaries give the following Preface for to-day:
... *Vere dignum* ... *Qui Ecclesiam tuam in tuis fidelibus ubique potentem, Apostolicis facis constare doctrinis; praesta quaesumus, ut per quos initium divinae cognitionis accepit, per eos usque in finem saeculi capiat regni caelestis augmentum. Per Christum.*

The Communion is the same as in the Mass of the vigil.

Post-Communion: "We who have received the sacraments beseech thee, O Lord, that what we have done to celebrate the glory of blessed Matthew, thine apostle and evangelist, may, through his intercession, avail us also for a healing remedy."

The Sacramentaries also assign the following *Oratio super populum* as a last benediction: "*praesta quaesumus, omnipotens Deus, ut qui iugiter Apostolica defensione munimur, nec succumbamus vitiis, nec opprimamur adversis. Per Dominum.*"

Sequere me. In order that we might be able to follow his call our kind Master set us an example which we all can follow. He abased himself, assuming our human nature, and desired that we should imitate his meekness, humility, and obedience.

SEPTEMBER 22

St Basilla, Virgin and Martyr

Station "ad coemeterium Basillae" on the Via Salaria vecchia.

The first documentary evidence which we have of this ancient sepulchral station is to be found in the Philocalian *Feriale* where it is entered thus to-day: *X. Kal. octobris. Basillae, Salaria vetere. Diocletiano IX et Maximiano VII consulibus* (A.D. 304).

The Cemetery of Basilla, or of Hermes, is well known. That the martyr was the object of widespread devotion can be deduced from the inscriptions in which her help is invoked as well as from the medieval Itineraries.

Thus, for instance, a sorrowing mother who lays her little

son Aurelius Gemellus in his grave, concludes his sepulchral inscription with this invocation :

COMMANDO · BASILLA · INNOCENTIA · GEMELLI

"I commend to thee, O Basilla, the innocent soul of Gemellus."

In another place two parents commend into the hands of the Saint the souls of their three children, Crescentius, Micina, and Crescens.

> DOMINA · BASILLA · COM
> MANDAMVS · TIBI · CRES
> CENTINVS · ET · MICINA
> FILIA · NOSTRA · CRESCEN
> QVE · VIXIT · MENS · X · ET · DES
> ⌀

It appears as though the date 304 recorded to-day in the Philocalian Calendar must refer to a translation of the body of Basilla in order to save it from profanation during the persecution of Diocletian. Her relics were transferred later to St Praxedes, and are therefore mentioned in the well-known inscription attributed to Paschal I.

SEPTEMBER 22

St Merita, Martyr

Station on the Via Ostiensis in the Cemetery of Commodilla.

This is also the *natalis* of St Merita, whose name, together with that of St Digna, was inserted by Baronius in the Martyrology. Digna, however, never existed, and this name was introduced through a mistake, which must have arisen in the deciphering of some inscription in which a defunct virgin was given the usual title *Dignae et Meritae*. An example of this is found in an inscription in the Lateran Museum :

ADEODATAE · DIGNAE · ET · MERITAE · VIRGINI

It is certain that the paintings in the Cemetery of Commodilla only represent St Merita, whose relics were transferred in the ninth century to a special oratory of the *titulus Marcelli*.

A *Pons sanctarum Dignae et Emeritae* on the Via Prenestina, ten miles distant from Rome, is mentioned in a Bull of St Gregory VII in favour of his ancient Abbey of St Paul's.

SEPTEMBER 22

SS MAURICE AND COMPANIONS, MARTYRS

The *cultus* of the martyrs who formed the *Legio felix Agaunensis* is both ancient and famous, and the Abbey which King Sigismund caused to be built over their tomb was the goal of devout pilgrims from all parts of Europe. It is not wonderful, then, that an altar should have been raised in the Vatican Basilica dedicated to the valiant leader of the Theban Legion, and that the festival of the martyrs of Agaunum should have been inscribed in the Roman Missal.

Indeed the name of St Maurice is to be found even in the coronation rite of an Emperor, for the *Ordo Romanus* attributed to Giacomo Gaetani prescribes that when three Collects have been recited over the new sovereign by the Bishops of Albano, Porto, and Ostia, the latter should advance with the Emperor-elect to the altar of St Maurice and anoint him with the oil of catechumens on the right arm and shoulder.

The Mass *Introit* is the same as for January 22, but the Collects are as follows:

Collect: " Grant, we beseech thee, almighty God, that we may be gladdened by the solemn festival of thy holy martyrs Maurice and his companions; so that we may glory in the birthday of those on whose prayers we lean."

The death of a martyr fills the whole Church with joy, for as St Paul says: *sicut abundant passiones Christi in nobis, ita et per Christum abundat consolatio nostra*. (2 Cor. i, 5.)

The Lesson is taken from the Apocalypse (vii, 13-17). The Apostle St John beholds in heaven a white-robed multitude and asks who these may be and whence they come. The Angel replies: These are martyrs, that is to say, they are those who arrive through sufferings at the gates of eternity. They have come through great tribulations and sorrows. Their tears, labours, and sufferings soon ended, and they now receive their reward and a prize which will endure for ever.

Secret: " We beseech thee, O Lord, to look upon the gifts which we bring to thee in memory of thy holy martyrs, Maurice and his companions; and grant that through the intercession of those for whose sake they are become well-pleasing to thee, they may bring us grace for evermore."

Post-Communion: " We who are refreshed and gladdened by the heavenly sacraments humbly beseech thee, O Lord, that we may be shielded and helped by those in whose triumph we glory."

In honour of the glorious Legion of Agaunum we may quote the following ancient antiphons from their Office: *Sancta legio Agaunensium Martyrum, dum resisteret adversariis, sacro duce Mauritio interveniente, immortalitatis compendium acquisierunt.*

Pretiosa sunt Thebaeorum Martyrum vulnera, sancti Mauritii cum sociis suis, qui sub Maximiano mortem decreverunt suscipere.

Ecce factus est sacer ille Agaunensium locus, per suffragia Sanctorum, salus praesentium, praesidium futurorum.

This prayer was fulfilled in history, for in the early Middle Ages the Abbey of Agaunum was famous for the holy lives of its inmates.

SEPTEMBER 22

St Thomas of Villanova, Bishop and Confessor*

The festival of this famous Bishop of Valencia, who was a great almsgiver and a father of the poor, was placed in the Missal by Alexander VII.

His death actually occurred on September 8, 1555, but as that day was consecrated to the Nativity of the Blessed Virgin Mary, the Office was deferred to September 22.

In order to give some idea of the generosity of St Thomas, it is enough to relate that when he died, the very bed on which he lay no longer belonged to him. He had given it a few days before to a poor man, who in his turn allowed him to keep it for the short time that it would still be of use to him.

The Mass is that of St Andrew Corsini on February 4.

The Secret and the Post-Communion are taken from the Mass of St Leo I on April 11.

The Collect is as follows: "O God, who didst endow blessed Thomas thy Bishop in a singular degree with the virtue of compassion for the poor; we beseech thee that through his intercession thou wouldst pour forth the riches of thy mercy on those who humbly pray to thee."

Almsgiving is a species of sacrament by which we exchange our temporal goods for immortal possessions and bestow them upon him who is the source of all good. This mystical sacrament is of so much value to the Church that the divine Founder ensured its permanence by a formal promise to his Apostles: *Pauperes semper habetis vobiscum.* The Church has always fully understood this word of Christ, and even from the days of the Apostles she has regarded the assistance of the poor and needy as one of the most important of her duties.

SEPTEMBER 23

ST THECLA, VIRGIN AND MARTYR

The *cultus* of this famous disciple of St Paul—who is honoured by the Greek Fathers as Protomartyr and equal to the the Apostles, πρωτομάρτυρος καὶ ἰσαποστόλου—is one of the most ancient and most celebrated. Many legends were connected with this martyr even from the second century. The tomb of St Thecla at Iconium was the goal of constant pilgrimages, and we know from the writings of Basil of Seleucia that numerous miracles were worked there.

Great devotion was shown at Rome, too, to St Thecla, and we find signs of this, especially, near the sepulchral basilica of her master St Paul, where, on the side of a hill near the *Ager* of Lucina, a cemetery was made and a basilica built which were dedicated to some person bearing the name of Thecla. We do not know who this Thecla was, but she may have been a Roman martyr, who was buried on that spot in memory of the relationship between St Paul and St Thecla. The case appears similar to that of the martyred priest Timothy, who was buried on another hill which overshadows the tomb of the Apostle, in order that *Paulo apostolo, ut quondam, Timotheus adhaereret.*

An inscription in the neighbouring Cemetery of Commodilla records the *natalis* of St Thecla.

The memory of the great martyr of Iconium occurs too in the very ancient litany of the *Ordo commendationis animae*, together with that of the most celebrated Patriarchs of the Old Testament, and of the two Princes of the Apostles, Peter and Paul : *Et sicut beatissimam Theclam virginem et martyrem tuam de tribus atrocissimis tormentis liberasti, sic liberare digneris animam huius servi tui, et tecum facias in bonis congaudere caelestibus.*

Besides the sanctuary of the Roman Thecla which stands on the hill over the Via Ardeatina, facing the Basilica of St Paul's—as though to recall how Thecla of Iconium kept her eyes fixed on the Apostle who instructed her—there exists an oratory with a monastery near St Peter's dedicated to the "great martyr who was like to the Apostles." The memory of this sanctuary is preserved by the little chapel of the convent of Santo Spirito *in Sassia*.

The Mass is the same as for St Martina on January 30, except the Collect.

Collect: "Grant, we beseech thee, that we who keep the birthday of blessed Thecla thy virgin and martyr, may both rejoice in her yearly festival, and profit by the example of such great faith."

The example of Christian fortitude which has so often been given by delicate women and young girls, whilst serving to illustrate the power of God, who enables the weaker sex to attain the palm of martyrdom, should also act as an incentive to us, for it is not fitting that we should allow ourselves to be outdone by women and children in our zeal for the Faith.

SEPTEMBER 23

St Liberius, Pope

The Martyrology of St Jerome records to-day the *natalis* of Pope Liberius (352–366), *Romae, depositio sancti Liberi episcopi*. The actual date of the Pope's death was September 24, of the year 366. Unfortunately legends soon gathered round the name of Liberius, and in these he was depicted almost as a renegade, who had joined the Arian party and had therefore persecuted Felix II. As a consequence of this, the early *cultus* which arose soon after the injured Pontiff's death, and which is still universally observed in Eastern Churches, gradually died out at Rome. To this day Liberius, who fell a victim to the perfidy of the Emperor Constantius, is regarded almost as a *lapsus*.

It is impossible to enter here into the much disputed question concerning the reasons which led Constantius to pardon the exiled Pontiff. It will suffice to note the monuments which give proof of the liturgical *cultus* once universal throughout the Church in honour of Liberius, and especially of the reputation for sanctity which he enjoyed at Rome in the period immediately following his death. Even during the Middle Ages it appears that his feast was celebrated in some Roman Calendars on May 17 and on September 23.

The Byzantine Calendar celebrates on August 27 the memory of τοῦ ὁσίου πατρὸς ἡμῶν καὶ ὁμολογητοῦ Λιβερίου Πάπα Ῥώμης, "Our holy Father, the Confessor of the Faith and Pope of Rome."

The Copts commemorate Liberius on October 9: "*The repose of St Liberius, Bishop of Rome and defender of the Faith.*" His name occurs again on the fourth day of their supplementary month: *Commemoration of Liberius, Bishop of Rome.*

The Sacramentary

After Liberius had been driven into exile because of his fidelity to the Nicene Faith, and that Felix II had taken his place at Rome, the inhabitants of the City separated into two parties. Tumults arose, blood was shed, and signs of the attachment of the greater part of the people to the rightful Pontiff may be found in certain inscriptions where the name of Liberius is intentionally included as a protest of devotion to his cause:

(de)FVNCTA · EST · EVPLIA · QVAE ·
VS · MAIAS · QVAE · FVIT · ANNORV
QVE · DEPOSITA · EST · IN · PACE · SVB · LIBE(rio episcopo)

* * *

RA
A · CVMPAVIT
ONVS · SEBIBO
(sedent)E · PAPA · LIBERIO

But the most important record of the veneration paid to Pope Liberius in early times, at the Cemetery of Priscilla, is his sepulchral inscription itself, which was fortunately transcribed by ancient collectors:

Quam Domino fuerant devota mente parentes,
Qui confessorem talem genuere potentem,
Atque sacerdotem sanctum, sine felle columbam !
Divinae legis sincero corde magistrum,
Haec te nascentem suscepit Ecclesia Mater,
Uberibus fidei nutriens devota beatum,
Qui pro se passurus eras mala cuncta libenter,
Parvulus utque loqui cepisti dulcia verba,
Mox Scripturarum lector pius indole factus,
Ut tua lingua magis legem quam verba sonaret ;
Dilecta a Domino tua dicta infantia simplex,
Nullis arte dolis sorde fucata malignis,
Officio tali iusto puroque legendi,
Atque item simplex aduliscens mente fuisti
Maturusque animo ferventi aetate modestus
Remotus, prudens, mitis, gravis, integer et equus,
Haec tibi lectori innocua fuit aurea vita.
Diaconus hinc factus iuvenis meritoque fideli
Qui sic sincere, caste, integreque pudice
Serviveris sine fraude Deo, quanta pectore puro
Atque annis aliquot fueris levita severus
Ac tali iusta conversatione beata,
Dignus qui merito inlibatus iure perennis
Huic tantae Sedi Christi splendore serenae
Electus fidei plenus summusque sacerdos,
Qui nivea mente immaculatus Papa sederes,
Qui bene Apostolicam doctrinam sancte doceres
Innocuam plebem caelesti lege magister.
Quis, te tractante, sua non peccata reflebat ?

September 23

In synodo, cunctis, victor, superatis iniquis
Sacrilegis, Nicaena Fides electa triumphat.
Contra quamplures certamen sumpseris unus
Catholica praecincte Fide possederis omnes
Vox tua certantis fuit haec sincera salubris :
Atque nec hoc metuo, neque illud committere opto.
Haec fuit, haec semper mentis constantia firma.
Discerptus, tractus, profugatusque Sacerdos,
Insuper, ut faciem quodam nigrore velaret
Nobili falsa manu portantes aemula caeli
Ut speciem Domini foedaret luce coruscam
En tibi discrimen vehemens, non sufficit annum ;
Insuper exilio decedis martyr ad astra,
Atque inter Patriarchas praesagosque prophetas
Inter Apostolicam turbam Martyrumque potentum
Cum hac turba dignus mediusque locutus adoras
Mite pium Domini conspectum, iuste Sacerdos.
Inde tibi merito tanta est concessa potestas.
Ut manum imponas patientibus, incola Christi,
Daemonia expellas, purges mundesque repletos,
Ac salvos homines reddas animoque vigentes
Per Patris ac Filii nomen cui credimus omnes,
Cumque tuum obitum praecellens tale vidimus
Spem gerimus cuncti proprie nos esse beatos,
Qui sumus hocque tuum meritum fidemque secuti.

" How devoted must those parents have been to the service of God,
Who gave life to this great Confessor of the Faith ;
To so holy a Bishop, who was guileless as a dove,
A teacher of Divine law, with a single heart.
At thy birth this Church received thee in her arms
And fed thee, O Blessed One, with the milk of Faith,
Who wast destined to suffer willingly for her sake.
When, as a young child, thou hadst hardly learnt to speak
Thou wert chosen to read the Scriptures because of thy piety,
And thy tongue learnt to pronounce the Law instead of empty words.
Thou wert simple and pleasing to God in thy childhood,
The sacred Text suffered no insidious alterations
When thou didst faithfully and rightly perform thine office.
As a young man, too, thou wert innocent, and with years
Didst show thyself wise, modest, mild, a lover of solitude,
Prudent, serious, single-minded and just.
These were the golden years of thy pure life as a lector.
Whilst still in thine early youth thou wert named deacon
By virtue of thy faith, and didst fulfil that office truly
Serving God faithfully, chastely, and with a sinless heart.
When some years had passed in this austere service,
Thou wert found worthy on account of thy holy life
To be called to the See of Christ, high-priest of the Faith,
Immaculate Pontiff whose heart was white as snow,
Thence to teach worthily the doctrine of the Apostles
And to instruct the faithful in the law of God.
Who did not bewail his sins, when thou didst upbraid ?
Victorious in the synod over sacrilegious heretics
Through thee the true Faith of Nicea prevailed.
Thou didst enter the battle alone against many,
And didst overcome through the force of thy Catholic Faith.
This was ever thy loyal battle-cry in the struggle :

'I fear no threats and will yield to no persuasions.'
Such was throughout the constancy of thy mind.
Thou wast torn from thy See, O Pontiff, and led into exile.
Then, in order that some stain should disfigure thine image,
They craftily present to thee a false confession
By which the glory of the Saviour is subtly offended.
And for near on two years this struggle endured.
At length death came, and thou didst enter heaven a martyr,
Because of the exile endured, and art seated amongst the Patriarchs,
Amongst the Prophets, the Apostles, and the powerful band of martyrs
Thou art held worthy to adore with this great company
The merciful presence of God, O holy Pontiff.
Thence hast thou fitly received that wondrous power
Of healing the sick, of casting forth devils by thy touch,
And of restoring health and sanity to all who invoke thee.
In the name of the Father and the Son, in whom we all believe,
We who were witnesses of thy glorious death expect
With confidence to attain also to that blessedness
Which thou dost enjoy, as thy followers who share thy Faith."

* * * * *

In the inscription on the tomb of Pope Siricius too, that Pontiff is praised because he followed Liberius into exile, at first as a simple lector and afterwards in the office of a deacon :

LIBERIVM · LECTOR · MOX · ET · LEVITA · SECVTVS

Therefore, although the report of the momentary weakness of the exiled Pope was accepted as a fact even by some of the Fathers of the Church,

Insuper, ut faciem quodam nigrore foedaret,

Catholic Rome threw the blame implied in this calumny upon those who had persecuted the supporters of the Nicene Faith, and especially the courageous Pontiff. The latter never allowed himself to be taken in by the *falsa aemula caeli*, but sustained for a long time the *discrimen vehemens*, and remained constant to the orthodox confession which he had made at Milan, and which had provoked Constantius to pass sentence of exile upon him.

After his death Liberius was hailed by the titles of Confessor and Martyr ; his tomb in the Cemetery of Priscilla became famous for the miracles which were worked there ; indeed, amongst the very portraits which exist of the early Popes, there is one dating from the second half of the fourth century, in the Cemetery of Pretextatus, which represents Pope Liberius with the two Princes of the Apostles and with the famous Martyr of the Appian Way, Sixtus II.

Indeed, we may truthfully say, that when St Ambrose wrote these words to his sister Marcellina concerning Pope

September 23

Liberius: *Tempus est, soror sancta, ea quae mecum conferre soles, beatae memoriae Liberii praecepta revolvere, ut quo vir sanctior, eo sermo accedat gratior,*[1] he was following the early tradition of the Roman Church, a tradition which, although it subsequently disappeared in the Eternal City, was preserved and handed down to us unaltered, by the most ancient Churches of the East.

In praise of Liberius, whose pontificate is commemorated at Rome by the classic monument of the Liberian Basilica on the Esquiline, we may quote the following lines which adorn the Grecian mosaics in honour of the great champion of the Nicene Creed:

Τὸν πλοῦτον ἀντλέιν Λιβέριος νῦν ἔχει
Ὃν οὐρανοῖς ἦν εὐφρώνως θησαυρίσας

" Liberius, who when he departed into exile at Berea sent back to the Emperor the fifty *solidi*, which the latter had offered him for the journey, can now dispose of the heavenly treasures."

SEPTEMBER 23

St Linus, Pope

The succession of the Popes of Rome from the apostle St Peter has been represented since very early times by the person of St Linus. His name occurs, therefore, not only in the most ancient Roman Calendars, but it follows those of the Apostles in the Canon of the Mass.

During the reign of Urban VIII the foundations designed to support the *baldacchino* of the altar of St Peter at the Vatican were excavated, and it was believed that the tomb of Linus had been found. Upon one of the sarcophagi which were then unearthed, the name LINVS, an uncommon one in classical nomenclature, was carved.

The identification of the relics with those of the successor of St Peter rests, however, upon the fact, impossible now to establish, whether the inscription was correctly read at the time or whether it may not have been the last syllables of some other name, such as *Tranquillinus* or *Marcellinus*.

Whatever may be the truth concerning the tomb discovered in the Vatican Basilica, it is certain that Linus was the immediate successor of St Peter in the Papal See, and that his name was included in the Canon of the Mass, nor is there any reason to reject the testimony of the *Liber Pontificalis* which

---
[1] *De virgin.* c. iv.

asserts that Pope Linus was buried near the tomb of the Prince of the Apostles. In the absence of any particulars concerning the life of St Linus, the fact of his having been chosen to succeed St Peter during the great Neronian persecution, is in itself a proof of his eminent sanctity, and is in keeping with the title of martyr under which he is honoured.

The Mass is the same as on December 10, for St Melchiades. The three Collects, however, are those of July 13, for the feast of St Anacletus.

We may well meditate upon a sentence which we read to-day in the Epistle of St James. Temptations and trials are regarded by us as misfortunes, and our human nature shrinks from them and prays for relief. The Holy Spirit, on the contrary, proclaims that the man is blessed who endures temptation, for as gold is tried by fire, and friendship is tried by adversity, so virtue is tried and purified by temptation. God is never so near to us as he is in the hour of trial, and that is why temptations increase and become fiercer as the soul advances in merit and sanctity in the sight of God.

SEPTEMBER 24

Our Lady of Ransom

This festival commemorates the favours granted by the Blessed Virgin Mary to St Peter Nolasco and to St Raymund of Pennafort when they founded the Order of Our Lady of Mercy. The feast was instituted by Pope Innocent XII.

Under the patronage of the Mother of Mercy the religious of this Order distinguished themselves by a devotion which the Christian religion alone can inspire, and even carried it so far as to give themselves up as hostages in order to deliver unhappy Christian prisoners from the hands of the Turks. The power of the Crescent no longer threatens us, but we should ask Mary to help us to deliver many souls from the chains of sin.

The Mass is the same as on August 5, but the Collect is as follows: "O God, who by means of the most glorious Mother of thy Son wast pleased to give new children to thy church for the deliverance of Christ's faithful from the power of the heathen; grant, we beseech thee, that we who love and honour her as the foundress of so great a work may, by her merits and intercession, be ourselves delivered from all sin and from the bondage of hell."

SEPTEMBER 26
St Eusebius, Pope and Martyr
Station at the Cemetery of Callixtus.

The Martyrology of St Jerome contains to-day this notice: *Romae, via Appia in Coemeterio Callisti, depositio sancti Eusebi Episcopi.* Damasus placed the following inscription on the tomb of this greatly tried Pontiff (310–311):

DAMASVS · EPISCOPVS · FECIT

D
A
M
A HERACLIVS · VETVIT · LAPSOS · PECCATA · DOLERE
S
I

P EVSEBIVS · MISEROS · DOCVIT · SVA · CRIMINA · FLERE
A
P
A
E SCINDITVR · IN · PARTE · POPVLVS · GLISCENTE · FVRORE

C
V
L SEDITIO · CAEDES · BELLVM · DISCORDIA · LITES
T
O
R EXTEMPLO · PARITER · PVLSI · FERITATE · TYRAMNI
A
T
Q
V INTEGRA · CVM · RECTOR · SERVARET · FOEDERA · PACIS
E

A
M PERTVLIT · EXILIVM · DOMINO · SVB · IVDICE · LAETVS
A
T
O
R LITORE · TRINACRIO · MVNDVM · VITAMQVE · RELIQVIT

F
V
R
I
V
S

D
I
O
N
Y
S
I
V
S

F
I
L
O
C
A
L
V
S

S
C
R
I
B
S
I
T

EVSEBIO · EPISCOPO · ET · MARTYRI

"Heraclius forbade those who had lapsed to do penance for their sins; Eusebius taught the unhappy ones to weep over their crime. The populace is divided into two parties by the increasing discord. Seditions follow, disputes, tumults, and loss of life. Both leaders were condemned by the severity of the tyrant, and were alike exiled from Rome, whereas the Pontiff had sought to keep the laws of peace. He endured exile serenely, trusting to the judgement of God, and passed from this life and this world on the shores of Sicily.

Damasus Bishop to Eusebius Bishop and Martyr.

Furius Dionysius Philocalus, full of reverence and affection for Pope Damasus, wrote this."

This inscription, which was damaged in the Gothic invasion and afterwards replaced on the tomb by Pope Vigilius, alludes to one of the saddest chapters of the history of the Church in the fourth century, when immediately after the persecution of Diocletian the rigorist party, known later in Africa as the Donatists, which already had many followers in Rome, wished to close the road of repentance to those who had denied their Faith through fear or under torment.

The epitaph of Pope Eusebius follows that which Damasus composed for Pope Marcellus, who under precisely the same circumstances had been held responsible by Maxentius for the tumults caused by the rigorist party in the city, and had suffered exile unjustly on this account.

We know from the inscription of Marcellus that Heraclius was himself a lapsed Christian:

CRIMEN · OB · ALTERIVS · CHRISTVM · QVI · IN · PACE · NEGAVIT

Some writers assert that the body of St Eusebius is still preserved in the Basilica *ad Catacumbas*.

SEPTEMBER 26

SS Cyprian and Justina, Martyrs

From very early times legendary stories gathered round the names of these two saints, on which account it is impossible to be certain of any of the facts described in their *Passio*.

The legend of Cyprian and Justina was very popular in the fourth century; indeed both St Gregory Nazianzen and Prudentius ended by identifying the Magician of Antioch, who was converted by the virgin Justina, with the celebrated Thascius Cyprianus of Carthage, who was converted by the priest Cecilius. Antoninus of Piacenza in the sixth century mentions the tomb of St Justina at Antioch, but the question still remains undecided whether the St Cyprian of this legend was, or was not, one and the same person as the Bishop of Carthage.

The Empress Eudoxia, the wife of Theodosius II, wrote an epic poem in three books on the martyrdom of St Cyprian.

Devotion to SS Cyprian and Justina was introduced into Rome during the Middle Ages, when tradition asserted that their relics were preserved near the Lateran Basilica.

The Mass *Salus autem* is the same as for the martyrs Faustinus and Jovita on February 15. The Collect is as follows: " Lord, let thy blessed martyrs Cyprian and Justina ever lend us strength and protection, for thou never ceasest to look with mercy upon those to whom thou givest the help of thy saints."

The Secret and the Post-Communion are taken from the Mass of St Symphorosa on July 18.

How supremely important is the salvation of souls! Not content with having given his only Son to save us, and with having instituted the Church and the Sacraments, God has also disposed that Heaven should co-operate with him in this most noble work of saving souls. Therefore he has given the angels and saints the duty of watching over us and praying for us, that they may be our advocates in the Court of Heaven.

SEPTEMBER 27

SS COSMAS AND DAMIAN, MARTYRS

Station at their Basilica on the Via Sacra.

These celebrated martyrs gave their lives for the Faith at Cyrus in Syria where they were buried, according to the explicit testimony of Theodosius. The fame of their sanctuary appealed to the generosity of Justinian, who built over it a great basilica, but the *cultus* of the *Anargyri* spread beyond the episcopal city of Theodoretus and reached Constantinople in the first half of the fourth century. In later days there were four basilicas in the Imperial City dedicated to the two brothers.

At Rome Pope Symmachus (498–514) built an oratory on the Esquiline, in honour of SS Cosmas and Damian, to which afterwards an abbey was added. Later, Felix IV (526–530) dedicated to them the Basilica of Romulus Augustulus and the *templum sacrae Urbis* on the Via Sacra, and in time this church became the most celebrated of the Roman sanctuaries consecrated to the wonder-working doctors.

We must, however, mention a few of the other churches built in honour of the *Anargyri* which prove the popularity of their *cultus* in ancient Roman Liturgy.

There was, for instance, a chapel in honour of SS Cosmas and Damian near the *titulus Marcelli;* another stood near Sta Lucia *de captu seccutae*, and a third, too, existed in the neighbourhood of St Apollinaris. In the " rione " *de pinea* there was a parish church in honour of the two saints, and lastly, about 935, the famous monastery of SS Cosmas and Damian in *Mica Aurea* was founded, which afterwards became one of the twenty-four privileged basilicas of the city.

The *cultus* of the two Eastern martyrs was so famous at Rome, that besides the two stational Synaxes on the Via Sacra which were held at Mid-Lent and on the night of the Octave of Easter, there were celebrated in the seventh century a third and a fourth station, not only on September 27, but on the preceding Sunday—*die domenico, ad sanctos Cosmae et Damiano ante natale eorum*. This was a kind of supplementary feast for the benefit of the working classes who were not able to attend the *natalis* of the two Saints during the week.

The Introit *Sapientiam* was composed, in early times, in honour of the two learned *Anargyri*, that is to say when Felix IV consecrated their Sanctuary near the Roman Forum.

The Collect is as follows: " Grant, we beseech thee, almighty God, that we who keep the birthday of thy blessed martyrs Cosmas and Damian, may, through their intercession, be delivered from all the dangers that threaten us."

The Lesson and the alleluiatic verse are the same as on the feast of the martyrs Primus and Felician on June 9. The Gradual *Clamaverunt* is that of the Mass of SS Faustinus and Jovita.

According to the Würzburg List, the Gospel to-day should be taken from St John xv, 17–25. But in the Missal we find that of St Luke vi, 17–23, which is also read on the feast of the martyrs Gervase and Protase, June 19. It harmonises with the title of wonder-working doctors and *Anargyri*, by which the Saints of to-day are known, and in honour of whom the following verse of Scripture is repeated: *Omnis turba quaerebat eum tangere, quia virtus de illo exibat et sanabat omnes.*

The Antiphon for the Offertory is the same as on June 17 for SS John and Paul, martyrs: " All they that love thy name shall glory in thee; for thou, O Lord, wilt bless the just: O Lord, thou hast crowned us with the shield of thy goodwill."

Secret: "May the loving prayers of thy saints never fail us, O Lord; may they make our gifts well-pleasing to thee, and ever win for us thy forgiveness."

The Antiphon for the Communion of the people is taken from the Mass of June 12, for the *natalis* of the martyrs Basilides, Cyrinus, etc.

Post-Communion: "May thy people, O Lord, we beseech thee, be shielded by the heavenly banquet of which thou sufferest them to partake, and also by the united prayers of thy saints."

The intention of Pope Felix IV, when he built the new basilica, near the Forum, in honour of SS Cosmas and Damian, is clearly seen in the dedicatory inscription to which we have already alluded. In those lines the holy Doctors' praise is thus expressed:

MARTYRIBVS · MEDICIS · POPVLO · SPES · CERTA · SALVTIS
FECIT · ET · EX · SACRO · CREVIT · HONORE · LOCVS

With what generosity does the Lord reward those who, possessing little, yet give all they have, even their lives, for the love of him!

SEPTEMBER 28

St Stacteus, Martyr

At the Cemetery " ad guttas " Ad aquas Salvias on the Via Laurentina.

To-day the Martyrology of St Jerome directs us to the Via Laurentina near the Aquas Salvias in the cemetery *ad guttam iugiter manantem*, where the martyr St Zeno, who is commemorated on July 9, also received burial. The notice for to-day in the Martyrology is expressed thus: *Romae, ad guttas, Sancti Stactei*.

This cemetery is unknown to us, and so, too, is the history of the martyrs who were interred there. An extremely ancient abbey, however, stands upon that spot, and the devout psalmody of the monks rises day and night in union with the prayers of the Saints whose relics rest beside it.

SEPTEMBER 28

St Wenceslas, Duke and Martyr

Pope Clement X first introduced into the Missal the feast of this holy Duke of Bohemia. The devotion of Wenceslas to our Lord in the Holy Eucharist is well known, and has been made familiar to all by the book of visits to the Blessed Sacrament composed by St Alphonsus de' Liguori.

Wenceslas was in the habit of sowing and reaping with his own hands the wheat from which the hosts were to be made, and he used to rise in the night even during the coldest seasons to visit the Blessed Sacrament. His virtue was the cause of his death, for it aroused the antagonism of his evil-minded mother and brother, who caused him to be assassinated.

The Mass *In virtute* is like that of St Canute on January 19.

The Collect is as follows: " O God, who by the palm of martyrdom didst remove blessed Wenceslas from an earthly princedom to the glory of heaven; keep us through his prayers from all harm, and grant that we may enjoy fellowship with him."

The Secret and Post-Communion are the same as on April 13 for St Hermenegild, King and Martyr.

If we study the Calendar of the Church we find there not a few names of kings who have entered heaven with their robes dyed in the blood of martyrdom. Indeed, their office itself often presents the occasion of winning the martyr's crown morally, if not actually, for the man who sets out to curb evil and to promote virtue must expect to face opposition and danger. It may have been on this account that in the Middle Ages the diadem worn by Christian sovereigns was always surmounted by a cross.

SEPTEMBER 29

THE DEDICATION OF THE BASILICA OF ST MICHAEL THE ARCHANGEL ON THE VIA SALARIA

The festival of to-day—*Natale basilicae Angeli in Salaria*—is mentioned in the Leonine Sacramentary as well as in the Martyrology of St Jerome. This is the original Roman feast in honour of the leader of the heavenly armies, in contradistinction to that of May 8, which only relates to the sanctuary of Monte Gargano in Apulia.

The site of St Michael's Basilica is noted with great precision as being the seventh milestone on the Via Salaria; and in the biography of Leo III it is therefore merely called: *Archangeli basilica in septimo*. It is also mentioned in the Itinerary of Salzburg: *Per eadem quoque viam venitur ad ecclesiam sancti Michaelis, septimo milliario ab Urbe*, and may thus be regarded as the earliest and most important Roman sanctuary built in honour of the great Archangel. In the Leonine Sacra-

September 29

mentary no less than five Masses are assigned to the feast of St Michael on this day.

The Captain of the heavenly armies, the Angel named in the Canon of the Mass, held from early times the first place in the Liturgy among the other angels; wherefore many churches dedicated to St Michael in the Middle Ages were simply known as churches " of the holy angel."

Within the Eternal City many sanctuaries rose in honour of the great defender of the Church of God against the assaults of the legions of Satan.

Near the " rotonda " of St Petronilla in the Vatican there was an oratory dedicated to St Michael; another, *sanctae Mariae in monasterio Michaelis,* is mentioned in the biography of Leo III, and can easily be identified with the Church of St Michael *in palatiolo* or *in schola Frisonum,* on the further slope of the Janiculum facing the right wing of the great colonnade of Bernini in front of the Vatican Basilica.

An Oratory of St Michael existed too, in the Lateran, and was, indeed, the origin of the great Hospital of St John founded by Cardinal Giovanni Colonna, about the year 1216. Near Monte Giordano we also find the little Church of Sant' Angelo *de Renizo,* better known now by the name of San Giuliano. There were besides these, Sant' Angelo *in piscina,* Sant' Angelo *de augusta,* Sant' Angelo *in nubibus* in the Mausoleum of Hadrian, Sant' Arcangelo, near Sta Pudenziana, etc.

The Benedictine monks especially contributed to the diffusion of the *cultus* of the holy Angels, as befits those who in their magnificent liturgical psalmody imitate on earth that which the Angels do in heaven; wherefore in the East, the monastic life and the monastic habit are commonly described by the title " angelic," which is applied to them.

It will be easy to understand the important place which St Michael fills in the Liturgy if we consider the office which the Archangel holds and the prominent part which he plays in the combat with Satan. The battle waged in heaven immediately after Lucifer's first rebellion is but a single episode in a long and bitter struggle which has endured through the ages, and on which the history of creation is founded.

The Word of God descended from heaven as a strong man to avenge his Father's honour and to place his enemies as a footstool at his feet. In this combat between good and evil, before which no creature can remain neutral, he has as his allies Michael and his angels, the Church and the Saints, who fight under his standard uttering the war-cry: *Quis ut Deus?* On the opposing side are Lucifer and his fallen Angels, with all their supporters, foremost among whom are the modern secret societies which endeavour to bring about on earth that which the Apostle calls " the mystery of iniquity that already worketh," and which will attain its full development shortly before the end of the world, and the final parousia of Christ. The accomplishment of this infernal design is, however, retarded, says St Paul, in order that God may carry out his merciful plan of salvation. According to the Apostle, it is a personal influence which frustrates the efforts of Satan, and Catholic theologians identify this influence with that of St Michael or of the Catholic Church. The devil who is preparing for the final battle which he will wage against Christ at the end of the world, cannot at present do all that he wishes, for the Church is protected by the invisible patronage of Michael and his Angels.

The Mass is the same as on May 8. The Gradual, however, is taken from Psalm cii : " Bless the Lord all ye his angels : you that are mighty in strength, that do his will."

The alleluiatic verse : " Holy Archangel Michael, defend us in battle, that we may not perish in the tremendous judgement. Alleluia."

We copy from the Leonine Sacramentary one of the splendid Prefaces assigned to the feast of to-day : *Vere dignum . . . Teque in omni factura tua laudare mirabilem ; in quo principaliter angelica natura praecellit, quae etsi humano generi conspectu subtrahitur, negatur adspectu, fidei tamen videtur intuitu. Dignumque est per honorificentiam nos eorum tuam suspicere maiestatem ; per quos multa praesidia nostrae salutis operaris ; tuamque magnificentiam hoc potius predicare, quod praeexcelsarum atque caelestium potestatum te Dominum confitentur. Per . . .*

It may be asked why, in this combat with the devil, God has entrusted our defence to the Angels. The reason of this is easily understood. The devil is a spirit who has lost none of the powers inherent to his nature. In order, therefore, that the struggle should not be unequal, God has placed at our side defenders of the same nature as Lucifer, that is to say pure spirits, who are, however, greater and more powerful than he is.

SEPTEMBER 30

St Jerome, Confessor and Doctor of the Church

The Martyrology of St Jerome notes to-day in the Province of Jerusalem : *castello Betlehem, depositio Ieronymi presbyteri.*

Sophronius Aurelius Ieronymus was born at Stridonium, and was universally renowned, even during his life, as a doctor

September 30

and interpreter of Holy Scripture. The greatest Doctors of the Church, including St Augustine and St Gregory, give special praise to his wisdom and virtue.

Although St Augustine may surpass him in doctrinal knowledge, St Jerome was certainly the most learned among the early Fathers of the Church. But he is best known by the powerful polemical writings in which he defended Catholic teaching against the crop of heresies which had arisen in the fourth century throughout the greater part of the Roman Empire. As the figure of St Augustine of Hippo appears to us to be almost inseparable from the episcopal dignity which surrounds it, so in the case of St Jerome, the monastic life is the background against which his virile virtues stand forth. His chief aim was to be a perfect monk, and before he would consent to be raised to the priesthood, he exacted a promise from Paulinus, Bishop of Antioch, that this new dignity should in no wise interfere with his monastic vocation.

Jerome, clad in a hair-shirt and emaciated by fasting like a second Baptist, calls up the image of a tall palm tree standing alone in the midst of the desert. But his words were carried to the ends of the earth, for whilst bands of the faithful led by their bishops arrived daily at Bethlehem to see Jerome and to take counsel with him, his writings reached those who could not come to him, and spread abroad his interpretation of the Scriptures and his polemics against heretics. An eye-witness, Sulpicius Severus, writes about him as follows : " He is continually absorbed in his books and studies ; he allows himself no rest either by night or by day ; he is incessantly occupied with reading or writing."[1] St Jerome died at an advanced age, probably about ninety years old, on September 30, 420, and was buried at Bethlehem, near the stable where our Lord was born.

Rome owes many things to St Jerome, who first entered her gates as a young student, and was afterwards the co-adjutor of Pope Damasus in dealing with the ecclesiastical matters of the whole world, and at one time actually a candidate for the See of Peter. Among these benefits are his translation of the Holy Scriptures, the introduction of the alleluiatic chant into the Sunday Mass, the spread of monastic life among the aristocracy, and lastly the daily recital of the Divine Office.

Several churches in the Holy City perpetuate the memory of the great Teacher of the Scriptures. Besides the altar dedicated to him in the Liberian Basilica near the Saviour's Crib, there was an Oratory of St Jerome on the Quirinal ; another still exists in the neighbourhood of St Lawrence *in*

---
[1] *Dialogues* I, 9, 5.

Damaso, where St Philip Neri founded his Congregation of the Oratory, and lastly, in the fifteenth century, a famous church was built in the " rione " of the *Campus Martius* by some natives of Dalmatia in honour of the holy Doctor who was their compatriot.

The Mass is the same as on January 29, with proper Collects.

Collect : " O God, who in blessed Jerome, thy confessor, didst vouchsafe to provide for thy church a great teacher in expounding holy scripture : grant, we beseech thee, that, by his merits which plead for us, we may be able with the help of thy grace to practise what he taught both by word and by example."

With the exception of the holy Sacraments there is nothing for which we should have greater veneration than the Scriptures, which contain the message of God to his people. Out of reverence for their contents the Scriptures were transcribed in letters of gold on painted parchment and encased in tablets of ebony or silver, studded with pearls and other precious stones. To this day in the Byzantine Churches the Codex of the Gospels is always kept upon the altar in the same manner as the Blessed Sacrament.

Secret : " Grant, O Lord, we beseech thee, that we may freely serve thee by thy heavenly grace ; let the offerings which we bring, through the intercession of blessed Jerome thy confessor, work in us both healing and glory."

Liberty of spirit consists in freeing ourselves from the tyranny of sin and of our passions. In order to obtain it, therefore, it is necessary to be watchful and to practise mortification.

Post-Communion : " We who are filled with thy heavenly food, beseech thee, O Lord, that, by the intercession of blessed Jerome thy confessor, we may be found worthy to win the grace of thy mercy."

Thus we, who because of the luxurious habits of modern life are unable to deny ourselves anything, must now have recourse to this holy monk, worn with fasting and tormented by cold during his lifetime, in order that he may cover our spiritual nakedness with the mantle of his immense merits.

The following words in which St Jerome expressed his devotion to the Faith of the Apostles and the Holy See in a letter to Damasus, are characteristic of the Saint : " I am joined in Communion with your holiness, that is with the chair of Peter ; upon that rock I know the Church is built. Whoever eats the lamb out of that house is a profane person. Whoever is not in the Ark shall perish in the flood."[1]

[1] *Ep.* XIV *alias* LVII *ad Damas.*

PART IX

THE SAINTS IN THE MYSTERY OF THE REDEMPTION

(THE FEASTS OF THE SAINTS FROM THE DEDICATION OF ST MICHAEL UNTIL ADVENT)

O · FORTVNATVM · NOSSET · SVA · SI · BONA · REGNVM
CVIVS · ROMA · ARX · EST · ET · CAELI · CLAVIGER · AVCTOR
QVI · TERRESTRE · VALET · IN · CAELVM · TOLLERE · REGNVM

Florus Lugdun.

FEASTS IN OCTOBER

OCTOBER 1

THE TRANSLATION OF ST REMIGIUS, BISHOP*

The precise date of the death of this great Apostle of the Franks, who administered Baptism to King Clovis and who occupied the See of Rheims for more than seventy years (459-533), was January 13. But from the time of St Gregory of Tours his feast was kept on this day, which is the date of the first translation of his relics. Later, under St Leo IX, the same day was chosen for a second translation of the body of the saint.

The words which Remigius is said to have addressed to Clovis when he was about to baptise him, are well known: " Bow down your neck with meekness, O Sicambrian prince: adore what you have hitherto burnt, and burn what you have hitherto adored."

The long line of the Most Christian Kings began that day, and the Eldest Daughter of the Roman Church received the waters of baptism as they fell upon the fleur-de-lis of her royal crown.

St Remigius was celebrated for his doctrine and for his miraculous powers, as well as for his holiness. His homilies have been lost, but four of his letters are extant, as well as some verses written by him and intended to be engraved on a chalice, and also his last testament.

The Mass is the same as on February 4, but the Collect is like that for St Liborius on July 23.

OCTOBER 2

FEAST OF THE HOLY GUARDIAN ANGELS*

The Roman feast of September 29 included, indeed, together with St Michael, the whole of the heavenly armies, and the Collect of that Mass declares that the special Office entrusted by God to the Angels is that of watching faithfully over us. This profound teaching of the Doctors of the Church establishes a wonderful unity between the visible and the invisible world, and between mortal and angelic beings. The higher orders of creatures are in close communion with the lower orders, whom they enlighten and protect.

A second feast of the Guardian Angels distinct from the primitive one of September 29 could only have originated at a far later date when the spirit of the Liturgy was no longer fully comprehended. As St Michael had his own festival, so, it was thought, the Guardian Angels must have theirs.

It was with this idea that Paul V in a decree of September 27, 1608, declared the feast of the Guardian Angels *duplex ad libitum*, and ordered that it should be kept on the first vacant date after the feast of St Michael. Clement X assigned it, later, to October 2.

The Mass is largely taken from earlier Masses in honour of the Archangel St Michael. The Introit is that of September 29.

Collect : " O God, who in thine unspeakable providence dost vouchsafe to send thy holy angels to keep watch over us ; grant, we humbly pray, that we may always be defended and shielded by them, and may rejoice in their fellowship for evermore."

The guardianship of the faithful is given by God into the hands of the angels, not only for the sake of the unity and harmony which bind together the orders of creation, but also on account of the duty owed by the angels to Christ. It is from Christ that they receive their glory, therefore out of gratitude to him who is *caput hominum et angelorum* these blessed spirits watch over the Church, the chosen Bride of the Saviour, and over the faithful who are the members of his mystical body.

The Epistle is taken from Exodus xxiii, 20–23, in which the Lord promises to the people of Israel journeying towards Palestine the guidance and help of his angel.

The angel represents God himself ; he is overshadowed by his ineffable name, wherefore the children of Israel cannot offend him with impunity. He is also the avenger of the outraged sanctity of God, and has power to punish that carnal people and bring them to obedience and fear of him.

In many stories of the saints we notice the same severity shown towards them by their guardian angels, who punished the slightest imperfection of which those chosen souls were guilty.

The motive of this loving discipline may be sought, perhaps, not only in the wise counsels of Providence aiming at the purification of certain predestined souls who were inspired to attain extraordinary sanctity through the ministry of the

October 2

angels, but also in the exquisite perfection of the angelic nature itself, which is less able to understand human nature than are Jesus Christ and his Blessed Mother, having no personal experience of human weakness. "*Non habemus Pontificem qui non possit compati infirmitatibus nostris, probatus per omnia, absque peccato.*"

The Gradual is taken from Psalm xc, and tells of the command given by God to his angels to watch over us in all our ways. It is the same as on the First Sunday in Lent.

The alleluiatic verse is from Psalm cii: "Bless the Lord all ye his hosts: you ministers of his who do his will. Alleluia."

The angels, then, are the ministers of divine Providence, which in order to lead us to our predestined end makes use of rewards and punishments. These blessed spirits ascend into heaven and present to God the incense of our prayers, descending again with the precious balsam of the divine graces. At other times they accuse us of ingratitude and infidelity, and God places in their hands the scourges destined to recall his earthly children to the observance of his laws.

The Gospel is that of May 8. The Saviour's words clearly reveal the wonderful mystery of his mercy, which forms the object of to-day's festival. Every Christian, no matter how small or humble he may be, has an Angel to guard and watch over him.

This great truth should fill us with love and respect for our neighbours, and more especially for the weak and for the little ones, who cannot rely upon their own powers and influence. Let us be careful not to grieve our neighbour, lest the anger of his angel be aroused against us.

The Antiphon for the Offertory is taken from Psalm cii: "Bless the Lord, all ye his angels: you ministers of his who execute his word, hearkening to the voice of his orders."

If the entire glory of these blessed spirits consists in the exact performance of the Divine Will, should we not, too, consider that obedience to the commands of God confers upon us a great honour?

Secret: "Receive, O Lord, the offerings which we bring in honour of thy holy angels; and grant in thy mercy that by their unceasing watchfulness we may both be freed from present dangers and may win everlasting life."

The following is the Antiphon for the Communion (Dan. iii, 58) from the canticle formerly known as the canticle of benediction: "All ye angels of the Lord, bless the Lord: sing a hymn, and exalt him above all for ever."

The Fathers of the Church remind us that the word "angel" refers to a certain office. The angels are of their nature pure spirits, they become angels or messengers when they are sent to us, or when they communicate to us a message from God.

Post-Communion: " We have received thy divine mysteries, O Lord, in joyful celebration of the feast of thy holy angels; let them so watch over us, we beseech thee, that we may always be kept safe from the wiles of our foes and guarded from all harm."

We should have a great veneration for the holy angels, to whom God has assigned the care and government of creation. St Paul had so great a feeling of reverence for the angels, that when he directed that Christian women should cover their heads in church, as a sign of modesty, he desired that this should be done *propter angelos*, that is to say out of respect for the blessed spirits.

St John, too, in the Apocalypse, addresses the seven letters for the Bishops of Asia to the angels of those churches, that is, to the angelic spirits who had been appointed by God to watch over those new centres of Christianity.

The ancient Liturgies often make mention of the Angel of Sacrifice, by whom our mystical gifts are carried from the altar on earth to that in heaven; this is the Angel who, whilst Tobias was employed on his labours of charity and mercy, *obtulit orationem Domino*.

St Benedict, following the tradition of the Fathers, whilst he speaks of the angels *nobis deputati*, who announce *die noctuque Domino factorum nostrorum opera*, desires that his monks shall have the greatest respect for the Divine Office, on account of the presence *Divinitatis et Angelorum eius* in the sanctuary.

OCTOBER 3

St Candida, Martyr

Station on the Via Portuensis, at the Cemetery of Pontianus.

To-day the Martyrology of St Jerome directs us to the road to Porto: *Romae, ad Ursum Pileatum, Candidae*.

The notice is not absolutely correct, for the martyr who is one of the group formed by the saints Pollio, Candida, and Pygmenius mentioned in the Passion of SS Peter and Marcellinus, reposed in a small basilica dedicated to her at the cemetery of Pontianus.

Adrian I restored this sanctuary, but soon after, owing to the dreary solitude to which the cemeteries outside the walls were abandoned at that time, he was obliged, against his will, to remove the relics of St Candida and placed them in the *titulus* of St Praxedes.

OCTOBER 4

St Balbina, Martyr

Station at the Title of Balbina.

The Martyrology of St Jerome invites us to seek the Via Appia to-day, where, in the Cemetery of Pretextatus, beside the martyr St Cyrinus, rested Balbina, whom the Acts declare to have been his daughter : *Romae, Via Appia, Balbinae.*

It is impossible to determine whether there is any connection between this Balbina and the second Balbina who gave her name to a part of the cemetery of Callixtus, and lastly the third St Balbina after whom a *titulus* on the Aventine was called. The difficulty which historians have been unable to solve, has been disposed of by legends which assert that the body of the martyr was transferred from the cemetery of Pretextatus to the *titulus Balbinae*, changing its name to *titulus Sanctae Balbinae.* We may conclude that the saint whose ancient liturgical *cultus* is celebrated to-day, is the Balbina who was originally buried beside the martyr Cyrinus. All other identifications, though possible, are only conjectural.

OCTOBER 4

St Francis of Assisi, Confessor*

Pope Innocent III is said to have beheld in a dream a poor man, bare-footed and girded with a cord, who upheld the falling Basilica of the Lateran. That dream was at once a prophecy and a symbol. In an age of factions and misrule, when Christian society had almost forgotten the Sermon on the Mount, and when even the Church and the Cloister had become tainted with the evils of feudalism, Francis, the poor man of Assisi, the bearer of the stigmata, appeared in the streets and market-places announcing the Gospel of the Kingdom and preaching Christ crucified to the people.

The magnitude and the Catholicity of the work achieved by the son of Pietro Bernardone, and the supernatural character of his mission all rest upon one circumstance. Before him numerous heretical sects had arisen, especially in France, to reproach the Church for her secular pomp and increasing riches. They wished to bring about a violent revolution in order to reform the clergy and to compel them by force to return to the state of evangelical poverty, in which SS Peter and Paul found themselves in the prisons of Nero.

The mission of these sects was not inspired by God and therefore did not succeed. That of St Francis was successful because instead of preaching revolt against his Mother the Church, he began by setting the example of detachment from worldly honours and conversion which was longed for, not by heretics only, but also by the faithful.

The Church has no need to look beyond her own fold in order to reform herself, for she possesses all the principles and the energy required to maintain a powerful supernatural life which defies the ages. Thus in the thirteenth century through the simple example and plain evangelical preaching of Francis, the Christian world was reformed, and a current of mystical spirituality moved with extraordinary force through the Church.

Different ages have different needs and require different remedies. In the preceding centuries of the early Middle Ages a great part was played by the higher clergy, the powerful Benedictine abbeys, the feudal system; but the people, weighed down by an endless list of duties with no corresponding rights, seemed hardly to exist. The society of that age, consisting of an ecclesiastical and secular aristocracy who still wrote and spoke the language of Virgil and Leo the Great, and was learned in Greek philosophy and Patristic theology, readily understood the symbols of God's essence, of his Unity and Trinity, which were painted on the walls of the basilicas.

But those times had passed away. At the end of the eleventh century, in the chronicles and day-books, we see the awakening of a new life throughout the country. The working classes, the *minores*, of the municipalities, emancipating themselves from the *maiores*, affirm their rights, and realize that with the passing away of the feudal system the future of Christian democracy has already dawned.

It was necessary to use a new spiritual language suited to its intelligence when speaking to this new generation, still in its childhood, which had the simplicity and the imaginative powers of a child. Before it could rise to Johannine contemplation of the Divinity it must rest upon the sacred humanity. Therefore we see St Francis at San Damiano, at Greccio, and at La Verna, leading the people to a more fervent devotion towards the person of the Redeemer, a devotion which from now onwards will continue to increase in the Catholic Church until it reaches its culminating point in the great revelations of Paray-le-Monial.

This is the special mark which gives a new character to the early Franciscan movement as we see it reflected in literature, in art, in the universities, and in municipal life,

October 4

in such a manner that St Francis may be regarded as the divinely appointed leader of the ecclesiastical reform in the thirteenth century, when a new epoch opened in the history of the Church.

Here, again, we find another characteristic mark of the mission of St Francis. His reform was carried out not by exterior agencies, as the heretics desired, but in the very bosom of the Catholic Church, by one who represented in his own person the head and the heart of the household of Christ. Cardinal Ugolino, afterwards Gregory IX, the friend, the confidant of the Poverello, who was later to raise him to the altars, was placed at his side by Divine Providence, as we must believe, in order to protect the simplicity of St Francis. And thus it was the papal authority and no other which directed from the first that overwhelming current of new life and evangelical mysticism loosed by the saint, and incorporated it in the service of the Church.

Francis died at sunset on Saturday, October 3, 1226, and was canonized three years later by Gregory IX, who caused the marvellous church to be built over his tomb, which is a noble monument of religious art, and which bears witness to the sublime greatness of his friend.

The Mass is almost the same as that for the feast of the Stigmata of St Francis. The following prayers are proper to this festival.

Collect: "O God, who through the merits of blessed Francis gavest increase to thy church by enriching her with new children; may we so follow his example as to despise the things of this world and always to rejoice in partaking of thy heavenly gifts."

We pray here for two things: the heavenly gifts of God's grace, and the joy which will be complete in the next world. These can only be ours on one condition. If our hands are full we can grasp nothing more, and if we carry a heavy burden we cannot run in the race. In order to reach heaven laden with graces we must abandon the useless luxuries of the world, and, as St Jerome says, we must follow naked the naked Christ.

The Gospel is the same as for the feast of St Matthias. We all seek rest for our souls, and this rest is only to be found by imitating the Sacred Heart of Jesus who is meek and humble.

Post-Communion: "Let grace from heaven, O Lord, we beseech thee, give increase to thy church; which thou didst vouchsafe to make illustrious by the glorious merits and example of blessed Francis thy confessor."

Ancient writers render a special tribute of praise to St Francis as being *vir catholicus et totus apostolicus*. His rule begins with a solemn promise of obedience to Pope Honorius III. Indeed, in order that the work begun by the "poverello" should appear as it truly was, a movement of reform from within the Church herself, Francis, in obedience to the Pope's wish, received the tonsure from the very outset, and later was raised to the rank of deacon.

OCTOBER 5

St Placidus and Companions, Martyrs*

On this day the Martyrology of St Jerome attributes to Sicily a group of thirty-two martyrs, among whom are named Placidus and Eutychius with thirty companions, whose festival also recurs on September 29.

Peter of Monte Cassino in the twelfth century mistook this Saint Placidus, who lived in the fourth century, for St Benedict's disciple St Placidus, who lived in the sixth century. He wove a whole romance about the saint, in which the pirates appear who finally put Placidus to death in the Port of Messina, together with his brothers Victorinus and Eutychius, his sister Flavia, and thirty monks. This invention of Peter's obtained credence, and when under Sixtus V there were discovered in the Church of St John at Messina on the spot which tradition indicated as the burial-place of Placidus, a large number of bones, showing traces of a violent death, the history related by the chronicler of Cassino was immediately remembered. It was on this occasion that the Pope caused the Office of St Placidus and his companions to be observed throughout the Church.

Whatever foundation there may be for the story of Peter the Deacon, the testimony by the Martyrology of St Jerome concerning the ancient group of the Martyrs of Messina remains unaltered: *In Sicilia, Placidi, Eutici et aliorum XXX*.

The Mass is the same as for SS Faustinus and Jovita on February 15, but the Collects are taken from the feast of St Symphorosa and her Sons, July 18.

OCTOBER 5

St Placidus, Disciple of St Benedict, Abbot*

The tradition of the Benedictine Order bears witness, from the tenth century, to the liturgical *cultus* of St Placidus, who was brought as a child to St Benedict by his father, Tertullus,

October 5

and was miraculously saved by Maurus from the lake of Nero. This *cultus* is quite separate from that of Placidus, the martyr of the Sicilian group. The name of Placidus appears regularly together with those of Benedict and Maurus in the Litany of the Saints, from the tenth century onwards.

In this the disciples of St Benedict imitated the example of their Master. On one occasion the great Patriarch, whilst at Subiaco, journeyed during the night to a precipitous height upon which he had built one of his twelve monasteries, and there, like Moses or Eliseus, he begged of the Lord to cause a spring of water to flow from the rock. He had with him as his companion the young child Placidus, who knelt beside him under the stars, uniting his prayers to those of the great Patriarch which obtained from heaven the miracle they implored.

Once, when Placidus had been sent with a pitcher to fetch water, he fell into the lake and was in danger of drowning, when St Benedict, seeing in spirit his young disciple's peril, sent Maurus to save him.

Miracles were common occurrences at that time at Subiaco, where the supernatural seemed to fill the air that surrounded the first Benedictine family. Maurus received the Abbot's blessing, and in a kind of ecstasy he ran to the lake, walked with dry feet upon the water, and, seizing Placidus by the hair, brought him safely to the bank. Then only was he aware of the miracle which had occurred.

After this great example of obedience, Maurus gives us a great example of humility. The question arose whether it were Benedict or Maurus who had worked the miracle. Each sought to attribute the merit to the other, and at last both the master and the disciple appealed to the decision of Placidus himself. He was, even then, so far advanced in the knowledge of heavenly things that Benedict and Maurus could rely upon him to solve the question. Placidus, whilst giving credit to Maurus for his obedience, decided that the miracle was due to the prayers of St Benedict, whose great sanctity caused his disciples to put implicit faith in his intercession. Indeed, at the moment when the young novice was overwhelmed by the waves, his thoughts turned to Benedict, and he seemed to see the *melotis* of the Abbot stretched over him as a sign of his protection. Maurus had no doubt seized him by the hair and drawn him out of the water, but the child, who was also in a kind of ecstasy, saw the Patriarch Benedict come and lead him to the bank in safety : *Ego cum ex aqua traherer, super caput meum Abbatis melotem videbam, atque ipsum me ex aquis educere considerabam.*[1]

[1] St Gregorii I, *Dialog.*, Lib. II, c. vii.

We may quote here in honour of St Placidus a beautiful Collect from the Gelasian Sacramentary (In Monasterio):

Deus, qui renunciantibus saeculo mansionem paras in caelo; (meritis beati Placidi) dilata sanctae huius congregationis habitaculum temporalem caelestibus bonis; ut fraternitatem teneant compagine charitatis unanimiter; continentiae tuae praecepta custodiant; sobrii, simplices et quieti, gratis sibi datam gratiam fuisse cognoscant; concordet illorum vita cum nomine; professio sentiatur in opere. Per Dominum.

May St Placidus, who as a child united his prayers with those of the Patriarch of Monte Cassino in order to obtain for the monks a spring of fresh water from the dry rock, ever obtain for their spiritual descendants the waters of divine grace. And may the sons of St Benedict, to whom the Church has especially entrusted the solemn interpretation of her Liturgy, always be truly sons of benediction: *concordet illorum vita cum nomine; professio sentiatur in opere.*

OCTOBER 6

St Bruno, Confessor*

We have here another son of the Patriarch of Western Monasticism who grafted the semi-eremitical branch of his rule upon the tree of monastic life.

This great reformer, who lived at the end of the eleventh century, has a special claim to be remembered in the *fasti* of the Saints of the Roman Church. For many years he resided at Rome by desire of Urban II, whom he assisted by his advice and by his labours. In order that the Saint should find, at least to some extent, the same atmosphere of peace and seclusion in the Eternal City that he enjoyed at the first house of his Order near Grenoble, the Pope permitted Bruno to found a Charterhouse in 1091 near the *titulus Cyriaci* at the Baths of Diocletian, then entirely abandoned and deserted.

The monastery of Sta Maria degli Angeli survived until the latter half of the last century, when, owing to the confiscation of Church property, it ceased to exist.

The Mass is the same as on January 23 for St Raymund of Pennafort, with the exception of the Collect.

Collect: " May we be helped, O Lord, we beseech thee, by the intercession of St Bruno, thy confessor, so that we who by sinning greviously offend thy divine majesty may, through his merits and prayers, gain forgiveness of our sins."

The Post-Communion is the same as for St Cajetan on August 7.

St Bruno, who left the world and its pleasures and withdrew into a desert to fast, pray, and prepare for death, sets before us a great example of Christian fortitude. There are, in the world, many occasions which lead to sin, and which make it difficult for us to preserve our innocence and to sanctify our souls. A way of escape from these dangers has been found by the more generous spirits. As Israel fled from the corruption of Egypt, as the dove of Noah finding no place of rest on the earth returned to the ark, so those who seek to assure their salvation by the most certain means, leave the world and take refuge in the cloister. In this way they save their souls, and by their example they have the immense merit of leading others on the way to salvation.

OCTOBER 7

St Mark, Pope

Station at the Cemetery of Balbina.

We learn from the *Liber Pontificalis* that Pope Mark, during his lifetime, caused a basilica to be erected in the Cemetery of Balbina in which he desired to be buried, and which was subsequently richly endowed by the Emperor Constantine. The building itself has disappeared, but the crypts even in very early times came to form part of the great Necropolis of Callixtus on the side which opens on to the Via Ardeatina.

Therefore the indication which we find to-day in the Martyrology of St Jerome is correct: *Romae, via Ardeatina, in cimiterio Balbinae, Marci episcopi.*

An inscription placed by Pope Damasus upon the tomb of a certain Mark, is supposed to refer to the Pope of this name. Professor De Rossi has accepted this identification.

Insons) VITA · FVIT · MARCI · QVAM · NOVIMVS · OMNES
Plenus am) ORE · DEI · POSSIT · QVI · TEMNERE · MVNDVM
Actis mon) STRAVIT · POPVLVS · QVOD · DISCERET · OMNIS
Parvus) HONOR · VITAE · GRANDIS · CONTEMPTVS · HABENDI
Intima sed) VIRTVS · TENVIT · PENETRALIA · CORDIS
Iusti) TIAE · CVSTOS · CHRISTI · PERFECTVS · AMICVS
Te colit) ET · DAMASVS · TVMVLO · CVM · REDDIT · HONOREM
HIC · MARCVS · MARCI · VITA · FIDE · NOMINE · CONSORS
ET · MERITIS

"Blameless was the life of Mark which we all witnessed. He was full of the love of God and therefore despised the world. By his acts he set an example to the people that all might follow. He cared little for honours and despised earthly things, for his inmost heart was attached to virtue alone. He was the champion of justice and the perfect lover of Christ. Damasus, too, whilst he adorns thy sepulchre, pays homage to thee. This Mark in his faith and his life imitated the evangelist Mark whose name and merits he shares."

Pope Mark built a second basilica in the City near the *Terme Pallacine* which was endowed by Constantine with revenues and sacred vessels. At the time of the great translation of relics the body of the founder was brought there from the Via Ardeatina. In time, however, the *titulus Marci* was held to be dedicated, not to the Pope of that name, but to the Evangelist of Alexandria, and on account of this, in the late Middle Ages, the Roman clergy were wont to meet there on April 25 for the procession of the *Robigalia* which had St Peter's as its objective.

The feast of St Mark appears not only in the Philocalian Calendar, but also in the Gospel List of Würzburg.

In the Missal, the Mass is *Sacerdotes* as on July 3, for St Leo I ; but the Collects are different.

Collect : " Graciously hear our prayers, O Lord, and being appeased by the intercession of blessed Mark, thy confessor and bishop, grant us forgiveness and peace."

A bishop should be distinguished by such a high degree of virtue in the sight of God and of the people that his sanctity should protect his flock from the scourges of divine justice, according to the words of Ecclesiasticus : *et in tempore iracundiae, factus est reconciliatio* (xliv, 17).

The Secret is that of December 13.

Post-Communion : " Grant, O Lord, we beseech thee, that thy faithful people may ever rejoice in the veneration of thy saints, and be strengthened by their continual prayers."

St Mark governed the Church for eight months only ; that is, from February 15 to October 7, 336 ; but in this short time he gave such striking proofs of holiness, that in preference to several other Popes of that age, his *cultus* forms part of the original Gregorian Calendar. We see by this that a man is not sanctified by heroic undertakings but by fidelity to the daily duties of his state. It is this simple unobtrusive holiness which Damasus praised in the inscription quoted above.

OCTOBER 7
SS Marcellus and Apuleius

These two martyrs mentioned in the Gelasian Sacramentary to-day, whom a legend actually describes as having been disciples of Simon Magus at Rome, were, as a matter of fact, inhabitants of Capua.

Marcellus is one of a group which includes Castus, Emilius, and Saturninus. We do not find the name of Apuleius, who appears in our Missal, in any ancient list, and it is merely a medieval tradition which asserts that he was the servant of Marcellus and shared the crown of martyrdom with his master.

Apuleius is unknown even to the ancient hagiography of Capua; no writer ever mentions him, nor is his picture to be found in the mosaics of St Priscus dating from the fifth or sixth century, where at least thirty-two saints are represented, the greater part of whom belong to the Province of Campania.

Because of this a doubt arises whether the name Apuleius has not been derived from an error in copying the topographical indication in the Martyrology to-day: *in Apulia, natale Casti et Emeli, Marcelli.*

The following lines may still be read on the Lombard façade of the Church of St Marcellus at Capua:

MARCELLVS · SANCTVS · COMTEMNENS · CAESARIS · ACTVS
EST · CAPVAM · LATVS · PRO · CHRISTO · DECAPITATVS

" St Marcellus, because he despised the command of Caesar, was brought to Capua and beheaded here for Christ's sake."

OCTOBER 7
SS Sergius and Bacchus, Martyrs

The fame of these two martyrs can only be compared with that of the *Anargyri*, Cosmas and Damian. The tomb of St Sergius was at Rosapha, and was the object of such continual pilgrimages from all parts of the Eastern world, that the Emperor Justinian surrounded the city with walls, in order to defend the sanctuary and its treasures from the barbarians. The name of Rosapha was changed to that of Sergiopolis in honour of the celestial patron of the city.

Tradition joins the name of the martyr Bacchus to that of

Sergius, but according to Antoninus of Piacenza the former saint was buried in another place. *In civitate Barbarisso.*

St Gregory of Tours relates the numerous miracles which occurred at Rosapha, on account of which many churches and monasteries were dedicated to St Sergius. The nomadic tribes of Syria honour him as their special patron.

At Rome, too, several churches were named after these celebrated Eastern martyrs. The Convent of SS Sergius and Bacchus *post formam aquaeductus* at the Lateran had been left empty and abandoned when Paschal I caused it to be restored, and, endowing it once more, established there a monastic community whose duty it was to chant the day and night Offices in the Lateran Basilica.

The Vatican likewise possessed an oratory dedicated to the martyrs Sergius and Bacchus; indeed, we know that it was restored by Gregory II, who added to the sanctuary a *diaconia* with a hospital for the poor.

The Basilica of St Paul counted amongst the sanctuaries affiliated to it, the Church of SS Sergius and Bacchus *in Suburra*, the ancient monastery *Canelicum*, which is still in existence. Another basilica in honour of these Syrian martyrs rose at the foot of the Capitol, between the Arch of Septimius Severus and the Julian Basilica. It was restored in the thirteenth century by Innocent III, who attributed his elevation to the Papacy to the intercession of the martyrs. He caused the following inscription to be placed in the porch of the church:

POENE · RVI · QVASI · NVLLA · FVI · SED · ME · RELEVAVIT · LOTHARIVS
PRIVS · POSTQVAM · RENOVAVIT · DEQVE · MEO · PRAEMIO · SVMPTVS · PATER · VRBIS
ET · ORBIS · HOC · TAMEN · EX · PROPRIO · FECIT · MIHI · SIC · RENOVOR · BIS

"I was almost in ruins and destroyed when Lotharius raised me up. After he had restored me he received an immediate reward and became the Father of the City and the world. He performed this work at his own expense; thus I have been twice renewed."

The martyrs Sergius, Bacchus, Marcellus, and Apuleius are all commemorated in one Mass in the Missal, *Sapientiam* as on July 2. The Collects are the following:

Collect: "May the blessed deeds of thy holy martyrs Sergius, Bacchus, Marcellus, and Apuleius plead for us, O Lord, and may they make us ever burn with love for thee."

The Catholic doctrine of the share which the faithful enjoy in the merits of the saints whom they invoke is founded on the consoling dogma of the Communion of Saints. In the Church as in the human body the nourishment, the life, and the strength of the various members are conducive to the general welfare of the whole organism.

Secret : " Receive, O Lord, the offerings made by thy holy people in honour of thy saints, from whose merits they acknowledge that they receive help in tribulation."

The martyrs had a greater share in the Chalice of Christ's Passion, and therefore God has granted to them above all others the power to bestow upon the faithful the treasures which that Passion purchased.

Post-Communion : " May we be strengthened, O Lord, by the mysteries we have received, and through the intercession of thy holy martyrs Sergius, Bacchus, Marcellus, and Apuleius, may we be shielded by heavenly armour against all wicked assaults."

We hear in this prayer a faint echo of the turbulent days of the Middle Ages, and of the confidence which the nomadic tribes of Syria placed in the intercession of St Sergius.

OCTOBER 7

THE MOST HOLY ROSARY OF THE BLESSED VIRGIN MARY*

October 7 is the anniversary of the glorious victory won in 1571 by the Christian forces over the Turkish fleet at Lepanto. This triumph of the Cross over the Crescent was universally attributed to the powerful intercession of the Mother of God, whom Pope Pius V fervently invoked with her Rosary in his hand, and to whom the prayers of all Christendom were addressed. Two years after this great favour had been obtained Gregory XIII instituted an annual feast of thanksgiving to be celebrated on the First Sunday of October in all churches where an altar *sub invocatione beatae Virginis Rosarii* had been erected. From being a local festival this celebration gradually spread and became general, until Leo XIII, ever zealous in devotion to the Rosary, raised it to the rank of a double of the second class for the whole Church.

The devotion of the Rosary of the Blessed Virgin Mary dates from at least the twelfth century. The prayer *Ave Maria*, etc., was recited on a string of beads divided into fifteen decades, between each of which the *Pater noster* was said. This form of prayer, consisting of one hundred and fifty *Aves*, was called the Lay Folks' Psalter. The early biographers of St Dominic do not attribute to him the institution of the Rosary, for this devotion was a tradition of Catholic piety long before his time. Indeed, the first writer to ascribe the merit to St Dominic appears to be Alain de la Roche at the end of the fifteenth century.

However, the glory of having spread this form of prayer with such extraordinary success is certainly due to the Dominican Order, and, owing to their zeal, the Rosary soon became the most popular devotion throughout the Christian world.

In the fifteenth century the Carthusians of Trêves introduced the custom of naming a particular mystery from the life of Jesus or Mary after the holy Name of Jesus in the Hail Mary, and thus the Rosary came to be divided into three parts, commemorating respectively the Joyful, Sorrowful, and Glorious mysteries.

The Holy Rosary as it is now recited, and enriched with great indulgences, represents, after the Divine Office, what may be described as a popular Breviary of the Gospel. By meditating on the appropriate mysteries, it may be adapted to the Liturgical Cycle, and because it unites vocal with mental prayer the Rosary is regarded as the most beautiful and approved devotion of the Latin Church.

To-day's feast of thanksgiving, by its connection with a special form of prayer to the Blessed Virgin, that of the Rosary, recalls the feast kept by the Greeks on the Saturday before Passion Sunday when the " Hymnos Akathistos " is sung. This festival was instituted in memory of the many occasions on which Constantinople was delivered from barbarian invaders through the intercession of Mary. In both cases the patronage of the Blessed Virgin and a Christian victory are connected with a special form of prayer to the Mother of God.

If we consider the " Hymnos Akathistos " more attentively, we find other points of resemblance with the Rosary, for in the Byzantine hymn, divided as it is into four parts, the mysteries of the infancy of Christ are commemorated, i.e. the Angelic Salutation, the Visitation, St Joseph's doubts, the adoration of the Shepherds and the Magi, the flight into Egypt, the prophecy of Simeon, precisely as in the Joyful Mysteries of the Rosary.

The " Hymnos Akathistos " in the East, the Rosary in the West are two admirable forms of devotion to Mary, somewhat resembling each other, but entirely independent. They arose from the same faith and the same love borne by the Universal Church for her who is the Mother of God and of men, the co-redemptress of the human race.

October 7

Although the Divine Office to-day commemorates the fifteen mysteries of the life of Christ venerated in the Rosary, the Mass is distinctly a Mass of the Blessed Virgin.

The Introit *Gaudeamus* is the same as on July 16.

The Collect, classic in its simplicity and restraint, sets forth clearly the nature, object, and benefits of the new Psalter of the Blessed Virgin.

Collect: " O God, whose only-begotten Son by his life, death, and resurrection hath purchased for us the rewards of eternal salvation; grant, we beseech thee, that, meditating upon these mysteries in the most holy Rosary of the blessed Virgin Mary, we may both imitate what they contain, and obtain what they promise."

The Lesson consists of two quotations from Proverbs (viii, 22–24, and 32–35) and has already been read on September 8. The Blessed Virgin is the

   . . . *termine fisso d'eterno consiglio.*

Blessed are those, therefore, who, following the Word of God, contemplate and study her. To find Mary is to find the gate of wisdom and of life.

The Gradual is taken from Psalm xliv, and mingles the Messianic triumphs of Christ with the glories of the Immaculate Spouse of the Holy Ghost.

The alleluiatic verse is taken from a well-known Antiphon referring to the genealogy of the Blessed Virgin, and therefore forms part of the Office of her Nativity. We are tempted to wish that another passage had been chosen for to-day's feast, more in keeping with the true character of this solemnity and the ancient title given to it: *Sancta Maria de Victoria.*

" Alleluia, alleluia. The feast of the glorious Virgin Mary, sprung from the seed of Abraham, from the tribe of Juda, from the noble house of David. Alleluia."

The Gospel, consisting of the story of the Annunciation (the first Joyful Mystery), is the same as on March 25.

According to the concise phrase of the Collect we should have two objects before our mind when we meditate upon the Gospel mysteries: *imitemur quod continent, et quod promittunt assequamur.* They contain, therefore, two species of grace: first they teach us to live a holy life, following the example of Christ, our divine model; secondly, they hold out to us the assurance that our conformity with this model will by the assistance of grace be brought to perfection one day through the brightness of eternal glory.

The Antiphon for the Offertory is taken from Ecclesiasticus, and hymns the praises of Divine Wisdom: " In me is all grace of the way and of the truth, in me is all hope of life and of virtue. I have budded forth as the rose planted by the brooks of waters."

The Church applies these words to the Blessed Virgin because she has been made the Mother and advocate of mankind, and every grace by which Jesus raises us to a supernatural life passes through the hands of Mary.

The first part of the Secret is taken from that of Ash Wednesday; the connection between this and the second part is strained and appears to be a modern addition to an archaic text. This will be more clearly appreciated if the Latin words of the Missal are examined.

Secret: "Make us meet, O Lord, to offer up these gifts; and by means of the mysteries of the most holy Rosary may we so keep in mind the life, passion, and triumph of thine only-begotten Son that we may be made worthy of his promises."

The Antiphon for the Communion also contains an allusion to flowers like that of the Offertory: (Ecclus. xxxix, 19): "Send forth flowers as the lily, and yield a smell, and bring forth leaves in grace, and praise with canticles, and bless the Lord in his works."

The beauty of creation is a universal hymn in praise of its Maker. St Paul tells us that the odour of virtue in a Christian soul is that of Christ, acquired by his grace and the imitation of his life.

The latter portion of the Post-Communion is taken from the ancient Collect of the Mass *in dedicatione altaris*: "May we be helped, O Lord, we beseech thee, by the prayers of thy most holy Mother, whose Rosary we are celebrating; so that we may draw strength from the mysteries which we reverence and receive grace from the sacraments which we have taken."

As a liturgical composition this Mass is inferior to the Divine Office for to-day, for the latter is not devoid of grace and devotion, especially in the hymns.

This inferiority is greatly to be deplored on the occasion of so great a feast, and in connection with a beautiful and popular devotion marking the progress of Christian piety towards the Mother of God. The Rosary, like the Crucifix, is always to be found in the Catholic household, and in many countries they are placed together in the hands of the dead. Christian art makes use of the Rosary as one of the favourite emblems of sanctity. Pius V, kneeling in prayer at the Vatican whilst the Battle of Lepanto is being fought, holds a Rosary in his hand. St Alphonsus Liguori tells his beads for the flock committed to his care; St Benedict Joseph Labre has two Rosaries, one in his hand and one about his neck; lastly, the Immaculate Virgin clothed in a white robe with a blue girdle who appeared to Bernadette in the Grotto of Massabielle also has a Rosary hanging on her arm.

OCTOBER 8

St Bridget, Widow*

This Prophetess of the New Law bears some resemblance to St Paula, the mother of Eustochium in the days of St Jerome, on account of the numerous pilgrimages she undertook together with her daughter St Catherine, to visit the various sanctuaries of Italy and Palestine. After having exerted her influence in the cause of the Church's reform in the courts, the episcopal palaces, the abbeys, and even at the papal court, St Bridget died at Rome on July 23, 1374, and was buried at St Lawrence *in Panisperna*. A year later, when the cause of her canonisation was introduced, her daughter procured that her relics should be transferred to Sweden, to the monastery of Wadstena founded by her.

The great basilicas of Rome still keep many records of the noble Swedish mystic who was once rapt in ecstasy in the catacombs of the Appian Way, and who prayed so often beside the tombs of the Apostles and the martyrs of old. In the Basilica of St Paul, for instance, a marble statue represents St Bridget listening to the words of Christ, who speaks to her from the ancient crucifix preserved in that venerable sanctuary of the Apostles. Beneath the statue of the saint these lines are inscribed:

PENDENTIS · PENDENTE · DEI · VERBA · ACCIPIT · AVRE
ACCIPIT · AT · VERBVM · CORDE · BIRGITTA · DEVM

Near the spot where she spent her last days, not far from the *titulus* of St Lawrence *in Damaso*, a small church was built soon after her canonisation, and adjoining it was a hostel for Swedish pilgrims.

St Bridget was canonised by Boniface IX on October 7 and 8 of the year 1391; the latter day, on which the Pope celebrated Mass in honour of the new Saint, was chosen for the date of her feast.

The Mass is the same as on March 9, for the feast of St Frances of Rome; but the Epistle is that of St Monica, May 4.

The Collect alone is proper to the feast, for in it the Church makes mention of the numerous revelations with which the Saint was favoured.

This reference made by the sacred Liturgy to the *Liber revelationum Sanctae Birgittae* is the highest recommendation of a book often examined and praised by ecclesiastical authority.

Collect: "O Lord our God, who, through thy only-begotten Son, didst reveal secrets of heaven to blessed Bridget; grant, through her loving intercession, that we thy servants may rejoice with gladness at the revelation of thine eternal glory."

OCTOBER 9

SS Genuinus and Companions, Martyrs

In the Cemetery ad duas lauros on the Via Labicana.

The Martyrology of St Jerome is extremely confusing to-day. It contains this notice concerning the Saints of Rome: *Romae Marcellini, Ienuini, Novii et inter duas lauros, sanctae Priminae.* Yet, of all these names, Genuinus only is mentioned in ancient itineraries. Therefore we should probably read the entry thus: *Romae, inter duas lauros (in coemeterio sancti) Marcellini, Genuini, Novii,* etc. We know nothing of St Primina or Firmina at Rome, whereas Genuinus is mentioned in *De locis Sanctis,* as one of the martyrs interred beside SS Peter and Marcellinus on the Via Labicana, and may belong to that group of thirty or forty soldier-martyrs who are recorded at that spot by the *Itinerari.*

OCTOBER 9

SS Denis, Rusticus, and Eleutherius*

The confusion which arose between Denis the Areopagite, converted by St Paul, the saint of the same name martyred at Paris, and the pseudo-Areopagite of Syria in the fifth or sixth century, contributed to the spread of the *cultus* of St Dionysius or Denis in the Middle Ages, and finally his feast was inscribed in the Roman Calendar.

The Basilica of St Denis at Paris was built at the suggestion of St Geneviève, and is often mentioned by St Gregory of Tours. Venantius Fortunatus regards St Denis as the most celebrated saint of the *urbs Parisiaca,* and therefore in the sixth century Bordeaux too desired to erect a sanctuary within her walls in honour of the martyr of Paris. Rusticus and Eleutherius have been associated with St Denis ever since the seventh century.

Besides an altar in the Basilica of St Paul—the erection of which was probably due to the confusion between the Martyr

October 9

of Paris and the Athenian convert of St Paul—there exist several churches at Rome dedicated to St Denis, whose *cultus* in the eternal City is founded upon an ancient tradition and flourished especially during the Carlovingian period.

As early as the eighth century, Paul I dedicated to St Denis and St Sylvester at the Campus Martius the new monastery founded by him in his own house *inter duos ortos*.

The Franks, too, in the Middle Ages erected an oratory in honour of their great martyr in the very shadow of the Vatican Basilica. It is mentioned in the *Catalogus Magnus* of Zaccagni.

We know of the existence of another Church dedicated to St Denis in the Forum, which Armellini located near the *diaconia* of St Adrian; and lastly, a fourth church called after the martyr still stands upon the Quirinal, but it was only built in the seventeenth century.

Amongst the Greeks the *cultus* of St Dionysius the Areopagite is famous. The Greek Menologies keep his feast on October 3, but he is also commemorated on Septuagesima Sunday in the Canon:

τῶν Ἁγίων Πατέρων : Ὁ πολὺς τα θεῖα Διονύσιος νῦν τιμάσθω, ὡς τῶν οὐρανίων μύστης.

The Mass *Sapientiam* is like that of July 2 for the martyrs Processus and Martinianus, except the following portions.

The Collect is turgid and clumsy in composition, especially where, after recording the martyrdom of the three saints, it returns to their evangelisation of the city of Paris.

"O God, who this day didst endow blessed Denis, thy martyr and bishop, with the virtue of constancy in his martyrdom, and didst join Rusticus and Eleutherius with him in preaching thy glory to the heathen; grant, we beseech thee, that we may follow their example by despising the good things of this world for the sake of thy love, and by fearing not its adversities."

The Epistle to-day is taken from the Acts of the Apostles (xvii, 22-34) where St Paul makes his magnificent speech to the Areopagites. St Ambrose points out the power of adapting himself to his surroundings shown here by the Apostle. For the moment he abandons the field of scriptural theology and meets his pagan audience on their own ground. Paul brings forward arguments and cites authorities recognized by the Greeks themselves as indisputable. For this reason he quotes the poet Aratus, he appeals to the testimony of an Athenian inscription, indeed in order to win the favour of the assembly he touches the most sensitive chord of the Grecian character by exalting the piety of the people of Athens above that of the other cities of Greece. Paul does not come to the city of Athens in order to censure or to revolutionize. No, he comes merely to satisfy the religious mind of the Athenians so eager for new things by making known to them that unknown God of whom they were aware in their inmost heart.

The Gospel is the same as on June 26, for the martyrs John and Paul. The fear of God drives out the fear of man. He who is filled with this fear which leads to holiness will not quail before the threats of the whole world in arms against him.

Secret: "Graciously receive, O Lord, we beseech thee, the gifts which thy people offer up to thee in honour of thy saints, and make us holy through their intercession."

The Christian must aim at more than the mere avoidance of evil. He has received the call to sanctity at the moment of his baptism; therefore in early apostolic times the followers of the Gospel, before the name of Christian had been given to them at Antioch, were simply known as the "Saints." For this reason we have received no other spirit but the Holy Spirit himself, who comes to develop in us that sublime fulness of sanctity which our incorporation with Christ the "Holy One of God" demands.

Post-Communion: "May the holy sacrament which we have received, O Lord, we beseech thee, avail us more and more to eternal salvation."

The redemption is like a magnificent design which the Divine Genius has conceived and in which he desires that we should co-operate with him. God wills our eternal salvation, but this salvation before it can be ours in the radiance of his glory must first be worked out on earth through obedience to his grace. Glory comes from God alone, but co-operation with grace depends on us with God's help, as St Paul says: *Non ego, sed gratia Dei mecum.*

OCTOBER 10

ST FRANCIS BORGIA, CONFESSOR*

Yesterday the solemn rites of the Church celebrated the Martyrs with their unfading palms and crowns, but to-day the name of the Duke of Gandia appears in the Calendar adorned with the precious merits of humility, zeal, and evangelical poverty.

Trained in the school of Ignatius, Francis Borgia was filled with a sense of his own unworthiness, and whilst it was the Will of God to entrust him with the direction of the new

Society of Jesus, and to raise him up to be the oracle of Pontiffs and of Princes, he still considered himself as the least of men. In this he followed the teaching of Christ, who 'spoke through the lips of the Prophet: *Ego . . . sum vermis et non homo ; opprobrium hominum et abiectio plebis.*

The Mass *Os justi* is the same as on March 21 for the feast of St Benedict, with the exception of the Collect: " O Lord Jesus Christ, who art both the pattern and the reward of true humility; we beseech thee that, even as thou madest blessed Francis follow gloriously in thy footsteps by spurning earthly honours, so thou wouldst suffer us also to become his companions alike in following thee and in his glory."

St Peter teaches that God rejects the proud and bestows his grace on the humble. The reason of this should be sought in the fact that when God desires to accomplish some great and wonderful work he seeks pliable and submissive instruments who will allow themselves to be moved and guided according to his good pleasure, in order that the result may be attributed only to the Divine intervention.

The self-sufficiency of the proud and the unbending character of the arrogant man impede divine grace, and God cannot make use of such inappropriate instruments.

OCTOBER 12

St Aedistus, Martyr

On the Via Laurentina.

In spite of the fact that the Martyrology of Baronius names Ravenna as the burial-place of St Aedistus, that of St Jerome directs us to the road to *Laurentum* : *Romae, via Laurentina, natalis Hedisti.* The sepulchral sanctuary of this martyr was in fact near the twenty-sixth milestone on that road, and is mentioned in the Itinerary of Salzburg: *deinde etiam in aquilone parte ecclesiae sancti Pauli, paret ecclesia sancti Aristi et sanctae Christinae et sanctae Victoriae, ubi ipsi pausant.* According to the *Acta*, Aedistus with his companions in martyrdom, Priscus, Termantia, Christina, and Victoria, was interred near *Laurentum* : *iuxta iter viae Laurentinae, ad aram Dianae, in quodam arenario.*

St Gregory the Great in a Bull of January 25, 604, addressed to the subdeacon Felix in favour of the Basilica of St Paul, mentions a *Monasterium Sancti Eristi* in that quarter of the town, and it was probably that sanctuary which possessed the tomb of the five Saints.

Adrian I, in the eighth century, ordered the erection of a *domus culta*, there, with *magnae constructionis fabricis*, as the *Liber Pontificalis* tells us. Therefore he restored the holy place *quae et domum cultam sancti Edisti vocatur usque in hodiernum diem*.[1]

The *cultus* of St Aedistus spread to Mount Soracte, which on account of the church dedicated to the martyr gradually lost its ancient classical name and was called Mount St Orestes.

The fate of the relics of the five martyrs of *Laurentum* is doubtful. As the name of Aedistus was converted into that of Edistus or Orestes, he was soon identified with St Orestes of Cappadocia, who is venerated with SS Eustratius, Assentius, Mardarius, and Eugenius. Baronius declares that the remains of this group of Eastern martyrs were taken to Rome and laid in the Church of St Apollinaris. This translation is difficult to prove, whereas it is easy to justify the hypothesis that the St Orestes who is buried at St Apollinaris is the St Aedistus or Eristus of *Laurentum*, and that the other relics are those of his companions in martyrdom.

OCTOBER 13

ST EDWARD, KING AND CONFESSOR*

This famous King of England died on January 5, 1066, but by order of Innocent XI, his feast is celebrated to-day, when the translation of his relics is commemorated. The example of St Edward proves that sanctity, distinguished by the most exceptional graces of the mystical life, may be united to the privileges and cares of royalty.

Our state of life can never be an obstacle to holiness; it is our want of generosity which prevents us from denying ourselves and giving all to God.

The Mass is the same as on January 23 for St Raymund of Pennafort, with the exception of the Collect.

Collect: "O God, who hast crowned blessed King Edward thy confessor with the glory of eternal life; make us, we beseech thee, so to honour him on earth, that we may be able to reign with him in heaven."

In olden days divine privileges were often attributed to anointed sovereigns: *Deus stetit in synagoga deorum; in medio deos dijudicat.* (Psalm lxxxi). Christian art, too, sometimes placed a halo about the head of a monarch like

---

[1] *Lib. Pontif.*, ed. Duchesne I, 505.

that used to denote a saint. Thus for example Justinian and Theodora are represented with halos in the mosaics of San Vitale at Ravenna, and King Herod in the mosaic of Sixtus III at St Mary Major also has a halo.

The reason for this is that the royal power is given by God to those who are his representatives in the government of the people, and this confers upon them a certain sacred majesty, together with the graces needed for the just exercise of that power.

Therefore the man who is raised to the throne is called by God to a state of sanctity of a most sublime kind ; and on account of this the few feasts of canonised kings celebrated in the Roman Liturgy possess a beauty and meaning all their own.

OCTOBER 14

St Callistus, Pope and Martyr

Station on the Aurelian Way at the Cemetery of Calepodium.

The Philocalian Calendar notes to-day the deposition of Pope Callistus on the Aurelian Way : *Calisti in via Aurelia, milliario III.* In spite of the fact that the Pontificate of Callistus was one of the most important and most glorious in the early history of the Church, the life of this Pope is not devoid of obscurity, for it is extremely difficult to reconcile the *Liber Pontificalis* with the *Philosophumena.*

The first disputes on the Trinity at Rome date from the time of Callistus, and even when he was only the archdeacon of Zephyrinus he possessed a violent adversary in the person of Hippolytus.

Callistus affirmed energetically the Unity of the divine essence and accused Hippolytus of heresy because by exaggerating the distinctions of the three Persons of the Trinity he appeared to compromise the Unity of substance. When, at the death of the aged Pontiff, the archdeacon Callistus succeeded him, according to the Roman custom, the indignant Hippolytus placed himself at the head of the opposing faction and was acclaimed Pope by his followers, thus winning the inglorious distinction of being the first of the anti-Popes.

The early discipline of the Church, which abandoned to the judgement of God alone the graver sins against faith and morals, was not adapted to society in the third century. The Christians had increased in number, but their zeal had declined. Therefore Callistus, in a famous edict, violently attacked by Hippolytus and Tertullian, promised absolution to all those who should have performed the canonical penances. His action roused a storm of opposition. The fiery Apologist of Carthage held up to scorn the *Pontifex Maximus, id est episcopus episcoporum;* as he called Callistus in a satirical pamphlet, whilst he described how the Pope, having admitted the sinner into the Church, caused him to prostrate before the priests and the virgins in order to move them to compassion for the unhappy culprit. Hippolytus, on his side, declared that the excessive mildness of Callistus was a scandal, and would break down the barriers of public morality. Many Romans were won over by the arguments of the austere author of the *Philosophumena* to abandon the cause of Callistus, and to join the ranks of the schismatics.

The saintly Pope, who in his sermons appealed to the example of the Good Shepherd, was not moved by the violence of his enemies, and continued to the end in his mission of peace. According to some writers, Callistus perished in a riot which took place in Trastevere, near the *titulus* founded by him in the neighbourhood of the *Taberna emeritoria* of Alexander Severus. His body, thrown at first into a well, must afterwards have been secretly buried in the cemetery of Calepodius, which was not far off on the Aurelian Way.

In the *Philosophumena* Hippolytus completely ignores the Pope's violent death at the hands of the mob, and explains the title of martyr given to Callistus by recounting the story of the imprisonment and exile in Sardinia which he endured for the faith when a young man.

Hippolytus, however, was the bitter opponent of Callistus, and it is possible that he did not mention the murder of the Pope by the pagan mob, either because it was carried out by order of the authorities of the city, or else because he wished to deprive his adversary of the glory due to a martyr. The silence of Hippolytus is not, therefore, sufficient to invalidate the tradition of the murder of Callistus, which can be divined under the legendary narrative of the Saint's *Acta*. Indeed if the story were not true it would be difficult to understand why the founder of the great necropolis of Callistus and the Papal crypt on the Appian Way, should alone have been denied the honour of resting among the other Pontiffs and beside his own master Zephyrinus in the Papal mausoleum which he had erected. Instead of which, Callistus was buried in the cemetery of Calepodium, where no Pope had been interred before his time.

It is evident that this unusual burial, contrary as it was to the tradition of the sepulture of the Popes on the Appian Way, must have been imposed upon the faithful by special circumstances which made it impossible for them to transport the

October 14

corpse as far as the second milestone of the *Regina viarum*. That the circumstances arose from the revolution and disturbance among the people is clear to us, indeed the *Acta* suggest as much.

Pope Julius caused an Oratory to be built over the sepulchral crypt of Callistus, and desired to be buried there. The foundations of this sanctuary were discovered by Stevenson, together with part of the apse, which however cannot be seen, as it is incorporated in a building belonging to what was formerly the Lamperini vineyard.

The Basilica of Sta Maria *in Trastevere* founded by Pope Julius I *juxta Callistum*, which has absorbed all the fame of the primitive Church of Callistus of the third century, has for centuries boasted the possession of the mortal remains of St Callistus.

Beside this basilica there still exists a small titular church which preserves the memory of the early *Callistum* of the third century. In this sanctuary, beside the martyr's altar, may be seen the mouth of an ancient well, and this well was venerated in the Middle Ages as it was traditionally believed to be that into which the body of Callistus was thrown during the riot. The inscription by a slave, noted by Fabretti,[1] tells us that the part of Trastevere on which the Church of St Callistus stands was commonly known as the *area Callisti* :

REVOCA · ME · AD · DOMINVM · VIVENTIVM · IN · AR(e)A
· CALLISTI.

Here we find a mention of the same building which was later called simply *Callistum* even by the biographer of Pope Julius.

Another small church in honour of the great Pope Callistus rose on the Coelian Hill, and we find reference to it until the sixteenth century.

The Mass takes the Introit *Sacerdotes* from the Common, as on December 11.

Collect : " O God, who seest that we fall from our own very weakness, mercifully restore us to thy love by the example of thy saints."

We read in the life of the great St Augustine of Hippo that when, before his conversion, he heard of the wonderful examples set by St Anthony and his followers, he kept saying within himself : *Tu non poteris quod isti et istae ? An vero isti et istae in semetipsis possunt, et non in Domino Deo suo ?*[2]

---

[1] De Rossi, *Bollettini*, 1866, p. 94 ; 1874, pp. 42–50.
[2] *Confessiones*, Lib. VIII., cap. xi.

The Epistle is taken from Hebrews (v, 1-4) and describes the qualities required in a priest. Like Aaron he is chosen by God, and does not claim the honour of the ministry through his own ambition. Moreover he is withdrawn from the multitude, and thus becomes as it were a bridge between creation and the Creator. He serves his brethren by his ministry, but is detached from earthly affairs, and is occupied only with the interests of God and the salvation of souls. His mission is not so much to judge and punish sin as to pour the oil of divine mercy upon the countless wounds of human nature. In so doing, it will be well that the priest should always bear in mind his own weakness and insufficiency, and should not demand of others a degree of perfection which he can himself only attain with a great effort.

The Gradual which follows is that of the feast of St Nicholas on December 6. These words should greatly comfort those whom God has chosen to carry the *onus* of the priesthood or of the episcopal dignity. Nature is too weak to bear it, but God has solemnly promised: " My hand shall help him, and my arm shall strengthen him."

The alleluiatic verse is the same as on January 14, from the Common of Doctors.

According to the Würzburg List the Gospel to-day was the same as for St Damasus on December 11 (Matthew xxiv, 42-47). Whereas in the present Missal the Gospel is taken from Matthew x, 26-32, as for St Saturninus on November 29.

Christ and the Martyrs preached the Gospel amid the dark shadows of persecution, but God glorified their words and testified to the divine origin of their teaching by the honour with which he has surrounded them even on earth.

The Antiphon for the Offertory is that of December 6.

Secret: " May this mystical offering be wholesome for us, O Lord ; may it free us from our sins, and confirm us in eternal salvation."

The Psalmist described man as *spiritus vadens et non rediens*. Everything changes, indeed, here below and our inconstancy is great, especially in doing good. The grace of the Eucharistic Sacrifice, however, corrects this weakness, and confirms us in virtue, bestowing upon us conformity with the divine will and that strength of mind, both in favourable and in adverse circumstances, which reflects in some manner the changeless calm of God.

We observe this in the lives of the saints ; they were always cheerful and even-tempered, because, as the office of the Church says on the feast of a Virgin: *Deus in medio eius: non commovebitur*. God was in the centre of their heart, and no created thing could move or trouble them.

October 14

This thought is illustrated in an ancient antiphon taken from the writings of St Gregory the Great, describing the appearance of the Patriarch St Benedict:

Erat vir Domini Benedictus vultu placido, moribus decoratus angelicis; tantaque circa eum claritas excreverat, ut in terris positus, in caelestibus habitaret.

The Antiphon *Beatus servus* (Matthew xxiv, 46-47) for the Communion of the people corresponds with the Gospel prescribed by the Würzburg List, but is not in keeping with that in our present Missal. The same Antiphon is read on December 3, for the feast of St Francis Xavier.

Post-Communion: "We beseech thee, almighty God, that these holy offerings may cleanse us from our sins and bring us grace to live righteously."

The Holy Eucharist, therefore, bestows on us two graces. It is the sacrament of our redemption and washes away our sins in the blood of the Lamb; moreover it is the bread of supernatural life, and confers upon us strength, joy, and youthfulness in order that we may grow like Christ in the fulness of his youth: *in mensura aetatis plenitudinis Christi.*

OCTOBER 15

St Teresa, Virgin*

"Had I not already created Heaven, I should create it for thee," Jesus said one day to St Teresa of Avila, who merited the sublimest graces of the mystical life by the docility with which she abandoned herself to the fire of divine love.

Transfixed by an angel with the dart of charity, Teresa became from that day a victim immolated to the love of God. Jesus united her to himself as his spouse, as his trusted friend, and as his victim. As his spouse, Teresa had no desire but that of serving him, and feared neither dangers nor labour. In spite of poverty and opposition, she succeeded in founding over thirty convents of her Carmelite Reform before her death.

As his trusted friend, Teresa was initiated into the secrets of that mystical science set forth in her writings, which have earned for her the title of a Doctor of the spiritual life.

Lastly, as victim, for when the fire of divine love had filled and consumed her heart, nature could no longer endure the strain, and her spirit was set free to seek the embrace of her spouse in Heaven.

The feast of this seraph of the Carmelite Order, canonized by Gregory XV in 1622, was introduced into the Missal by Urban VIII.

The Mass is the same as on February 10 for St Scholastica, but the Collect appears to be proper to the feast. It is, however, merely that of the Common of Virgins, and is also used on the feast of St Lucy. The modern compiler has introduced one new sentence in order to allude to the doctrinal writings of the Saint.

Collect: " Graciously hear us, O God our Saviour; that as we rejoice in the festival of thy blessed virgin Teresa, so we may be fed with the food of her heavenly teaching and grow in loving devotion towards thee."

This allusion to the doctrinal work of St Teresa is worthy of notice, for it is a unique case in the whole Liturgy that the office of teaching and feeding the faithful, *caelestis eius doctrinae pabulo*, should be entrusted to a woman.

OCTOBER 16

St Sosius, Deacon and Martyr

To-day the Martyrology of St Jerome records at Baiae the martyr Sosius, deacon of Misenum, who belongs to the group of St Januarius and his companions, already mentioned on September 19. Pope Symmachus introduced the *cultus* of this saint into Rome, and dedicated an oratory to him near St Peter, as has already been noted.

OCTOBER 17

St Hedwig, Widow*

Not many days ago we celebrated the feast of a great king; to-day we name among the saints a queen of Poland who preferred the discipline of monastic life in the Convent founded by her at Treibnitz to the splendour of the throne. St Hedwig died on October 15, 1243, and her name was included in the Roman Calendar by Innocent XI. Prior to this, however, Clement IV had proposed her to the Poles as the celestial Patroness of their country.

The Mass is that of St Frances of Rome on March 9, but the Collect is proper.

Collect: " O God, who didst teach blessed Hedwig to renounce the pomps of this world with her whole heart, so that she might humbly follow thy cross; grant that, through her example and merits, we may learn to trample under foot the perishable delights of this world, and, by cleaving to thy cross, overcome whatever may withstand us."

October 17

St Hedwig fasted and prayed and took the discipline; she heard several Masses daily and distributed alms with great generosity. The Saints have all laboured and suffered in order to reach the harbour of salvation. We cannot expect to get to heaven without suffering, especially when we remember that Jesus too *oportuit pati et ita intrare in gloriam suam*.

OCTOBER 18

St Luke, Evangelist

This glorious disciple of St Paul, who according to many of the early Fathers deserved the martyr's palm, has undoubtedly a right to figure in the Roman Missal, for during St Paul's first imprisonment at Rome he preached the word in the Eternal City, and it was here that he wrote the Gospel and the Acts of the Apostles.

Perhaps for this reason an early painter drew a picture of St Luke holding a case containing surgical instruments, in the cemetery of Commodilla, near the sepulchral basilica of the Doctor of the Gentiles. In the same manner another cemetery on the opposite side of the basilica was called after Thecla, and another after Timothy, in order to evoke the memory of the first disciples of St Paul beside the tomb of the Apostle.

St Luke died and was buried at Thebes in Bœotia, whence his relics were brought, together with those of St Andrew, to Constantinople, on March 3, 357. The feast of St Luke has been kept on October 18 from very early times, and has always had a place in the Calendars.

A small church was dedicated to St Luke at Rome near St Mary Major on the spot where Sixtus V subsequently caused the obelisk to be erected. As, however, this had been the meeting-place since the time of Sixtus IV of a pious association of painters, in order that this excellent work should not cease, Sixtus V assigned to this guild the Church of St Martina in the Forum, which when it had been renovated also took the name of St Luke, the patron of the Society of Christian Artists.

Many churches claim the honour of possessing the body of St Luke, at Venice, at Padua, and elsewhere. It is worth noting, too, that at Leprignano, in the diocese of the Abbot of St Paul's, there existed until a few years ago an ancient *tricorum* or basilica with three apses, dedicated to St Luke, who is the patron of that village. Here, in an ancient silver casket, is preserved a relic of the great Evangelist, the constant companion of St Paul.

The Introit of the Mass is the same as on November 30.

Collect: "Let blessed Luke thine evangelist, O Lord, we beseech thee, intercede for us, who for the honour of thy holy name continually bore in his body the mortification of the cross."

The wording of the prayer is not very definite, for a later tradition asserted that St Luke ended his life in peace at an advanced age.

The Lesson is taken from the second Epistle to the Corinthians, in which St Paul announced that he had sent Titus and Luke to restore peace to that church disturbed by contending factions, and also to make a collection for the Christians in Palestine.

The terms he applies to Luke are remarkable. The praises of the Evangelist are spoken through all the churches; he was specially ordained as the companion of Paul's travels and apostolate for the greater glory of God. This is the reason why the Greeks give to St Luke the title Ἀποστολοῦ καὶ Εὐαγγελιστοῦ.

We should note, too, the enthusiasm with which Paul speaks of the dignity of the apostolic ministry. Those who participate in it are called *apostoli ecclesiarum, gloria Christi*. Their vocation is one of mercy, for they are heralds and dispensers of grace: *in hanc gratiam quae ministratur a nobis*. This grace is so great that St Paul describes it as an "abundance," for the preacher of the Gospel seeks to give to souls the fulness of Christ.

The Gradual, the alleluiatic verse, and the Communion are those of St Barnabas on June 11.

The Gospel, taken from St Luke, is the same as that of December 3, and describes the first mission of the seventy-two disciples of the Lord. These are labourers sent by the master into the fields to toil and to reap, rather than prelates or dignitaries. Their material necessities must therefore be the master's care, and his divine Providence will succour them in their need. Who, asks St Paul, would consent to make war at his own expense? Yet the apostle must be poor, must limit his requirements as much as possible, for the less he needs the more free he will be, and the more independent in following his heavenly vocation. Let him not consider the judgements of men in announcing the word of God, and let him speak, not in his own name, but as the herald of another. The blame, if there be any, must fall on him whose envoy he is, for *ambasciator non porta pena*. . . . Indeed, so true is it that he does not speak or act in his own name (St Paul says: *pro Christo legatione fungimur . . . tamquam Deo exhortante per nos*) that even if he should work miracles and heal the

October 18

sick, the apostle must not accept any reward: *gratis accepistis, gratis date*.

The Offertory *Mihi autem* is the same as on November 30.

Secret: " By these gifts from heaven grant, O Lord, that we may serve thee with a free mind; so that through the intercession of thy blessed evangelist Luke the offerings which we bring may avail us both unto healing and glory."

To serve God with a free spirit means to rule our flesh and the impulses of our corrupt nature, bridling them by the practice of continual mortification.

The medieval Sacramentaries assigned the following Preface to this day: *Vere . . . Deus; et te in tuorum sanctorum meritis gloriosis collaudare, benedicere et predicare; qui eos dimicantes contra antiqui serpentis machinamenta et proprii corporis blandimenta, inexpugnabili virtute, Rex gloriae, roborasti. Ex quibus beatus Lucas evangelista tuus, assumpto scuto Fidei, et galea salutis et gladio Spiritus Sancti, et viriliter contra vitiorum incentiva pugnavit, et evangelicae nobis dulcedinis fluenta manavit. Unde petimus immensam, Domine, pietatem tuam, ut qui eum tot meritorum donasti praerogativis, nos eius et informes exemplis, et adiuves meritis; per Christum Dominum nostrum. Per quem. . . .*

The Antiphon for the Communion, *Vos qui secuti*, is that of the feast of St Matthias, February 24.

Post-Communion: " Grant, we beseech thee, almighty God, that what we have received at thy holy altar may, by the prayers of thy blessed evangelist Luke, sanctify our souls and keep us in safety."

There is a deep meaning beneath these words, that the gift is taken from the holy altar. Upon the altar is laid the sacrifice, and therefore the Holy Eucharist, whilst it is a sacrament of the New Law, is at the same time truly a sacrifice. Now, he who participates in the sacrifice enters into solidarity with the victim, with the altar, and with the divinity to whom it is dedicated. For this reason St Paul forbade the first Christians to eat the flesh which had been sacrificed to idols, or to take any part in such sacrifices. Thus when we receive Holy Communion we share the intentions and the merits of the passion of Christ.

OCTOBER 19

St Asterius, Martyr

The Martyrology of St Jerome indicates at Ostia to-day: *In Hostia, Asteri*. The *cultus* of this saint must have been popular at Rome too, for to-day's feast is mentioned in an epigraph of the Cemetery of Commodilla : *Paschasius vixit plus minus annus XX fecit fatum IIII idus Octobris VIII ante natale domni Asterii. Depositus in pace.*

The importance attributed to the octave preceding the *natalis domni Asterii* is worthy of notice.

The basilica of the martyr at Ostia is also mentioned in the *Libellus precum* of the priests Faustinus and Marcellinus against Pope Damasus.[1]

OCTOBER 19

St Peter of Alcantara, Confessor*

Peter Garavito, or Peter of Alcantara as he is called from the city of his birth, died on October 18, 1562, and his feast was introduced into the Missal by Clement X. This saint is distinguished by three characteristics. The first of these is the incredible severity of the mortification by which, like St Paul, he sought to fill up that which was wanting in the Passion of Christ, for the good of the Church. The spirit of the Franciscan Reform, initiated in the new so-called province of St Joseph by his endeavours, is one of great penance and extreme poverty.

The second characteristic of St Peter of Alcantara is the abundance of mystical gifts and the grace of sublime contemplation received by him in reward for his austerities.

Thirdly, St Peter is distinguished by the active part he took in the reform of the Carmelite Order initiated by St Teresa. He was the first to examine and approve of the spirit of this reform.

St Teresa, for her part, declared that she had never asked anything of the Lord through the merits of Brother Peter which she had not obtained.

The Mass *Justus* is the same as on January 31, for St Peter Nolasco, except the following parts.

Collect : " O God, who didst vouchsafe to make thy blessed confessor Peter illustrious by the grace of marvellous penance and lofty contemplation ; grant, we beseech thee, that, by his merits, which plead for us, we may so mortify our bodies as to embrace the more readily the things of heaven."

The Collect is inspired by the words of St Paul in which he declares that the earthly man cannot discern the things of the spirit. Blessed are those whose interior sight is pure, for they shall understand the things of God.

[1] *P.L.* XIII, c. xxii, p. 99.

The Epistle, in which the Apostle speaks of his renunciation of the privileges of his race in order to win Christ, occurs also on January 15 for the feast of St Paul the Hermit.

The Secret and the Post-Communion are those of July 19, the feast of St Vincent de Paul.

We should bear in mind certain memorable words spoken by St Peter of Alcantara. After his death he appeared to St Teresa and said to her: " Blessed be the penances which earned for me such great glory."

OCTOBER 20

St John of Kenty, Confessor*

St John of Kenty died on December 24, 1473, but Clement XIV appointed his feast to be kept on this day.

The life of this saint is distinguished in Catholic hagiography by a characteristic which causes it to be of actual interest to us to-day, and well suited to be a model to the present generation. St John was a parish priest and a missionary, but, above all, he is remarkable for having fulfilled during many years the duties of a professor at the University of Cracow. There may be many who hold that the position of a teacher at a university, who is apt to be enamoured of his own learning, is scarcely suited to the practice of Christian perfection. John of Kenty has dispelled this illusion, and has proved that the example of a holy life lends authority to a master's teaching far more than would self-sufficiency.

More than once this holy professor visited the Eternal City and spent long hours in prayer at the tombs of the Apostles and martyrs. He was once asked why he set out on such a dangerous journey, as he did not intend to seek for benefices or honours at the Roman court, and he replied that he did so in order to accomplish his purgatory upon earth, and to gain the numerous indulgences granted to those who visit the basilicas of the Apostles in Rome.

John of Kenty was marked during his life-time by a great generosity towards the poor, and, after his death, God distinguished him by a number of miracles.

The following Mass dwells upon the charity of the holy professor.

The Introit is taken from Ecclesiasticus xviii, 12, 13. The charity of man only stretches forth to those about him, whereas the mercy of God embraces the whole world. The Lord is merciful, and, like a shepherd, he guides and directs his flock.

Apart from the allusion which this verse contains to

St John's teaching and almsgiving, we should consider the contrast between human and divine goodness set forth in this passage. Men are slow to love, and when they love it is generally without fervour and often from interested motives and only for a time. God alone loves for ever and with his whole being. We should, therefore, put more confidence in the love of God and trust less in that of man.

The first verse of Psalm i follows, and has evidently been chosen because of the allusion to the seat of learning.

Psalm i. " Blessed is the man who hath not walked in the counsel of the ungodly, nor stood in the way of sinners, nor sat in the chair of pestilence."

The Epistle is taken from the Canonical Letter of St James, ii, 12-17, where the Brother of the Lord explains that faith is nourished by charity, as a flame feeds on that which it consumes. Christianity is not merely a theory, then, but a life. Faith is light, it is the eye of the spirit, but the light would shine in vain, the eye would be useless if there were no object to be illuminated, none to be seen.

The Gradual is taken from Psalm cvi, where the mercy of Providence is praised, and illustrated in four beautiful images of the wayfarers, the prisoners, those who suffer hunger, and of those who go down to the sea in ships.

The alleluiatic verse is taken from Proverbs xxxi: "Alleluia, alleluia. He hath opened his hand to the needy, and stretched out his hands to the poor. Alleluia."

The Offertory is chosen from Job xxix, 14-16: "I was clad with justice, and I clothed myself with my judgement, as with a robe and a diadem: I was an eye to the blind and a foot to the lame: I was the father of the poor."

Secret: " Graciously receive these victims, O Lord, we beseech thee, for the sake of the merits of the holy John thy confessor; and grant that by loving thee above all things, and all mankind for thy sake, we may become well-pleasing to thee both in will and in deed."

The teaching of the Church, and that of the holy Scriptures, insist upon the necessity of practising the works of mercy. We should impress upon our minds that it is not enough to be faithful to our resolutions concerning our spiritual life, the frequenting of the sacraments, and the time devoted to prayer. We must also devote ourselves to the poor, as to God himself, for he has willed that the needy should represent him on earth.

The Communion is taken from St Luke vi, 38: " Give, and it shall be given to you: good measure and pressed down, and shaken together, and running over, shall they give into your bosom."

October 20   187

He who gives to the poor, lends to God at a high rate of interest, and the Lord often gives back the capital and the interest in this world. In any case, even if God withholds the full payment until the next life, he gives to us here instead of the material bread which we bestow on the poor, the sacred bread of angels which nourishes our souls for immortality.

Post-Communion: "We who have been fed with the delights of thy precious body and blood, humbly beg thy mercy, O Lord; so that through the example and merits of blessed John thy confessor we may follow him in his charity and share with him his glory."

The Holy Eucharist stimulates our charity, for St John says that as Christ sacrificed himself for us, so we, too, should sacrifice ourselves for our brethren.

OCTOBER 21

St Hilarion, Abbot*

This disciple of St Antony, who spread the monastic observance through Palestine, Greece and Sicily, died in 371, and became popular in the Middle Ages owing to his miracles and also to the fact that his biography was written by the great St Jerome. The last words of St Hilarion have been recorded: "Go forth, O my soul, what do you fear? You have served Christ for seventy years, do you now fear death?"

The famous hermit had fought for so many years under the banner of Christ and yet he was not sure of his salvation. We who do so little for God should not expect to enter Heaven easily.

The Mass is that of St Sabbas, on December 5.

OCTOBER 21

St Ursula and her Companions, Martyrs*

The most ancient document concerning the *cultus* of this group of virgins is an inscription composed by a certain Clematius, who caused the sepulchral basilica at the place of their martyrdom at Cologne to be restored.

DIVINIS · FLAMMEIS · VISIONIB · FREQVENTER
ADMONITVS · ET · VIRTVTIS · MAGNAE · MAI
IESTATIS · MARTYRII · CAELESTIVM · VIRGIN
IMMINENTIVM · EX · PARTIB · ORIENTIS

EXHIBITVS · PRO · VOTO · CLEMATIVS · V. · C. · DE
PROPRIO · IN · LOCO · SVO · HANC · BASILICAM
VOTO · QVOD · DEBEBAT · A · FVNDAMENTIS
RESTITVIT · SI · QVIS · AVTEM · SVPER · TANTAM
MAIIESTATEM · HVIIVS · BASILICAE · VBI · SANC
TAE · VIRGINES · PRO · NOMINE · XPI · SAN
GVINEM · SVVM · FVDERVNT · CORPVS · ALICVIIS
DEPOSVERIT · EXCEPTIS · VIRGINIB · SCIAT · SE
SEMPITERNIS · TARTARI · IGNIB · PVNIENDVM

"Clematius, descendant of a senatorial family and an Eastern by birth, having been admonished many times by celestial lights and visions to honour the merit and the majesty of the martyrdom of the holy Virgins, fulfilled his vow by restoring from the very foundations this basilica erected on his own land. If therefore any man should lay the body of another besides those of the Virgins within the venerable precincts of this basilica where the holy martyrs shed their blood for Christ, let that man know that he will be punished in the eternal fire of hell."

At Rome, too, there were two churches dedicated to St Ursula. The first of these is mentioned in the *Mirabilia*, and stood near the bridge of Sant' Angelo: *secretarium Neronis fuisse, ubi deinde fuit Ecclesia sancti Ursi. . . .*[1] It was destroyed towards the end of the nineteenth century.

Legends grew up around the history of the martyrdom of Ursula and her companions, and converted it into a most complicated drama. The truth probably is that this group of virgins suffered for the faith in the territory of *Colonia Agrippina* towards the end of the third or the beginning of the fourth century.

Their names, according to the ancient Martyrologies, were: Martha, Saula, Brittula, Gregoria, Saturnina, Sambatia, Pinnosa, Ursula, Sentia, Palladia, Saturia, Clementia and Grata.

The well-known legend grew up much later, for Ado does not mention it. After the eleventh century popular tradition only kept the names of Ursula and Pinnosa.

The Mass is that of St Barbara on December 4, but with the Collect and Secret of the *natalis* of the Martyrs Perpetua and Felicitas on March 6.

The Post-Communion is as follows:

"Grant, O Lord, we beseech thee, through the intercession of thy holy virgins and martyrs Ursula and her companions, that what we take into our mouths we may receive with a clean heart."

[1] Armellini, *Le Chiese di Roma* (ii Ed.), 354.

October 21

The Church continually insists upon the spiritual import of the sacraments and the rites of our religion. We must not be like the Jews whom God rebuked by the mouth of Isaias in these words: *populus hic labiis me honorat; cor autem eorum longe est a me.* God is a spirit, and we must adore him in spirit and in truth, especially by approaching the Sacraments with the proper dispositions, in order to receive together with the visible sign also the invisible grace which the Sacrament signifies and conveys.

OCTOBER 24

St Raphael, Archangel*

In the same manner that the Archangels Michael and Gabriel were honoured with particular offices, so in later times devotion to St Raphael was widely spread. This Archangel is known to us chiefly through the Book of Tobias, but he is also mentioned by the Fathers in early Christian times and in many inscriptions. St Ambrose mentions besides Raphael, also Gabriel and Uriel, because the latter is named in the Apocalypse of Enoch: *non moritur Gabriel, non moritur Raphael, non moritur Uriel.*[1] The union of these three angels' names recalls the inscription on a tablet of gold found in the Vatican chapel of St Petronilla in the tomb of Maria the wife of Honorius and daughter of Stilicho. Upon this was written:

MICHAEL · GABRIEL · RAPHAEL · VRIEL

These four angels as the *maiores* are frequently invoked in the *Canon universalis* of Ethiopia, in the Eastern Calendars, and in several medieval Liturgies.

In an inscription on an amethyst described by Le Blanc,[2] around the image of Christ with his hand raised to bless, the following names may be read:

ΡΑΦΑΗΛ
ΡΕΝΕΛ
ΟΥΡΙΗΛ
ΙΧΘΥΟC
ΜΙΧΑΗΛ
ΓΑΒΡΙΗΛ
ΑΖΑΗΛ

---

[1] *De Fide*, L. III. P.L. XVI, col. 616.
[2] *Le premier chapitre de St. Jean et la croyance à ses vertus secrètes*, in the *Revue Archéologique*, vol. II, p. 8, 1894.

Raphael, Gabriel, Michael and Uriel are familiar names, but the others accompanying the divine Ichthys are taken from the Apocrypha, as is also the third spirit named in the following inscription from Kodya-Genzlar. (Thiounta): ΚΥΡΙΕ ΒΟΗΘΙ ΑΑΑΑΑ ΜΙΧΑΗΛ Ε ΓΑΒΡΙΗΛ ΙΣΤΡΑΕΛ ΡΑΦΑΗΛ.

The Introit is the same as on September 29.

Collect: " O God, who gavest blessed Raphael the Archangel to thy servant Tobias to be a companion on the journey; grant that we thy servants may always be sheltered by his guardianship and strengthened by his help."

The Lesson is from the Book of Tobias (xii, 7–15) where the Archangel reveals his spiritual nature and his heavenly office. He is none other than Raphael, that is to say " the healing of God," one of the seven blessed spirits who stand before the throne of God. When Tobias exercised charity towards his companions in captivity the Angel offered to the Lord the incense of his prayers. The blindness by which the just man was smitten was allowed by God for a divine purpose: *necesse fuit*. The trial perfected his virtue. But now the Archangel has come to restore his sight, to deliver Sarah his son's wife from the demon, and to fill the house of Tobias with blessings even of a material kind.

The Gradual which follows betrays the hand of a modern compiler who has been satisfied to put together two verses from Scripture without considering the special structure of this ancient responsorial chant, which holds the place with regard to the Lesson that the Greek chorus held with regard to the tragedy.

Tobias, viii, 3. " The angel of the Lord, Raphael, took the devil and bound him."

Psalm cxliv. " Great is our Lord and great is his power. Alleluia."

The alleluiatic verse is taken from Psalm cxxxvii.

Alleluia. " I will sing praise to thee in the sight of the angels; I will worship towards thy holy temple, and I will give glory to thy name. Alleluia."

We may ask why the Psalmist mentions the presence of the holy angels as a special motive for the respect we should show at our prayers. The reply given by exegetes is that those blessed spirits are models of the fervour with which we should perform our devotions. Moreover, they are appointed by God as the special protectors and ministers of our prayer. Theirs is the duty of offering up in their golden thuribles the incense of our prayers, as St John describes in the Apocalypse: *incensum sunt orationes Sanctorum.*

A third meaning may be attributed to the Psalmist's words

October 24

when he praises God in the sight of his angels. These blessed spirits surround God and are the seat of his majesty, the throne of his glory; they rejoice in the triumph of his omnipotence, and therefore the Prophet is filled with awe and reverence at the sight of the angels who stand before God, and, joining in the hymns which they sing perpetually in heaven, he also cries : *In conspectu Angelorum psallam tibi ; adorabo ad templum sanctum tuum et confitebor nomini tuo.*

The Gospel which tells of the angel who moved the healing waters of the Pool of Bethsaida (John v, 1–4) is also read on Friday of Ember Week in Lent, as a symbol of baptism and the grace of the Paraclete who breathes upon the sacramental waters and infuses life into them. The angel who stirred the pool is often identified with St Raphael by the Fathers of the Church; indeed some hold that it was this archangel who appeared to our divine Redeemer in the Garden of Gethsemani in virtue of his attribute of *medicina Dei : Apparuit autem illi Angelus de caelo confortans eum.*[1]

The Antiphon for the Offertory, *Stetit Angelus*, is celebrated because it is set to a magnificent and impressive melody in the Gregorian collection, and occurs also on May 8. It is connected with the passage from Tobias read above, and we have already spoken of the office of the angels who offer to God the incense of our prayers.

The Secret and Post-Communion are the same as on the feast of St Michael on Monte Gargano on May 8.

Post-Communion. " Vouchsafe, O Lord God, to send holy Raphael the archangel to help us; and may he whom we believe ever to stand before thy majesty, present our poor prayers to be blessed by thee."

Concerning the *cultus* of the angels we may record here the great veneration which the early Christians professed towards the angels appointed by God to watch over the graves of the faithful. In the Island of Thera in the Archipelago there may be seen many tombs on which this angel is mentioned. The following are examples of this.

ΑΝΓΕ	ΑΓΓΕ	ΑΒΑΤΟΝ
ΛΟC	ΛΟC	ΑΓΓΕΛΟΥ
ΕΠΙ		
ΚΤΟΥC	ΒΑCΙΛΙΟCΦ	
ΠΡΕCΒΥ	ΙΡΜΙΟ	
ΤΙDΟC		

The inscription on another tomb ends thus : ἐνορκίζω ὑμας τοὺ ὧδε ἐφεστῶτα ἄγγελου μή τίς ποτε τολμη(ση) ἐνθὰ δε τινὰ καταθέσθε.

" I adjure you by the Angel above this grave that no one should dare to lay another corpse within it."

[1] Luke xxii, 43.

OCTOBER 25

SS Chrysanthus and Daria, Martyrs

Station at the Cemetery of the Giordani on the Via Salaria Nuova.

The Martyrology of St Jerome mentions these two martyrs on several different dates, for instance on August 12, October 25, November 29, and December 19 and 20. However, their feast which in the ninth century was kept on March 19, was at last definitely fixed on October 25, the date on which the Martyrology commemorates, together with a group of sixty-two soldiers, a number of Christians who had met on the *natalis* of the martyrs to celebrate the holy Sacrifice on their tomb. The pagans discovered this and filled up the crypt with stones and sand, burying the courageous martyrs alive.

The place hallowed by this massacre was held later in great veneration. At the time of Gregory of Tours, an iron gate closed the entrance to the sacred crypt, but through the openings in it could be seen the bones which strewed the ground, and the altar with the silver ampollae for the holy Sacrifice, placed there by the martyrs.

The following is the notice in the Martyrology on October 25: *Romae, Via Salaria, Maximi et aliorum centum viginti militum, quorum nomina soli Deo cognita sunt, in cimiterio Trasone.*

Pope Damasus speaks, in an inscription, of a group of sixty-two martyrs, who may perhaps be the *milites* mentioned in this record.

TEMPORE · QVO · GLADIVS · SECVIT · PIA · VISCERA · MATRIS
SEXAGINTA · DVO · CAPTI · FERITATE · TYRAMNI
EXTEMPLO · DVCIBVS · MISSIS · TVNC · COLLA · DEDERE
CONFESSI · CHRISTVM · SVPERATO · PRINCIPE · MVNDI
AETHERIAM · PETIERE · DOMVM · REGNAQVE · PIORVM

"At the time when the sword pierced the heart of our Mother the Church, sixty-two of the faithful were captured by the fierce tyrant, and immediately offered their necks to the soldiers. They confessed Christ, overcame the prince of this world, and sought the heavenly mansion and kingdom of the saints."

Another epitaph by Pope Damasus which, according to the Codex of Verdun, must once have been in the neighbourhood of the tomb of Chrysanthus and Daria, appears to refer to the second group of martyrs buried alive in the crypt.

October 25

SANCTORVM · QVICVMQVE · LEGIS · VENERARE · SEPVLCHRVM
NOMINA · NEC · NVMERVM · POTVIT · RETINERE · VETVSTAS
ORNAVIT · DAMASVS · TVMVLVM · COGNOSCITE · RECTOR
PRO · REDITV · CLERI · CHRISTO · PRAESTANTE · TRIVMPHANS
MARTYRIBVS · SANCTIS · REDDIT · SVA · VOTA · SACERDOS

" Whosoever thou art who readest this, venerate the tomb of the saints. Time has not preserved their names or their number. Know that Damasus the bishop adorned this sepulchre on the occasion of his triumph when the schismatic clergy through the help of Christ returned to him. The Pontiff now gives thanks to the holy martyrs."

We know, too, from Gregory of Tours[1] that Pope Damasus caused some work to be executed at the crypt of the saints and placed an inscription there.

Lastly, we have the lines in honour of Chrysanthus and Daria, recording the restorations executed by Vigilius after the Goths had profaned the tomb of the saints.

HIS · VOTIBVS · PARIBVS · TVMVLVM · DVO · NOMINA · SERVANT
CHRYSANTI · DARIAE · NVNC · VENERANDVS · HONOR
EFFERA · QVEM · RABIES · NEGLECTO · IVRE · SEPVLCHRI
SANCTORVM · TVMVLVS · PRAEDA · FVRENTIS · ERAT
PAVPERIS · EX · CENSV · MELIVS · NVNC · ISTA · RESVRGVNT
DIVITE · SED · VOTO · PLVS · PLACITVRA · DEO
PLANGE · TVVM · GENS · SAEVA · NEFAS · PERIERE · FVRORES
CREVIT · IN · HIS · TEMPLIS · PER · TVA · DAMNA · DECVS

"Two names of equal merit are recorded on this tomb. The glory of Chrysanthus and Daria is now revered. The sacred right of the tomb was once violated by the fury of those who sought treasure. The sepulchre formerly poor and unadorned rises in greater beauty through generous gifts and is more pleasing to God. O fierce barbarians, weep over your crimes, your fury has passed, and as a result of your devastations, the beauty of this temple has been increased."

According to the inscription of Paschal I at St Praxedes, the bodies of the sixty-two *milites* as well as those of Chrysanthus and Daria were translated to that church. It must, however, have been only a portion of the relics which were placed there, for the *Notitia Nataliciorum* of the martyrs interred at St Sylvester *in Capite* mentions those of SS Chrysanthus and Daria on March 19.

The Lateran Basilica and that of St Paul also boast of important relics of the two martyrs of the Cemetery of the Giordani; this proves that the *cultus* of Chrysanthus and Daria was once widely popular at Rome.

---
[1] *De Gloria Martyrum*, C. xxxviii.

Indeed this festival might almost be described in the words of an ancient inscription : *dies martyrorum*, for the eucharistic Sacrifice offered to-day in the *Coemeterium Jordanum* was intended to commemorate not only Chrysanthus and Daria, but the sixty-two soldiers who were buried in the neighbourhood, and the multitude of the faithful as well, who had come to assist at the Mass of the *natalis* of Chrysanthus and Daria and met their death at the martyrs' tomb. Thus to-day's sacrifice is indeed rich by reason of the number of victims immolated with Christ, and the altar erected in the depths of the catacombs may be said to be red with the blood shed by the saints in their victorious confession of faith.

The Introit *Intret* is the same as on January 20.

Collect : " Let the prayer of thy blessed martyrs Chrysanthus and Daria intercede for us, O Lord, we beseech thee ; that we who honour them by this service may continually enjoy their loving help."

The Lesson (II Cor. vi, 4–10) and the Gradual are those of July 30, for SS Abdon and Sennen. We are the ministers of God, and therefore we must imitate our divine model. That is to say, we must be prepared to be treated with ingratitude and contempt, and in return we must bless and serve those who curse and revile us.

The alleluiatic verse is the same as on the feast of St Basilides, June 12. The rage of the persecutors, like a storm, is soon over. But the bones of their victims rest in peace, and their memory echoes through the ages.

The Gospel is the same as for the martyrs Marcus and Marcellianus on June 18, and contains the rebuke which Christ addressed to the Pharisees, who hypocritically erected monuments to the prophets slain by their forefathers. These words had a special significance when read in this crypt of SS Chrysanthus and Daria, where the bodies of so many martyrs still lay unburied.

The Offertory and the Communion are exactly the same as those of July 28, for the martyrs Nazarius and Celsus.

Secret : " We beseech thee, O Lord, let the victim which thy people solemnly offer up on the festival of SS Chrysanthus and Daria be well pleasing to thee."

We should note the phrase : *solemniter immolatur*, which alludes to the ancient stational Mass and reveals the spirit in which the feasts of the martyrs are celebrated in the Liturgy. We should always strive to make our devotion accord with that of the Church. When, therefore, the Church mourns we should fast and mourn with her ; when she

October 25

celebrates the festivals of her heroes we too should join in her solemn rites, *solemniter immolatur* as the Missal expresses it to-day.

Post-Communion: "We whom thou hast filled with sacramental gladness, beseech thee, O Lord, that through the intercession of thy holy martyrs Chrysanthus and Daria the actions which we do may bring grace to our souls."

St Thomas expressed this thought of the Liturgy with scholastic exactitude in a well-known prayer: *Da mihi, quaeso, Dominici Corporis et Sanguinis non solum suscipere Sacramentum, sed etiam rem et virtutem Sacramenti.*

We may quote here in honour of the two martyrs this verse from the Byzantine Liturgy.

Ζῶσι Χρύσανθος καὶ Δαρεία ἐν πόγῳ
Κἂν ἐκπνέωσι ζῶντες εἰσθύντες βότρῳ
Χῶσαν συζυγὴν δεκάτῃ ἐνάτῃ ὁμόλεκτρον.

"Chrysanthus and Daria live in heaven, though they are dead, having been buried alive in one grave. The inseparable pair were entombed on March 19.

OCTOBER 26

St Evaristus, Pope*

The name of this holy Pope, the successor of Clement in the government of the Roman Church, was first inscribed in the martyrology by Ado. The *Liber Pontificalis* attributes to him the credit of having divided the various ecclesiastical regions of Rome among the titular presbyters and of having desired that seven deacons should surround the Pope when he preached: *propter stylum veritatis*, that is to say because of the supreme dignity of the Roman Pontiff, who is here spoken of, in words borrowed from St Paul, as a column of truth.

St Evaristus (111-121) according to an ancient Roman tradition, was buried at the Vatican beside the Prince of the Apostles, and was succeeded by Alexander.

The Mass *Statuit* is the Common of a Martyr and Bishop, as for Pius I, on July 11.

OCTOBER 27

Vigil of the Holy Apostles Simon and Jude

The Martyrology of St Jerome notes the names of three martyrs at Rome on this day: *Romae, Marciani, Luci, Victi,* of whom, however, nothing is known. On the following night the Laterculus of Berne registers the synaxis of the vigil of SS Simon and Jude, Apostles.

The Introit is the same as on January 20.

Collect: "Grant, we beseech thee, almighty God, that even as we are approaching the glorious festival of thine apostles Simon and Jude, so may they approach thy divine majesty in our behalf, to win for us thy good things."

Anticipation is a sign of solicitude and zeal, and therefore the Church, because she is full of love, anticipates the liturgical solemnities in her prayers. In the daily round of prayer she even anticipates the rising of the sun according to the word of the Psalmist (Psalm cxviii): *Praevenerunt oculi mei ad te diluculo*. A typical example of this zeal is found in the lives of some of the early saints like St Nicholas of Myra and the Patriarch St Benedict, of whom we are told that in their prayer they even anticipated the liturgical night vigils.

The Epistle (I Cor. iv, 9–14) is like that of January 31, for St Peter Nolasco. St Paul alludes sarcastically to the excessive sensitiveness of the Corinthians, and compares their luxury to the humiliations and labours of his missionary life.

The Gradual *Vindica* follows as on the feast of St Basilides, June 12. It has often happened that God has avenged the blood of his saints by permitting those who shed it to be converted to the Faith through the merits of the martyrs, as in the case of Saul, of the executioners of SS Peter and Marcellinus, of those of SS Processus and Martinianus, and of the murderer of St Peter Martyr, etc.

The Gospel, containing the similitude of the vine and the branch, is also read on April 23 for the feast of St George.

The Offertory and the Communion are the same as in the Mass of St Basilides.

Secret: "We who celebrate the coming festival of thy holy apostles SS Simon and Jude with our gifts, humbly beseech thee, O Lord, that whereas they are hindered by the guilt on our souls, nevertheless by the merits of these thy saints they may become well pleasing in thy sight."

It is sin, then, which withholds from us the special graces of God. Even when its guilt is forgiven, sin leaves behind it painful consequences in the punishment and expiation due to it. The Holy Sacrifice, and the intercession of the saints joined to our own mortification are powerful in counteracting the *virus* of our sins.

Post-Communion: "We who have received thy sacraments, humbly entreat thee, O Lord, that through the

October 27

intercession of thy blessed apostles Simon and Jude, what we now do in time may bring us grace for life everlasting."

Every moment of this life is precious on which our immutable eternity depends. We have only one span of mortal existence, and it must be spent in serious and unremitting endeavour, for if we fail at the hour of death we shall have no second chance.

OCTOBER 28

SS Simon and Jude, Apostles

According to an ancient tradition recorded in the pseudo-Abdia, these apostles after having preached the Gospel during thirteen years in Armenia and Persia received the crown of martyrdom at Suanir on July 1, in the year 47. Their festival is kept on that day in some Western martyrologies.

The most ancient of the Roman Sacramentaries do not contain the names of SS Simon and Jude, but their feast is noted in the later copies. Indeed, the *cultus* of these apostles must have been popular at Rome during the twelfth century, since as Benedict the Canon[1] tells us, their relics were believed to rest under two particular altars in the Vatican Basilica, and because of this these altars were incensed during solemn night vigils : *duo altaria in mediana ad Crucifixos, ubi ab antiquis patribus audivimus requiescere apostolos Simonem et Judam.*

When St Peter's was rebuilt the relics of the two apostles were translated on December 27, 1605, and laid under a new altar erected in their honour, on which occasion Paul V granted a plenary indulgence to all present. This altar, over which a painting representing the crucifixion of St Peter is now to be seen, is of great importance, for it stands on the spot (*inter duas metas*) marked by tradition as that where the cross of the Prince of the Apostles was erected.

There was another small church at Rome dedicated to SS Simon and Jude, and this stood near Monte Giordano, close to the Orsini palace.

St Jude, whose feast we celebrate to-day, has a special prerogative besides that of the apostleship common to our Lord's first twelve disciples upon whom, as St Thomas says, God had poured forth the firstfruits of the Spirit. In the holy Scriptures Jude is described as the brother of James the first Bishop of Jerusalem, and was therefore cousin to the Saviour. This close relationship endeared him to Christ

---

[1] *P.L.* LXXVIII, col. 1029.

and won for him special graces. On account of this the *fratres Domini* were greatly honoured in the early Church at Jerusalem, and St Paul in his first Epistle to the Corinthians appealed to their authority as having great weight.[1] It was fitting that the relations of the Saviour should be worthy of all praise even in the eyes of the Jews.

We possess a short Canonical letter written by St Jude, who is daily commemorated in the Roman Canon of the Mass under the name of Thaddeus. It is directed against the false mysticism which was then just beginning to appear. The second and third chapters of St Peter's second Epistle seem to be inspired by this letter which is an example of the Gospel preaching of the *Frater Domini*, and is therefore read not only in the Divine Office but also at the Mass of St Silverius, Pope, on June 20.

We read in the life of St Bernard that having received some relics of St Jude from Jerusalem in the year of his death, he commanded that these should be laid upon his dead body and that he should be enclosed in his coffin with this precious treasure upon his breast. Geoffrey, the Saint's biographer, tells us that his order was obeyed.

Very little is known about the apostle St Simon of whom St Matthew says that he was a Cananean, whilst St Luke adds: *qui vocatur Zelotes*.[2] From this it is evident that, before Christ called him to be an apostle, Simon belonged to the patriotic party known as Zealots, who, impatient of foreign rule, prepared for a war of independence. This circumstance was not forgotten, and even after he had become a disciple of the Lord, he was still known by the appellation of the Zealot.

The Introit is that common to all feasts of the Apostles, as on November 30.

The Collect, Secret, and Post-Communion are those which the Gelasian Sacramentary assigns to the collective feast of the Apostles, which at that time must have been kept in France within the Octave of the festival of SS Peter and Paul.

Collect: "O God, who through thy blessed apostles Simon and Jude hast brought us to the knowledge of thy name; grant that by advancing in virtue we may celebrate their everlasting glory, and also that by celebrating their glory we may advance in virtue."

The Latin text is strikingly expressive: *proficiendo celebrare et celebrando proficere.*

In the Epistle (Eph. iv, 7–13) St Paul explains to his disciples at Ephesus the manner in which the grace of God

---

[1] 1 Cor. ix, 5. [2] Luke vi, 15.

is bestowed upon the various members of the Church. It is the Church, rather than the individual, who represents Christ in the fulness of his sanctity on earth; each one of us, as a single member of this mystical body, is called to fill a special place and is given a certain measure of grace. Therefore all graces are not given to all; but to one this gift is given, to another that, and thus by working together the whole community shows forth the life of Christ.

This Epistle is also read on the Vigil of the Ascension.

The Gradual *Constitues* is the same as for the feast of St James, July 25.

The alleluiatic verse is from Psalm cxxxviii and treats of the secret thoughts of divine Providence, and not, as in the Vulgate, of the friends of God.

The Gospel (John xv, 17–25) is taken from our Lord's discourse at the Last Supper. The world has rendered hatred to God in return for his love. Although this hatred is a sin against the Holy Ghost, God did not cease to love his creatures. He loved them beyond measure even to giving his life for those who hated him. Indeed, he did more than this, he overcame hatred with infinite love and enveloped the world in an atmosphere of love, commanding his disciples to love without ceasing as he had loved.

The Offertory and the Communion are the same as for the feast of St James.

The following prayer appears in the Gelasian Sacramentary during the vigil in preparation for the feast of the twelve apostles. The version given in the Missal has been slightly altered and loses some of its meaning.

Secret: " We who pay honour to the eternal glory of thy holy apostles Simon and Jude, beseech thee, O Lord, that we may celebrate it the more worthily now that we have been cleansed by thy holy sacraments."

Post-Communion: " We who have received thy sacraments, O Lord, humbly pray that through the intercession of thy blessed apostles Simon and Jude what we do in honour of their martyrdom may avail us for a healing remedy."

We should notice that in all these prayers of great antiquity the people are intimately associated with the sacred action of the priest. As the latter offers up to God, before the Preface, the oblations of the faithful, so too after Communion he words his prayer as if the people, too, had taken part in the Sacrifice by receiving the Body of the Lord.

Therefore the Council of Trent followed the early liturgical tradition, when it declared that the Church desired that the faithful should always, at Holy Mass, participate in the reception of the sacred mysteries.

SUNDAY BEFORE THE FEAST OF ALL SAINTS

Feast of the Kingship of Our Lord Jesus Christ*

The Messianic Kingdom is essentially the universal and glorious reign established by Christ for the glory of God and the salvation of the world. The Holy Scriptures are clear on this point, and whilst they describe with great reserve the character of the "Servant of Jahvè wounded for our iniquities," they are eloquent in telling us of the glories of the King whose brow is crowned with many crowns, and who bears written on his royal mantle the title of *Rex regum et Dominus dominantium*.

The holy Sacrifice and the divine Office form the solemn daily tribute paid by the Church to Christ, who is both High-priest and King. The very feasts of the Liturgy such as the Epiphany, Easter and the Ascension are intended to glorify those mysteries in which Christ appears to us more especially under the figure of a King.

It is as a King that on the Epiphany he is sought by the Magi from the distant Eastern lands, and that he receives the firstfruits of the adoration soon to be rendered to him by all the powers of the earth.

At Easter he bends beneath his feet all the forces which are arrayed against him: *curvat imperia*, and opens the Messianic reign by triumphing over death and Satan. It is as King and supreme arbiter of the earth's destiny that Christ, heeding no temporal authority, sends his apostles to preach freely in every place *Evangelium Regni. Data est mihi omnis potestas in caelo et in terra. Ite ergo; docete omnes gentes, baptizantes eos.*

Lastly, on Ascension Day we contemplate him seated on the throne of the Godhead at the right hand of the Father, and we say in the words of the Creed: *cujus regni non erit finis*.

Nevertheless, in spite of the solemn affirmations of the Kingship of Christ contained in Scripture and in Holy Liturgy, for more than fifty years, a pernicious heresy has spread throughout the civilized world which some call liberalism and others " laicisme." This error has many aspects, but consists chiefly in the denial of the supremacy of God and the Church over Society and the State. The latter officially declares itself to be independent of any other authority (a free Church in a free State), when it does not go further and claim divine prerogatives requiring like Moloch of old the sacrifice of every other right both of the individual and the family. The State is the supreme expression of the absolute.

Sunday before the Feast of All Saints 201

As in the past many liturgical feasts originated from the ardour with which the Faith of the Church opposed certain errors then in vogue, so now, too, the Apostolic See has considered that the most efficacious way of making the condemnation of "laicisme" widely known was that of instituting a solemn feast of the Messianic Kingship of Christ. This forms at once a protest and an act of reparation to atone for that idolatry of the State which has joined in a great conspiracy: *reges terrae et principes . . . in unum, adversus Dominum et adversus Christum eius.*

At first many different dates were proposed by liturgists: the Sunday within the Octave of the Epiphany, the Ascension, the Octave of the feast of the Sacred Heart, but it seemed wiser not to join this feast to one already in existence but to give it a particular character of its own and a special place in the Missal. Finally the new festival was fixed on the Sunday preceding the feast of All Saints in order to connect it with the Office of November 1, and with the thoughts inspired by that collective feast of all the saints, the veneration of the Heavenly Jerusalem and the court of the King of Glory. It is fitting that the Liturgy, drawing near to the end of the cycle of Sundays after Pentecost, which represents the labours and struggles of earthly life, before turning her thoughts to the various choirs of the *ecclesia primitivorum* and the Heavenly City, should pay homage to him who is the cause and the end of that glory, and to whom the saints all offer their crowns and sing their joyful Alleluia.

This is the reason why in the Office of All Saints the first responsory of Matins describes the throne of the Omnipotent One, the hem of whose garment rests upon the holy temple in sign of sanctification. *Vidi Dominum sedentem super solium excelsum et elevatum . . . et ea quae sub ipso erant replebant templum.*

The Introit is taken from the hymn which St John heard in heaven: "Worthy is the Lamb that was slain to receive power, and divinity, and wisdom, and strength, and honour. To him be glory and empire for ever and ever."

The exaltation of Jesus Christ is, according to St Paul, in proportion to the humiliation he endured in obedience to his Heavenly Father. Wherefore St John before speaking of the glory of the Lamb recalls his sacred Passion, and says that he was immolated and slain.

The first verse of Psalm lxxi follows, which is distinctly Messianic: "Give the King thy judgement, O God: and to the King's Son thy justice."

This is the Messianic office conferred upon Jesus in the

world. He as "splendour of the substance of the Father" will govern the House of David until such time as he shall have conquered the enemy and established the kingdom of God in peace. Death and the devil having been overcome, the temporal mission of Christ will end, and he like a glorious conqueror will lay at his Father's feet the sceptre and the crown, the trophy of his victory.

Collect : "Almighty everlasting God, who hast willed to restore all things in thy beloved Son, the King of the whole creation ; mercifully grant that all the communities of the nations that are scattered by the wound of sin may be subjected unto his most sweet dominion."

This Collect is inspired by the words of St Paul, and therefore is full of meaning. The unity of the human race, indeed that of the whole of creation, has been ruined by sin which is a disruptive force. God has willed to restore the original unity and has done so through Jesus Christ, whom he has established as the centre and end of creation, the new Adam from whom all the peoples of the earth can receive life, unity, and grace.

The Lesson is taken from the Epistle to the Colossians (i, 12–20) where St Paul describes the primacy of Christ over all creation, which finds in him the object of its existence. This primacy of Christ is founded on the hypostatic union of his human nature with the divine nature in the person of the Word, but it is universal and includes not man alone, but also the angels who derive grace and glory from him. His primacy concerns the Church especially, for Christ's dominion over her is similar to that which in the human body is exercised by the head over the other members.

The Gradual is taken from Psalm lxxi and describes the extent and the glory of the Kingdom of Christ. "He shall rule from sea to sea, and from the river even unto the ends of the earth. And all the Kings of the earth shall adore him ; all nations shall serve him. Alleluia."

This prophecy is gradually being fulfilled as the Church extends her peaceful conquests among the pagan nations, and the Gospel of the kingdom will be preached throughout the whole earth. In the history of the Church this kingdom of Christ is complete and absolute *de jure*, but is still opposed and incomplete *de facto*. It will be entire, final, and glorious at the day of judgement, when, having conquered death, Christ will fulfil his office as judge, condemning the wicked and calling the just to the immortal life of the blessed resurrection.

The alleluiatic verse is taken from the passage in Daniel (vii, 14), when the prophet describes the various reigns dividing

Sunday before the Feast of All Saints 203

the history of humanity into different periods : " His power is an eternal power, which shall not be taken away ; and his kingdom shall not be made void."

It is easy to recognize the partial accomplishment of this prophecy even now, if we compare the history of the Church already covering nearly two thousand years with those of other empires and dynasties. All these have passed like the leaves which unfold in the Spring and fall with the coming of Autumn.

In the double chant after the Epistle the threefold catholicity of the Kingdom of Christ is placed before us. First that of place : *a mari usque ad mare,* thus embracing the whole world. Then that of the subjects : *omnes reges . . . omnes gentes* including all men, be they kings and princes or wretched pariahs humbled in the dust. Finally the universality of the ages : *potestas aeterna . . . non auferetur,* that is to say a power which shall never end.

The Gospel is taken from St John (xviii, 33–37) and contains the solemn declaration made by Christ before Pilate concerning the nature and origin of his kingdom. This kingdom does not depend upon the world : *regnum meum non est hinc,* but it comprehends the world. Jesus does not come to dethrone the sovereigns of the earth, and to take from them the domains over which they rule. He comes, rather, to give to human society the last and most perfect rule, and lays down in the Gospel the supreme laws of truth and justice to guide both rulers and subjects in the exercise of their mutual duties. God is the supernatural end of man. It is the obvious task of civilized society and of those who govern it to collaborate with the Church and to help her, always of course within the bounds of civil authority, to accomplish with greater security and ease her divine mission of enlightening, guiding, and governing souls, establishing in them the kingdom of Christ.

This supremacy of the Catholic Church and the Pope over nations and their monarchs formed part of the international law of Christian states in the Middle Ages. Therefore it happened more than once that the Popes deposed kings who were unworthy of their office and released their subjects from the oath of fidelity by which they were bound.

The Offertory is taken from Psalm ii. To the nations and the kings who rise up against his divine design of establishing the Messianic Kingdom for the salvation of the world, Christ shows the solemn deed of investiture which he has received from his Father : " Ask of me, and I will give thee the Gentiles for thy inheritance, and the ends of the earth for thy possession."

Secret: "We offer unto thee, O Lord, the Host of man's reconciliation; grant, we beseech thee, that he whom we immolate in these present sacrifices, may grant unto all nations the gifts of unity and peace, even Jesus Christ our Lord thy Son."

The Preface is proper to the feast and has some of the grandeur and lyrical quality of the ancient Prefaces. *Vere dignum . . . Qui Unigenitum Filium tuum Dominum nostrum Jesum Christum, sacerdotem aeternum et universorum regem, oleo exsultationis unxisti; ut seipsum in ara Crucis hostiam immaculatam et pacificam offerens, redemptionis humanae sacramenta perageret; ut suo subjectis imperio omnibus creaturis, aeternum et universale regnum immensae tuae traderet maiestati; regnum veritatis et vitae; regnum sanctitatis et gratiae; regnum justitiae, amoris et pacis. Et ideo . . .*

The conception of Christ as Pontiff and King who reconquers and restores to his Heavenly Father the realm of creation which had been taken from him by sin, in order that God might eternally be all in all, is borrowed from St Paul. The compiler, however, has the merit of having given to his liturgical composition the lyrical character of a triumphant hymn of thanksgiving so characteristic of the primitive eucharistic *Hymnus*, as our anaphora of the consecration was then called.

The Antiphon for the Communion is a prelude to the final effect of the eucharistic Sacrifice which ends with the divine blessing. At the moment of Holy Communion Jesus is enthroned in the faithful heart and fills it with his presence: He who is "Blessed" among all and through whom, according to the promise given by God to Abraham, all the nations of the earth shall be blessed. Psalm xxviii: "The Lord shall sit as King for ever, the Lord shall bless his people with peace."

Post-Communion: "Having received the food of immortality, we beseech thee, O Lord, that we who glory in our warfare under the banners of Christ the King may come to reign with him for ever in his heavenly dwelling-place: who with thee."

The Royal Standard of Jesus Christ is the Cross: *Dicite in nationibus: regnavit a ligno Deus;* for the kingdom of Christ is that of obedience, humility and sacrifice.

OCTOBER 31

Vigiliary Mass of All Saints

The celebration of a festival in honour of all the Saints at this season of the year, appears to have passed from the Gallican into the Roman Liturgy. As a collective feast of all

October 31

the blessed inhabitants of Heaven it has precedents in various liturgies, especially in the East. This feast was only adopted at Rome in the ninth century; we find no mention of it in the earlier Sacramentaries.

The vigiliary Mass, which at the time of its institution was not celebrated in the night, but in the afternoon preceding the feast, after None, belongs to an age when the true liturgical spirit was still universal. The predominant idea is the triumph of those who once were afflicted, judged, and condemned by the world.

In the Introit, the Antiphon from Wisdom (iii, 8): "The saints judge nations and rule over people: and the Lord their God shall reign for ever," is placed before the first verse of Psalm xxxii: "Rejoice in the Lord, ye just: praise becometh the upright. Glory be."

Collect: "Multiply thy grace upon us, O Lord, and grant that we may be gladdened at the holy confession of those to whose glorious festival we are looking forward."

The Lesson is taken from the Apocalypse (v, 6-12). For a moment the veil is lifted and John first contemplates and then paints in rapid strokes the vision of the Church triumphant. There, too, a Liturgy exists, an altar, golden candlesticks, incense and a victim. The centre of this Liturgy is the Lamb, immolated in the eternal design of God from the beginning of the world. The choir of angels, of ancients, and of saints form his court; the Church Triumphant is merely the halo which shines about his head. As all have reached heaven by his grace and have washed their garments in his blood, so now they continually bless his mercy and his love.

The Gradual is taken from Psalm cxlix and is the same as for St Vitus on June 15. After the labours and humiliations of this life the saints rest with Christ in the heavenly mansions. We must not anticipate events. Now is the time to work and suffer until the Holy Spirit calls us away. In heaven we shall know no more sorrow or tears, but joy, triumph and glory will take their place.

The Gospel (Luke vi, 17-23) is that of the Beatitudes as on June 19 for the martyrs of Milan, Gervase and Protase.

The beatitude of the saints is wholly spiritual and can never be touched by the malice or cruelty of those who persecute them. These may indeed reduce them to poverty and may even tear out their eyes or strike off their limbs, but they will never reach that inner sanctuary which the Holy Ghost has consecrated within their souls. Here are serene peace, holy joy, and unshaken trust.

The Antiphon for the Offertory is that of June 12, for St Basilides.

Secret: "We offer our gifts upon thy altar, O Lord; grant, we beseech thee, that by the prayers of all thy saints, to whose approaching festival we look forward, they may avail for our salvation."

The sentence in the Missal *altare muneribus cumulamus* refers to the ancient liturgical custom by which the people themselves presented the offerings of bread and wine to be used for the sacrifice.

The Antiphon from Wisdom (iii, 1-3), *Justorum animae* which was sung during the Communion of the faithful, is the same as for St Vitus on June 15.

Post-Communion: "When we have taken the sacraments and been gladdened by the festival which we desire, O Lord, may we be helped by the prayers of those in memory of whom these things are done."

When we pray to the saints in heaven they do as Joseph did when his brothers arrived in Egypt. He went before Pharaoh and, full of joy, announced: *Fratres mei et domus patris mei . . . venerunt ad me.*[1] And the King out of love for Joseph gave to them the land of Gessen.

FEASTS IN NOVEMBER

NOVEMBER 1

ST CAESARIUS, DEACON AND MARTYR
COLLECTA AT SS COSMAS AND DAMIAN

Station at St Caesarius " in Palatio " on the Palatine.

On this day the festival was celebrated at Rome of the famous deacon of Terracina, Caesarius, to whom several churches in the City were dedicated. One was on the Via Appia: St Caesarius *in Turri*, which still exists, near the title *de fasciola*. This was a diaconia with a convent attached to it dedicated to St Simitrius. Another stood near the Tiber in the *regio* of the Arenula; a third in the Lateran near the papal "guardaroba," and finally a fourth with a monastery adjoining it rose beside the Basilica of the Apostle of the Gentiles. Indeed, the present Basilica of St Paul, the *coenobium sacratissimum* of the Papal documents, is really the ancient monastery of St Caesarius which was restored by Gregory II from its foundations, and joined to another equally ancient one standing beside it, but formerly dedicated to St Stephen.

Rome possessed a fifth sanctuary of St Caesarius, and

Genesis xlvi, 31.

this one was actually on the Palatine. Thus Christian devotion took the place of the pagan tradition which connected that spot with the *cultus* of the Cæsars.

The Gregorian Sacramentary, contrary to custom, indicates to-day the church where the *Collecta* was held. This was the Basilica of the Anargyri on the *summa sacra via* in the Forum near the Arch of Titus. Therefore the procession which started from there did not go to the Lateran, nor to the Appian Way, both of which were too far from the top of the Via Sacra; but was directed instead to the Palatine hill overlooking the narrow valley of the Forum, and to the monastery of St Caesarius *in Palatio* which on account of the Greek monks who inhabited it was also called *Sancti Caesarii Graecorum*.

We know from the Epistles of St Gregory that the oratory of the martyr on the Palatine had so completely absorbed the traditions of the worship of the *Augusti* connected with this spot, that it was here and nowhere else that the portraits of the new Emperors were brought processionally by the Pope and the Roman people, and deposited on their arrival from Byzantium. St Caesarius *in Palatio* became in this manner the domestic sanctuary of the *domus augustana*, the court church.

In the Martyrology of St Jerome, St Caesarius is recorded on April 21, as well as on November 1. It is possible that this date was connected with the Palilian festivals on the Palatine, and the *natalis* of Rome, but another hypothesis is not to be excluded, i.e. that the feast of November 1 represents the true Roman solemnity of the famous Deacon, the *dedicatio* of one of the churches named after him in the City.

* * * * * *

Collecta ad Sanctos Cosmam et Damianum.

The Introit having been sung, before the procession began to ascend the Palatine, the Pontiff recited the following Collect: *Adesto, Domine, Martyrum deprecatione Sanctorum, et quos pati pro tuo Nomine tribuisti, fac tuis fidelibus suffragari.*

Station at St Caesarius " in Palatio."

The Introit was the same as on the feast of St Lawrence: *Confessio et pulchritudo*, with the Gradual *Justorum animae* of January 19; the Offertory *In virtute tua*, of January 15, and the Communion *Qui vult venire*, of January 19, for the feast of St Canute.

Collect: *Deus, qui nos beati martyris tui Caesarii annua solemnitate laetificas, concede propitius, ut cujus natalitia colimus, etiam actiones imitemur.*

To-day the Würzburg List prescribes the passage from St John (xii, 24–26), *Amen, amen dico vobis: nisi granum frumenti,* as on the feast of St Lawrence.

Super Oblata. Hostias tibi, Domine, beati Caesarii martyris tui dicatas meritis benignus assume, et ad perpetuum nobis tribue provenire subsidium.

Ad Complendum. Quaesumus omnipotens Deus, ut qui caelestia alimenta percepimus, intercedente beato Caesario martyre tuo, per haec contra omnia adversa muniamur.

Even after the ninth century, when Rome introduced the feast of All Saints on the calends of November, the commemoration of St Caesarius remained in all the medieval Missals almost until the time of the Tridentine reform.

This is, therefore, a distinctly Roman feast, confirmed by the tradition of many centuries and only removed from the calendar when the Eternal City had forgotten the ancient *cultus* of St Caesarius. At the present time the festival of the holy Deacon is only kept at the monastery once dedicated to him near the tomb of St Paul.

NOVEMBER 1

Feast of All Saints

The progress of Autumn with the fall of the withered leaves, the long cycle of Sundays after Pentecost inspiring that feeling of sadness and weariness which pervades the latter part, call our minds to the solemn thoughts of eternity and of the world beyond the grave, to which we draw ever nearer as years and months pass by.

The Seer of Patmos comes to-day to anticipate the close of that long cycle symbolizing the arduous life of the Church militant: he raises a corner of the veil and shows us the Church triumphant in all her splendour.

At the beginning of this liturgical period which extends from Pentecost to Advent, it was said that the Holy Spirit would glorify Jesus: *Ille me clarificabit.* To-day we see in what manner he has kept his promise and has poured forth upon the mystical body of the Saviour such sanctity as now bears fruit in this great glory.

A collective feast of all martyrs, connected with the triumph of Christ's Resurrection, was known in Syria in the fourth century. At Byzantium, however, it was celebrated on the

November 1

Sunday following Pentecost, a custom which at one time was introduced at Rome, as is proved by the ancient *Comes* published by Morin from the well-known Codex of Würzburg : *Dominica in natale Sanctorum*.

This festival brought from Byzantium to the banks of the Tiber was short lived. An ancient tradition prescribed that the Romans should keep the solemn fast of Ember days in the week following Whit Sunday, and also the great vigil of St Peter's. It was, therefore, impossible after so fatiguing a night Office to celebrate the feast of All Saints on the same morning. The Byzantine custom was abandoned, and the festival of May 13 in honour of the martyrs instituted by Boniface IV, when he consecrated the Pantheon as a Christian Church, alone remained.

The idea of a collective feast of all the saints and not of the martyrs only, continued, however, to gain ground. At a time when the Iconoclasts in the East were destroying the sacred ikons and relics and that in Italy, in Lazio, the cemeteries of the martyrs were deserted on account of the raids of the Lombards in the campagna round Rome, Gregory III built an oratory at St Peter's in honour of all the Saints, confessors as well as martyrs, who had died in all parts of the world. A choir of monks carried out the liturgical offices of that Vatican sanctuary, and in the Mass a daily commemoration was made of all the saints whose *natalis* was celebrated on that day in the various churches of Christendom.

The reason which determined the choice of November 1 for the feast of All Saints is not certain. The change occurred under Gregory IV (827–844), with the co-operation of Louis the Pious and the Frankish episcopate ; but it has not yet been proved whether it was the Pope or the Emperor who took the initiative in the matter. Sixtus IV subsequently added the celebration of an octave to the feast.

The Introit *Gaudeamus . . . sub honore Sanctorum omnium*, is an ancient one, originally assigned to the feast of St Agatha on February 5.

On all other days of the year the Liturgy celebrates the memory of one or more individual saints. To-day the Lord *multiplicavit gentem et magnificavit laetitiam*, as Isaias says. Thus the glorification of Christ and of the Church is complete on this feast.

The Spirit of the Lord like the mysterious aromatic oil described by the Psalmist is diffused through the entire mystical body of Christ, sanctifying even the most lowly member, and preparing it thus for the highest glory.

Apostles and martyrs, clergy and laity, labourers and even slaves, all these have received the Paraclete and have been raised to heroic sanctity. This is the thought which inspires the Introit to-day.

The Collect is already to be found in the Gelasian Sacramentary, and is assigned to a collective feast of the Apostles, celebrated within the Octave of SS Peter and Paul.

Collect: " Almighty and everlasting God, by whose grace we pay honour to the merits of all thy saints on this single festival day; inasmuch as so many are pleading for us, grant us, we beseech thee, the fulness of thy mercy, for which we long."

The Lesson, and this is significant of the origin of the feast, is the same as for the dedication of the Pantheon, May 13 (Apocalypse, viii, 2–12). The Seer of Patmos beheld a gate opened before him, through which an immense multitude entered heaven. Not only the hundred and forty-four thousand predestined sons of Abraham, but a *turba magna* of every age, sex, and condition enter through Jesus, who is the gate of heaven. It is not then so hard to be saved, as St John writes that he could not count the number of the elect.

One condition is however essential. Those who reach the port of salvation are sealed on the forehead with a seal which is a sign of membership or conformity with the Eternal Father and his Christ. This seal, according to Ezechiel, has the shape of a Tau and is impressed upon the forehead of those who weep and lament. *Signa Tau super frontem virorum gementium et dolentium.* The Apostle explains the meaning of this when he teaches us that *sicut socii passionum estis et consolationis eritis*, that is to say, the future glory will be in proportion to the share we have had here in the passion of Christ.

The Gradual *Timete Dominum* is the same as on August 8 for St Cyriacus. The alleluiatic verse is a preparation for the Gospel. Jesus invites those who faint beneath the cross to come to him and he will give them refreshment.

On the day when the Church keeps the feast of All the Saints the Gospel can be no other than that of the Beatitudes (Matt. v, 1–12). All are included in it and to each is granted a special blessing. Illustrious birth, a distinguished position, ability and knowledge are not necessary here; on the contrary those who have least according to the world receive a larger share of the heavenly gift, and therefore the first Beatitude is promised to the humble and poor in spirit, that is to say to those who have stripped themselves and have become lowly like the child whom Jesus set as a model before his disciples.

The Antiphon for the Offertory is set to a fine Gregorian melody somewhat resembling that of the *Stetit Angelus*, and is the same as for St Hippolytus, August 13.

The persecutor believes that the lives of the martyrs are in his hands, but they are in the hands of God. The wicked are merely his instruments which he uses to perfect his works of art. Thus, rage and hatred only exist in the heart of the persecutor, but the divine artist and his living masterpiece absorbed in the ideal which they pursue are full of the undisturbed peace which is necessary for the perfecting of every work of supreme genius.

The Secret is as follows: "We offer to thee, O Lord, the gifts of our devotion; let them be well-pleasing to thee for the sake of all the saints; and of thy mercy let them avail also for our salvation."

The medieval Sacramentaries contain this Preface to-day: *Vere dignum . . . aeterne Deus : et clementiam tuam suppliciter obsecrare, ut cum exsultantibus sanctis in caelestis regni cubilibus gaudia nostra subiungas. Et quos virtutis imitatione non possumus sequi, debitae venerationis contingamus affectu, per Christum*, etc.

The Antiphon for the Communion is taken from to-day's Gospel of the Beatitudes. The world has an insatiable thirst for happiness and here the Eternal Truth teaches men how to attain it, as standing on the Mount, he sets forth as it were the decalogue of happiness. Blessed are those whose heart is clean, for they shall see God; blessed are those who keep their hearts untroubled, for they shall be known as the true sons of God, the author of peace; blessed are those who endure persecution for the cause of virtue, for they will receive endless life and joy in exchange for the life and joy they have sacrificed here.

This is the Post-Communion: "Grant, we beseech thee, O Lord, that thy faithful people may ever rejoice in paying reverence to all the saints, and may be helped by their unceasing prayers."

Let us consider the expressive word by which the Liturgy describes the Church militant. "The faithful people," that is to say the people journeying towards eternity with the eyes, and in the light of faith. What is the reward of this Catholic faith, professed and practised without wavering, and which alone gives a man the right to be called "faithful"? *Fides quid tibi praestat ?* the Church still asks her catechumens. And they reply: *vitam aeternam.*

We take pleasure in reproducing here the beautiful inscription composed by Pope Damasus in memory of all the saints interred in the Cemetery of Callixtus.

HIC · CONGESTA · IACET · QVAERIS · SI · TVRBA · PIORVM
CORPORA · SANCTORVM · RETINENT · VENERANDA · SEPVLCHRA
SVBLIMES · ANIMAS · RAPVIT · SIBI · REGIA · CAELI
HIC · COMITES · XYSTI · PORTENT · QVI · EX · HOSTE · TROPHAEA
HIC · NVMERVS · PROCERVM · SERVAT · QVI · ALTARIA · CHRISTI
HIC · POSITVS · LONGA · QVI · VIXIT · IN · PACE · SACERDOS
HIC · CONFESSORES · SANCTI · QVOS · GRAECIA · MISIT
HIC · IVVENES · PVERIQVE · SENES · CASTIQVE · NEPOTES
QVIS · MAGE · VIRGINEVM · PLACVIT · RETINERE · PVDOREM
HIC · FATEOR · DAMASVS · VOLVI · MEA · CONDERE · MEMBRA
SED · CINERES · TIMVI · SANCTOS · VEXARE · PIORVM

" Here are gathered, if you would know, a number of the just, for these venerable sepulchres hold the bodies of many saints. The kingdom of heaven possesses their sublime souls. Here are the companions of Sixtus bearing the trophies of their victory. Here are the Pontiffs who serve the altars of Christ. Here lies the priest whose life was spent in constant peace. Here are the holy confessors sent from Greece. Here are youths, children, old men, and their chaste descendants who chose to keep their virginal purity intact. I, Damasus, too, desired to lay my bones here, but I feared to disturb the holy ashes of the Saints."

This inscription was placed in the vault of the Popes of the third century where the four deacons beheaded with Sixtus II were buried beside him (*Comites Xysti*.)

The *numerus procerum* mentioned in the fifth line, refers to the series of Popes from Zephyrinus to Miltiades who with the exception of Callixtus, Marcellinus, and Marcellus were interred in the Cemetery of Callixtus.

The *Sacerdos* who spent his days in *longa pace* is generally supposed to be Pope Militiades, the Pontiff who finally beheld the Church at peace under Constantine the Great.

The *Confessores Sancti quos Graecia misit* are without any doubt the martyrs Hippolytus, Neonus, Maria, Hadria, Paulina, etc., buried in the so-called " arenaria " of Hippolytus, whilst of the *juvenes castique pueri* who kept their virginity undefiled, especial mention may be made of the acolyte Tarcisius and the martyr Cecilia who rest near by.

Damasus, from humility, refused the honour of burial beside his predecessors in the papal vault. But in order to be near the martyrs, he imitated the example of Pope Marcus, and caused a special crypt to be made for himself in the vicinity, where his mother Laurentia, and Irene his sister, a virgin consecrated to God, were also interred.

NOVEMBER 2
Commemoration of All the Faithful Departed

When, at the hour of death, a man finds himself on the threshold of eternity, his thoughts turn naturally to religion and his mind assumes a humble and reverent attitude in the sight of his Creator who is about to judge him according to his divine law.

Therefore we trace even among the most sensual and materialistic of the ancient civilizations, a feeling of religion at least towards the dead, and many are known to us chiefly through their mortuary inscriptions and prayers for the departed.

In ancient times, no sooner had the soul left this world, than the contact with God, indeed its appearance before the judgement seat, surrounded it in the eyes of the survivors with a kind of sacred atmosphere enveloping the corpse and the sepulchre itself. Human passions, anger, and revenge were arrested and disarmed by the sacred majesty of the tomb: *parce sepulto*.

The *Manes* no less forcibly than the civil laws ensured the inviolability of the sepulchre, and to refuse honourable burial to a culprit was, among the Greeks and the Romans, the worst punishment that could be inflicted on him, for his soul was believed in consequence to wander for ever, lonely in space, without finding rest.

The Romans, especially, loved to surround their dead with the memories of domestic life. Far from regarding sepulchres as places of evil augury, they buried their dead either in their own properties, *in ortulis nostris secessimus*, as one inscription has it, or by the side of the great consular roads, which ran from the Eternal City like so many great arteries traversing the *imperium*. Here the ashes of the ancestors, collected in caskets and sarcophagi, were continually cared for by the affection of their descendants. The living resided in their small country houses around these tombs, and upon those memorials covered with roses and violets, sacrifices were periodically offered, after which the living united themselves in a certain manner with the dead by consuming funeral meats in memory of them.

The Christian religion, instead of weakening this devotion of the ancients towards the departed, only purified and strengthened it, especially in virtue of the dogma of the Resurrection, the essential corollary, according to St Paul, of the fundamental truth of the Gospel; the fact that Christ our model and example is risen from the dead.

Thus we see that from the days of the Apostles the faithful at Rome constructed their places of burial at the side of the great consular roads. In those early tombs excavated in the vineyards of Domitilla, of Priscilla, of the Cecilii, of the Christian branch of the Acilii Glabriones, of Pudens, of Lucina, etc., we know that beside the most noble victims of Nero and Domitian were laid also the bodies of their brothers in the faith, whether rich or poor,—*ad religionem pertinentes meam*,—according to an ancient inscription.

Their Mother the Church, giving to each a place carved out of the tufo which forms the Roman subsoil, instead of celebrating the usual *parentalia* of the pagans, came on certain fixed days to offer upon those tombs that which St Augustine beautifully described later as *sacrificium pretii nostri*:[1] the Sacrifice of our Redemption. The custom of offering the Eucharist in suffrage for the faithful departed was associated with the first beginnings of the Church, long before St Thomas explained in his theological works the reason why the Sacrifice of our common redemption was applied to the souls of the dead. At the time of St Ignatius of Antioch and St Polycarp it was spoken of as a traditional usage, and when in later days the custom degenerated into an abuse, the authority of the Church was needed to control it and bring it within the proper limits. So, for instance, it was decreed that Holy Mass should only be celebrated on the tombs of the martyrs, and it was forbidden to celebrate the *Sacrificium pro dormitione* for those among the faithful who had forfeited the privilege through some fault. An example of this occurred in Africa at the time of St Cyprian in the case of an individual who had ventured to establish a *presbyterium* in favour of his testamentary executor. It was also forbidden to place the Holy Eucharist on the breast of the defunct person and to bury him with that token of resurrection upon him. Lastly, in the fourth century, it was forbidden in Italy to celebrate funeral banquets on the tombs of the dead.

The Church, however, with her usual sublime economy preserved all that was innocent, tender and inspired in the funeral rites of classic antiquity. She purified and spiritualized them, handing them on to the new generations of the Middle Ages transfigured by a new thought which gave a sense of joy and life to the Liturgy of the departed, the thought that they would rise once more like the risen Redeemer.

[1] *Confessiones*, Lib. IX: cap. xii.

November 2

Therefore all that was dismal or frightening disappeared. There were no more emblems of death, skulls or cross-bones traced upon the draperies; all spoke instead of peace and serene hope.

The ancient Roman cemeteries, then, were not merely graveyards, there were country houses with baths and gardens adjoining them, where even the Popes themselves often resided. The "graffiti" of the cemetery *ad Catacumbas* show the *refrigeria* or feasts celebrated in that place in honour of the two Princes of the Apostles.

In a "graffito" dating from 373 in the cemetery of Priscilla, three of the faithful announce that on the day preceding the ides of February:

AD CALICE BENIMVS

Prudentius mentions the flowers which used to be scattered on the tombs, and the libations of perfumes poured upon the sepulchres of the beloved dead. Sometimes these precious unguents were sprinkled upon the body through holes pierced in the cover of the sepulchre.

Tertullian speaks of the large sums spent by the Christians on the purchase of oriental perfumes for embalming the dead. A few years ago a body was found near the crypt of St Sebastian ad *Catacumbas* with the hands fastened behind the back, entirely covered with a thick coating of balsam which still preserved its fragrance when burnt.

The barbarian invasion of Italy caused some changes to be made in this classical Liturgy of the dead, as we may call it. The approach to the extra-mural cemeteries having become too dangerous owing to the raids of the enemy, the catacombs ceased to be used as places of burial, and it became the custom to inter the dead within the city, in a church, or in the narthex. In consequence of this the traditional funeral banquets with the libations of perfume and scattering of flowers were no longer possible, if indeed they had not already ceased before that time. Devotion to the dead no longer found expression in the ancient familiar and domestic rites, but was confined within the clearly-marked limits of sacred Liturgy. At last, this came to mean simply the burial within a hallowed place, the offering of the eucharistic Sacrifice on the day of deposition, on the seventh, on the thirtieth day, and on the anniversary, as well as (in later times) the singing of the *officium defunctorum*, consisting of a brief votive office used in the monasteries. Vespers, with Nocturns and Lauds still form part of this office.

In the present *Pontificale Romanum* of Clement VIII another rite is mentioned which also dates from the Middle

Ages. At certain specified times the Bishop must visit the various parishes within his jurisdiction, and among the objects of this visitation we find mentioned in the first place *ad absolvendas defunctorum*. This refers to a non-sacramental absolution from the ecclesiastical censures which the departed may have incurred during their lifetime, and on account of which they might be deprived in the next world of the suffrages of the faithful, as Dante describes so finely in the case of Manfred. The Bishop who has inflicted the penalty can also recall it, and, therefore, in his pastoral visitation he grants *per modum suffragii* to his former sheep now passed into eternity a full indulgence for their sins.

These absolutions were already regarded as being of traditional use in the eleventh century, and are noted in the various *Ordines* of that period.

In order to show examples of this rule of the Church concerning absolutions or indulgences for the dead—apart from the question of baptism for the departed of which St Paul writes (1 Cor. xv, 29), and which has been treated by exegetes—it is useful to recall here the stories told by St Gregory the Great concerning the Patriarch of the West, St Benedict. Gregory is generally recognized as the most reliable exponent of Catholic devotion at the period which marked the decline of the Roman Empire and the first dawn of the Middle Ages.

A certain monk had died whilst under the censure of the great Abbot of Monte Cassino, and after his burial, it was found that the earth repeatedly cast forth the corpse. The relatives had recourse to St Benedict, and he, in token of pardon, consigned to them a small particle of the sacred Host, instructing them to lay it with great reverence on the dead body, and thus to replace it in the grave.

On another occasion St Benedict had merely threatened some scandal-mongering nuns with excommunication. These women died and were buried in a church, but each time that the deacon, after the Gospel, warned the catechumens and penitents to depart, according to the custom of the age, the nuns were seen to leave their tombs and to go out of the sacred building. The fact was recounted to St Benedict, who raised his censure and in token of this reconciliation caused a Mass to be offered for their souls. From that day the gossiping nuns found peace at last, and no longer left the church during the holy Sacrifice.

The memento of the dead in the Mass is common to all Liturgies since the third century. That is to say that besides the Masses offered specially at the grave of the departed in suffrage of their souls—a rite from which the daily private

Mass said by every priest is largely derived—at all other eucharistic synaxes, both in the diptychs and in the prayer after the Consecration known as the "great intercession," a general memento is made of the faithful departed. The reason of this commemoration is that as Christ is present on the altar as victim, in the words of St Cyril of Jerusalem: *maximum iuvamen pro quibus offertur precatio sancti illius ac tremendi Sacrificii.*[1] St Thomas expressed this concisely in later days: *Ut omnibus prosit quod est pro salute omnium institutum.*[2]

Indeed the Liturgy becomes more expressive and more tender in that part of the Eucharistic Action where intercession is made for the dead. "Be mindful, O Lord," we pray in the Roman Anaphora, "of thy servants who are gone before us with the sign of faith and sleep the sleep of peace. To these and to all that rest in Christ, we beseech thee grant a place of refreshment, light and peace."

The Byzantine Liturgy celebrates annually on the Saturday before Sexagesima Sunday an Office for all the faithful departed. Τῷ σαββάτῳ πρὸ τῆς ἀπόκρεω· μνημην ἐπιτελοῦμεν πάντων τῶν ἀπ' αἰῶνος κεκοιμημένων ὀρθοδόξων Χριστιανῶν πατέρων καὶ ἀδελφῶν ἡμῶν.

"On the Saturday before Carnival (*carnis privii*) we commemorate all orthodox Christians, our fathers and brothers, who have left this world."

The Latin Liturgies also introduced a similar Office towards the eleventh century. Abbot Hugh of Farfa records that even in the preceding century his Abbey possessed a precious altar frontal for the *dies judicii*, the sight of which filled the faithful with awe and caused their minds to dwell for many days on the thought of death.[3]

In the eighth century we find among the customs of the monastery of Fulda that of celebrating each month a commemoration of the faithful departed with a special Office and special prayers. To pass from a monthly celebration to an annual one was easy, and thus we find that towards the tenth century, especially in Benedictine monasteries, the custom prevailed of commemorating every year the benefactors and friends of the house who had been taken from this world.

St Odilo, Abbot of Cluny, is generally recognized as having been responsible for the universal adoption of this custom, already in use in many churches. We know the rule issued

[1] *Catech.* V.　　[2] *Opusc.* LVII.
[3] *Destruc. Pharph.* ed. Balzani I, 30.

by St Odilo. It dates from 998, but only concerns those religious houses which were dependent on Cluny and which numbered more than a hundred, being scattered through France, Spain, and Italy. In that document the saintly Abbot commanded that on November 1, after solemn vespers, the bells should toll, and the monks should chant the Office of the dead. On the following day all the priests were to offer the holy Sacrifice to God *pro requie omnium defunctorum*.

This custom was soon imitated, at first by the various Benedictine monasteries, and then by degrees in the diocesan rituals, as for instance at Liège (1008), and at Besançon, until at last it became a universal rite of the Latin Church.

In the *Ordines Romani* the *anniversarium omnium animarum* appears for the first time in *Ordo XIV* of the fourteenth century. On that day the consistory was not held and no sermon was preached at Mass. The day chosen was that appointed by St Odilo: November 2. But in *Ordo Romanus XV* we find traces of a far older liturgical custom, for on July 8 is noted an *officium defunctorum pro fratribus* (the cardinals) et *Romanis Pontificibus*,[1] precisely as in the *Ordo* of Farfa of the tenth century.

In the same *Ordo Romanus* we find a description of the ritual observed in the Papal Chapel under Martin V, for the commemoration of the faithful departed. The second vespers of the Saints being ended the Pope resumed his scarlet cope, the *camaurus* and the white mitre, and the cantors intoned the psalms of the vespers for the dead. This was followed by Matins. Both at the *Magnificat* and at the *Benedictus* of Lauds the Pope *accedit ad altare et thurificatur, et cophinum ubi stat Corpus Christi. Reverso vero ad cathedram suam, sibi soli et nulli alteri incensum datur*.[2] The Collect *Fidelium Deus* was chanted by the Pope, who ended the rite with a solemn benediction.

On the following day the Pope assisted at Mass, which was celebrated by one of the Cardinals. At the Gospel the usual candles were carried by the acolytes, but without the thurible, and at the Offertory, after the incensing of the altar, the Pope, too, was incensed. The compiler of the *Ordo* notes that it is no longer the custom for the Pope to celebrate solemnly the Mass for the dead, but only to do so in his private oratory.

Devotion to the suffering souls in Purgatory has developed considerably during the last centuries, as indeed may be said of Catholic piety in general. The Church is like a flourishing tree, which, as it continues to grow and to throw out branches, is covered with a profusion of leaves and flowers.

[1] *P.L.* LXXVIII, col. 1343.   [2] *P.L.* LXXVIII, col. 1346.

November 2

So it came about during the recent terrible war, when every town, not to say every family, mourned its dead, that Benedict XV extended to the entire Catholic Church a privilege granted by Benedict XIV centuries ago to the States which were at that time under the crown of Spain. This was the permission for every priest to celebrate three Masses for the faithful departed on November 2. It was not only the thought of the " useless slaughter " as he termed the war which prompted Benedict XV to grant this privilege.

The devotion of our ancestors had endowed churches, altars, and Chapters, in order that at their death Masses should be celebrated for the repose of their souls. The revolution and the confiscation of Church property had in many cases done away with such endowments, and because of the poverty of the clergy the Pope found himself obliged constantly to dispense Chapters, religious communities and priests from fulfilling these ancient obligations which could no longer be carried out.

Therefore Benedict XV, accustomed to the liturgical usage of Spain where he had spent some time in the suite of the Papal Nuncio, the late Cardinal Rampolla del Tindaro, granted to every priest the permission of celebrating three Masses on the day of the commemoration of the faithful departed. The following conditions were made. One of the Masses might be offered by the celebrant for a private intention, but the Pope desired that of the other two, one should be offered for the souls in Purgatory in general, and the other in satisfaction for an immense number of legacies left for Masses which could not be fulfilled because of the confiscations.

The celebration of these three Masses on November 2 constitutes a privilege in modern Church discipline which is not only rare but almost unique, and places the commemoration of the faithful departed on a level with Christmas Day. It is indeed the Christmas of the Holy Souls.

In medieval times, however, such a privilege was not so extraordinary, and we know that some saints and even some of the Roman Pontiffs celebrated more than one Mass a day, merely to satisfy their own devotion.

Purgatory represents the last supreme effort made by God's love to rescue the sinner and save him from the clutches of the devil. It may be compared to a temple erected to the sanctity of God where the avenging flames destroy everything in the creature, opposed to conformity with the divine beauty and perfections. *Estote perfecti, sicut et Pater vester caelestis perfectus est.* When the holy Scriptures speak of the flames which form the throne of God and surround him like the walls of his sanctuary, we see in this an image of Purgatory where our feeble virtue will be tested like gold in the furnace of that ineffable sanctity.

Again, when St Paul tells us that God dwells in inaccessible light, we must remember the poor souls in Purgatory, who with eyes still dim from the dust of this world, are too weak to be able to gaze like the eagle on that dazzling brightness. The same apostle warns us to choose carefully the material with which we build : gold, precious stones, wood or straw, for the fire of divine judgement will try it (1 Cor. iii, 13). Then the solid substance will remain, but the weak will be destroyed, and the foolish builder, if he desires to be saved, will be forced to escape through the flames, not without grave peril and suffering. The Apostle adds that he may indeed be saved but only through the fire.

In this comparison chosen by St Paul to explain the purity of the Gospel teaching to the Corinthians, Catholic exegetes have rightly seen an allusion to the dogma of Purgatory. According to the Apostle there are certain sins which, whilst they are not grave enough to close the gates of heaven to us, and to cast us into hell, must be atoned for either in this world or the next. The divine Judgement tries our moral actions as the fire tries the builders' material. If the house burns, the builder, seeing the flames, rushes from the building, escaping through the fire and thus suffers great loss and even wounds.

The suffering souls in Purgatory cannot even pray for mercy. God has created all things in order and everything has its proper time. The time for mercy has passed with this earthly life to give place to justice in eternity. When the building is on fire there can be no discussion or hesitation ; he who would save his life must face the flames in order to escape.

Purgatory is a temple, but one which has neither priest nor altar of propitiation. Happily, however, the Communion of Saints unites the Blessed in heaven, the wayfarers on earth, and the suffering souls in one mystical body, and the eucharistic Sacrifice by which Christ *una oblatione consummavit in sempiternum sanctificatos,* as it gives glory to the elect, also washes in the Blood of the Redemption the stains of those predestined members who are united to Christ by faith, hope, and charity.

The following three Masses only differ in the Lessons and the Collects as the Graduals and Antiphons are the same in all.

The First Mass

The antiquity of the Antiphon for the Introit is proved by the fact that it is inspired by a text from the apocryphal fourth Book of Esdras. The use of the Apocrypha in the Liturgy is rare, and cannot be later than the sixth century.

Ant. *Requiem aeternam dona eis Domine, et lux perpetua luceat eis.*

(IV Esdras ii, 34, 35). *Requiem aeternitatis dabit vobis . . . quia lux perpetua lucebit vobis.*

The first verse of Psalm lxiv follows: "A hymn, O Lord, becometh thee in Sion; and a vow shall be paid to thee in Jerusalem. hear my prayer; all flesh shall come to thee."

There is no *Gloria Patri* but the Antiphon is repeated immediately. The hymn which is becoming to God in Sion, and the vows paid in the temple of Jerusalem, are symbols of the life of glory in heaven, where in the light of the Beatific Vision all our supernatural aspirations will be fulfilled. It may be noted that some Antiphonaries give the following Antiphon for the Introit which is now only used at the burial service before the beginning of Mass.

Subvenite, Sancti Dei, succurrite, Angeli Domini, suscipientes animam eius, offerentes eam in conspectu Altissimi.

Psalm xxiv. *Anima eius in bonis demorabitur, et semen eius haereditet terram.*

Collect: "O God, the Creator and Redeemer of all the faithful, grant to the souls of thy servants departed the remission of all their sins; that through pious supplications they may obtain the pardon which they have always desired."

This very ancient Collect is a little masterpiece and contains a complete spiritual treatise. First, the motive is set forth why God is so good to us, and this is because he is our Creator. We are the work of his hands, and more than this, we are also the fruit of his Passion, the property bought or rather redeemed by his Blood.

Next, the Collect alludes to the Communion of Saints which unites the Church militant and suppliant to the Church suffering and expiating in Purgatory. Further, the special reason which draws down the divine mercy on the souls in Purgatory is—even more than our intercession—the hope they place in God. Both during life and in death they have hoped and trusted, not in their own justice, but in his mercy. As the Apostle says: *spes non confundit*, for God never denies us those things for which his grace has led us to hope.

The Lesson is taken from the first Epistle to the Corinthians (xv, 51–57), where St Paul writes of the destinies of the just who will survive the final persecution of Antichrist, and who by a special privilege will still be living at the moment of the *parousia*. The Apostle wishes to reveal a secret thing to the Corinthians. When, at the end of the world, Christ will return to judge the living and the dead, he tells them, we shall not all die, but all, even those who at the time of the *parousia* are still alive (*qui relinquimur, qui residui sumus*), shall be changed. This change, considered by some theologians to be a kind of death similar to that undergone by the Blessed Virgin, will take place in an instant: *in momento, in ictu oculi*. Christ's victory over death and sin will then be final and complete, when death is swallowed up in life, and the body becomes incorruptible and immortal like that of the prototype of the elect, Christ Jesus.

The Gradual in its first verse repeats the Antiphon of the Introit. R̷. *Requiem*. The second verse is taken from Psalm cxi: " The just shall be in everlasting remembrance; he shall not fear evil hearing."

That blessed destiny is not always fulfilled in this world, but will be made manifest at the judgement-seat where nothing will remain hidden and where the light of truth will penetrate our hearts. Then all our most secret deeds will be revealed before the whole world at the supreme tribunal of the human race.

The Tract follows, which, however, is usually omitted from the Sacramentaries as this votive Mass has a mournful character. The reader must remember that the Tract originally marked the Sunday Stations or those which were especially solemn, until the time when St Gregory instituted the alleluiatic chant on all the Sundays except those in Lent.

Tract: " Absolve, O Lord, the souls of the faithful departed from every bond of sins. ℣. And by the help of thy grace may they be enabled to escape the avenging judgement. ℣. And enjoy the happiness of everlasting life."

The Liturgy in this, as in many other prayers for the dead, refers to the supreme moment of the individual judgement of the soul, the moment in which its fate is decided for all eternity. The prayers of the Church follow the body to the grave, but God, with whom there is neither past nor future, has already beheld the mediation of the Church whose suffrage has a powerful influence on the divine judgement. Her prayers are those of a Spouse and a Mother, and the heart of the Father of all men cannot be deaf to them.

The sequence *Dies irae*, composed by the Minorite Thomas

of Celano, describes the Last Judgement in words which have Michelangelo's realistic colouring. By this we intend only to describe their style, for in the matter of derivation it was Michelangelo who, composing the terrible scene reproduced on the walls of the Sistine Chapel, was inspired by the vivid words of the medieval friar.

The painter has certainly borrowed from the Franciscan not only the apocalyptic elements of the picture, but also the dramatic intensity which distinguishes it, and that feeling of terrific force dominating almost all the figures, not excepting that of the Virgin Mother.

Originally this Sequence or *Dies Irae* was sung on the First Sunday in Advent in connection with the Gospel describing the end of the world and the universal judgement. Subsequently owing to the addition of the last two verses of intercession for the dead, it came to be inserted in the Masses *de requie*. In this place it should not be called a Sequence, as the Sequence was originally merely a composition in prose or in verse adapted to the extremely lengthy vocalization which followed the alleluia in medieval times. Instead of this simple vocalization, verses were set to the notes and were therefore described as *sequentia* or *acoluthia* in the Byzantine manner. It is plain that where there is no alleluiatic verse there cannot be a true Sequence.

We may consider, here, the religious psychology of medieval society at the time when Thomas of Celano composed his great hymn, and the gulf which lies between his muse and the calm and serene inspiration of the inscriptions in the catacombs, or the ancient vesper hymn *Jucundum lumen* of the Byzantine *Lucernarium*.

It might even be said that the $\Phi\hat{\omega}\varsigma\ \iota\lambda\alpha\rho\delta\nu$ and the *Dies Irae* mark the two extremes between the beginning and the end of Christian hymnody. Eleven centuries have passed between the two. The dogmas are unaltered, but a great change has come over the spirit of the masses who profess them in the thirteenth century. The vesper hymn is the song of serene light, *jucundum lumen*, of joy, of the life of union with God, proper to the first centuries of Christianity, the centuries of sacrifice and martyrdom. Whereas the *Dies Irae* betrays the remorse of a generation steeped in fratricidal wars and disputes between those " che un muro ed una fossa serra ; "[1] a century of indifference and forgetfulness of God. The *jucundum lumen* is joyous because it is full of love ; the *Dies Irae* is sad and fearful because the generation which dictated it knew the pangs of a guilty conscience.

[1] *Purgatorio* VI.

Sequentia.

Dies irae, dies illa,
Solvet saeclum in favilla:
Teste David cum Sibylla.

Quantus tremor est futurus,
Quando judex est venturus,
Cuncta stricte discussurus!

Tuba mirum spargens sonum
Per sepulcra regionum,
Coget omnes ante thronum.

Mors stupebit et natura,
Cum resurget creatura,
Judicanti responsura.

Liber scriptus proferetur,
In quo totum continetur,
Unde mundus judicetur.

Judex ergo cum sedebit,
Quidquid latet, apparebit:
Nil inultum remanebit.

Quid sum miser tunc dicturus?
Quem patronum rogaturus,
Cum vix justus sit securus?

Rex tremendae majestatis,
Qui salvandos salvas gratis,
Salva me, fons pietatis.

Recordare, Jesu pie,
Quod sum causa tuae viae:
Ne me perdas illa die.

Quaerens me, sedisti lassus:
Redemisti crucem passus:
Tantus labor non sit cassus.

Juste judex ultionis,
Donum fac remissionis
Ante diem rationis.

Ingemisco, tamquam reus:
Culpa rubet vultus meus:
Supplicanti parce, Deus.

Qui Mariam absolvisti,
Et latronem exaudisti,
Mihi quoque spem dedisti.

Sequence.

Nigher still, and still more nigh
Draws the day of prophecy,
Doomed to melt the earth and sky.

Oh, what trembling there shall be,
When the world its Judge shall see,
Coming in dread majesty!

Hark! the trump, with thrilling tone,
From sepulchral regions lone,
Summons all before the throne.

Time and death it doth appal
To see the buried ages all
Rise to answer at the call.

Now the books are open spread;
Now the writing must be read,
Which condemns the quick and dead.

Now, before the Judge severe,
Hidden things must all appear;
Nought can pass unpunished here.

What shall guilty I then plead?
Who for me will intercede,
When the saints shall comfort need?

King of dreadful majesty,
Who dost freely justify,
Fount of pity, save thou me!

Recollect, O Love divine,
'Twas for this lost sheep of thine
Thou thy glory didst resign:

Satest wearied seeking me:
Sufferedst upon the tree:
Let not vain thy labour be.

Judge of justice, hear my prayer;
Spare me, Lord, in mercy spare;
Ere the reckoning-day appear.

Lo, thy gracious face I seek;
Shame and grief are on my cheek;
Sighs and tears my sorrow speak.

Thou didst Mary's guilt forgive;
Didst the dying thief receive;
Hence doth hope within me live.

November 2

Preces meae non sunt dignae :	Worthless are my prayers, I know :
Sed tu bonus fac benigne,	Yet, oh cause me not to go
Ne perenni cremer igne.	Into everlasting woe.
Inter oves locum praesta,	Severed from the guilty band,
Et ab haedis me sequestra,	Make me with thy sheep to stand,
Statuens in parte dextra.	Placing me on thy right hand.
Confutatis maledictis,	When the cursed in anguish flee
Flammis acribus addictis :	Into flames of misery ;
Voca me cum benedictis.	With the blest then call thou me.
Oro supplex, et acclinis,	Suppliant in the dust I lie ;
Cor contritum quasi cinis :	My heart a cinder, crushed and dry;
Gere curam mei finis.	Help me, Lord, when death is nigh.
Lacrymosa dies illa,	Full of tears and full of dread
Qua resurget ex favilla	Is the day that wakes the dead,
Judicandus homo reus.	Calling all with solemn blast
Huic ergo parce, Deus :	From the ashes of the past.
Pie Jesu Domine,	Lord of mercy, Jesu blest,
Dona eis requiem. Amen.	Grant the faithful light and rest. Amen.

It may be said of to-day's Gospel (John v, 25-29) that it contains the very text of the " good news " of the *mysterium* referred to above by St Paul in his beautiful letter to the Corinthians.

Christ is the new Adam, and the human race is his inheritance. As God, he has one and the same divine nature as the Father, and therefore his saving mission is to vivify, to uphold, and to judge. Through him God has willed to repair the ruins caused by sin ; this is the reason of the glorious resurrection of the just according to their prototype Jesus Christ. The wicked, indeed, will also rise again to appear before the judgement-seat, but the eternal life of punishment will be worse than death, and therefore Scripture speaks of it as *mors secunda*. Their reprobation does not detract from the glory of Christ, for by their own wilful secession they no longer belong to him. The integrity of the mystical body of the Saviour is complete without them, for they are in no way a part of it now.

To-day the Offertory with the repeated hemistich has kept the ancient musical character of the antiphonic chant. The Offertory should really be a psalmodic hymn and not a *prex* as is the *Domine Jesu Christe* described in the Missal to-day. But we must remember that the entire Mass *pro defunctis* is a compilation made in later times from older elements contained in various Sacramentaries.

In some Antiphonaries, indeed, Psalm l (*Miserere*) is

assigned to the Offertory for the Dead; or the beautiful Antiphon *Dextera Domini* from Psalm cxvii, which occurs in the Missal on the Third Sunday after the Epiphany.

The following Offertory was also used. R̟. *Erue, Domine, animas eorum ab omni vinculo delictorum, ut in resurrectionis gloria inter Sanctos tuos resuscitari mereantur.* ℣. *Tuam, Deus, piissime Pater, deposcimus pietatem, ut eis tribuere digneris placidas et quietas mansiones.*

The Offertory given in to-day's Missal attributing the office of *signifer* to St Michael is certainly of the early Middle Ages. The dignity of *psychopompus* given to St Michael is paralleled in many documents of early Christian literature where he is called simply *Praepositus paradyso, princeps Angelorum*, and is represented weighing the merits of the dead in the balance before introducing them into the Heavenly Kingdom.

In the Arabian History of St Joseph the carpenter, the Saint prays thus: " If my life, O Lord, is at an end; if the moment has come for me to go forth from this world, send unto me Michael the Prince of thine Angels. May he remain beside me that my poor soul may go out of this suffering body in peace, without pain or fear." This apocryphal book is certainly earlier than the fourth century.

In the Gelasian Sacramentary, too, we find the following prayer for the Dead: . . . *suscipe, Domine, animam servi tui . . . revertentem ad te. Adsit et Angelus Testamenti tui, Michael.*

Offertory.

O Lord Jesus Christ, king of glory, deliver the souls of all the faithful departed from the pains of hell and from the deep pit: deliver them from the lion's mouth, that hell may not swallow them up and they may not fall into darkness, but may the holy standard-bearer Michael lead them into the holy light; which thou didst promise to Abraham and to his seed of old.

℣. We offer to thee, O Lord, sacrifices and prayers; do thou receive them on behalf of those souls whom we commemorate this day. Grant them, O Lord, to pass from death to that life; which thou didst promise to Abraham and to his seed of old.

Libera eam, Domine, de principibus tenebrarum et de locis poenarum . . .

. . . Adsit Angelus testamenti tui Michael . . . Maneatque in mansionibus Sanctorum, et in luce sancta, quam olim Abrahae promisisti et semini eius.

(*Sacramen. Gelas.— Orat. post obit. hominis.*)

· This is the ancient Collect which precedes the Anaphora of the Consecration: " Mercifully look down on this sacrifice which we offer to thee for the souls of thy servants, O Lord, we beseech thee; that to those to whom thou didst grant the merit of Christian faith, thou mayest also grant its reward."

The Liturgy of the Dead dwells persistently upon the merit of the Catholic Faith, as though the Church desired that after death it should cover the misery of weak humanity like a veil in pity laid over it.

The reason of this is that the Catholic Faith professed and practised is the true means of drawing near to God, and together with charity and grace is the source of every supernatural merit we may possess, according to the words of St Paul: *Accendentem ad Deum oportet credere.*

The Preface for the Dead was inserted in the Roman Missal by Benedict XV. It is, however, a fine adaptation of an ancient Preface in use in some of the Gallican Churches: *Vere dignum . . . per Christum Dominum nostrum. In quo nobis spes beatae resurrectionis effulsit, ut quos contristat certa moriendi conditio, eosdem consoletur futurae immortalitatis promissio. Tuis enim fidelibus, Domine, vita mutatur, non tollitur, et dissoluta terrestris huius incolatus domo, aeterna in caelis habitatio comparatur, per Christum. Et ideo cum Angelis,* etc.

This ancient liturgical composition is a gem, and puts the funeral inscriptions sometimes seen in modern cemeteries to shame. Where human nature is tempted to draw a sorrowful picture of death and grief, the Church rises to sublime contemplation of resurrection and true life. *Vita mutatur, non tollitur.* Why should we mourn when those who have left us have suffered no loss but have rather gained all? Instead of earthly life they have gained eternal life; they have exchanged a house of earth for a heavenly mansion; in place of the world they have found God. Because of this the early Christians avoided the word *mortuus* in their inscriptions, and instead made use of the expressions *dormit, depositus, defunctus.* To this day the Greeks intone the *Alleluia* at their funerals, and during Easter week they make use at the burials which may occur at that time, of the Office of the Resurrection of Christ.

The Antiphon for the Communion in some Sacramentaries is taken from the Gospel of St John (xi, 25-26): *Ego sum resurrectio et vita, dicit Dominus. Qui credit in me, etiam si mortuus, vivet.*

In to-day's Missal, however, the Communion is taken from a responsory which bears a slight resemblance to that of Esdras quoted above: " May light eternal shine upon them, O Lord. With thy saints for ever, because thou art merciful.

℞. Eternal rest give to them, O Lord, and let perpetual light shine upon them. With thy saints for ever, because thou art merciful."

Post-Communion: "We beseech thee, O Lord, that the prayer of thy suppliants may benefit the souls of thy servants; that thou mayest deliver them from all their sins, and make them partakers of thy redemption."

The sacrament of Redemption produces in us conformity with Christ, our mystical head. This likeness is prepared here by grace, but it is in the light of glory that the effect of the eucharistic Sacrifice, foreshadowed during our mortal pilgrimage, attains its complete fulfilment.

In the second and third Mass the Antiphons and Graduals are the same as in the preceding one. Only the Lessons are proper to the day and are taken from the collection of Masses *pro defunctis*.

THE SECOND MASS

Collect: "O God, the Lord of mercies, grant to the souls of thy servants a place of refreshment, rest, and happiness, and the glory of thy light."

The word *refrigerium* was used by the ancients to describe both the funeral Agape celebrated in memory of the deceased, and the heavenly banquet which Jesus promised in the Gospel to the faithful servant: *Faciet illos discumbere, et transiens ministrabit illis.* (Luke xii, 37.)

The Epistle and Gospel are taken from the Mass *in anniversario defunctorum*.

The former is derived from the Book of Machabees (xii, 43-46), and tells of the collection made by Judas after the battle for a sacrifice to be offered at Jerusalem for the souls of the slain. The sacred writer calls this a holy and wholesome thought and a token of faith in the future resurrection. If this resurrection had not been promised, it would indeed have been useless to take thought for the fate of the dead.

This text is important, for it confirms the Catholic dogma of Purgatory and the ancient and universal practice of the Church of offering the divine Sacrifice in suffrage for the departed souls, together with prayers and alms.

In connection with this subject we may quote here a beautiful inscription from the Cemetery of Priscilla, possibly dating from the third century.

EVCHARIS · EST · MATER · PIVS · ET · PATER · EST
VOS · PRECOR · O · FRATRES · ORARE · HVC · QVANDO · VEN(itis)
ET · PRECIBVS · TOTIS · PATREM · NATVMQVE · ROGATIS
SIT · VESTRAE · MENTIS · AGAPES · CARAE · MEMINISSE
VT · DEVS · OMNIPOTENS · AGAPEN · IN · SAECVLA · SERVET

November 2

"My Mother is Eucharis and my dear Father is . . .
I beg you, O my brothers, when you come here to pray
And when together you intercede with the Father and the Son
Let it be your care to remember the dear Agape
That the omnipotent Lord may preserve Agape in eternity."

In this beautiful inscription it is interesting to note especially those sentences which concern the ancient liturgical assemblies: *orare huc quando venitis, et precibus totis Patrem Natumque rogatis*, as well as the desire of the departed that the faithful assembled in the Cemetery of Priscilla should pray for the beloved Agape.

The Gospel is taken from St John (vi, 37–40). It is the will of the Father from whom we receive Jesus Christ, that he should give to us that which he himself possesses: light, life, salvation and resurrection. Christ is, then, himself the measure of the marvellous promise which the Lord has made us: *ut digni efficiamur promissionibus Christi*.

Secret: "Be favourable, O Lord, to our humble prayers on behalf of the souls of thy servants for whom we offer up to thee a sacrifice of praise, that thou mayest vouchsafe to grant them fellowship with thy saints."

The Mass is called, both here and in the Canon, *Sacrificium laudis*, because it contains the precise adoration and thanksgiving which Christ renders to his Father for us: *gratias agens*.

Post-Communion: "Grant, we beseech thee, O Lord, that the souls of thy servants, purified by this sacrifice, may obtain pardon and everlasting rest."

This is how *legem credendi lex statuat supplicandi*, according to the words of Pope Celestine I, and why the venerable formulae of the ancient Collects assert that the eucharistic Sacrifice has a satisfactory and propitiatory value for the Dead.

This has ever been the belief and practice of the Church, a belief reflected in a text of the apocryphal *Actus Johannis* which date from the second century. Here the Apostle goes with Andronicus to the sepulchre of Drusiana on the third day after her death, ὅπως ἄρτον κλάσωμεν ἐκεῖ.[1]

THE THIRD MASS

This Mass is like the first, with the exception of the Lessons and Collects. The former are taken from the *Missa quotidiana pro defunctis* and the prayers from those *pro defunctis fratribus, propinquis et benefactoribus*, which are also used in the Common Mass for the dead.

Collect: "O God, who grantest forgiveness and desirest

---

[1] *Act. Johannis* 72. Bonnet, p. 186.

the salvation of mankind, we beseech thee in thy mercy to grant that the brethren of our congregation with their kinsfolk and benefactors who have passed out of this life, by the intercession of blessed Mary ever a virgin and of all thy saints, may partake of everlasting bliss."

The Lesson is taken from the Apocalypse (xiv, 13). The Seer of Patmos is ordered to write: "Blessed are the dead who die in the Lord." They are blessed because like men who have worked untiringly in the Lord's vineyard, they have not ceased from labour until the Spirit said: Come. Then they left the world, naked, as Job says, abandoning their houses, lands, and goods. They take with them only one possession, their good deeds.

We may draw two practical considerations from this passage of Scripture. First, we should labour here unceasingly, for no man has the right to judge that he has done enough until the Holy Spirit calls to him at the hour of death. Secondly, we should prepare for our journey towards eternity by laying up a store of the only possessions which we shall be allowed to take with us: a great number of good works.

The Gospel is also taken from St John (vi, 51, 52). It is part of the beautiful discourse on the Eucharist pronounced by Jesus in the Synagogue at Capharnaum.

As all things were created in the beginning by the Word of God, so it is by him, too, that man receives life and is directed to his last end, the beatitude of heaven. Christ is the bread of divine life come down from heaven. He who eats this bread, who is made one with him in the sacraments and lives in him by Faith *quae per dilectionem operatur*, possesses the true life, and even in this world receives and keeps in his heart the seed of life everlasting.

The early belief of the Catholic Church concerning the doctrine of Purgatory is described with great simplicity in the *Acta* of the martyrs Perpetua and Felicitas.

Perpetua was praying, and happened to name her little brother Dinocrates who had died a short time before at the age of seven, of an ulcer in his face. The same night she saw Dinocrates in a vision coming out of a dark place, pale and sad, and suffering from thirst. There seemed to be a wide space between Perpetua and the child, so that it was impossible for them to reach one another. The saint, however, saw Dinocrates make a great effort to drink from a vessel full of water which stood beside him, but the brim was higher than the boy's stature and he could not reach it. Perpetua then understood that the soul of the child was still suffering in Purgatory, and began to pray for him with tears, night and day. *Et experrecta sum, et cognovi fratrem meum laborare . . .*

et feci pro illo orationem die et nocte, et lacrymans ut mihi donaretur.

Later the martyr and her companions were transferred from the proconsular prisons to those contiguous to the amphitheatre where they were to be exposed to the wild beasts. One day when the fearless heroine had been suffering for many hours in the stocks or *nervus*, she had another vision. This time she saw Dinocrates with a cheerful countenance and the wound in his face healed, leaving only a scar. He was clad in festal garments, and when he approached the fountain, she saw with joy that it only reached to his chest and he was able easily to drink the water. Perpetua observed a small phial of gold, also full of water, standing beside the fountain. The child drank eagerly and then ran away to play, after the manner of children. His sister understood that this dream was symbolical, and that Dinocrates had at last attained the possession of God, and slaked his thirst in the beatific vision of the uncreated Essence.

Video . . . et Dinocratem mundo corpore, bene vestitum, refrigerantem . . . Tunc intellexi translatum esse de poena.

When we reflect that this vision concerned the fate of a child of only seven years, we realize how mysterious are the judgements of God, and how pure a soul must be before it can be admitted to his presence.

THE LITURGY AT THE GRAVESIDE IN CHRISTIAN ANTIQUITY

In the early Sacramentaries the various Collects *pro defunctis* are all grouped together. We shall preserve this liturgical tradition, and shall describe here a few out of a great number of Masses and Collects for the Dead still contained in the Missal.

From the earliest times, our Mother the Church accompanied her children to the grave with liturgical rites, which soon became traditional. We have already spoken of these in the first volume of this work, and it will suffice if we repeat that the Liturgy did not destroy but elevated and sanctified the funeral traditions and classical customs of the Greeks and Romans, who were used to surround their dead with such poetical demonstrations of piety and affection.

The deceased having been buried outside the city, but not so far as to prevent his friends from frequently visiting the grave, the burial service was followed in ancient times by nine days of mourning known, therefore, as *novemdialia*. The third and the ninth of these days were the most solemn, for then the relatives celebrated the funeral banquet and sacrifice at the tomb. But throughout the year, the *parentalia*—a kind of annual commemoration of all the dead—the *rosalia*, the *dies violationis*, the birthday, etc., were all occasions when the relations assembled round the tomb of their dear one, and scattered flowers, perfumes, aromatic herbs upon it, mingled with their tears.

It is significant that whilst the pagans celebrated as the chief anniversary the *dies natalis*, or birthday of the dead, the Christians always meant by the *dies natalis* the day of death, or rather the birth of the faithful to eternal life.

According to the *Apostolic Constitutions*, the third, ninth, and fortieth day after the decease were celebrated with liturgical rites. St Ambrose mentions this tradition, but the great Doctor of Milan knew, too, that another existed by which the third and the thirtieth day instead of the seventh and the fortieth were observed: *Alii tertium diem et trigesimum, alii septimum et quadragesimum observare consueverunt.*[1]

It appears, indeed, that at Milan the offices of the seventh day were commonly celebrated during the lifetime of St Ambrose: *die septimo ad sepulchrum redimus, qui dies symbolum quietis futurae est.*[2] Whereas at Hippo, St Augustine did not tolerate even the *novemdialia*, because he considered that they savoured of paganism.[3] *Nescio utrum inveniatur alicui Sanctorum in Scripturis celebratum esse luctum novem dies, quod apud Latinos novemdial appellant. Unde mihi videntur ab hac consuetudine prohibendi, si qui Christianorum istum in mortuis servant, qui magis est in Gentilium consuetudine.*

Although these frequent pilgrimages to the grave, the *psalmi ex Christiana traditione*, mentioned by St Jerome on the occasion of the burial of St Paul the Hermit, the funeral Agape, the libations of perfumes, the *rosalia* and *violationes* were a suggestive part of early Christian observances, yet the central rite of the Liturgy for the dead was the eucharistic Sacrifice. It was to the holy Sacrifice only that the thoughts of St Monica turned when she was dying at Ostia, and her sons lamented that her remains should lie in that foreign soil and not in her own native Africa: *Ponite, inquit, hoc corpus ubicumque; nihil vos eius cura conturbet. Tantum illud vos rogo, ut ad Domini altare memineritis mei, ibi ubi fueritis.*[4]

Augustine tells us that after the death of his saintly mother there was offered *pro ea sacrificium pretii nostri iam iuxta*

---

[1] *De obitu Theodosii*, 3. P.L. XVI, col. 1386.
[2] *De Fide resurrect.*, I. P.L. XVI, col. 1315.
[3] *Quaest. in Heptateuchum*, I, 172. P.L. XXXIV, col. 596.
[4] *Confessiones*, Lib. IX, cap. xi.

sepulchrum posito cadavere, priusquam deponeretur, sicut illic fieri solet.[1] And the saint concludes this memorial of his Mother with the wish that the Lord might inspire those who read it *quotquot haec legerint, meminerint ad altare tuum Monicae, famulae tuae.*[2]

In spite of the doubts felt by some of the Fathers of the Church, the tradition concerning the offices on the day of burial and on the third, seventh, and thirtieth day, as well as on the anniversary, were preserved by the Liturgy, and the Missal still contains the venerable forms of prayer used on these occasions.

We must repeat with regard to the dead of all classes what we said in another volume about the martyrs—that the funeral liturgy always took place at the graveside. The dead were prayed for at every Mass, but the commemoration on the days specified above would have had no meaning in the eyes of the early Christians if the rites then used had been performed elsewhere. So true is this, that, when it was impossible to bury the dead in the case of death occurring at sea or in a fire, the Romans were in the habit of erecting a cenotaph to represent the tomb, of such importance in their eyes was the custom of visiting the grave of their beloved dead: *die septimo ad sepulchrum redimus*, as St Ambrose attests. They loved, too, to pour perfumes and flowers on the tomb, to celebrate the holy Sacrifice beside it, and to hold there the funeral banquet, for by these observances the living could almost imagine that the dead had returned to share with them the good things of this world. Nor was this merely an illusion to the early Christians, for at the Agape which they celebrated, the beloved dead and Christ himself were almost always present as guests in the person of the poor and needy.

Holy Mass for the Day of Death and Burial of the Departed.

The eucharistic Sacrifice is the *sacrificium pro dormitione* mentioned by St Cyprian. It was celebrated at Rome from the third century upon the tomb of the departed, and in the days of St Augustine was still offered at Ostia *iam iuxta sepulchrum posito cadavere, priusquam deponeretur, sicut illic fieri solet.*

According to the Confessions, this would appear to have been a special custom of the Church at Ostia, where the cemeteries, instead of being underground, were *sub divo* as in Africa. If they preferred to leave the body unburied *iuxta*

---

[1] *Op. cit.*, Lib. IX, cap. xii.
[2] *Op. cit.*, Lib. IX, cap. xiii.

sepulchrum during the Mass, it is evident that it was not celebrated in church but in the cemetery *sub divo*. Therefore Ostia had preserved the ancient Roman custom, forbidden in the city by Pope Felix I, or rather restricted to the burial of martyrs only, on whose tombs, but on no others, it was allowed thenceforth to celebrate Holy Mass.

The Antiphons, Graduals, and the Sequence of this, as of the following Masses *pro defunctis*, are the same as on November 2. The sung portions are alike in all, and only the Epistle, Gospel and Collects are proper to the day.

Collect: "O God, whose property is ever to have mercy and to spare, we humbly beseech thee on behalf of the soul of thy servant N., whom thou hast this day called out of this world, that thou wouldst not deliver him (*or* her) into the hands of the enemy, nor forget him for ever, but command the holy angels to take him and lead him to the home of paradise, that forasmuch as in thee he put his hope and trust, he may not endure the pains of hell, but may come to the possession of eternal joys."

The phrase *ne obliviscaris in finem* is taken from Psalm lxxiii, and it signifies God's final abandonment of the wicked when they have left this world. During this life it seems sometimes as though God had abandoned the good as well as the wicked. It may appear so to us, but in reality he only withholds his consolations from the just and exposes them to trials in order to try their virtue and to encourage them to fight on with the sole help of his grace. *Sufficit tibi gratia mea, nam virtus in infirmitate perficitur.* As to the wicked, God does not refuse even to them the graces necessary to salvation. If, in his secret judgements, he does not always give them greater graces, it is because they have not deserved them, or they would not profit by them. It is not fitting to cast pearls before swine.

The Epistle is taken from 1 Thessalonians (iv, 13-18) in which St Paul exhorts the Christians not to mourn for the dead as the pagans do *qui spem non habent*. Christ sanctified Christian life. Therefore as we unite our agony with his in order that it may be sanctified and rendered meritorious, so, too, one day we shall share with him in the joy of resurrection.

St Paul then proceeds to answer a question which his disciples had asked him. Those who will be living at the last day will have no advantage over the faithful who have preceded them, for at the sound of the trump those who are "dead in Christ" will rise first. Then, says the apostle, we too who remain, the living—οἱ ζῶντες, οἱ περιλειπόμενοι—will be raised up to meet Christ and to be with him for ever.

According to St Paul, therefore, the spirit which should be dominant at a Christian burial is the spirit of joyful hope and of resigned expectancy, entirely opposed to the grief of pagans who mourn and give away to despair because death, in their eyes, puts an end to all hope.

The Gospel is taken from St John (xi, 21–27). Martha laments that Jesus was not with them when Lazarus fell ill, for had the Lord been there, her brother would not have died. Jesus comforts her with the promise of the resurrection. Then, since this hope seems too far off to the sister's affection, he prepares her for the miracle he is about to work by raising her thoughts to the more sublime conception of his saving mission. He is the resurrection and the life ; the resurrection of the body and the life of the soul. In him is life, and those who are united to him by faith participate in this supernatural and everlasting life of the spirit, though in this world their bodies must undergo the universal law of death " from which no man may escape " as St Francis sings.

Secret : " Be merciful, O Lord, we beseech thee, to the soul of thy servant N., for which we offer up to thee the sacrifice of praise, humbly beseeching thy majesty that, by these holy peace-offerings, it may be found worthy to win everlasting rest."

We should note the phrase *piae placationis officia*, which describes the funeral rite and the object for which it is offered. The sanctity of God is offended by human sin. The dead can no longer make atonement, therefore it is to the Church, the sinners' mother, that the Lord, beholding her weeping, says as he once said to the widow of Naim : *Noli flere : Adolescens . . . surge.*

The Gelasian Sacramentary contains this beautiful Preface for the departed : *Vere dignum . . . per Christum Dominum nostrum. Per quem salus mundi, per quem vita omnium, per quem resurrectio mortuorum. Per ipsum te, Domine, suppliciter deprecamur, ut anima famuli tui N. cuius diem . . . celebramus, indulgentiam largiri perpetuam digneris, atque contagiis mortalitatis exutam, in aeternae salvationis partem restituas cum Angelis et Archangelis,* etc. . . .

The ancient Sacramentaries contain, as a rule, the prayer *infra actionem* in the Masses *pro defunctis* with a memento of the dead. The following are examples of this :

For the Pope. Infra actionem. *Hanc igitur oblationem servitutis nostrae, quam tibi offerimus pro anima famuli tui N. episcopi, quaesumus, Domine, placatus accipias ; et cum praesulibus Apostolicae dignitatis, quorum est secutus officium, habere tribuas sempiternae beatitudinis portionem. Diesque nostros,* etc . . .

For all the Faithful Departed. Infra actionem. Hanc igitur oblationem servitutis nostrae, quam tibi pro requie et animabus famulorum famularumque tuarum offerimus; quaesumus, Domine, propitius intuere; et concede ut et mortuis prosit ad veniam, quod cunctis viventibus preparare dignatus es ad medelam.

The ancient Roman Liturgy was varied and rich in the extreme. It was greatly reduced by the copyists of the later Middle Ages, who, in order to save sheets of parchment, merely transcribed those formulae which were more generally used at the time.

Post-Communion: "Grant, we beseech thee, almighty God, that the soul of thy servant N., which has this day departed out of this world, may be cleaned by this sacrifice, and delivered from sins, may receive forgiveness and everlasting rest."

The beatific life is also called eternal rest, not in the ordinary sense of the *Sheol* of the Jews, as though the activities of the soul ceased after death, but because the labours of this life being ended, the soul aspires and unites itself to God, without any effort but with incomprehensible joy.

The Commemoration of the Departed on the Third, Seventh, and Thirtieth day after Burial.

On the third, seventh, and thirtieth day the Mass is the same as on the day of death, except the Collects.

Collect: "We beseech thee, O Lord, that thou wouldst vouchsafe to grant fellowship with thy saints and elect to the soul of thy servant N., whose burial three (*or* seven *or* thirty) days since we commemorate, and wouldst pour upon it the everlasting dew of thy mercy."

We may note that in all these Collects the Church prays for peace and light not simply for John, Thomas, etc., but for the soul of God's servant N., and for this there is a good reason.

Man, the *servus* of God, consists of body and soul and, as Tertullian would add, of the Holy Ghost. Now, the soul we pray for is in an unnatural state of separation from the body of which it is the form. The Liturgy therefore no longer speaks of it, as when in life, as John or Thomas, etc., but with a philosophic distinction as the soul of thy servant John, etc.

Secret: "Look down favourably, we beseech thee, O Lord, upon the offerings we make on behalf of the soul of thy servant N.; that, being cleansed by heavenly remedies, it may rest in thy mercy."

This expression *remedium celeste* used to describe the holy Eucharist offered for the dead, is a very beautiful one.

November 2

Post-Communion: "Receive our prayers, O Lord, on behalf of the soul of thy servant N., that, if it is still soiled by any earthly stains, they may be wiped out by thy merciful forgiveness."

In this Liturgy for the dead we see the Church like a loving mother excusing the sins of her sons before the tribunal of God. Here she attributes their stains to the contagion pervading the world: lately in the burial service she asserted that during their life they had borne upon them the seal of the Blessed Trinity. In the *Commendatio animae* she attributed their sins to the *furor sive fervor mali desiderii*, and pleaded that *licet enim peccaverit, Patrem et Filium et Spiritum Sanctum non negavit*. The Saints are always ready to palliate and excuse the faults of their neighbours, and the spirit of the Church is not a spirit of harshness but of tenderness and mercy, in which she imitates the example of Jesus, who is meek and humble of heart.

On the Anniversary of the Departed.

This may be considered as a Christian equivalent to the classical γενέσια when as Tertullian declares: *Oblationes pro defunctis, pro nataliciis, annua die facimus*.[1]

This commemoration, according to St Ambrose, had a certain festive and solemn character: *nos quoque ipsi natales dies defunctorum obliviscimur, et cum obierunt, diem celebri solemnitate veneramur*.[2]

Indeed, in the case of the martyrs and holy bishops these *natalitia* and *depositiones* furnished the rudiments of the ancient Martyrologies. Besides the lists of Saints observed by the Liturgy, however, every Church or Abbey in the Middle Ages had its own *liber obituarius*; and day by day at the Office of Prime commemoration was made of the dead, whose γενέσια occurred on that day, as is still the custom in Benedictine monasteries.

The Mass *anniversario defunctorum* has been adopted as the second Mass on November 2. To the Collects, however, should be added the words excised on that occasion, "whose anniversary we are keeping."

Daily Masses for the Dead.

There remains a third category of *Missae defunctorum*, which includes those not connected with any of the occasions we have described, but which at a later date, during the Middle Ages, came to be celebrated either daily, or at certain

---

[1] *De Corona* III, Oehler, Vol. I, 422.
[2] *De Fide resurrect*. V. P.L. XVI, col. 1516.

periods of the month, according to the devotion of the priest. These Masses were very common in Benedictine monasteries, where the monks daily offered the holy Sacrifice and recited psalms for the repose of the faithful departed. The rubrics have now limited the celebration of these Masses for the Dead to certain days when the Divine Office has a less solemn character.

The Mass is that indicated above as the third Mass on November 2. Instead of one Collect, however, it has three, as in all Masses of lower rank than a double. The first prayer is for the higher orders of the hierarchy, as those who are most severely judged because they have to render an account to God of their flock as well as their own souls; the second, characteristic of medieval monasteries, is for the defunct brethren, parents and benefactors; lastly, the third is for all the faithful departed.

Collect: (a) For Bishops and Priests deceased.

This Collect is found in the Gelasian Sacramentary, but as the *Sacerdos* and *Apostolicus* refers to the Pope, it is probable that this prayer was intended originally only for the Roman Pontiffs.

" O God, who didst raise thy servants to the dignity of bishops or priests in the apostolic priesthood; grant, we beseech thee, that they may be joined in fellowship with thine apostles for evermore."

When in later times the titles of *sacerdos apostolicus* or of *domnus apostolicus*, or simply of *Apostolicus*, originally reserved to the Pope, were no longer understood, and this Collect was used for bishops and priests, another prayer was composed for the supreme Pontiff which is more modern in its wording: *Deus qui inter summos Sacerdotes famulum tuum N.N. ineffabili tua dispositione connumerare voluisti; praesta quaesumus: ut qui Unigeniti tui vices in terris gerebat, sanctorum tuorum Pontificum consortio perpetuo aggregetur.*

Collect: (b, c) The second Collect which is read in the common Masses for the Dead is the same as in the third Mass on November 2, whilst the third Collect is taken from the first Mass of the Commemoration of all the faithful departed.

Secret: For Bishops and Priests.

" Receive, O Lord, we beseech thee, the sacrifice which we offer up on behalf of the souls of thy servants who are bishops or priests; so that those whom in this world thou didst raise to episcopal or priestly rank may, by thy command, be gathered to thy saints in the kingdom of heaven."

Post-Communion: For Bishops and Priests.

" We beseech thee, O Lord, that thy clemency, which we implore, may benefit the souls of thy servants who are bishops

November 2

or priests; that by thy mercy they may partake of that in which they hoped and believed."

Another Mass for the Anniversary of the Departed.

The Missal *defunctorum* has a large collection of prayers for the dead. We shall only quote a few examples of these.

For a man deceased: "Incline thine ear, O Lord, to our prayers, in which we humbly entreat thy mercy; bring to the country of peace and light the soul of thy servant, which thou hast summoned to go forth from this world, and bid him to be numbered with thy saints."

Secret: "Hear us, O Lord, we beseech thee, and let the soul of thy servant profit by this sacrifice, by the offering of which thou didst grant that the sins of the whole world should be loosed."

Post-Communion: "Absolve, O Lord, we beseech thee, the soul of thy servant from every bond of sin, that he may be raised up in the glory of the resurrection and live amongst thy saints and elect."

This Collect may be regarded as intended to correct the error of the schismatic Greeks who hold that the saints do not enjoy the beatific vision until the day of Judgement. The Church prays, it is true, that the deceased may receive *resurrectionis gloria*, but she does not deny that this commences immediately after death with the beatific vision enjoyed by the soul alone, until the body is united to it at the final resurrection.

For the Parents of the Celebrant.

Collect: "O God, who hast commanded us to honour our father and mother; in thy lovingkindness have mercy on the souls of my father and mother, and forgive them their sins; and bring me to see them in the joy of eternal brightness."

Secret: "Receive, O Lord, we beseech thee, the sacrifice which I offer up to thee on behalf of the souls of my father and mother; grant them everlasting joy in the land of the living, and in company with them let me share in the happiness of the saints."

Post-Communion: "We beseech thee, O Lord, that this heavenly sacrament, of which we have partaken, may win rest and light everlasting for the souls of my father and mother, and by means of it may I be crowned with them by thy grace for evermore."

This filial devotion reflected in the Roman Liturgy is beautifully expressed by St Augustine in his "Confessions."

He prayed every day and solicited the prayers of others for his deceased parents: *meminerint ad altare tuum Monicae famulae tuae cum Patricio quondam eius coniuge, per quorum carnem introduxisti me in hanc vitam.*[1] In this he resembled St Peter Damian who, when a boy and in great poverty, happened once to find a coin, and instead of using it to buy bread, took it to a priest and begged him to say a Mass for his parents.

For all the Departed lying in a Cemetery.

From the earliest times the faithful sought to bury their dead beside some renowned martyr or in a famous sanctuary, and cherished the hope that this vicinity would benefit the soul of the deceased.

In the Middle Ages when the Benedictine Abbeys enjoyed a great reputation for sanctity, it was regarded as a privilege among the nobles to be allowed to possess a tomb in the shadow of one of the great monastic basilicas, and so to obtain a share in the prayers of the monks.

These tombs were generally in the *claustrum*, the *capitulum* or the *narthex*, and the monks when they passed before them after Prime, were in the habit of singing the *De Profundis*, as is still the custom in Benedictine monasteries.

The following Collects are found in the Gelasian Sacramentary under the title: *Alia missa, in cymiteriis.*

Collect: " O God, by whose mercy the souls of the faithful find rest; mercifully grant forgiveness of their sins to thy servants and handmaids, and to all here and elsewhere who sleep in Christ: that being freed from all sins, they may rejoice with thee for evermore."

Secret: " Graciously receive, O Lord, the victim which we offer up on behalf of the souls of thy servants and handmaids and of all Catholics who sleep in Christ, whether in this place or elsewhere, so that by this excellent sacrifice they may be freed from the terrible bonds of death and may be found worthy of life everlasting."

Infra actionem. Hanc igitur oblationem quam tibi offerimus, Domine, pro tuorum requie famulorum N.N. (et omnium fidelium catholicorum orthodoxorum in hac basilica in Christo quiescentium, et qui in circuitu huius ecclesiae tuae requiescunt); quaesumus, Domine, placatus accipias, ut per haec salutis humanae subsidia, in tuorum numero redemptorum sorte perpetua censeantur; diesque nostros, etc.

Post-Communion: " O God, who art the light of faithful souls, hearken to our humble prayers, and grant to thy servants and handmaids, whose bodies here or elsewhere

---

[1] *Confessiones*, Lib. IX, cap. xiii.

November 2

rest in Christ, a place of refreshment, rest, and happiness and glorious light."

At the Burial of an Abbot.

There is a great variety of prayers *pro defunctis* both in the Sacramentaries and the Missal of to-day. We may quote here a beautiful prayer assigned in the Gelasian Sacramentary *pro sacerdote, sive abbate.*

Deus, qui famulum tuum N.N. sacerdotem atque abbatem et sanctificasti unctione misericordiae tuae, et adsumpsisti consummatione felici; suscipe propitius preces nostras et praesta; ut sicut ille tecum est meritis, ita a nobis non recedat exemplis.

Alia. Omnipotens, sempiterne Deus, majestatem tuam supplices exoramus, ut famulo tuo N.N. abbati atque sacerdoti, quem in requiem tuam vocare dignatus es, dones sedem honorificatam, et fructum beatitudinis sempiternae; ut ea quae in oculis nostris docuit et gessit, non judicium nobis pariant, sed profectum attribuant, ut pro quo nunc in te gaudemus in terris, cum eodem apud te exultare mereamur in caelis.

These Collects resemble prayers in honour of a saint rather than prayers offered for a deceased person.

We shall conclude these examples of the Liturgy for the faithful departed on the day of their solemn commemoration with this fine inscription composed by St Ambrose for his brother Satyrus, who was buried by his command near the martyr Victor close to the Ambrosian Basilica.

VRANIO · SATYRO · SVPREMVM · FRATER · HONOREM
MARTYRIS · AD · LAEVAM · DETVLIT · AMBROSIVS
HAEC · MERITI · MERCES · VT · SACRI · SANGVINIS · VMOR
FINITIMAS · PENETRANS · ADLVAT · EXVVIAS

"To Uranius Satyrus his brother Ambrose rendered the last honours, laying him on the left hand of the martyr. May this be the reward of his merits: that some drops of the venerable blood may penetrate the tomb and may moisten his remains."

NOVEMBER 2

DEDICATION OF THE GREATER BASILICA OF ST LAWRENCE

To-day the Martyrology of St Jerome notes: *Dedicatio basilicae sanctorum Xysti, Yppoliti et Laurentii.* This refers to the *basilica major* erected by Sixtus III near the tomb of St Lawrence, which only in part corresponded with the present building raised by Honorius III.

The remains of the apse of the *basilica speciosior of*

Pelagius II were discovered a few years ago near the existing ambo of St Lawrence. Therefore the apse of the Basilica of Sixtus III, to the dedication of which the Martyrology of St Jerome refers to-day, must have been in the middle of the present church, and the basilica must have extended on to the Via Tiburtina far beyond the *narthex* now existing. The church was dedicated to the Blessed Virgin, and for this reason Leo IV ordered that a Station should be celebrated there on the Octave of the Assumption.

NOVEMBER 3

ST SYLVIA, WIDOW*

The Martyrology of Clement VIII notes to-day the feast of St Sylvia, widow, the mother of Gregory the Great. Her *cultus* is of great antiquity but is purely Roman, for it was connected with the history of the Aventine, where in the ninth century John the Deacon saw the *oratorium nomini ejus*, a chapel adjoining the celebrated monastery of St Sabbas. The Oratory of St Sylvia, standing upon that piece of land belonging to the Greeks in the Capital of the world, proved the Roman origin of that sanctuary. Long before the first exiled monks of the laura of Mar Saba at Jerusalem had built their *Cella Nova* on the hill, the mother of St Gregory spent the last years of her widowhood there in retirement, and in the practice of ascetic virtue. She continued, however, to watch over her son's health, and when she became aware that the food prepared at the neighbouring monastery of Sant' Andrea did not suit him, she took upon herself to send him every day a dish of vegetables, which she knew he could eat. The dish used was a silver one, a relic of the former luxury of the family of the Gordiani, but one day it was not returned to Sylvia. Gregory having nothing left to give, had bestowed his mother's silver dish upon a beggar.

We know from the letters of the great Pope that Sylvia was present at the holy death of his aunt the virgin Tarsilla, sister of Gordianus, and that, with the other persons present, she heard her converse with St Felix III who was a relative of hers, and then exclaim joyfully : " Go, now, go, for behold Jesus cometh." As she said these words the holy virgin gave up her soul to God, and a mysterious fragrance pervaded the chamber of death. This happened on Christmas Eve.

Three weeks later, on the Epiphany, the family vault of Gordianus in the Basilica of St Paul was again opened to receive the coffin containing the remains of another aunt of

November 3

Gregory the Great, the virgin Emiliana, who was laid beside St Felix III, St Tarsilla, and the other members of that saintly family.

The fragments of the great inscription which once covered the sepulchre of the family of Felix III are still preserved at St Paul's.

The father of that Pope, a priest who was also called Felix, was entrusted by Leo the Great with the great work of restoration undertaken by him at the Ostian Basilica.

The result was extremely satisfactory, and Leo congratulated Felix on his achievement. The latter, at his death, which occurred shortly after, was buried in the sanctuary of the apostle in recognition of his services. In his sepulchral inscription, still extant in the museum of epigraphs of the Abbey of St Paul's, the praises of the noble work of restoration carried out under his directions are expressed.

The ownership of the family tomb passed from Felix the priest to his son who bore the same name. He was still a deacon when his wife died in 472, and he naturally caused her to be interred in the family sepulchre beside his father, placing upon it the following inscription:

LEVITAE · CONIVNX · PETRONIA · FORMA · PVDORIS ·
HIS · MEA · DEPONENS · SEDIBVS · OSSA · LOCO
PARCITE · VOS · LACRIMIS · DVLCES · CVM · CONIVGE · NATAE
VIVENTEMQVE · DEO · CREDITE · FLERE · NEFAS
DP · IN · PACE · III · NON · OCTOB · FESTO · V · C · CONS

Twelve years later, in 484, when the quondam deacon had been raised to the Papacy under the name of Felix III, the tomb was again opened to receive the body of Paula, his daughter. This inscription was added to the former one upon the same marble slab:

HIC · REQVIESCIT · IN · PACE · PAVLA · CL · F · DVLCIS · BENIGNA
GRATIOSA · FILIA · SS · DP · VII · KAL · SEPT · VENANTIO · V · C ·
   CONS

In the following year 485 her young brother was laid beside Paula, and these words were inscribed on his tomb:

HIC · REQVIESCIT · DVLCISSIMVS · PVER · GORDIANVS · FILIVS · SS
   DP · V · ID · SEPT · SYMMACHO · V · C · CONS

But even then, death had not ceased to visit the house of Felix III. In 489, Emiliana, *sacra Virgo*, a consecrated virgin, apparently another daughter of Felix, followed her mother and his other two children to the grave. Her epigraph, which was inscribed on the same slab as that of Petronia, ran as follows :

HIC · REQVIESCIT · AEMILLIANA · SAC · VG · DP · V · ID · DEC · PRO BVIO · V · C · CONSS

Last of all, Pope Felix himself died at the end of February 492, and alone among all the Roman Pontiffs was buried in the Basilica of St Paul beside his father, his wife, and the children who had gone before him.

St Gregory the Great speaks of Pope Felix III as *atavus meus* or great-grandfather, as his father Gordianus was the grandson of the Pontiff. It is remarkable that we find in the *domus* of the *Clivus Scauri* the same names as those of the family of Pope Felix. Thus the father of Gregory was called Gordianus, one of his sisters was Emiliana, and she too was a *sacra virgo* like her namesake, in 489. At the death of his sister Tarsilla, St Felix appeared to help her in her agony. It is therefore evident that the patrician house of Gregory the Great was one where family traditions were cherished, and handed on from father to son and from uncle to nephew.

We do not know where the immediate relatives of Gregory were interred, but it is natural to suppose that Gordianus, Sylvia, Emiliana, and Tarsilla were buried in the family tomb near their grandfather Felix III.

Another family record of St Sylvia and of Gordianus still existed on the Coelian Hill in the ninth century. Near the ancient *nymphaeum* of Gregory's home, where classical tradition demanded that the *effigies maiorum* or portraits of the ancestors should be preserved, at the entrance of the *domus* of Gordianus, Gregory the Great caused the portraits of his parents, founders of the monastery of Sant' Andrea, to be painted. Gordianus, the *defensor*, clothed in a penula, stood beside the Prince of the Apostles, who was represented enthroned, in the act of conferring upon him his high ecclesiastical office. St Sylvia, on the other hand, was seated majestically in a chair, clad like a noble matron, and held the Psalter open at the words in Psalm cxviii : *Vivet anima mea et laudabit te.* About the picture ran the inscription :

GREGORIVS · SYLVIAE · MATRI · FECIT

According to the Bollandists St Sylvia died about 590, when her son had already been raised to the Papacy. The fame of her virtues endured, and the Romans, according to their own liturgical tradition, dedicated a chapel *oratorium nomini ejus* on the spot sanctified by her life of retirement on the Aventine, near the " Porta muraria " of St Paul.

NOVEMBER 4

SS VITALIS AND AGRICOLA, MARTYRS

The *feriale* of Bologna for this day is contained in a line of St Paulinus:

Vitalem, Agricolam, Proculumque Bononia condit.[1]

The two first-mentioned saints, sometimes together, sometimes separately, appear on several dates in the Martyrology of St Jerome: as, for instance, on November 3 and 27, December 3, April 29, etc. These feasts all refer to the same two martyrs Vitalis and Agricola, whose bodies were discovered at Bologna in 393, and at whose translation St Ambrose was present. From that time their *cultus* spread throughout the Christian world, and many bishops, such as Victricius of Rouen and Namatius of Clermont, procured their relics and dedicated celebrated churches to them.

At Rome, in the time of Innocent I, the matron Vestina built a title dedicated to St Vitalis *in Vico longo*, where the station of the second Friday in Lent is still celebrated. A century later, Justinian and Theodora gave enormous sums of money in order to erect a church to St Vitalis, enriched with mosaics and precious marbles, which is to this day an object of wonder and admiration to artists and archaeologists.

The martyrs Vitalis and Agricola originally reposed in a Jewish cemetery at Bologna. Paulinus relates in the life of St Ambrose that God " revealed the place of their sepulture to the bishop." He does not say to which bishop he refers, whether to the Bishop of the diocese or the Bishop of Milan, who apparently was merely invited to assist at the festival. In any case the presence of the great Bishop of Milan added to the solemnity of the martyrs' translation, especially as St Ambrose immediately after leaving Bologna proceeded to Florence for the consecration of a church in that town, and placed there some relics of the martyrs, lately discovered at Bologna.

Rome commemorates St Vitalis first on April 29, the date given in the Martyrology of St Jerome: *Bononiae, Vitalis.* To-day's feast of both martyrs is wanting in the ancient Sacramentaries, and was only introduced later in the Roman Liturgy when two saints of the name Vitalis were venerated, one, contrary to the testimony of Peter Chrysologus, being attributed to Ravenna, and the other, the companion of Agricola, to the rival city of Bologna.

[1] *Carm.* XXIII, 432.

The Mass is the same as on July 2, for SS Processus and Martinianus, except the Collects.

Collect: "Grant, we beseech thee, O almighty God, that we who keep the festival of thy holy martyrs Vitalis and Agricola, may be helped by their intercession with thee."

Secret: "Be appeased, O Lord, we beseech thee, by the gifts which we offer up; and by the intercession of thy holy martyrs Vitalis and Agricola keep us from all danger."

Post-Communion: "May this Communion, O Lord, cleanse us from guilt; and by the intercession of blessed Vitalis and Agricola, thy martyrs, may it win for us healing grace from heaven."

NOVEMBER 4

St Charles Borromeo, Bishop and Confessor

The city of Milan looks upon St Charles as the most illustrious of her Bishops since the time of St Ambrose, but the Mother Church of Rome, too, regards him as one of the greatest and most worthy of her sons.

The life-work of St Charles may indeed be considered under two aspects, and divided into two periods. First the activities he discharged beside his uncle Pius IV which embraced not only Rome but the universal Church. Secondly, the pastoral office which he filled at Milan, as the Bishop and Apostle of that diocese.

As Secretary of State to Pius IV, St Charles was at the Pope's side in one of the most decisive epochs in the history of the Papacy. The question still hung in the balance whether the Holy See would resolutely initiate the ecclesiastical reform so long desired and so widely advocated, or whether the difficult undertaking should still be delayed, and only half-measures attempted, as had been done unfortunately by some of the Popes of that century.

It was under the personal influence of St Charles that Pius IV decided on the reform, and from that day Cardinal Borromeo in the name and with the authority of his uncle carried on the work without sparing himself. He may be said to have directed from Rome the last phase of the Council of Trent; and what was more difficult, no sooner was the Council approved by the Pope, than St Charles devoted all his energies to insure the realization of its plan of reform.

✝ Here the second period of the great Archbishop's life began. After the death of Pius IV, he returned to the Church of Milan where he was obliged to remedy many evils due to the absence of the rightful pastors.

November 4

In order to sanctify the flock committed to his care St Charles began by sanctifying himself, and as Christ when he came to redeem the world did so not only by preaching and working miracles but by his Passion, so Cardinal Borromeo offered himself as a victim to God for his people. He was in the habit of saying that one must win souls on one's knees, alluding to the long hours he spent kneeling before his crucifix and in the crypt of the Church of the Holy Sepulchre at Milan.

The zeal displayed by St Charles in fulfilling his pastoral duties is almost incredible. His field of action as Archbishop of Milan and Legate of the Holy See was very extensive. Yet there was no deserted Alpine village which was not included in his pastoral visitation. His biographers tell us that in three weeks he consecrated no less than fifteen churches.

At that period it was no easy task to be Archbishop of Milan. The heresy which had spread through the Swiss Cantons threatened to communicate itself to that diocese. It was necessary to arrest its progress, and St Charles accomplished this. Further, it was urgent to train the clergy to higher ideals, and therefore the Saint built colleges and seminaries, assembled councils, promulgated canons, and encouraged the opening of religious houses for the education of the young.

The weakening of religious spirit among the clergy is almost always encouraged by the civil authorities, as it enables them more easily to obtain the mastery. St Charles boldly upheld the episcopal authority, and was obliged to struggle not only with canons, monks and nuns who had lost their first fervour—of these we may cite the Umiliati, who even attempted the life of the Archbishop—but also found a more formidable adversary in the governor of Milan who jealously defended the prerogatives usurped by Spain.

Thus did the great Cardinal Borromeo live, labour, and struggle, a worthy champion of the Church for whom he gave his life. Worn out before his time by his arduous labours, he died at his post on November 3, 1584, aged only forty-six years.

The Church in the Collect of the Mass sums up his praises in a few eloquent words: *Pastoralis sollicitudo gloriosum reddidit.*

Rome has many records of St Charles, at San Martino ai Monti, for instance, and at St Praxedes, his titular church. His heart is preserved in the great church dedicated to him near the Porta Flaminia, the special sanctuary of the Lombards in the Holy City. Besides the Church in the Corso, two other churches bear the name of this saint: San Carlo ai

Catinari, and San Carlo at the Quattro Fontane. The room occupied by him in the Palazzo Altemps is still held in veneration, and the purple worn by the great Cardinal is treasured at the title of St Cecilia.

The Mass is that of February 4, except for the Collect: " Ever keep thy church, O Lord, we beseech thee, under the protection of St Charles, thy confessor and bishop; so that through the intercession of him who became glorious by his watchful care over his flock, we may ever burn with love for thee."

NOVEMBER 6

St Leonard, Confessor

The *cultus* of this celebrated abbot, from whom the village formerly called Nobiliacum in Aquitania, near Limoges, took its present name of St Leonard, entered into the Roman Liturgy after the eleventh century, at the time when so many saints of France and Aquitania, such as St Pellegrinus, St Egidius, St Brixius, etc., became very popular in Italy.

This occurred, too, in the case of St Leonard, and there are many churches and oratories dedicated to him throughout the Peninsula. At Rome, alone, at least four are known: San Leonardo *in Settignano*, San Leonardo *de Porta Flaminia*, San Leonardo *de Albis*, San Leonardo *in Carinis*.

The popularity of the *cultus* of St Leonard, to the diffusion of which, both at Rome and in the Marche, the monks of Farfa may have contributed, gave to his name a place of honour in the Roman Missal.

Indeed, in some dioceses this was even a holiday of obligation, as for instance at Rimini, where the Cathedral Chapter possessed the privilege of freeing a condemned prisoner from the gaol or galleys on this day.

At Venice, too, St Leonard was venerated both at the church which bears his name and at St Mark's. The Crusaders carried the devotion to St Leonard to the East, and at St Mary's of Bethlehem the picture of the saint may be seen with the bilingual inscription: *Sanctus Leonardus*—'Ο ἅγιος Λεονάρδος.

St Leonard lived in the sixth century, but the greater popularity of his *cultus* dates chiefly from the eleventh century, when kings and princes journeyed to visit his tomb, before which St Bruno of Segni one day came to pray.

The intercession of this Saint was invoked especially in order to obtain the miraculous liberation of prisoners and slaves.

NOVEMBER 7

ST WILLIBRORD, BISHOP, APOSTLE OF FRISIA

To-day the *Laterculus* of the Martyrology of St Jerome, preserved at Heptemach, which was actually used by St Willibrord, founder of the monastery, has a note transcribed: *hic domus, Apostolicus vir, Willibrordus episcopus, migravit ad Christum.* This refers to the death on November 7, 739, of the famous Apostle of Frisia.

St Willibrord, in a manner, is connected with Rome, for he, together with St Boniface, St Willibald, and St Sturmius, was one of the band of apostles who were sent by the Holy See to Germany in the eighth century, to spread the Catholic Faith in those regions and to bring them into unity with the Roman Church. St Willibrord was consecrated Bishop by Pope Sergius in the Basilica of St Cecilia on November 21, 695.

This important date was inserted in the Abbot's own handwriting on the margin of the *Laterculus* of Heptemach. It was on the same occasion that the Pope changed Willibrord's Anglo-Saxon name to the Roman one of Clement, after the saint of that name whose *natalis* occurs two days later.

NOVEMBER 8

THE HOLY CROWNED MARTYRS

Station on the Via Labicana, " in Comitatum," and later at the Title of the Holy Crowned Martyrs.

We must draw attention here to the following fact. Both the Leonine Sacramentary and the Philocalian Calendar, instead of noting the *natalis* of the *Coronati* to-day, mark it on *V. id. Nov.*, that is to say on November 7. The following is the text of the Calendar: *V. id. Nov.: Clementis, Semproniani, Claudi, Nicostrati, in Comitatum,* that is to say in the neighbourhood of the imperial gardens *ad duas lauros*, on the Via Labicana.

The history of these martyrs who have been known from the earliest times by the simple title of *Coronati* is a most intricate one. Some archeologists have gone so far as to distinguish three separate groups of *Coronati*. The first is that of the five sculptors of Pannonia, Sempronianus, Claudius, Nicostratus, Castorius, and Simplicius, who were put to death under Diocletian for having refused to carve a statue of Esculapius. Then follow the four Roman *Corniculari Coronati*, named in the Philocalian Calendar and interred on the Via Labicana.

Last of all come the four saints of Albano mentioned in the same Calendar on August 8: *Secundi, Carpofori, Victorini et Severani in Albano.*

The question arises: to which of these three groups do the *Quatuor Coronati* named in the Calendar and the Sacramentaries to-day belong? Were the relics of the sculptors of Pannonia translated to Rome as early as the fourth century? It would appear not. As, however, the Calendar and the ancient Itineraries only mention a group of four or five crowned martyrs on the Via Labicana (those named in the Philocalian Calendar), it becomes difficult to account for the other two groups of the Pannonian martyrs and the saints of Albano.

This is the complicated problem to which, at present, we have found no solution. One thing is certain, that in order to decide the question, it must be studied by examining the records of the Roman cemeteries and the local monuments, and not merely by consulting the Acts.

We find, then, that the ancient pilgrims to the cemetery of SS Peter and Marcellinus venerated only one group of martyrs under the title of *IV Coronatos*. It is thus described in the Itinerary of Salzburg.

The *De Locis SS Martyrum* on the other hand has a curious manner of expressing itself, for while attempting to explain more clearly who the Crowned Ones are, it confuses the hagiographical tradition of the four *corniculari* of Rome with the five martyrs of Pannonia. This is the text: *Quatuor Coronati, id est: Claudius, Nicostratus, Simpronianus, Castorius, Simplicius.* It announces four, and proceeds to enumerate five, and those five are the Pannonian sculptors.

This anomaly can only be explained by examining the two Passions. When the story of the Roman martyrs is compared with that of the martyrs of Sirmium it becomes evident that one is copied from the other. The fact that the dates of their martyrdom almost coincided made it more easy for the biographers to bring the two groups together, and whilst at first the Liturgy united them in a single *cultus*, the Pannonian martyrs at length superseded the Roman ones, and the early tradition which preserved the names of the *corniculari* of the Via Labicana was lost to the Sacramentaries.

Such is the derivation of the legend as represented in the Sacramentaries and the Itinerary *De Locis Sanctis*. The Roman custom of naming this festival after the Four Holy Crowned Ones of the Via Labicana still persists, but the four have really become five, as the four Romans have been identified with the five Pannonian martyrs: *idest Claudius,* etc.

November 8

The original sepulchre of the *Martyres corniculari* of Rome was discovered in the cemetery *ad duas lauros* during the excavations of 1912. At the end of a passage a large tomb was found which by the graffiti and the decorations still discernible had evidently remained in use until the ninth century. A door from the left-hand wall of the vault led through another tomb to a second crypt, where in a deep niche the remains of a large sarcophagus were still to be seen. This sarcophagus had originally been protected by a marble *transenna* placed in front of it. On the walls, blackened by the earth which had filled them, was inscribed in two places ✠*Leo Presbyter*, the signature of a well-known pilgrim to the Roman cemeteries in the early Middle Ages.

Lastly, not far off, appeared another inscription: ✠ SCE · CLE (mens). This, then, is the Clement of the Philocalian Calendar who reposed in this sanctuary, together with his "Crowned" companions—*idest, Sempronianus, Claudius, and Nicostratus*.

The Mass *Intret* is the same as on January 22, but the Epistle is taken from the feast of St Sebastian, January 20.

The Gospel is that of the feast of All Saints. Thus only the Collects (and originally the Preface) are proper to the feast.

The first Collect is now the same as on July 10, but formerly included the names of the martyrs.

Collect: "Grant, we beseech thee, almighty God, that we who acknowledge the boldness of thy glorious martyrs (Claudius, Nicostratus, Symphorian, Castorius and Simplicius —these are the Pannonian sculptors—) may enjoy their loving intercession for us before thee."

The passage from the Gospel for to-day in the Würzburg list is not the one described in the Missal, but that of the feast of St Sebastian.

Secret: "We offer up to thee, O Lord, these gifts for our sacrifice; for the sake of thy righteous ones may they be well-pleasing to thee; and out of thy compassion may they become healthful for us."

This Collect sets before us the two aspects under which we may consider the Holy Eucharist. It is a true Sacrifice and therefore we pray God to look graciously upon it; it is also, as the Missal tells us, *nobis Sacramentum redemptionis*, and its increased efficacy depends upon the dispositions of faith and love which we bring to it. This gives force to the word *perficiat* in the Latin text.

The liturgical tradition of Rome, beginning with the Leonine Sacramentary, assigns to the *Coronati* a special Preface. The following is from the Gregorian Sacramentary: *Vere dignum*

... *aeterne Deus : celebrantes Sanctorum natalitia Coronatorum, quia dum tui nominis per eos gloriam fraequentamus, in nostrae fidei augmento succrescimus. Per Christum.*

Post-Communion : " We who are filled with thy healthful sacraments, beseech thee, O Lord, that we may be helped by the prayers of those whose festival we are keeping."

At the stational Mass which the Pope formerly celebrated on this feast at the Basilica of the Four Holy Crowned Ones on the Caelian Hill, he was, according to the *Ordines Romani* of the thirteenth century, crowned with the *regnum* or pontifical tiara in honour of the saints.

The title given to this group of martyrs in ancient times is significant. They are the " Crowned " Ones. But as no one can be crowned unless he has fought, as St Paul says : *nisi legitime certaverit,* it follows that we, too, must look upon the world as a battlefield, and our life as the term of our *militia* under Christ our captain. *Regnante Domino nostro Jesu Christo.*

NOVEMBER 8

Octave Day of All Saints

That this Octave only dates from the time of the Renaissance can be deduced from the fact that there is no special Mass for it in the Missal, and that the Roman Sacramentaries only mark to-day as the feast of the Crowned Saints.

It is well to repeat, on account of the modern tendency to multiply octaves, that originally the celebration of the Octave was a characteristic of the Paschal solemnity. Because of the sublimity of that mystery and the share we claim in it to live again with Christ our Pasch, it was fitting that the Church should employ seven days in solemnizing it.

The seven days *in albis paschalibus* were symbolical of the immortal and glorious life of Christ, conqueror over death and hell.

The Octaves of Christmas, of the Epiphany, of SS Peter and Paul, of St Lawrence, and of the Assumption, etc., only followed later as the special meaning of the Easter Octave with its processions of white robed neophytes *ad fontes* gradually weakened.

The Octaves of various saints introduced in the early Middle Ages, were, however, very quietly celebrated, with a simple Mass on the Octave of the feast and no commemoration on the intervening days. It was not until the thirteenth century that a great number of octaves pervaded the *Breviarium de Curia,* all marked with unusual importance and with each intervening day raised to the rank of a double.

NOVEMBER 9

St Theodore, Martyr

This is one of the most celebrated of the Eastern Saints who were venerated throughout the world in ancient times. St Theodore was a soldier martyr, and suffered death at Amasea where an enormous concourse of pilgrims met each year on his festival, notwithstanding the rigour of the season.

It was in that venerated sanctuary that on one occasion St Gregory Nazianzen delivered his magnificent panegyric on St Theodore.

The Greek hagiographers generally distinguish Theodore Euchaita, "ὁ Στρατηλάτης," from Theodore τοῦ τύρωνος in whose honour the Byzantines keep the feast known as "Κολλύβων" on the first Saturday in Lent. Modern historians, however, consider that the two names refer to the same person.

While nearly all the great cities of the Byzantine world desired to have sanctuaries dedicated to the "megalomartyr" Theodore, Rome, too, followed their example in the seventh century. The place chosen was in the midst of Eastern or rather of imperial surroundings—for it was at the foot of the Palatine. Between the title of Anastasia and Santa Maria *Antiqua* an ancient rotonda was consecrated to the martyr, who was patron of soldiers (ὁ Στρατηλάτης), and this has been identified by some archeologists as the *templum divi Augusti*.

The round Church of St Theodore, on account of numerous restorations, has little of the first Byzantine period left, except the mosaic in the apse. Here we see an image of the Saviour seated upon the terrestial globe, surrounded by SS Peter and Paul, St Theodore, and another saint whom it is not possible to identify with certainty.

The traditional devotion to St Theodore survives at Rome, and pious women still carry their sick children to the round church in order to invoke the help of the great martyr.

It was as the patron of soldiers and of the sick that St Theodore was admitted into the Gregorian Sacramentary, and, therefore, into the Missal in the Middle Ages, long before the feast of the dedication of the Lateran Basilica took the place of that of the Megalomartyr, once the patron of the Imperial forces on the Palatine.

The Mass *Laetabitur* is the same as for St Saturninus on November 29, but the Collects are proper.

Collect: " O God, who dost encompass and shield us by the glorious confession of blessed Theodore thy martyr;

grant that we may profit by his example, and be strengthened by his intercession."

To-day the Würzburg list contains the passage from St Luke (xxi, 14–19), which in our Missal is assigned to the feast of SS Vincent and Anastasius, January 22.

Secret: "Receive, O Lord, the prayers of the faithful with the victims which they offer up; and through the intercession of blessed Theodore thy martyr, may this service of love and devotion bring us to the glory of heaven."

The Latin form is sometimes so concise that it is almost necessary to make use of a periphrasis in order to translate it. Thus in this prayer the expression *haec piae devotionis officium* signifies that the eucharistic Sacrifice corresponds on our part to the fulfilment of a duty: *officium;* and this duty is the consequence of our *devotio*, or baptismal consecration to the service of God.

Post-Communion: "Grant, O Lord, we beseech thee, through the intercession of blessed Theodore thy martyr, that what we take with our mouth, we may receive with a clean heart."

This is an admirable Collect, and it expresses a well-known opinion of St Augustine, adopted by St Thomas Aquinas: *aliud est Sacramentum, aliud virtus Sacramenti.* (*Tract. XXVI in Joan.*)

The *Sacramentum* is indeed the bread of life, but in order to have its full effect it must be received, as it were, by a healthy organism.

NOVEMBER 9

Dedication of the Lateran Basilica of the Saviour

This feast, destined to become so important, only appears in the Latin ritual towards the twelfth century; that is to say when the *Ordines Romani* note that on this occasion the church was adorned with garlands, and that the Pope himself celebrated Mass and vespers of the festival.

We do not know at what exact date, or for what reason this anniversary of the encænia of the Lateran, at first ignored by the classical tradition of the Liturgy, arose. Considering, however, that they occur ten days before the encænia of SS Peter and Paul, the hypothesis is not altogether to be excluded that they were instituted in connection with the celebration of the foundation of the two chief Apostolic Sanctuaries, and in order to commemorate within fifteen days the dedication of the three Constantinian Basilicas of Rome.

The fact remains that while the Martyrology of St Jerome

mentions the dedication of the Basilicas built or restored by Sixtus III, for instance St Mary Major (August 5), St Peter *ad vincula* (August 1), SS Sixtus, Hippolytus, and Lawrence (November 2), it makes no mention of the encænia celebrated by Pope St Sylvester on the Via Cornelia, on the Ostian way, and *in Lateranis*.

We do not know, therefore, why November 9 was chosen at Rome as the anniversary of the dedication of the Basilica of the Saviour. It may be that this was the date of the dedication of San Salvatore *in Thermis*, a church connected with Constantine the Great, who was its first founder. In time, however, the *dedicatio Sancti Salvatoris* may have come to be regarded as referring to all the churches in the city dedicated to the Saviour, including the Lateran Basilica.

There is another hypothesis. On this day the Eastern churches celebrate the memory of a miraculous picture of the Saviour, which, on being profaned by Jews at Beirut, shed drops of blood. It is possible that this Eastern feast of the Saviour having become popular among the Latin peoples and inscribed in the Martyrologies, was the first origin of the Roman solemnity of the Basilica of the Saviour at the Lateran. But instead of attempting to trace the history of to-day's feast back to the time of Pope Sylvester, it would seem more simple to connect it with the ceremony held by Sergius III (904–911) at the Lateran, when he restored from its foundations the venerable Basilica of Constantine which had collapsed in 897.

These are all questions which at present must be left unanswered, and all we can safely assert is that the *Dedicatio Sancti Salvatoris* has a tradition of eight centuries behind it, and is therefore of respectable antiquity.

The Lateran was first mentioned in ecclesiastical history in the year 213, when according to Optatus of Milevis a council against the Donatists was held within its walls. *Convenerunt in domum Faustae in Lateranis*.[1] It was about this time that Constantine gave to the Church of Rome the ancient Palace of the Laterani, which had probably come into his possession as part of the dowry of his wife, Fausta, sister of Maxentius.

From that time onwards the Lateran became the ordinary residence of the Popes, and may, therefore, be regarded as a memorial of that long series of holy Pontiffs who inhabited it during the course of nearly ten centuries. Those walls, now nearly two thousand years old, have seen many important events in history and have figured in poetry and in art,

[1] *De schism. Donat.* I, 23, P.L. XI, col. 931.

whilst they sheltered a dynasty of Pontiffs who ruled longer than any dynasty of kings.

It was here that, at the suggestion of Pope Sylvester, Constantine the Great transformed or constructed the first basilica dedicated to the Saviour at Rome, and so it came about that the baths of the ancient palace of Plautius Lateranus, a victim of the cruelty of Nero, were transformed into a Christian Baptistery, marking the triumph of the cross which the pagan Emperor had endeavoured to obliterate in the city of the seven hills. The palace he had seized became, three centuries later, the inheritance of the successors of St Peter.

In the early centuries to which we are now referring, the question would not arise whether the Lateran or the Vatican Basilica was the cathedral of Rome. To speak of a cathedral at Rome in the early Middle Ages would be an anachronism; for, on account of the liturgical system of stations, the Pope officiated not at one church only, but in all the basilicas and titles within and without the city. He certainly resided at the palace of Fausta in the early Middle Ages, but when he celebrated some solemnity, such as the Epiphany, the Easter baptism, the Ascension, Pentecost, or the ordinations and the coronations, the station always took place at St Peter's, for it was in the baptistery there that the *Cathedra* of St Peter was preserved. It was there that the Pope began his pontificate and it was there that he was buried when that pontificate ended.

When the stational system of the Liturgy declined, and the exterior power of the Pope increased, the idea was adopted that as the Lateran was the papal residence, it must also rank as a cathedral with regard to the other titles of the city. This idea developed by degrees and was confirmed in the eighth century when the *episcopium* became the seat of government as well, and the successor of Sylvester held in his hands the double inheritance of Peter and of Constantine.

Against the various monastic, capitulary, and episcopal jurisdictions which then disputed the many sanctuaries of Rome, the Basilica of the Saviour became the symbol of the universal authority of the Pope. Because of this it was not considered fitting that the divine praises should be celebrated by simple monks or clerics in that sacred place. As it had already been the custom for many centuries that the priests of the neighbouring titles should daily take it in turn to celebrate Mass at the tomb of the Princes of the Apostles, so now at the altar of the Lateran the bishops " suburbicari " officiated as celebrants in the cathedral of the Pope. The

November 9

first beginning of the college of Cardinals around the Pope was thus founded.

All this is expressed in the famous inscription in Leonine verses carved over the portico of the Lateran:

DOGMATE · PAPALI · DATVR · AC · SIMVL · IMPERIALI
QVOD · SIM · CVNCTARVM · MATER · ECCLESIARVM
HIC · SALVATORIS · CAELESTIA · REGNA · DATORIS
NOMINE · SANXERVNT · CVM · CVNCTA · PERACTA · FVERVNT
QUAESVMVS · EX · TOTO · CONVERSI · SVPPLICE · VOTO
NOSTRA · QVOD · HAEC · AEDES · TIBI · CHRISTE · SIT · INCLYTA · SEDES

" It is decreed by both the Papal and Imperial authorities that I am the mother of all the churches. When the building was completed they gave me the name of the Saviour, of him who bestows the kingdom of heaven; we turn to thee with humble prayer and beseech thee, O Christ, that thou wouldst make of this temple thy glorious throne."

As Papal Cathedral and mother of all the Churches, the Basilica of the Saviour has been clothed with the dignity of a symbol of the Pontifical authority in the eyes of the Catholic world. Dante expressed it in his time in the lines:

> *Vedendo Roma e l'ardua sua opra*
> *Stupefaceansi, quando Laterano*
> *Alle cose mortali andò di sopra.*[1]

The Liturgy has also consecrated in her ritual this belief held by the household of the faith, and Pius X raised the encænia which we celebrate to-day to the same rank of a double of the second class for the entire Latin Church, which is held by the great feasts of the religious year.

Therefore the question once raised whether the Vatican or the Lateran Basilica has the best claim to the dignity of the Pontifical Cathedral has been solved by the Liturgy in favour of the Basilica of the Saviour.

We should be filled with reverence when we cross the threshold of this sanctuary where after Constantine's great victory *ad saxa rubra* the Romans first beheld the gleaming labarum of the victor: EN · TOYTO · NIKA. *In hoc vinces.* Here indeed, the Roman See through long centuries of struggle and of triumph, of humiliation and of victory, has fought the world and has conquered it. EN TOYTO, with the sign of the Cross, nor have the gates of hell, the *portae inferi*, ever prevailed against the Church.

We have said that the festival is not of great antiquity, so

---

[1] *Paradiso* XXXI, 34.

the Mass is not a primitive one, and is taken entirely from that of May 13 for the dedication of the Pantheon.

In early Roman Liturgy the encænia were always regarded as feasts in honour of the saints to whom the church was dedicated, and whose Office was therefore celebrated. The festivals of SS Philip and James on May 1, of St Peter in Chains on August 1, of St Mary Major on August 5, of St Michael on September 29, of St Cecilia on November 22, etc., originally commemorated the encænia of their basilicas at Rome. If to-day's feast had been primitive, the Sacramentaries would have possessed a fine Mass of Christ the King, for instance, in honour of the Saviour, instead of making use of the Common *dedicationis ecclesiae*. Whereas the Lateran Basilica has been obliged to adopt the feast of the Transfiguration, which was only instituted under Callixtus III, as its titular feast.

The Collects are those described in the Gregorian Calendar: " O God, who year by year bringest round once more the day of the consecration of this thy holy temple, and summonest us, still hale and well, to take part again and again in these holy mysteries, graciously hear thy people's prayer, and grant that whosoever shall enter into this holy temple to ask good things from thee, may receive with joy whatever he shall ask."

It is not the same thing to pray in private, or to pray in the sacred sanctuary and to take part in the rites of Catholic Liturgy. By reason of its consecration the Church is the throne of God's mercy, the place chosen by him, and where he chiefly condescends to work our salvation. Here we know he listens to our prayers; here Jesus is pleased to receive from the assembly of believers that solemn, public, and united adoration which is due to him.

Secret: " Give ear, O Lord, unto our prayers, and let all those who within the precincts of this temple are keeping the anniversary day of its dedication become well-pleasing unto thee both in body and in soul by full and true devotion; so that we who offer up this sacrifice to thee may by thy help be found worthy to win thy everlasting reward."

As a lightning-conductor by attracting the lightning protects the inhabitants of a building, so the Church, through the efficacy of the consecration of a sanctuary, raises up in every place an altar of propitiation where the anger of God is placated, where his heart is ever present, and the power of his adorable name is felt.

For this reason, our ancestors never failed to consecrate an altar, and to dedicate solemnly every church or oratory, no matter how small. We know that St Charles Borromeo consecrated fifteen churches within less than three weeks, and Pope Benedict XIII, who consecrated many hundreds of altars both in Rome and elsewhere, exhorted the bishops to consecrate at least all the parish churches in their dioceses.

At the present time, through an exaggerated desire to simplify everything, old altar stones are inserted into new altars, and modern buildings dedicated to the worship of God are often opened after having been merely blessed by a priest. This seems to denote want of faith and of religious enthusiasm, and many do not realize that it is not altogether desirable that the same edifice should serve as a place of worship and a parish hall.

All this is not in keeping with the spirit of the Church. It not only deprives the people of the special graces and efficacy attached to consecrated buildings and altars, but causes them to lose the sense of devotion due to the house of God.

The office for the consecration of a church is not only magnificent, but very instructive. If, in our day, the populace ignores the sacredness of the holy place, it is that it no longer hears the voice of the Liturgy which in former years expounded the catechism. *Legem credendi lex statuat supplicandi.*

We have travelled a long way since the days of faith when veneration for sacred things was so great that the cloths which covered the altar were used as relics.

The Gregorian Sacramentary contains a splendid Preface to-day: *Vere dignum . . . aeterne Deus: et pro annua devotione tabernaculi hujus, honorem tibi debitum referre per Christum Dominum nostrum, cujus virtus magna, pietas copiosa. Respice, quaesumus, de caelo, et vide, et visita domum istam, ut si quis in ea nomini tuo supplicaverit libenter exaudias, et satisfacientibus libenter agnoscas. Hic tibi sacerdotes tui Sacrificium laudis offerant; hic fidelis populus vota persolvat; hic peccatorum onera deponantur; hic fides sancta stabiliatur; hic pietas absoluta redeat; hic iniquitas emendata discedat. Inveniat apud te, Domine, locum veniae, quicumque satisfaciens huc confugerit, et conscio dolore victus, altaria tua rivis suarum eluerit lacrymarum. Hic, si quando populus tuus tristis maestusque convenerit, acquiesce rogari, et rogatus indulge petentibus. Per quem,* etc.

Post-Communion: " O God, who out of living and chosen stones buildest up an everlasting dwelling-place for thy majesty: help thy people, who humbly pray to thee, and whatever material room thy church may set apart for thy worship, let it bring also spiritual increase."

In this prayer we see how noble a thing is our Catholic worship, our perfect adoration in spirit and in truth. A new church has been built and the encænia are annually celebrated. But the Liturgy looks beyond this material gain and warns the faithful that religion does not consist in multiplying churches, statues and processions—the pagans, too, did this—but requires above all that the soul should become the temple of God and that the life of a Christian should correspond with the dignity of this temple or altar where sacrifice is offered to the Father and the Son in the sanctity of the Paraclete *qui datus est nobis*.

Mass for the Dedication of a Church.

The ritual for the dedication of a church has already been described in Volume I, in which we explained that in the spirit of the early Liturgy the essential rite for the dedication of a new church was the celebration of the eucharistic Sacrifice.

At the present time the Mass which follows the lengthy office of consecration ordered by the *Pontificale Romanum* is that which we have just described for the encænia of the Lateran. The Collects on the day of Dedication are, however, as follows:

Collect: " O God, who though unseen, upholdest all things and yet for the salvation of mankind showest them visible signs of thy mighty power; give glory to this temple by virtue of thy dwelling therein; and let all who come hither to pray, in whatever trouble they shall cry to thee, win comfort and blessings from thee."

When, therefore, we go into the church of God and make known to him the desire of our heart, our prayer does not rise alone in his sight, but is accompanied by that of the sacred Liturgy. The voice of the Church, his spouse, has great power with God and obtains for us grace and mercy.

Secret: " O God, who art thyself the giver of whatever we dedicate to thee, pour forth thy blessing upon this house of prayer; so that all who shall call upon thy name herein may enjoy thy protection and help."

The name given to the church or house of prayer, *domus orationis*, should help us to understand the theological importance of the Liturgy, the public prayer of the Church. Besides the private prayer which each of us *in cubiculo, clauso ostio*, makes to his heavenly Father, there exists another prayer, public and collective, which Christian society as a public body raises to God. This public prayer so often recommended by Christ and his apostles, is of so much importance and is so sacred that it pervades with its sanctity the place where it is celebrated, and therefore the house of God is called *domus orationis*, the house of prayer.

November 9

The Gregorian Sacramentary assigns a very beautiful Preface for this occasion: *Vere dignum . . . aeterne Deus; qui cum ubique sis totus, et cum universa tua majestate contineas, sacrari tamen tibi loca tuis Mysteriis apta voluisti, ut ipsae orationum domus supplicum mentes ad invocationem tui Nominis incitarent. Effunde, quaesumus, super hunc locum gratiam tuam, et omnibus te invocantibus auxilii tui munus ostende, ut hic Sacramentorum virtus omnium fidelium corda confirmet, per eumdem Christum, etc. Per quem.*

Post-Communion: "We beseech thee, almighty God, to lend the ears of thy lovingkindness to all who pray to thee in this place which we, all unworthy, have dedicated to thy name."

It is well to consider attentively the classic conception of the *dedicatio*. We moderns, absorbed by the idea of practical utility, erect places of worship chiefly because the needs of the population require it. They are inaugurated with a religious rite, suggested by the ritual, but this is often regarded as a secondary matter, and though it is not omitted is certainly not the primary consideration. The Church—we are apt to think—exists for the people. In the eyes of the ancients the position was quite different. The Church existed for God. Without any thought of public utility, the altar and the temple were votive gifts offered to the divinity through a sacred and official rite which dedicated them to him—*Dedicatio*. In many classical temples the people did not enter into the sanctuary inhabited by the divinity, and the altar of sacrifice stood outside at the top of a flight of steps. In the early Middle Ages at Rome, Ravenna, Milan and Bologna, several basilicas were grouped together or at a short distance one from another, as was especially the case in Benedictine Abbeys. The number of these holy places did not arise from any need on the part of the population, they merely had a votive character. The Lombards multiplied churches and oratories all over the country, and to this day there are to be found in the ancient cities of Italy a quantity of religious buildings which were certainly not erected for the convenience of the population, for the limited proportions of some of these chapels did not admit of the presence of many worshippers.

The founders of these oratories could only have had one object in view. This was the ancient intention of making an offering, a *dedicatio*. All those sacred buildings, altars and chapels represent *munera*, monuments or votive gifts presented to the majesty of God in thanksgiving for his benefits, or in memory of some saint.

We may quote here in honour of the Basilica of the Saviour

the Leonine verses which adorned the papal throne erected within the apse of the Lateran:

> HAEC · EST · PAPALIS · SEDES · ET · PONTIFICALIS
> PRAESIDET · ET · CHRISTI · DE · IVRE · VICARIVS · ISTI
> ET · QVIA · IVRE · DATVR · SEDES · ROMANA · VOCATVR
> NEC · DEBET · VERE · NISI · SOLVS · PAPA · SEDERE
> ET · QVIA · SVBLIMIS · ALII · SVBDVNTVR · IN · IMIS

"This is the Papal and Pontifical throne whence the Vicar of Christ rules according to his right. It is also called the Roman See rightfully established, whereon the Pope alone may sit. As this is the greatest of all thrones, all others must be subject to it."

NOVEMBER 10

SS Trypho and Respicius, Martyrs, and St Nympha, Virgin and Martyr

Station at St Trypho.

St Trypho and the boy saint Respicius are believed to have suffered martyrdom at Nicea during the persecution of Decius (250). A church was dedicated to St Trypho at Constantinople under Justinian, and at Rome a very ancient church also bore his name, where the station on the Saturday before the First Sunday in Lent was celebrated. The fact proves the fame enjoyed by the Saint, who belongs to the band of Anargyri or wonder-working Saints of the East.

It is significant that the Gospel for the Lenten station at St Trypho describes the miraculous cures worked by Jesus when those who touched even the hem of his garment were healed. The allusion to the holy Anargyri is evident.

St Trypho was commemorated at Constantinople on February 1, and in Armenia on the following day. The *cultus* of the martyr spread from the East to Italy.

It is uncertain at what period his relics were brought to Rome. They are said to be preserved at the old church of Santo Spirito in Sassia, whence a portion of them was removed by Benedict XV a few years ago and given to the cathedral of Cerignola of which St Trypho is the Patron.

St Nympha, according to her *Acta*, was a martyr of Palermo. She was included in the Roman Calendar because her relics were venerated in the church of Sta Maria *in Monticelli*, in the Arenula, together with those of SS Mamilianus or Marcellianus, Eustatius, and Quodvultdeus which were brought there from Porto by Urban III.

It appears probable that two saints existed who bore the

same name, Nympha. However this may be, Clement VII granted to the Senate of Palermo a portion of the relics of the Martyr Nympha then preserved at Arenula, and in gratitude for this favour the Senate bestowed five thousand scudi on the church, which were used to restore the building and the tomb of the Martyrs interred at Sta Maria *in Monticelli*.

The Mass was evidently composed in the early Middle Ages when the true liturgical tradition still existed.

The Introit *Clamaverunt* and the Epistle are the same as on June 2, for the martyrs Peter and Marcellinus.

Collect: " Grant, O Lord, we beseech thee, that we may ever honour the festival of thy holy martyrs Trypho, Respicius, and Nympha ; that through their intercession we may always enjoy thy protection."

The guilty man will not dare to present himself before the judge unless he has found a powerful mediator who will plead for him. In the same manner we who are so cowardly in the service of God seek the patronage of the martyrs, and trust that their merits may cover our unworthiness.

The Gradual *Posuerunt* is taken from the Mass of St Basilides (June 12) whilst the alleluiatic verse is taken from the Mass of Martyrs at Eastertide as on April 22.

The Gospel is the same as for the martyrs SS John and Paul on June 26. Christ continually exhorts us not to fear the anger of man and those who can do us material injury only. Fear must be driven out by fear, and in order not to yield to the anger of man we must dread the anger of God.

The Offertory and the Communion are those of March 10, whilst the Secret and Post-Communion are taken from the Mass of St Symphorosa on July 18, changing the names of the martyrs.

NOVEMBER 10

St Andrew Avellino, Confessor*

This celebrated Neapolitan missionary, one of the most distinguished members of the Congregation of Canons Regular founded by St Cajetan of Thiene, belongs to that group of saints who, like St Charles Borromeo, Blessed Paul of Arezzo, and St Cajetan himself promoted the vigorous Catholic Reform, the result of which was manifested in the Council of Trent.

St Andrew Avellino was at one time spiritual director at the seminary of Piacenza, where he is still venerated. His patronage is invoked by the faithful against apoplectic seizures and sudden death. He died of an attack of apoplexy as he was standing at the foot of the altar repeating the words: *Introibo ad altare* (✠1590).

The Mass is the Common of Confessors, *Os justi*, as on January 23 for St Raymund. The Collect only is proper to the feast, and according to modern usage, it alludes to the virtues of the Saint, drawing from them a moral applicable to the faithful.

Collect: " O God, who didst marvellously lift up to thyself the heart of blessed Andrew, thy confessor, by means of his steadfast vow to advance in virtue daily; grant, we beseech thee, that through his merits and intercession we may share in the like grace; so that, by ever following the more perfect way, we may happily be brought to thy glory on high."

Sanctity is not a form or habit which can be adopted at choice and adhered to. The grace of baptism sows in us the seed of Christ—*quos iterum parturio, donec formetur Christus in vobis*—whom we must reproduce in our spiritual life. This seed grows and develops until it reaches *mensura aetatis plenitudinis Christi*, determined by God for each of us.

When we have attained that measure of conformity with our model we have no longer any reason to remain in this world, and are ready for eternity. We are like the statues in a sculptor's studio; when the artist has given the finishing touches, the work of art is removed from the studio, and set up in the place for which it was designed.

NOVEMBER 11

St Mennas, Martyr

Station at St Mennas on the Via Ostiensis.

The station to-day was held on the Ostian Way, where between the first and second milestone the numerous colony from Alexandria had erected a sanctuary in honour of the national martyr Mennas. The sepulchral church of this saint, " the glory of Libya," stood about nine miles from Alexandria, and on account of the miracles worked there, a village had risen up around it for the accommodation of pilgrims, as has been the case at Lourdes in our own days. A number of accounts have been written describing the marvels which occurred there, but even apart from this curious collection attributed to the Patriarch Timothy, proof of the immense number of devout persons who visited the tomb of St Mennas from all parts of the world may be found in the quantity of ampullae or mementos of St Mennas existing in almost all the museums of Europe. On these little phials, made of earthenware, there is always represented the image of the saint between two kneeling camels, with the inscription ΕΥΛΟΓΙΑ ΤΟΥ ΑΓΙΟΥ ΜΗΝΑ, "The blessing of St Mennas."

In spite of the fact that various legends call St Mennas a Phrygian martyr from Cotyaeus, he was certainly an Egyptian and suffered under Diocletian. His *cultus* spread from Alexandria through the greater part of the world, but was most popular in Phrygia. There were, however, many other basilicas dedicated to St Mennas, especially at Jerusalem, at Constantinople, at Rome, and perhaps, too, in Africa, where apparently it was not unusual that his relics should be placed under altars.

The importance of St Mennas' feast at Rome is shown by the fact that although his sanctuary on the Ostian Way is at some distance from the town, St Gregory the Great went there to celebrate the station on the *natalis* of the martyr. The Pope began his homily on this occasion by informing the people that on account of the distance from the city he would not keep them as long as usual.[1] In the seventh century the feast of St Mennas was more important even than that of St Martin, whose *natalis* was deferred to the following day.

The Mass *Laetabitur* is the same as for St Saturninus on November 29. The Collects are taken from the Mass *In virtute*, as for St Vitalis on April 28. The Würzburg List assigns to the station of to-day the passage from the Gospel of St Luke (ix, 23-27), which now no longer appears in the Liturgy.

De Rossi discovered the following important inscription, showing that there existed in Rome in 589, under Pelagius II and Julian Exarch of Italy, a corporation of Alexandrians whose patron was St Mennas.[2]

τῶν Ἀλεξανδρέων ἐπὶ Ἰουλιάνῳ τῷ ἐξάρχῳ Ἰταλίας
θω καί τοῦ ἁγιότατου Μηνᾶ τοῦ σωματίου
ἐγένετο τοῦτο τό ἀγαθὸν ἔργον ἐπί τῷ μακαριωτάτῳ καὶ αγιωτάτῳ
πατριάρχ ἡμῶν Πελαγίῳ Ἐγράφη Φαρμουθι ε ἰνδικτ ἐβδόμης

This inscription may have been connected with the Church of St Mennas in the Ostian Way, where the society named after the Saint had its headquarters.

---

[1] Hom. XXXV. P.L. LXXVI, col. 1259.
[2] *Inscrip. Christ. Urbis Romae*, II, 456.

NOVEMBER 11 (OR 12)

ST MARTIN, BISHOP OF TOURS

During the Byzantine period the fame of St Mennas eclipsed that of St Martin at Rome, and the great Bishop of Tours was commemorated on the following day. This, however, did not continue very long, and after the eighth century the feast of St Martin became one of the most popular at Rome, while the Egyptian martyr only received a commemoration in the Mass.

The origin of the *cultus* of St Martin at Rome dates from the Pontificate of Pope Symmachus (498–514), who built a basilica dedicated to St Martin near the ancient title of Equitius on the Esquiline. Therefore at a time when liturgical honours were reserved almost exclusively to martyrs only, the Apostle of Gaul was the object, at a very early period, of the veneration afterwards extended to all Confessors.

St Martin died at Candes towards the end of the year 396 or the beginning of 397, after a life marked by many miracles, and by the apostolic zeal with which he laboured to root out paganism in his diocese and to establish in it the ideals of the monastic life. His asceticism and his simple habits did not find favour with his brother bishops, or even with his own clergy whilst he lived, but in 397, immediately after his death, his biography, written by Sulpicius Severus, entirely rehabilitated his memory.

This little book became a kind of Gospel of the monastic life, and in a very short space of time it was read in Rome, Alexandria, and Carthage, and even in the desert of the Thebaid, and contributed enormously to the growth of a movement towards the religious life.

St Martin had been famous for his miracles during his life, and after his death his tomb became the goal of many pilgrimages. During the entire Middle Ages the faithful visited the tomb of St Martin as they visited that of SS Peter and Paul, or as they now visit Lourdes: and those afflicted with every kind of infirmity were carried there in hope that

> *Quolibet morbo fuerint gravata,*
> *Restituuntur,*

as we sing in the hymn *Iste Confessor* which was originally written in honour of St Martin.

The first chapel built over the sepulchre of the Saint was erected by his former opponent, afterwards his successor in the See of Tours, St Brice. This was done in 437. A simple transenna separated the tomb from the altar, and from it hung a metal crown with lamps attached to it. There was also a font in which, according to the custom prevalent in the sanctuaries of the Eastern Anargyri, the sick were bathed, that their health might be restored.

This chapel was, however, too small for the ever-growing fame of St Martin, and in 461 the bishop Perpetuus, putting an end, as the ancient inscription says, to the jealousies which pursued the great bishop beyond the grave :

LONGAM • PERPETVVS • SVSTVLIT • INVIDIAM[1]

undertook the erection of a new basilica in honour of his illustrious predecessor.

After the book of Sulpicius Severus, the most ancient reference to St Martin in Gaul is to be found in the epigraph of a certain *Foedula*, who prided herself on having received baptism at his hands.[2]

FOEDVLA • QVAE • MVNDVM • ⳩ DOMINO • MISERANTE • RELIQVIT
HOC • IACET • IN • TVMVLO • QVEM • DEDIT • ALMA • FIDES
MARTINI • QVONDAM • PROCERIS • SVB • DEXTERA • TINCTA
CRIMINA • DEPOSVIT • FONTE • RENATA • DEI
AD • NVNC • MARTYRIBVS • SEDEM • TRIBVENTIBVS • APTAM
CERBASIVM • PROCEREM • PROTASIVMQVE • COLIT
EMERI • TAM • REQVIEM • TITVLO • SORTITA • FIDELE
CONFESSA • EST • SANCTIS • QVAE • SOCIATA • IACET

" Foedula who has left this world, through God's mercy rests in this tomb prepared for her by her holy faith. Baptised by the hand of Martin she was born again to God at the font where her sins were washed away. Now, through the venerable martyrs Gervase and Protase whom she reverenced, she has obtained a worthy place, and has been admitted to eternal rest by the merits of her faith, and is now among the saints."

St Martin had, during his lifetime, so much intercourse with Rome and with Italy, that at his death his *cultus* spread rapidly beyond the Alps. St Paulinus of Nola was one of his most zealous admirers, and asserted on his death-bed that St Martin of Tours and St Januarius of Naples were come to help him in his last agony.

Besides the Church of St Martin built by Pope Symmachus on the Esquiline, there was, in the seventh century, a famous monastery dedicated to the same saint at the Vatican. It

---

[1] Le Blanc, *Inscript. Chrét.*, Vol. I, 181.
[2] *Op. cit.*, Vol. II, n. 412, pl. 292.

stood *juxta ferratum*, that is to say, near the Confession of the Prince of the Apostles, and during the solemn vigil of Saturday night in Ember week, whilst the people sang the Litanies in the basilica, the Pope withdrew into the Oratory of St Martin and performed the ceremonies of the ordination of priests.

At the Basilica of St Paul, also, a chapel was dedicated to the Bishop of Tours in the Middle Ages. It had an apse and corresponded with what is now the lesser choir on the left of the apse in the great transept.

In order to give the reader some idea of the great devotion inspired by the Patron of monastic life in ancient times, we shall merely give here a list of the churches dedicated to him at Rome. They included San Martino *in Exquiliis;* San Martino *juxta ferratum;* San Martino *in Scorticlaria;* San Martino *de Maxima;* San Martino *in Monteria;* San Martino *in Panarella;* San Martino *de Pila;* San Martino *de Posterula*. To these must be added innumerable chapels and altars dedicated to the great Bishop in the various titular churches, and especially in the Benedictine monasteries.

As to those outside Rome, it is a significant fact that the Patriarch of Western Monasticism dedicated to St Martin the ancient temple which stood on the height of Cassino. It became the first church of the Benedictine order, where the new community of Monte Cassino recited the divine Office, and where St Benedict desired to yield up his soul before the altar of St Martin.

The founders of the famous Abbey of Farfa followed the example of the Patriarch of Monte Cassino, and St Lawrence of Siro also converted a pagan ruin on the Monte Acurziano in Sabina into a Christian oratory, and dedicated it to St Martin. In the accounts of the estates of the Abbey of Farfa in the eleventh century, we find about thirty churches named after the Bishop of Tours.

It is not only in monastic surroundings that the name of Martin is recorded, but in every place throughout Italy, France and Spain we still see churches, crosses, bridges, fountains, hills, and villages named after him. St Martin was regarded as the patron of the oppressed, the terror of the tyrant, the most popular saint in Europe whom the Middle Ages regarded as the embodiment of its genius and its religious spirit.

It is therefore not to be wondered at, that the feast of St Martin was formerly a holiday of obligation, when all abstained from servile work. We find it entered as such at the synod of Aix-la-Chapelle in 809, and it held this position during the greater part of the Middle Ages.

The Mass *Statuit* is like that of St Andrew Corsini on February 4, except the followng portions.

The Collect is taken from Sexagesima Sunday: " O God, who knowest that we stand not by any strength of our own, mercifully grant that, by the intercession of blessed Martin thy bishop and confessor, we may be kept from all harm."

We should note the phrase: *ex nulla nostra virtute subsistimus*, which strikes a blow at the Pelagian heresy, and proves that without grace we cannot raise ourselves towards God, or perform those works which will merit eternal life. The Catholic doctrine of grace so clearly and fully explained by St Augustine and St Thomas, gives to our spiritual life a character of humility and confidence.

The alleluiatic verse is proper to the feast: " The blessed man St Martin, Bishop of the City of Tours, went to his rest. and the Angels and Archangels, the Thrones, Dominations, and Powers received him." The ministers of Christ on earth imitate in a manner the angelic choirs. They are the angels of the Church, which they serve as the angels of God serve the heavenly altar and temple. They fulfil on earth the duties which the blessed spirits fulfil in heaven. Like the Angels and Archangels they announce the word of God to men; like the Thrones they uplift their sacramental Lord in their hands; they form the sacred Hierarchy on earth, and rule over the family of Christ in which they resemble the Dominations, Principalities and Powers. Like the Virtues they open and close the gates of heaven, they bind and subdue Satan; they distribute the treasures of divine grace, they sanctify by their word and the gesture of their hand the lifeless elements in order that as sacraments or sacramentals they may co-operate in the sanctification of souls.

The Gospel in the Würzburg List is from the Mass *Os justi* of Confessors only (Luke xii, 35–40), but in the present Missal is taken from St Luke (xi, 33–36). The candle is intended to be set up in the candlestick and the marvellous graces of pastoral zeal and the power to work miracles are ordained by God for the edification of the Christian people. The Saviour uses the same illustration to draw another lesson. As the eye is the light of the body, so a pure intention is the eye of the soul. The man who desires only to please God has a single eye and a pure intention.

The Offertory and the Communion are taken from the Mass *Os justi* as on January 23. The Antiphon *Beatus vir* for the Communion is connected with the passage in the Gospel given in the Würzburg List.

The Secret in the present Missal is that of the feast of St Nicholas of Bari on December 6. Formerly it was taken from the twenty-second Sunday after Pentecost and had a general character, the name of the Saint being omitted.

The Gregorian Sacramentary gives the following Preface for to-day: *Vere dignum . . . aeterne Deus: cuius munere beatus Martinus confessor pariter et sacerdos, et bonorum operum incrementis excrevit, et variis virtutum donis exuberavit, et miraculis coruscavit. Qui quod verbis docuit, operum exhibitione complevit, et documento simul et exemplo subditis ad caelestia regna pergendi ducatum praebuit. Unde tuam clementiam petimus, et eius qui tibi placuit exemplis ad bene agendum informemur, meritis muniamur, intercessionibus adiuvemur, qualiter ad caeleste regnum, illo interveniente, te opitulante, pervenire mereamur. Per Christum . . . per quem maiestatem tuam*, etc.

The Post-Communion is as follows: " Grant, we beseech thee, O Lord our God, that these sacraments may avail to our salvation, through the intercession of those on whose festival they are offered."

That Communion is truly salutary in which the soul becomes one with Christ and takes part in his sorrows and his death, and so shares in that salvation of which he is the fount.

The medieval Sacramentaries also contain a blessing or *oratio super populum: Exaudi, Domine, populum tuum tota tibi mente subiectum, et beati Martini Pontificis supplicatione custodi, ut corpore et corde protectus, quod pie credit appetat, et quod juste sperat, obtineat. Per Dominum.*

We quote here the verses in honour of the great St Martin, which in the early Middle Ages could be read on the Eastern tower adorning the façade of his basilica at Tours. The first line is also written over one of the doors of the Basilica of St Paul at Rome.

INGREDIENS · TEMPLVM · REFER · AD · SVBLIMIA · VVLTVM
EXCELSVS · ADITVS · SVSPICIT · ALTA · FIDES
ESTO · HVMILIS · SENSV · SED · SPE · SECTARE · VOCANTEM
MARTINUS · RESERAT · QVAS · VENERARE · FORES
HAEC · TVTA · EST · TVRRIS · TREPIDIS · OBIECTA · SVPERBIS
ELATA · EXCLVDENS · MITIA · CORDA · TEGENS
CELSIOR · ILLA · TAMEN · QUAE · CAELI · VEXIT · AD · ARCEM
MARTINUM · ASTRIGERIS · AMBITIOSA · VIIS
VNDE · VOCAT · POPULOS · QUI · PRAEVIVS · AD · BONA · CHRISTI
SYDEREVM · INGRESSVS · SANCTIFICAVIT · ITER

" Lift up thine eyes, thou who dost enter this temple,
For its lofty walls are symbols of great faith.
Be humble in mind, but follow, in hope, him who calls.
Martin opens to you these venerable doors.
This tower is a refuge to the weak, but resists the proud.
But far higher and more glorious is that which raised Martin

November 11 (or 12)

Amongst the stars to the heavenly mansion.
Thence he calls his people to the joys of Christ
Having preceded them to heaven and sanctified the way."

NOVEMBER 12
St Martin, Pope*

We have already spoken of this famous Confessor of Catholic orthodoxy against the Monothelites who died on September 16, 655, at Sebastopol, and was buried there in the basilica outside the walls, dedicated to the Virgin Mary.

Greek authorities record the great number of miracles worked at his tomb, and because of these the *cultus* of the fearless bishop of Rome was more popular among the Byzantines than it is now among the Latins. That his festival was entered on this day in the Roman Calendar is due partly to a curious mistake.

As the feast of St Mennas was kept at Rome on November 11, there was some difficulty in fixing a date for the commemoration of St Martin of Tours.

In some of the Roman Calendars the feast of St Martin was marked on November 11, in others on November 12. Finally both feasts were kept. But, as in the case of St Peter's Chair, one date was fixed for that of Rome and the other for that of Antioch, so it occurred too for the double festival of St Martin. November 11 was dedicated to the Bishop of Tours, and November 12 to the Pope of the same name, also a Confessor, who died in exile at Sebastopol.

The Mass is *Sacerdotes Dei*, as for St Eusebius on December 16. The Epistle, however, is taken from the feast of the martyrs Gervase and Protase on June 19, whilst the Gospel is that of St Melchiades on December 10.

The Lesson is from the first Epistle of St Peter (iv, 13–19), and was evidently chosen because the special character of the persecution suffered by St Martin caused him to resemble Christ when in his passion he became an object of derision to his persecutors. The following are some of the praises addressed to St Martin in the Greek Liturgy:

τί σε Μαρτῖνε προσφθέξομαι; ὀρθοδόξων διδαχῶν καθηγητὴν πανευκλεῆ· κορυφαῖον ἱερὸν δογμάτων θείων ἀψευδῶς; τοῦ ψεύδους ἀλεθέστατον κατήγορον;

... Ἀρχιερέων σε ἔγνωμεν κρηπίδα, ὀρθοδοξίας τε στήλην καὶ εὐσεβείας διδάσκαλον.

Ἐπεκόσμησας τὸν Πέτρου θεῖον θρόνον καὶ τῇ αὐτοῦ θείᾳ πέτρᾳ τὴν ἐκκλησίαν ἀσάλευτον συντηρήσας σὺν αὐτῷ δεδόξασαι.

"By what name shall I call thee, O Martin ? Shall I salute thee as a most illustrious teacher of the orthodox faith ?

"Shall I call thee the infallible and holy exponent of the divine dogmas ? Shall I proclaim thee the most sincere opponent of error ? . . . We recognize in thee the foundation of the sacred episcopate, the column of the orthodox faith, the teacher of religion.

"Thou didst adorn the See of Peter, for after having defended the Church established on that divine rock, thou dost share the glory of Peter."

We cannot help wondering what the thoughts of our separated Eastern brethren may be, when they pronounce this solemn profession and acknowledgement of the papal supremacy in their Liturgy, as they do to this day. Such was the faith of the Eastern Churches before a disastrous schism caused them to break away from the Rock on which Christ founded his Church.

NOVEMBER 13

St Brice, Bishop

St Brice, who was first the rival and later the successor of St Martin of Tours, became the object of a universal *cultus*, principally because of his connection with the celebrated bishop. Sulpicius Severus describing the trials suffered by Martin at the hands of his clergy and fellow-bishops, envious of his sanctity and miraculous gift, makes no exception of the priest Bricius. The Saint supported all this ill-will with incredible patience and was content to remark : " If Christ endured Judas, why should I not endure Brice ? "

After the death of the Master, a reaction set in, and in 397 Brice was elected as his successor in the See of Tours. In the fulfilment of that difficult office the former rival of St Martin learnt to realize his own errors, and generously expiated all his faults. He carried the burden of the episcopacy in a manner worthy of praise for the space of forty-seven years. Needless to say that when placed in a position similar to that of Martin, his former hostility towards his predecessor was changed into veneration, and Brice erected in 437 a chapel over the tomb of St Martin, where he, too, was buried. From that moment, devotion towards St Brice was united with that to St Martin, and his feast was regularly inscribed even in the Missals of the Roman Curia until the end of the fifteenth century.

In the ancient accounts of the Abbey of Farfa, there is

mentioned in the eleventh century an *Ecclesia Sancti Bricii in fundo occiano*[1] in the Sabine district of Scandrilia.

The history of St Brice teaches us never to despise anyone, and never to despair of a man's conversion. Those who at the present moment appear degraded by vice or evil qualities, may by the help of divine grace become in a short time far better than we are.

NOVEMBER 13

St Didacus, Confessor*

This humble Franciscan friar, famous for the miracles he performed, deserves a place of honour in the calendar of the Mother Church, for Rome witnessed his virtues when in the year of the Jubilee, 1425, Fra Didacus resided at Ara Coeli where he had care of the infirmary. He died at Alcalá de Henares on November 12, 1463, and was canonized by the Franciscan Pope Sixtus V, who placed his name in the Roman Calendar in 1585.

The Mass *Justus* is the same as on January 31.

The Collect is as follows: "Almighty everlasting God, who by thy wonderful providence choosest the weak things of the world to confound the strong; mercifully grant to us, thy humble servants, that through the prayers of blessed Didacus, thy confessor, we may become worthy to be raised to everlasting glory in the heavens."

Pride is the lust of the soul which takes pleasure in itself. God does not make use of the proud to accomplish his greatest works, for they would appropriate the glory and would not abandon themselves as obedient instruments in his hands. On the contrary, God confounds the proud by overthrowing them as the giant Goliath was overthrown by a stone cast from a sling; that is to say by lowly and inefficient things, in order that the glory of the victory should belong to God alone.

The Secret and Post-Communion are of the Common, as on the feast of St Philip Benizi on August 23.

NOVEMBER 14

St Josaphat, Bishop and Martyr

There is scarcely one of the truths of the Catholic Faith which has not had its martyr. St John Nepomucene is the martyr of the seal of Confession, St Tarcisius is the martyr of

---

[1] *Chron. Farf.* I, 296, ed. Balzani.

the Eucharist, St Peter of Verona the martyr of the Holy Office of the Inquisition. It was fitting then that a Ruthenian, a representative of the venerable Eastern Churches, should seal with his blood the ancient faith of Catholic Byzantium concerning the primacy of the See of Peter.

The labours of this martyr for the union of the Ruthenian Church with that of Rome are almost incredible. After a youth of singular innocence mortified by voluntary penance, Josaphat, remembering the powerful support lent to the orthodox cause by the monastic orders, entered religion, and with the help of Velamin Rutski, devoted himself to the restoration of the rule of St Basil.

In 1619 when he had already gathered round him a zealous community of monks, Josaphat was raised from being Archimandrite of Vilna to the archiepiscopal See of Polotsk.

As superior of a monastery the Saint had succeeded in keeping his disciples free from any schismatic taint; so, too, as metropolitan he devoted himself to the conquest of error with ardent and enlightened charity. He gave to all the example of a holy life, and laboured for souls by preaching, by teaching the catechism, and by the distribution of controversial works. As a result of his zeal many schismatics were reconciled to the Catholic Church. His opponents at last resolved to take his life, and he suffered martyrdom at their hands with great courage and serenity at the age of forty-three years.

In 1642, Urban VIII placed his name in the ranks of the Blessed, and Pius IX, on June 29, in 1867, on the occasion of the centenary of the Princes of the Apostles, canonized the zealous champion of the Primacy of the Roman Church. The Ruthenians celebrate his feast on September 16.

The Introit, Epistle, Gospel, and Communion of this Mass are like those of December 29 for the feast of St Thomas of Canterbury, whom this martyr resembles in many ways.

Collect: "Stir up within the Church, O Lord, we beseech thee, the Spirit, who did so fill blessed Josaphat, thy martyr and bishop, that he laid down his life for the sheep; by his intercession let us be so stirred and strengthened by the same Spirit, that we may not shrink from giving our lives for the brethren."

The Gradual *Inveni* has been quoted on December 6, and the alleluiatic verse is the same as for St Polycarp on January 26.

The Lord truly crowned his faithful servant even on earth. The martyr's head was split open with a blow from an axe, but God permitted that the liturgical crown of canonization should be placed upon it by Pius IX under the most solemn circumstances, when, for the centenary of SS Peter and Paul, the Pope was surrounded by a host of cardinals and bishops who gathered at Rome from all parts of the world.

The Offertory was chosen in accordance with the martyrdom endured by the Saint in the accomplishment of his duties as Bishop. (John xv, 13), " Greater love than this no man hath, that he lay down his life for his friends."

A Bishop gives his life for his sheep not only by dying for them but by living for them, and therefore his whole time and thought should be devoted to the spiritual care of those entrusted to him. It is in this sense that the Apostle defines the episcopate as *bonum opus*, and that the scholastics call it *status perfectionis acquisitae*. The fact remains that no state of life has given more saints to the Church than the episcopal state.

Secret : " O most merciful God, pour forth thy blessing on these our gifts, and strengthen us in that faith which thy holy martyr and bishop Josaphat upheld by shedding his blood."

The first condition essential to true sanctity is perfect orthodoxy. His biographers tell us that during the first years of Josaphat's religious life, the monastery was governed by an abbot who sympathized secretly with the schismatics, but who avoided any act likely to compromise him with Catholics. He exerted a very harmful influence in the monastery, but it was difficult to find an opportunity for breaking with such a deceitful superior. Josaphat and Rutski were obliged, therefore, to combine the obedience they owed their abbot, though a disguised schismatic, with their own fidelity to the Roman Church.

One day, however, the Archimandrite betrayed his true sentiments. He was in the act of celebrating the divine Sacrifice and Josaphat was participating in it as deacon. After the Consecration during the Litany of " great intercession " when the celebrant should have commemorated the Roman Pontiff, the Archimandrite omitted to do so. This was sufficient to reveal the truth, and the holy deacon immediately left the altar, and refused to take any further part in the sacrilegious service.

Post-Communion : " May this heavenly banquet impart to us, O Lord, the spirit of fortitude, which inspired thy holy martyr and bishop Josaphat to strive for the honour of the church throughout his life even until the hour of his triumph."

The Lord has entrusted to each one of us a mission of great importance to be carried out in the midst of difficulties of every kind. We feel ourselves, rightly, to be weak and incapable, but we must not despair on this account. Jesus has given himself to us in the Holy Eucharist in order to be our strength. The greater our insufficiency, the deeper our need, the more grace we must obtain to supply our wants and to atone for our inability.

We read in the life of St Josaphat that in the first years of his monastic reform Satan vented his rage on the monks by terrifying them when they rose in the night to recite the divine Office. At last the Saint determined to put an end to the fearful noises, and one night he took the Blessed Sacrament, and advancing against the devil, drove him from the sanctuary. The uproar was terrific, but at length Satan was obliged to yield, and the monks were able ever afterwards to sing the night Office in peace.

NOVEMBER 15

St Gertrude, Virgin*

Christian art is wont to represent the saints holding an emblem symbolical of some special characteristic of their holiness. Therefore St Gertrude is pictured with a flaming heart in her hands, for as she lived her mystical life in the most Sacred Heart of Jesus, so the Saviour lived in her by faith and love.

The mission of this celebrated Benedictine nun in the thirteenth century was very similar to that of Margaret Mary Alacoque, which indeed she recognized and foretold in a prophetic showing. There is this difference between the two mystics; the great revelations of the Heart of Jesus to the Benedictine saint were intended for a band of privileged souls; those of Paray-le-Monial were to enrich the whole Catholic world. The object of the apparitions granted to both mystics was the same: the ineffable love of Jesus, of which his Heart is the organ and the physical sign. But the manner of conceiving this devotion is as different in the two saints as was their spiritual education.

A member of an order which for more than seven centuries had been the heir of patristic tradition and in which the Liturgy was almost exclusively the source of spiritual life, Gertrude conceived devotion to the Sacred Heart not as a separate devotion, but as a deeper intelligence of the great all-embracing mystery of Christ living again in the Church by means of the Catholic Liturgy. It is essentially the love of Jesus which through the universal prayer of the Church explains and illustrates the whole drama of his Incarnation and the treasures of his Heart.

The mysticism of St Gertrude is entirely founded on the

liturgical life of the Church. She knew few religious practices except the divine Office and the solemn Masses at which she and St Mechtilde, the *cantrix Mechtildis*, sang daily in the choir, together with the community of the Abbey of Helfta. The revelations granted to her by God were generally in relation to these Offices, and Jesus explained to her their more hidden meaning, or taught her more sublime ways of following them and of nourishing her spiritual life upon them.

The atmosphere in Gertrude's mystical writings is almost always serene and radiant. Jesus revealed to her his Heart as a mystery of grace and love rather than as an abyss of sorrow. She did not see the divine Heart encircled with a crown of thorns, neither was she called to the special vocation of victim for the sins of the world, as was St Margaret Mary Alacoque. She sometimes beheld the Sacred Heart pierced for us, but that wound was a golden door through which she entered joyfully into the secret sanctuary of the Godhead, the chamber of the Spouse.

Like John, who at the Last Supper rested calmly on the breast of the Saviour, whilst the other apostles were alarmed and distressed by the announcement made by Christ of the treachery of Judas and of his own death, the mystic of Helfta found in the Sacred Heart a secret tabernacle, where nothing disturbed her profound contemplation.

At times she would see that Heart like a golden cup at which all the saints slaked their thirst. At other times a chain of gold came from the Heart of Christ to bind the world in bonds of love. Again, the Divine Heart resembled a thurible sending up incense before the throne of the Heavenly Father, whilst at another moment it would appear like a precious casket containing all the merits of the Incarnation freely granted to souls.

Therefore the devotion of the Benedictine Virgin to the Sacred Heart as a symbol of sorrow and of love, reflects the attitude of fervent worship of the humanity of the Redeemer adopted by Catholic piety at the end of the Middle Ages, after the arid theological disquisitions of the Byzantines had died away.

Gertrude is one of the most remarkable representatives of this school, but she is not by any means the only one even in her Abbey of Helfta, where under the government of the holy abbess Gertrude of Hackeborn—too often confused with her namesake—St Mechtilde also lived and wrote mystical works, and where a second Mechtilde of great virtue, and favoured by celestial revelations, was her companion.

Although devotion to the Sacred Heart as expressed in the

convent of Helfta in the thirteenth century exactly reflects the ancient spiritual teaching of the Benedictine Order, the great revelations made to the mystic of Paray-le-Monial are more in keeping with the psychology of later times, and with the unusual conditions in which the Church found itself shortly before the French Revolution.

Gertrude had foreseen the important mission of the humble disciple of St Francis de Sales on an occasion when Jesus had bidden her to rest her head upon his Heart with St John the Evangelist. Listening to the beating of the adorable Heart, the Saint of Helfta asked St John why he had not made known in his Gospel the treasures of light and mercy revealed to him during his mystic repose on the Saviour's Heart at the Last Supper. John replied that this new and touching revelation would be made later when the world had reached the depths of malice, and that in order to rescue it God would employ the last resources of his invincible love.

In writing the history of the devotion to the Sacred Heart, it is right to consider the ancient spiritual tradition of the Benedictine order, as well as the zeal displayed in spreading the apostolate of the Heart of Jesus by more modern religious congregations, without setting one devotion against another, since all contribute to illustrate one Catholic Faith. In the same manner as the Incarnation or the Holy Eucharist, so too the most Sacred Heart of Jesus is a gift common to the whole Church and cannot be regarded as the exclusive possession of any particular order. St Gertrude therefore joins hands with Margaret Mary Alacoque, and her revelations find their complete fulfilment in those granted four centuries later to the heroic daughter of the Visitation.

Gertrude was born on January 6, 1256; at five years old she entered the monastery of Helfta, at the age of twenty-five she was favoured with celestial visions, and towards the end of her life she received the stigmata. She died in 1302, and her name was inserted in the Roman Calendar by Clement XII.

The Mass *Dilexisti* is the same as on February 10, except the Collect, which alludes to words spoken by Jesus to St Gertrude: "In no place am I so well pleased to dwell as in the bosom of my heavenly Father, in the sacrament of the Eucharist, and in thy heart, my beloved Spouse."

Collect: "O God, who in the heart of the holy virgin Gertrude didst provide for thyself a dwelling in which thou wast well pleased, through her merits and intercession mercifully wash away the stains from our hearts and grant that we may enjoy fellowship with her."

On one occasion when St Gertrude was unable to assist at the spiritual conference with the community, Jesus appeared to her and told her that he himself would instruct her. He then made her listen to the beatings of his Heart in which the Saint discerned two kinds of pulsations. Jesus explained to her that by this double pulsation he accomplished the salvation of mankind. " By the first," he said, " I placate the wrath of my heavenly Father against men, I excuse their malice and inspire them to repent. By the second I rejoice with my Father in the efficacy of my blood manifested in the salvation of the just, and I draw the virtuous to the desire of ever greater perfection. As the employment of a man's senses cannot impede the beating of his heart, so the government of the whole universe can never cause these two movements of my Heart of mercy towards the just and towards sinners, to be interrupted."

NOVEMBER 17

ST GREGORY THAUMATURGUS, BISHOP AND CONFESSOR

This Saint is one of the brightest lights of the Church of Pontus, and was at once an apostle and a doctor, a Thaumaturgus and Confessor of the Faith.

Gregory was born at Neocaesarea in Pontus about the year 213, and in his early youth was a disciple of Origen whom he praised in an enthusiastic panegyric. Having been made bishop of his native city, he converted it from idolatry to the true Faith, working a number of miracles, on account of which he received the title of Ὁ θαυματουργός. He died during the reign of Aurelian between 270 and 275, and the whole of Pontus, according to St Basil, venerated his memory with the greatest devotion as that of a teacher of the Faith.

The Mass *Statuit* is the same as on February 4. The Collect, *Da quaesumus*, etc., is that of St Liborius on July 23.

The Gospel taken from St Mark (xi, 22–24) is proper to the feast, and contains the words of Christ which promise that unshaken faith shall have power even to move mountains and cast them in the sea. This promise has been fulfilled many times as is shown in the lives of the saints. It happened at Neocaesarea at the word of St Gregory Thaumaturgus, and again, according to St. Gregory the Great, in the vicinity of Rome, on Mount Soracte, in the monastery where the monk St Nonnosus lived in the sixth century.

NOVEMBER 18

Dedication of the Basilicas of the Princes of the Apostles, Peter and Paul

"I can show the trophies of the Apostles; for if you will go to the Vatican on the Ostian Way you will find the trophies (τρόπαια) of those who founded this Church."[1]

These words, written by the priest Caius disputing with Proclus the leader of the Phrygian sect at Rome, prove that since the second century the memorials erected by Pope Anacletus over the tombs of the two Princes of the Apostles were regarded even by heretics as the foundation-stones of the Roman Church, the symbol of her apostolic origin and her divine pre-eminence.

It is not surprising, therefore, that as soon as Constantine granted peace to the Church, Pope Sylvester proposed to him to make of those two chief sanctuaries of the Catholic faith monuments of art and grandeur, in order that they should correspond externally with the importance of the two sepulchres in the eyes of the whole Christian world.

The son of St Helena readily assented to the Pope's request. He erected on the Via Cornelia and on the Via Ostiensis two *domus regales*, as the *Liber Pontificalis* calls them, dazzling with gold, and endowed with an extensive patrimony in land, some of the property being in the East.

The first care of the Emperor was to cause the tombs of the apostles to be enclosed in a thick casing of bronze. The result was to form a kind of bronze cube: *ex aere cypro . . . ad caput, ped. V., ad pedes, ped. V., ad latus dextrum, ped. V., ad latus sinistrum, ped. V., subter, ped. V., supra, ped. V.* The biographer of Pope Sylvester in the *Pontificalis* ingeniously assures us that within this enormous mass of metal the tombs of the apostles were indeed safe, for they are now immovable: *quod est immobile.*

Upon each sepulchre the devout Emperor placed a great cross of gold weighing a hundred and fifty pounds. On that of St Peter was inscribed:

CONSTANTINVS · AVG · ET · HELENA · AVG · HANC · DOMVM · REGALEM (*auro decorant quam*) SIMILI · FVLGORE · CORVSCANS · AVLA · CIRCVMDAT.

The *Liber Pontificalis* tells us that Constantine did the same on the Ostian Way in honour of the Doctor of the Gentiles.

[1] Euseb., *Hist. Eccles.*, II, 25-27.

November 18

In speaking of the tombs of the Apostles it is necessary to distinguish two monuments: the sepulchre itself, the *domus regalis*, from the *coruscans aula* or the basilica surrounding it. The sanctuary *ad corpus*, the *domus regalis*, or the two sepulchral cells, were since the time of Pope Hormisdas practically closed to the people, who were only permitted to touch the tombs with cloths (*brandea*) let down through the *cateractae* pierced in the stone covering them. The marble slab dating from the time of Constantine, with three holes in the centre for the passage of cloths and of incense, is still to be seen at the Ostian Basilica.

The dimensions of the Constantinian Basilica of St Paul were limited, no doubt because of the position of the Apostle's tomb situated between the Via Ostiensis and another *iter vetus* on the side towards the Tiber. The church was soon too small for the crowd of pilgrims who visited it, and in 386 the Emperors Valentinian II, Theodosius, and Arcadius, in a letter to Sallustius, Prefect of Rome, ordered its reconstruction on a larger scale. By this new design the orientation of the basilica was transposed, leaving the altar of Pope Sylvester over the tomb in the same place. The apse of the new building stood where the original door on the Ostian Road had been, and the church was lengthened by about a hundred metres towards the Tiber. The entrance was approached through a great atrium or "paradysus," in the centre of which Leo the Great caused the ritual font or *cantharus* for the ablutions to be replaced.

When the Emperors transferred their residence to Constantinople, Christian Rome became yet more attached to the Roman Pontiff, and regarded the two Basilicas of the Princes of the Apostles as the real Palatine, the new *regia—domus regalis*—of the Catholic religion. Peter and Paul were now the new sovereigns of Rome, and as in the ancient ceremonial the court chamberlains were called *cubiculari*, so Leo the Great when he instituted, according to the *Pontificalis*, a guard of honour about the sepulchres of the Apostles, granted to them the magnificent title of *cubiculari beati Petri*, *cubiculari beati Pauli*, still to be seen on some of the sepulchral inscriptions which have come down to us.

In the meantime the influx of pilgrims from all lands *ad limina Apostolorum* continued to increase, until Pope Simplicius was obliged to institute a permanent service of priests attached to the Vatican and Ostian Basilicas: *ut presbyteri manerent propter poenitentes et baptismum . . . regio I ad sanctum Paulum, regio VI vel VII ad sanctum Petrum.*[1]

This condition of things is reflected in the golden period

---
[1] *Lib. Pontif.* I, 249, ed. Duchesne.

of Roman Liturgy. There had not yet arisen in Rome the idea of the medieval cathedral, supreme over all lesser churches. On account of the stational Liturgy the Pope did not celebrate the sacred Offices regularly in any particular church, but went now to one, and now to another sanctuary, according to where the feast of the day was to be kept. If, however, we were determined to find a canonical institution in some manner anticipating the medieval conception of a cathedral, we should be obliged to recognize this pre-eminence in the Vatican Basilica.

It was there, around the tomb of the founder of the Roman Church, that his successors were always interred. It was there too, that, as we have seen, the eucharistic station was held on the feasts of the Epiphany, the Ascension, Pentecost, and for the great *pannuchis* following Saturday in Ember week. The Pope, the priests and deacons were all ordained at St Peter's. It was there that the new Pope inaugurated his Pontificate, it was there that he was laid to rest when that Pontificate ended. In the Baptistery of Damasus, the Pope always administered baptism, and it was on the wooden chair venerated as that once used by St Peter, that he sat when he admitted new sheep into the Christian fold by means of the sacrament of Confirmation.

For this reason Ennodius of Pavia, speaking of this ancient chair of St Peter preserved at the Vatican, called it : *sella gestatoria confessionis Apostolicae*,[1] and in a similar manner, the sepulchral inscription of Pope Siricius, describing his exaltation to the supreme Pontificate, says that he was enthroned amid the acclamation of the people, on the chair of St Peter, at that time preserved in the *Consignatorium* of Damasus.

FONTE · SACRO · MAGNVS · MERVIT · SEDERE · SACERDOS
CVNCTVS · VT · POPVLVS · PACEM · TVNC · SOLI · CLAMARET

" He merited to sit as Pontiff in the sacred Baptistery when the people had declared themselves in communion with him alone."

Venerated by generations of Catholics, enriched with all that genius inspired by faith could produce through long centuries of Christian civilization, the Vatican Basilica which Leo IV surrounded with the walled Leonine city as a defence against the Saracens, assumed in the medieval mind the significance of a symbol of the Primacy of the See of Peter. This thought is well expressed in the lines which could

[1] *Apolog. pro Synodo*, P.L. LXXIII, col. 206.

formerly be read under the mosaic of the apse restored by Innocent III.

SVMMA · PETRI · SEDES · EST · HAEC · SACRA · PRINCIPIS · AEDES
MATER · CVNCTARVM · DECOR · ET · DECVS · ECCLESIARVM
DEVOTVS · CHRISTO · TEMPLO · QVI · SERVIT · IN · ISTO
FLORES · VIRTVTIS · CAPIET · FRVCTVSQVE · SALVTIS

" This is the throne of Peter, and the temple consecrated to the Prince of the Apostles.

This is the Mother, the ornament, and the glory of all other churches.

He who pays devout service to Christ in this temple

Will obtain the flowers of virtue and the fruit of eternal salvation."

The history of the tomb of the Apostles on the Ostian Way is similar to that of the Vatican. When, in 410, Alaric sacked the city he issued a proclamation to the terrified Romans that those who would escape from the massacre should take refuge in the Basilica of the two Apostles. St Jerome tells us that St Marcella, with her companion Principia, fled from the Aventine, and sought shelter in the Basilica of St Paul " to find there either a refuge or a grave."

St Gregory the Great testified that in his day, the two apostolic sepulchres were famous for so great a number of miracles, that the faithful out of reverence scarcely dared to approach them.

After the invasions of the Saracens John VIII, imitating the example set by Leo IV for the defence of St Peter's, surrounded St Paul's with a fortified city, which he desired to be called Giovannipolis after himself.

In the meantime, throughout the early Middle Ages, besides the religious communities who had been entrusted by St Gregory II with the solemn celebration of divine Office at St Paul's, the hebdomadary clergy and the priests of the titles of Regio I continued to carry out uninterruptedly their original duties concerning the administration of the sacraments.

Pietro Mallio quotes the following list of priests who celebrated the solemn daily sacrifice at the Confession of the Apostles on the Ostian Way:

Tit. Sabinae
,, *Priscae*
,, *Balbinae*
,, *de Fasciola*
,, *S. Xysti*
,, *Marcelli*
,, *Susannae*

But the celebration of a single daily Mass on the altar of each church according to the ancient custom, was not sufficient when great crowds of pilgrims succeeded each other *ad limina Apostolorum*. Therefore, Gregory III established that five Masses should be said daily in the Ostian Basilica, but that these must be offered at five different altars, and with the condition that the monks of the abbey who administered the revenues of the Basilica should give to the officiating priests the stipend for the Mass.

On the more solemn festivals the honour of officiating at the tomb of the Doctor of the Gentiles was reserved to the Pope. After Christmas and Easter, before Lent, on the occasion of the scrutinies of the catechumens, on the feast of the Apostles, the Liturgy of Rome required that the Pope, the clergy, and the faithful should visit the Via Cornelia and the Via Ostiensis in order to celebrate the night vigils and the festive stations at the tombs of SS Peter and Paul.

The Sanctuaries of the sepulchres of the Apostles were then the true centre of the town, that which, above all, made Rome sacred and important in the eyes of the Catholic world. Therefore it is not surprising that on the greatest festivals, the Offices at the two Basilicas were performed by the whole clergy and people at Rome.

The ancient collections contain inscriptions referring to the Ostian Basilica similar to those of the Vatican, which illustrate the dignity of the sanctuary of St Paul. The following are examples of these :

HIC · POSITVS · CAELI · TRANSCENDIT · CVLMINA · PAVLVS
CVI · DEBET · TOTVS · QVOD · CHRISTO · CREDIDIT · ORBIS

" Paul who is buried here is raised above the heavens.
The whole world is indebted to him for his faith in Christ."

The following inscription could be seen formerly on the apse of the baptistery :

HAEC · DOMVS · EST · FIDEI · MENTES · VBI · SVMMA · POTESTAS
LIBERAT · ET · SANCTO · PVRGATAS · FONTE · TVETVR

" This is the throne of faith where the sovereign power
Frees the souls purified in the sacred font, and protects them."

Although the two Basilicas of the Apostles were held in great veneration from the earliest times we do not find any commemoration of their encænia in the ancient traditional Liturgy of Rome. The Martyrology of St Jerome and the Sacramentaries are silent concerning this point; the Calendar of the

November 18

Antiphonary of St Peter dating from the twelfth century ignores it, and it is not until the time of Mallio that we find a mention of the feast of the *dedicatio basilicarum Petri et Pauli*. The silence of the documents belonging to the Vatican Basilica is decisive.

The reason determining the date of November 18 is unknown. The fact however of the two encænia being celebrated on the same day points to the introduction of a symbolical meaning, when, originally, the feast was merely the commemoration of an anniversary.

On November 9, the dedication of the Basilica of the Saviour is celebrated at Rome; on November 18 that of the Basilicas of the Apostles. It would appear as though these feasts occurring within a few days of each other had been fixed by some conventional arrangement. It is impossible to affirm this positively, but the suggestion cannot be ignored.

However this may be, the festival had already acquired a solemn character in the *Ordo Romanus* of Cencio. The Pope and the Cardinals sang vespers and celebrated the vigil at St Peter's, where they spent the night, and where the stational Mass was offered the next morning. We find the following entry revealing the ingenious simplicity of the times: *XII den. pro implendo saccone domini papae, et III sol. pro lignis in camera domini Papae.*[1]

Neither the Vatican Basilica nor that on the Ostian Way are the identical churches so much admired by the pilgrims of the Middle Ages. The Church of St Peter's, decayed by age, was pulled down in the sixteenth century, and having been rebuilt with great magnificence, was again consecrated by Urban VIII on November 18, 1626.

In 1823 Pius VII was on his death-bed, and in his agony his mind wandered back to the happy days when he was a simple monk at the monastery of St Paul, whilst at the same time he was tormented by the mental vision of a great fire. At the same hour a terrible conflagration destroyed the greater part of the Basilica of the Doctor of the Gentiles. The flames only spared that part of the church where the altar of the Apostle stands under the triumphal arch of Leo the Great. The dying Pope was not told of the catastrophe; this was perhaps the only sorrow which he was ever spared! Leo XII, who succeeded Pius VII, immediately commenced to repair the disaster. In a short time, owing to the unwearying zeal of four Popes, the Basilica of St Paul rose from its ashes, more beautiful and more magnificent than before.

Pius IX reconsecrated the new Church on December 10, 1854, amid the largest assembly of cardinals and bishops ever

[1] *P.L.* LXXVIII, col. 1096.

seen, who had come to Rome for the proclamation of the dogma of the Immaculate Conception. In order, however, not to separate the names of the two Apostles in the Liturgy, it was decided that the annual commemoration of the *dedicatio Petri et Pauli* should still be celebrated, as in the past, on November 18.

So by the wonderful dispensation of Providence it came to pass that the Catholic Church celebrates annually the dedication of the four patriarchal Basilicas at Rome, that of the Saviour, of St Peter, St Paul and St Mary Major. As each diocese commemorates the encænia of its own cathedral, so the whole Catholic world celebrates annually the dedication of the fourfold Papal cathedral, and this festival is symbolical of the fact that in spite of the limits established to each diocese the Church of Christ is one, and is founded on Peter, who continues to feed his lambs from the seven hills, and to rule over the flock of Christ throughout the earth.

The Mass is that of November 9.

We take from the Leonine Sacramentary these two prayers which, however, belong to the dedication of another basilica of St Peter, quite distinct from the Vatican.

Deus, qui beati Petri Apostoli dignitatem ubique facis esse gloriosam; praesta, quaesumus, ut et doctrina semper ipsius foveamur et meritis.

Super Oblata. Suscipe, Domine, quaesumus, hostias quas maiestati tuae in honorem beati Apostoli Petri, cui haec est basilica sacrata, deferimus, et eius precibus nos tuere. Per Dominum.

We see by these prayers that in the ancient Roman tradition, in contrast to our modern ideas, the feast of the dedication of a church was not regarded as a *festum Domini*, but as a solemnity in honour of the saint who gave his name to the church.

In order to supplement what has already been said we may add this ancient inscription which once was on the façade of St Peter's.

QVI · ECCLESIAM · PETRI · SACRASTI · NOMINE · CVIQVE
AGNOS · MANDASTI · PASCERE · CHRISTE · TVOS
EIVSDEM · PRECIBVS · CONSERVA · HAEC · ATRIA · SEMPER
PRAESIDIO · VT · MANEANT · INVIOLATA · TVO

" O Christ, who hast willed that this church should be consecrated in the name of Peter, whom thou didst commend to feed thy flock, by his prayers preserve this building for ever, that under thy protection it may never be violated."

In the Abbey of St Paul, still rich in records of saints and famous Pontiffs who lived there as monks, we find these beautiful lines composed by Alcuin.

SERVA · PAVLE · TVI · VENERANDI · SACRARIA · TEMPLI
NE · LATRO · DEPOPVLANS · VASTET · OVILE · TVVM

" Guard thy sacred temple, O Paul, that no thief may enter to devastate thy fold."

NOVEMBER 19

St Pontian, Pope and Martyr*

Pontianus died in Sardinia on September 28, 235, but from the days of Pope Liberius his *depositio* was kept in the Eternal City, together with that of Hippolytus on August 13, that is upon the anniversary of the day on which Pope Fabian brought the two bodies to Rome. He interred the Pope in the Papal Cemetery of Callixtus, and Hippolytus in a special crypt near the Cemetery of Cyriaca : *Idib. aug. Ypoliti in Tiburtina et Pontiani in Calisti*. According to De Rossi a graffito in the papal crypt of the Appian Way records this translation of the relics of Pontianus : EN ΘΕΩ ΜΕΤΑ ΠΑΝΤΩΝ (τῶν ἐπισκόπων) ΠΟΝΤΙΑΝΕ ΖΗCΗC. If the addition suggested by the great archæologist is correct, the person who wrote the words intended them as an allusion to the posthumous *vindicatio* of Pontianus amongst the Roman Pontiffs.

As is well known, the sentence of exile according to the Roman law meant the loss of all civil rights ; this being the case, Pontianus, condemned with his rival Hippolytus to hard labour *in insula nociva*, and therefore unable to govern the Church, *discinctus est*, as the Liberian Catalogue says, that is, he abdicated. Perhaps the fact of his abdication contributed to bring to an end the schism which had divided the Church of Rome since the days of Callixtus. At any rate, the Pope and the Antipope joined hands and departed together into exile. Under Pope Fabian the entire Christian community unanimously received the venerated remains of the two exiled martyrs in Rome, and Hippolytus, formerly the enemy of Callixtus, became even more than Pontianus himself the object of a notable *cultus*, and statues were raised and inscriptions dedicated to him.

There appears to be no historical foundation for this date having been chosen to commemorate Pontianus. The Leonine Sacramentary as well as the Philocalian Catalogue testify that the martyr Pontianus was commemorated at Rome together with Hippolytus on August 13, and even contains the Collects of his feast.

According to the catalogue of relics transferred by Paschal I to St Praxedes those of Pope Pontianus are amongst them. The Basilica of San Lorenzo *in Lucina* also claims to possess the body, or at least some important relic of Pontianus, since the year 1112.

The Mass *Statuit* is the same as for St Pius I on July 11, except the Gospel, which is taken from the feast of St Callixtus, on October 14.

The mind of man is naturally inclined to wish to practise virtue among noble and honourable surroundings which add to the dignity of his acts, and increase his importance. The true spirit of Christ is rather that we should accomplish even the most heroic sacrifices with simplicity and humility. This holy Pope who was exiled from Rome, removed from his high office, condemned to hard labour in the mines of Sardinia, died only three months after his arrival there, worn out by the hardships he had endured, having drunk the chalice of martyrdom to the dregs. He had certainly experienced the depths of humiliation, but through his sufferings Pontianus became a glorious martyr and obtained the cessation of the schism.

ΕΝ ΘΕΩ ΜΕΤΑ ΠΑΝΤΩΝ ΤΩΝ ἘΠΙΣΚΟΠΩΝ ΠΟΝΤΙΑΝΕ ΖΗCΗC.

NOVEMBER 19

St Elizabeth, Widow* (1231)

The story of this gentle Saint, the daughter of the King of Hungary and wife of the Landgraf of Thuringia, has some points of resemblance with that of Pope Pontianus. Elizabeth, too, was dragged from her throne and humbled in the dust, after the death of her husband, but the virtues of this Tertiary of St Francis were greater than her misfortunes. The miracles obtained through her intercession after her death caused her *cultus* to spread rapidly, and she was canonized in 1235.

The Mass *Cognovi* is the same as for St Frances of Rome, March 9, but the Collect is proper to the feast.

Collect: " Enlighten the hearts of thy faithful, O God of mercy; and through the prayers of blessed Elizabeth, grant that we may despise worldly welfare and ever be gladdened by consolation from heaven."

Several churches at Rome were dedicated to this famous spiritual daughter of St Francis of Assisi. These were St Elisabetta " dei fornari tedeschi " on the Via papale ; Sant' Elisabetta " alle muratte " ; Sant' Elisabetta " a Pozzo Bianco " ; Sant' Elisabetta " in Banchi " ; Sant' Elisabetta *in Trastevere.* It will be seen by this how widely the Franciscan Tertiaries had spread the devotion to their celebrated patron.

NOVEMBER 20
ST FELIX OF VALOIS, CONFESSOR*

Innocent III was, without doubt, one of the greatest Popes who have occupied the See of Peter, and during his reign the Papacy may be said to have reached the height of its power and glory, realizing the ideals for which Hildebrand died in exile, but under new forms and in a manner appropriate to the times. The institution of the great modern religious orders coincides with the reform initiated by the young Lotharius of Segni. When he approved the rules of the Friars Minor, the Friars Preachers, and the order founded for the ransoming of captives, Innocent III infused into the body of the Christian community a new life full of energy and supernatural zeal, greatly needed in the dawning era of the Communi and of popular liberty.

The work carried out by St Felix of Valois forms part of this great plan of Catholic reform encouraged by Innocent, and it was at the feet of this Pontiff that he and St John of Matha knelt at the Lateran, to obtain the confirmation of the Institution for the ransoming of captives.

The conventional limits of Christian influence were not wide enough for these men, who in their youthful energy and sanctity longed to sacrifice themselves for the love of Christ. Whilst Dominic was preaching against the Albigenses in France, Francis had set sail for Palestine.

This awakening of missionary activity was soon followed by the two Founders of the Order of the Blessed Trinity for the redemption of slaves, with this difference, that while the Franciscans and Dominicans preached the Gospel to the infidels, the labours of Felix of Valois and John of Matha were devoted to saving the Christians, who under the tyranny of the Moors were in danger of loss of faith as well as of liberty.

The Mass *Justus* for this hero of charity who died November 4, 1212, and who bears such a resemblance to St Peter Nolasco, founder of another order for the redemption of captives, is exactly the same as that of January 31, with the exception of the Collect, Secret, and Post-Communion.

Collect: " O God, who by a voice from heaven wast pleased to summon blessed Felix from the desert to undertake the ransoming of captives; grant, we beseech thee, that through his intercession we may be freed from the bondage of our sins and may be guided by thy grace to our home in heaven."

The Secret and Post-Communion are the same as on July 19 for St Vincent de Paul.

NOVEMBER 21

PRESENTATION OF THE BLESSED VIRGIN MARY

The tradition that Mary when three years old was presented by her parents in the Temple in order to be brought up in the shadow of the Tabernacle is first found in the Apocrypha such as the *Protevangelium* of James, and the Gospel *de Nativitate Beatae Mariae*, It agrees, however, so completely with the sentiment of Catholic devotion concerning that part of the immaculate life of Mary not mentioned in the Gospel, that it found favour with Catholics too. We find upon an ancient paten adorned with biblical images the figure of the Blessed Virgin in the attitude of an " orante " with the rough inscription :

MARIA · MENESTER · DE · TEMPLO · CEROSALE

" Mary ministers in the Temple of Jerusalem."

The feast of the Presentation of the Blessed Virgin in the Temple was celebrated at Constantinople on November 21 long before Michael Comnenus, in 1166, included it among those feasts upon which the meeting of the law courts was forbidden.

The feast was introduced in the West by the agency of Philippe de Maizières, envoy of the King of Cyprus to the papal Court of Avignon. He described the festival as celebrated in the East in such glowing colours that Gregory XI introduced it into the Calendar of the Curia (1372).

The Mass is the same as on August 5, except the Collect.

Collect : " O God, by whose good will blessed Mary ever a virgin, being herself the dwelling-place of the Holy Spirit, was this day presented in the temple ; grant, we beseech thee, that through her intercession we may be found worthy to be presented before thee in the temple of thy glory."

Mary was brought by her parents to the Temple at Jerusalem in order that the Rod of Jesse from whence the Flower of Nazareth would blossom should be preserved from all danger in the shadow of the sanctuary. This should be a lesson to all, but especially to parents who cannot guard the innocence of their children more surely than by accustoming them from an early age to prayer and to frequent reception of the sacraments. Great care and infinite trouble are necessary in the education of the young, but above all it is most important to protect them from the dangers of evil surroundings.

NOVEMBER 22

Dedication of the Titulus Caeciliae in the Trastevere

According to the Martyrology of St Jerome the *natale et passio sanctae Caeciliae* should occur on September 16. As, however, on that day the feasts of SS Cornelius and Cyprian and of the virgin Euphemia are celebrated, it was the custom from early times to defer the festival of St Cecilia to November 22, the anniversary of the dedication of the *Titulus Caeciliae* in Trastevere. The Leonine Sacramentary illustrates this practice of Roman Liturgy, for we find in it, on November 22, under the title of *in natali sanctae Caeciliae*, at least five different Masses. The wealth and splendour of these formulas prove the fame of the Martyr's *cultus* at Rome, where in the fifth century the Pope was in the habit of celebrating the stational Mass at the Basilica in the Trastevere.

This fact connected with the place is attested by the biographer of Pope Vigilius in the *Liber Pontificalis*, where he describes how the Pope was taken prisoner by the soldiers of Justinian on account of the question of the Three Chapters, at the moment when Vigilius was celebrating on this day, in the year 538, the stational synaxis at the *Titulus Caeciliae* near the " ripa del Tevere."

The Pope was dragged into a boat, but as he had not pronounced the last benediction or *oratio super populum* after Communion, the people raised a tumult and demanded that he should at least be allowed to bless Rome before he was taken away. His captors were forced to consent, and Vigilius recited the *oratio super populum* from the ship, after which the people having responded *Amen*, the sailors bent to their oars, and the vessel was soon carried down the stream.

The *Titulus Caeciliae* built in the house of Valerian where she suffered martyrdom, appears in the list of Roman titles in 499. It stands upon an ancient Roman *domus*, and the *Acta* of St Cecilia in their topographical details have been substantially confirmed by the excavations made under the basilica. The date of St Cecilia's martyrdom is still uncertain, but the fact that the title in the Trastevere was called after her and that the encænia of the church were celebrated at Rome on November 22, inclines us to think that it took place at the end of the third century.

The remains of the Martyr were first laid in the Cemetery of Callixtus beside the papal crypt, but in 821 Paschal I removed them to the Basilica in Trastevere, where they are still venerated, together with those of Valerian and Tiburtius, her husband and brother-in-law, converted by her to the Faith. The tomb was opened in 1599, and the body of St Cecilia was found intact and clothed, with the pieces of linen beside her used to collect the blood shed in the last hours of her long agony.

The Introit *Loquebar*, the Gospel and the Antiphons for the Offertory and Communion are common with the feast of St Barbara, December 4.

Collect: "O God, who dost gladden us with the yearly festival of blessed Cecily thy virgin and martyr; grant that we who honour her with our service, may also follow the example of her godly life."

The feasts of the Saints are a cause of joy to the Christian people, for whilst by their death the places left empty in heaven by the rebel angels are filled, the Church militant also gains in them powerful patrons and noble examples of virtue.

The Epistle is taken from Ecclesiasticus (li, 13–17) and alludes to the Titulus where Cecilia suffered martyrdom.

"Thou, O Lord, hast exalted my dwelling-place upon the earth," the Martyr says. "I called upon the Lord that he would not leave me in the day of my trouble. My prayer was heard, and thou hast saved me from destruction and hast delivered my soul from evil men. My body only has remained in their hands like a mantle which is cast aside." *Et post haec non habent amplius quid faciant*, the Gospel adds.

The Gradual is taken from Psalm xliv, and describes the bridals of Christ and the Church. "Hearken, O daughter, and see, and incline thine ear; for the King hath greatly desired thy beauty. ℣. With thy comeliness and thy beauty set out, proceed prosperously and reign. Alleluia, alleluia.

It is impossible to speak too often of the necessity for recollection and generosity in souls who have consecrated themselves to God. In order to hear the invitation of the Spouse it is necessary to retire into solitude and to listen to his voice alone. Yet it is not enough to hear the divine inspiration, we must also follow it, and therefore the Psalmist says: *Audi filia et vide et inclina aurem tuam.* In the sixth century St Benedict, the Patriarch of Western monasticism, takes these words as his text in order to describe in seventy-two chapters the Rule of Monastic life: *Ausculta, o fili, praecepta Magistri, et inclina aurem cordis tui, et admonitionem pii Patris libenter excipe, et efficaciter comple.*

The alleluiatic verse is the same as for the feast of St Agnes on January 21.

Secret: " May this sacrifice of propitiation and praise, O Lord, we beseech thee, through the intercession of holy Cecily thy virgin and martyr, ever make us worthy of thy mercy."

The chief ends for which we offer the eucharistic Sacrifice are alluded to in this prayer. It is above all an oblation *placationis*, and therefore makes satisfaction for our sins; *et laudis*, and therefore is a perfect sacrifice of adoration. It renders us ever more worthy of the divine *propitiatio*, and thus has a supreme power of propitiation and impetration, equal to the power and dignity of the immaculate Victim.

The Sacramentaries contain Prefaces for to-day's feast. The following is one of the finest in the Leonine Collection: *Vere dignum . . . Quia vicissitudo nobis est hodie collata mirabilis ; quum ille noster inimicus, qui hominem paradisi felicitate conspicuum et totius mortis ignarum, dum propria integritate fidendo, praesidia divina non quaereret, viperea calliditate subvertit ; nunc inter huius mundi miserias, et in exilio damnatae conditionis humanae, a mortali fragilitate, sed in te fidente, prosternitur. Et quum prima mulier viro suo dux fuisse referatur ad lapsum, nunc confessio puellaris, virum praecedens, ducit ad praemium. Per Christum*, etc.

The Post-Communion is that of the feast of St Lucy on December 13.

In the inscription in verse placed by Paschal I under the mosaic in the apse of the *Titulus Caeciliae* the following lines are worthy of note :

AVREA · GEMMATIS · RESONANT · HAEC · DINDIMA · TEMPLI
LAETVS · AMORE · DEI · HIC · CONIVNXIT · CORPORA · SANCTA
CAECILIAE · ET · SOCIIS · RVTILAT · HIC · FLORE · IVVENTVS
QVAE · PRIDEM · IN · CRYPTIS · PAVSABANT · MEMBRA · BEATA
ROMA · RESVLTAT · OVANS · SEMPER · ORNATA · PER · AEVVM

" The interior of the church gleams with gold and gems where (Paschal I) inspired by the love of God brought together the holy bodies of Cecilia and her companions, whose youth blooms here like a flower. Their sacred limbs reposed in the darkness of the crypts, but now adorn Rome, who rejoices through the centuries."

The Eternal City has dedicated many churches to this noble Roman lady. Of these we may mention : Santa Caecilia *in Trastevere;* Santa Caecilia "della fossa" near the Circus Maximus ; Santa Caecilia *montis Farfae* near the Ghetto ; Santo Caecilia *a domo*, possibly to be identified with the former : Santa Caecilia *in Campo Martis;* Santa Caecilia *de turre Campi*, near the Parione. The latter church was consecrated by Callixtus II in 1123.

NOVEMBER 23

St Clement, Pope

Station at the Title of Clement.

The title of Clement is mentioned by St Jerome : *Nomini eius memoriam usque hodie Romae exstructa ecclesia custodit;*[1] and refers probably to a sanctuary named after him on the site of his dwelling-place which the *Liber Pontificalis* tells us was *de regione Caeliomonte*.[2] The *Acta* of St Clement are apocryphal, it is true, but his martyrdom was an undisputed fact, well known at Rome in the fourth century, for Rufinus and Pope Zosimus mention it, as also does the Leonine Sacramentary. There is accordingly no serious reason for doubting it. According to his *Acta*, he was buried at Chersonesus in Crimea ; and the pilgrim Theodosius in his Itinerary records that *ibi domnus Clemens martyrizatus est.*[3]

It is possible, as some archaeologists believe, that confusion has arisen between the Roman Clement and a martyr of Sebastopol of the same name.

When the Apostles of the Slavs, Cyril and Methodius, went to Rome in 868 to give an account of their mission to Adrian I they brought with them as a gift to the Pope the relics of St Clement discovered by them at Chersonesus. A painting in the ancient subterranean basilica of St Clement at Rome reproduces the triumphal procession of the Pope, the people, and the Roman clergy, who escort the holy relics from St Peter's to the ancient title on the Caelian :

HVC · A · VATICANO · FERTVR · PP · NICOLAO
IMNIS · DIVINIS · QD · AROMATIB · SEPELIVIT

The *dominicum Clementis*, as it is called on a slave's medal quoted by Baronius, stands upon the site of several ancient

---

[1] *De viris illustr.*, XV.   [2] Ed. Duchesne, I, 123.
[3] Geyer, *Itinera*, p. 143.

November 23

buildings. On the lowest level is a wall of *opus quadratum* of a very early period, which De Rossi considered to have been a mint. The second building is a fine house of the first century and may very probably be the place where Clement assembled his disciples. Beside the house has been found an altar dedicated to the worship of Mithras. Upon these buildings there rose in the early half of the fourth century the *dominicum Clementis*, which remained standing until the year 1084, when Robert Guiscard in his struggle against Henry IV, sacked and burnt the whole of the Caelian quarter around the Lateran.

At the beginning of the twelfth century, by desire of Paschal II, a titular Cardinal, Anastasius by name, undertook the reconstruction of the Basilica as it is at present, making use of the altar and the ambos of the earlier church.

The relics of Pope Clement, together with those of Ignatius of Antioch, which an ancient tradition asserts to be preserved in this church, are referred to in the following lines :

IMPIVS · INSANO · TE · MERSIT · IN · AEQVORA · CAESAR
HIS · POSITIS · ARIS · NVNC · PIA · ROMA · COLIT
VICINVM · TIBI · PROBRA · TVLIT · NVMEROSA · THEATRVM
HIC · TIBI · DELATVS · PROBRA · REPENDIT · HONOS

" An impious Caesar in his rage cast thee into the sea,
Now Rome venerates thee in prayer before these altars.
In the amphitheatre near this spot thou wert loaded with insults,
For this, the honours paid to thee here make amends."

The Introit is taken from Isaias lix, lvii. " The Lord saith, My words, which I have put in thy mouth, shall not depart out of thy mouth : and thy gifts shall be accepted upon my altar."

This is followed by the first verse of Psalm cxi : " Blessed is the man that feareth the Lord : he delighteth exceedingly in his commandments."

Collect : " O God, who dost gladden us with the yearly festival of blessed Clement, thy martyr and bishop ; grant that we who keep his birthday may also imitate his courage in suffering."

Are all Christians then destined to be martyrs, since the Church tells us all to pray that *virtutem passionis imitemur ?* Certainly not, for very few of us are called to shed our blood for the Faith, but the life of a Christian, by reason of the curb he is obliged to keep upon his passions, the mortifications he practises, and his self-denial in order to live to Christ, is compared by the Fathers to a slow and bitter martyrdom.

The Lesson to-day is from the Epistle of St Paul to the Philippians (iii, 17–21 ; iv, 1–3), which is also read on the Twenty-third Sunday after Pentecost.

It is chosen because after speaking of the worldly minded Christians who by their lives make a mockery of the cross of Christ, and comparing with these the lives of the faithful ones, Paul mentions among his fellow labourers a certain Clement, whose name is recorded in the book of life. Many suppose that this is the Pope of that name, and there is no real reason to doubt it. At the time that Paul during his first captivity at Rome (61–62) wrote the Epistle to the Philippians, Clement might have been a young man. He died in the reign of Trajan towards the beginning of the second century, and therefore the disciple of St Paul at Corinth, though old, would not have exceeded the average length of human life.

Towards the end of the first century the name of Clement again occurs in the first part of the Ποιμήν which Hermas, the brother of the future Pius I, was composing at Rome, on the much disputed question of penance. Clement was entrusted with the care of distributing copies of this little book in foreign cities, " for this is his office": ἐκείνῳ γαρ ἐπιτετράπται.

We have here another proof of the universal solicitude shown even in those days by the Roman Pontiffs for the whole Catholic Church.

The Gradual *Iuravit* is the same as on March 12 for St Gregory I, the alleluiatic verse *Hic est sacerdos* is that of St Eusebius on December 16.

The Gospel according to the Würzburg List is that containing the parable of the talents, but the actual Missal assigns another passage from St Matthew (xxiv, 42–47) generally read on the feasts of Bishops and Confessors : *Vigilate*.

The verse for the Communion justifies this second choice which we quoted on May 25, on the feast of Gregory VII.

The duty of keeping watch is especially incumbent on bishops, and their very name in Greek expresses this inspection of their flock.

In the history of St Guido, a monk of Farfa in the eleventh century and later Abbot of San Clemente di Casauria in the island of Pescara, we read that he died on the day dedicated to the titular saint of his Abbey. His happy death occurred at the hour when, in the church, the deacon chanted the Gospel Lesson of the faithful servant who distributed food to his companions in due season.

The Antiphons for the Offertory and the Communion are the same as for St Stephen of Hungary on September 2.

Secret : " Hallow the offerings consecrated to thee, O

Lord; and through the intercession of blessed Clement thy martyr and bishop, cleanse us with them from the stain of our sins."

In this prayer the satisfaction made for our sins by the holy Sacrifice of the Mass is beautifully expressed. Unhappily many people forget this, and hear Mass with little contrition, as though they had no sins to expiate, and the altar were not the throne of grace raised by God in the centre of his Church Militant.

The Sacramentaries contain several fine Prefaces in honour of the great Pope who, in a way, personifies all the direct followers of St Peter. *Vere dignum . . . Quoniam per Sancti Spiritus largitatem, beatus ille Clemens hodiernae nobis exultationis affectum magnificae passionis agone sacravit : qui mundo nobilis, amore Christi nobilior, pro labore conspicuus, et inter parentum vel inquisitione, vel receptione mirabilis, apostolicae praedicationis fidelissimus alumnus acceptus, sacerdos refulsit egregius et martyr insignis.*

Nearly all the Prefaces of St Clement, by allusions to the loss and subsequent discovery of his parents, show that they are inspired by the apocryphal books of the *Recognitiones*.

The Post-Communion is as follows : " We who have fed at the sacrifice of thy holy body and precious blood, beseech thee, O Lord our God, that through the intercession of blessed Clement, thy martyr and bishop, what we do with godly devotion may bring us sure redemption."

We may note the appropriate liturgical expression : *pia devotione gerimus*, that is the devout offering up of the Sacrifice ; *certa redemptione capiamus*, this is the effect of the Sacrament.

NOVEMBER 23

St Felicitas, Martyr

Station at the Cemetery of Maximus.

Two stations were held on this day, for, besides the commemoration of St Clement, the Martyrology of St Jerome indicates that on the Via Salaria the deposition of the martyr Felicitas was also celebrated. Her remains rested, as we have already said, in the Cemetery of Maximus with those of Silanus, the youngest of her seven martyred sons. Subsequently the bones of this Saint were placed in the title of Susanna where they still repose.

Another sanctuary dedicated to St Felicitas existed at Rome, and this was near the *Dominicum Clementis*. We referred to it on July 10, when we put forward the hypothesis that it may have occupied the site of the Saint's house. As we find in the Leonine Sacramentary a Collect common to both St Clement and St Felicitas, it appears probable that this prayer refers to the synaxis held on this day at the house of St Felicitas, in the very shadow of the title of Clement.

The Mass *Me expectaverunt* is the same as for the Martyrs of Carthage, SS Perpetua and Felicitas, on March 6, with the exception of the prayers.

Collect: "Grant, we beseech thee, almighty God, that we who are keeping the festival of holy Felicitas, thy martyr, may be shielded by her merits and prayers."

This is the true spiritual parentage promised in the Gospel to the man who accomplishes the will of the heavenly Father. He shall be to Christ as brother and sister, father and mother, because by his example and the efficacy of his intercession he will draw many souls to God. This is the secret of the spiritual fecundity we admire in the lives of the saints.

St Felicitas was favoured by God with a two-fold motherhood: for the seven sons whom she bore were nourished and educated by her not to enjoy earthly life only, but to attain the heavenly life through martyrdom. She was indeed a happy mother, rightly named Felicitas, for before giving her own life for the faith, she saw her seven children, her treasures, precede her to Paradise, testifying to her love as a Christian mother and a most courageous martyr.

On account of this, the Würzburg List prescribes for to-day the passage from the Gospel of St Matthew read on July 10, and this was the Lesson commented on by St Gregory the Great to the Roman people, on the occasion of the festal station celebrated at the tomb of St Felicitas.[1]

But the same List also assigns another Gospel to this day; that which is read on the feast of the Assumption, relating the visit of Jesus to Martha and Mary. It may have been merely a second passage to be used at choice, or it may have been the Gospel of the second Mass of the *natalis* of St Felicitas, celebrated in the sanctuary at her house, near the Church of St Clement.

Secret: "Be appeased, O Lord, and look upon the offerings of thy people; and grant that we may enjoy the intercession of her whose festival we are keeping by thy grace."

The Sacramentaries generally assign a Preface to-day in honour of the heroic mother. The following is a beautiful one taken from the Leonine Sacramentary: *Vere dignum . . . In exultatione festivitatis hodiernae, qua beata genitrix sacratum tibi gregem, carne procreatum, per tuam gratiam, morte perfecit.*

---

[1] Lib. I. Hom. III. P.L. LXXVI, col. 1087.

Ecce vere in qua, sicut scriptum est, fabricavit sibi Sapientia domum, septem columnis instructam. Ecce quae, quod nomine praelibavit, rebus implevit, et non solum foecunditatis prosperitate gloriosa, sed cum eadem etiam mansit et inter adversa felicitas; quam eidem nec mors auferre potuit, sed efficit potius sempiternam. Per Christum.

Post-Communion: "We humbly beseech thee, O God almighty, that through the intercession of thy saints thou wouldst increase within us thy gifts and order our lives by thy grace."

This thought should give us a great serenity in every circumstance, even the most adverse. Our lives are directed, not by chance, but by divine Providence, which disposes all things to our greater good with perfect wisdom, power, and love. All will be well with us; let us then trust entirely in God : *spera in Domino et fac bonitatem, et inhabita terram.*

According to the *Acta* of St Felicitas, when the prefect Publius urged her to deny her faith, she replied: *Viva te superabo, et si interfecta fuero, melius te vincam occisa.*

The *cultus* which has honoured her name through seventeen centuries shows how great a triumph this courageous Mother of seven martyrs won over the spirit of evil.

NOVEMBER 24

St Chrysogonus, Martyr

Station at the title of Chrysogonus.

Chrysogonus whom the Greeks call ΜΕΓΑΛΟΜΑΡΤΥΡ appears to have been a martyr of Aquileia, to whom a basilica was dedicated at Rome from the fourth century, as though to commemorate the sojourn of the Saint in that part of Trastevere.

There is no trace in any of the extra-mural cemeteries of a *cultus* at a sepulchral memorial of the martyr, and this is sufficient to show that he was not a Roman. Yet Chrysogonus is numbered among the martyrs who are regarded as Romans, only because their *cultus* was established in early times in one of the basilicas of the city.

It is thought that the *titulus Chrysogoni* may date from the fourth century; certainly the base of the statue of the Good Shepherd found on the spot in the seventeenth century may easily be of that period. It bore the following inscription:

FL · TERTVLLVS · DE · ARTE · SVA
AECLESIAE · DONVM · POSVIT

A few years ago the ancient apse and part of the nave of the *titulus* were discovered; the original level of the church coincides with the ancient *excubitorium* of the guard which belongs to the second century. The inscription copied by early collectors, *In throno sancti Chrysogoni*, is interesting:

SEDES · CELSA · DEI · PRAEFERT · INSIGNIA · CHRISTI
QVOD · PATRIS · ET · FILII · CREDITVR · VNVS · HONOR

"The emblems of Christ shine on the high throne of God,
For equal honour is due to Father and to Son."

The mosaic must have represented the customary *Etimasia* and the lines are a protest against the Arian heresy.

The name of Chrysogonus was placed in the Roman diptychs, and this testifies to the antiquity and celebrity of the *cultus* of the martyr, whose picture appears in mosaic at Ravenna, with the name Chrysogonus, both on the roof of the episcopal chapel of St Peter Chrysologus, as well as in the procession of saints adorning the nave of San Martino in *caelo aureo*.

The Mass *In virtute* is the same as for St Canute on January 19, except the prayers which are proper to the feast.

Collect: "Give heed, O Lord, to our humble prayers; so that we who acknowledge our own guilt, may be delivered by the intercession of thy blessed martyr Chrysogonus."

In the early discipline of the Church, during the first three centuries, the confessors and martyrs detained in prison possessed the privilege of interceding with the bishop in favour of public penitents, in order to obtain a remission of their penance, or their readmission to the Communion of the Church. The Liturgy attributes the same prerogative to the martyrs crowned by God in heaven. Their blood, through the merits of the blood of Christ for whom they had shed theirs, can wash away not only their own defects, but those of the faithful who have recourse to them.

According to the Würzburg List the Gospel read at the stational Mass to-day was the passage from St John (xv, 17–25): *Haec mando vobis, ut diligatis invicem . . . quia oderunt gratis* as on the feast of SS Simon and Jude, on October 28.

Secret: "Be appeased, O Lord, we beseech thee, by the gifts which we offer up to thee; and through the intercession of blessed Chrysogonus thy martyr keep us from all danger."

The Sacramentaries assign a proper Preface for to-day. We quote the following from the Leonine Sacramentary: *Vere dignum . . . quia pectora Martyrum beatorum sic ignis ille*

November 24

caelestis inflammat, ut omne quod in huius mundi luce iucundum est, amore tui Nominis refutetur, et subeatur quidquid temporaliter est acerbum, ut promissionis tuae praemia capiantur. Per Christum.

Post-Communion : " By partaking of thy sacrament, O Lord, may we be cleansed from our secret sins and delivered from the guile of our enemies."

The enemies referred to in this prayer may be the barbarians who at that time were surrounding Rome, and not the invisible forces of hell. We consider it possible that the words alluded to visible enemies, and that the sacred Liturgy implored a double grace, interior purity from every sin, and exteriorly, protection from the barbarians, and from Attila who called himself *flagellum Dei*.

NOVEMBER 24

St John of the Cross, Confessor and Doctor*

We have already noticed the fact that the traditional Liturgy of Rome has been overlaid by feasts added after the sixteenth century, feasts which, at Rome, assume a lesser degree of importance, compared with those written in letters of blood in her hagiographical record for so many centuries. We have an example of this to-day, for the Mass and station in honour of the martyr Chrysogonus have been practically suppressed in favour of the Office of St John of the Cross, although as a matter of fact the latter Saint did not die on this day, but on December 14, 1591.

The feast of the Mystical Doctor of Carmel was introduced into the Calendar by Clement XII, who desired to honour the great merits of this Saint, famous for the help he gave to St Teresa in the reform of her Order and for his mystical writings, in which he taught the science of the Saints for the good of souls.

It is through this second circumstance that St John of the Cross has acquired his celebrity, and the important place he holds in the ranks of those mystical writers, who, beginning with Origen, St Ambrose, Gregory the Great, down to St Francis de Sales, Father Faber, and Mgr. Gay, have described the secret workings of the Paraclete in the soul of the elect. It is indeed as a mystic that Pius XI included St Teresa's intrepid adviser among the Doctors of the Universal Church.

The following incident in the life of St John of the Cross is characteristic of the Saint, and sums up his life, embittered by anxiety, fatigue, persecution and painful illnesses. When Jesus asked him one day what reward he desired for the labours he had sustained, John replied: *Domine, pati et contemni pro te.* And his prayer was granted.

The Mass *in medio* is the Common of Doctors, as on May 27 for the Venerable Bede. The Collect is proper to the feast and contains allusions to the history of the Saint.

Collect: " O God, who didst endow holy John thy confessor with a wonderful love of self-denial and of the cross; grant that by ever cleaving to his example we may obtain everlasting glory."

The Collect records the two movements which mark the rhythm of our interior life. The first is denial of ourself, of all that is not love, truth and virtue, of all, therefore, which is the negation of goodness. The second is the love of the Cross in which is *salus, vita et resurrectio nostra.* In this love we find God, and he who remains in this love, remains in God and God in him.

NOVEMBER 25

St Catherine, Virgin and Martyr*

The legend of Αἰκατέριυα, or, as the Latins call her, *Catharina*, is unfortunately unsupported by any authority. The ancient Eastern and Egyptian Calendars do not mention her name. In the West the *cultus* of the Saint began only about the eleventh century. It was widely spread by the Crusaders, and St Catherine became one of the most celebrated saints of the later Middle Ages. The churches, altars, and ikons of the Saint are very numerous, and she was chosen as the patron of the schools of philosophy. We have still much to learn about the personality of St Catherine, but although the particulars of her life are uncertain, God has been pleased to glorify his Saint on Mount Sinai, where her tomb is still venerated by pilgrims.

St Gertrude, who from her childhood had had a great devotion to St Catherine, once asked of our Lord to be allowed to see the heavenly glory of her patron. Her prayer was heard, and she beheld the virgin of Alexandria on a golden throne surrounded by the sages whom she had led to a knowledge of the faith, and who formed her brightest crown in heaven.

Medieval Rome raised in honour of St Catherine μεγαλομαρτυρος και πανσόφου, not less than five churches, and these are: Santa Caterina *de Cavallerottis* near St Peter; Santa Caterina *ai Cenci;* Santa Caterina *de cryptis Agonis;* Santa Caterina *in Pallacinis;* Santa Caterina *sub Tarpeio.*

The Mass *Loquebar* is the same as for St Barbara, December 4, except the Collect which is proper to the feast.

Collect: "O God, who gavest the law to Moses from the top of Mount Sinai, and didst marvellously carry thither by thy holy angels the body of thy blessed virgin and martyr Catherine; grant, we beseech thee, that through her merits and intercession we may be able to reach that mountain which is Christ."

Christ is likened to a mountain, for he alone as God and Man is raised up above all created beings. He is the Mount that all men can see from far off, and to which their steps should be turned. Lastly, he is the Mount, because as Jerusalem the holy City is enclosed in a circle of hills, so the Lord surrounds his people *in circuitu populi sui*.

NOVEMBER 26

ST PETER, BISHOP OF ALEXANDRIA AND MARTYR

St Peter was the last martyr to suffer at Alexandria under the persecution of Diocletian (311), and therefore the Greeks give him the honourable title of σφραγις καὶ τέλος τοῦ διωγμοῦ, "the seal and limit of the persecution." He is first mentioned in the Syriac Martyrology, and, subsequently, in all those of the East, on November 24. The Martyrology of St Jerome, however, commemorates him to-day. His *cultus* was widespread in early times, and was very popular, even as far as Antioch. His fame is partly due to the fact that he was Patriarch of Alexandria, and partly to his personal qualities, for he was the director of the didascaleion of Alexandria, and a writer on sacred subjects. It is certain that Peter was "an admirable example of a bishop" as Eusebius attests.[1]

The Syrians have bestowed upon Peter a title derived from his Acts: hav d' fallĕs l-sâtâ van' faq, meaning "he who passed through the pierced wall." The *Acta* relate that the population of Alexandria mounted guard around the prison in order than no pagan soldier should be able to enter it to carry out the sentence of execution upon the Patriarch. Under these circumstances the danger arose that the soldiers might take vengeance on the unruly inhabitants. Therefore the holy bishop sacrificed his life for his flock, surrendering himself voluntarily to his executioners. He caused the tribune to be secretly warned that during the same night he would knock upon the wall to mark the place where it should be pierced in order to open a passage into the prison. That

---
[1] *Hist. Eccl.* IX, 6, 2.

night a great storm arose and favoured his plan, for the thunder, lightning, and heavy rain distracted the attention of the Christian watchers, and the soldiers of the tribune were able to make a break in the wall of the prison without being disturbed. The Patriarch passed through the opening, and allowed himself to be led away to the same spot where tradition asserts that St Mark suffered martyrdom. Here his head was struck off and the faithful gave him burial. " εἰς τὸ κοιμητήριον ὃ αὐτός ἦν οἰκοδομήσας, εἰς τὸ δυτικὸν τῆς πόλεως μέρος ἐν τοῖς προαστείοις."

The Mass *Statuit* is the same as for St Simeon on February 18.

NOVEMBER 26
St Sylvester, Abbot *

The feast of this holy Abbot of Monte Fano near Fabriano was introduced into the Calendar by Leo XIII, who in doing so paid him the honour rendered by the Church to the Founders of Religious Orders.

In the thirteenth century, when many Benedictine monasteries in Italy had lost much of their former holiness and learning, St Sylvester succeeded in infusing new vitality into the ancient order, by founding a monastic family which by the blessing of God transformed several religious houses, and was distinguished by the sanctity of its members.

The Mass *Os justi* is the Common of Abbots as for St Sabbas on December 5, but the prayers are proper to the feast and betray the modern liturgical taste. The two last have no special reference to the life of the Saint, and it is hard to say why the compiler preferred them to the prayers of the Common.

Collect : " O most merciful God, who, when the holy abbot Silvester stood within an open tomb in godly meditation on the vanity of the world, wast pleased to summon him into the wilderness and to make his life illustrious by signal virtue ; we earnestly beseech thee, that, like him, we may despise earthly things, and enjoy fellowship with thee for evermore."

This prayer alludes to an incident in the life of St Sylvester. He was one day assisting at the funeral of a relative, when gazing upon the disfigured features of the dead man, he began to say to himself : *Ego sum quod hic fuit ; quod hic est, ego ero ;* "I am now what he was ; what he is, I shall be." This thought made him resolve to leave the world and to become

November 26

a monk. One good inspiration can change a man's life, if he has the courage to follow it.

Secret: "We beseech thee, O Lord, that we who reverently offer up these gifts to thy divine majesty, by devout preparation and by cleanness of heart may become like to the blessed abbot Silvester and may receive worthily and holily the body and blood of thy Son."

Post-Communion: "Grant, O Lord, we beseech thee, that we who have been refreshed by thy divine banquet may so cleave to the footsteps of the holy abbot Silvester as to receive a plentiful reward with thy saints in the kingdom of thy glory."

Among the examples given to us by the saints, is that of perseverance in doing good, which we should try to imitate. St Sylvester died at nearly ninety years old, on November 26, 1267, and during the whole course of his long life in the monastery, he never faltered or failed in his fervour, through weariness or neglect.

NOVEMBER 27
St Optatus, Bishop
Synaxis at the Cemetery of Callixtus.

In some copies of the Martyrology of St Jerome we find to-day: *Romae, Optati episcopi.* The event recorded is the translation of the relics of this holy bishop from Numidia to the Cemetery of Callixtus. The Catholic clergy, driven from Africa by the persecutions of the Vandals, carried away the more famous relics of the Saints, among which were those of Optatus. Nothing is known of the history of St Optatus, but his bones were laid in the *cubiculum* of Pope Eusebius at Rome, together with those of another saint named *Polychamus*, also brought from Africa.

The name of Optatus occurs at the end of the list made by Sixtus III of the saints buried in the Cemetery of Callixtus. In the crypt of St Cornelius the image of St Optatus was painted beside that of St Sixtus II; and in the list of relics translated to St Praxedes by Paschal I his name occurs amongst those of other bishops. St Optatus is also commemorated, together with Polychamus, on November 27 in the *Notitia Nataliciorum* of San Silvestro *in Capite*.

Mense $\overline{\text{Nov}}$ $\overline{\text{D}}$. xxvii $\overline{\text{N.S.}}$ OPTATI ET POLYCHAMI

Very little is known about Polychamus, buried, too, in the Cemetery of Callixtus. Of his relics brought from Numidia with those of Optatus and laid in the Appian Cemetery, a part was taken to St Praxedes and the remainder to St Sylvester. Polychamus is represented in the *lucernarium* of the crypt of St Cecilia, and this work of art appears to be of the fifth century.

The Saint Optatus whose feast we keep to-day was probably Bishop of Yesceter; in any case he must not be confused with the Bishop of Milevis of the same name, who wrote a book against the Donatists, still extant. These words occurring in Book II of that work are remarkable: *Negare non potes, scire te in Urbe Roma Petro primam cathedram episcopalem esse collatam, in qua sederit omnium Apostolorum caput, Petrus, unde et Cephas est appellatus, in qua una cathedra, unitas ab omnibus servaretur.*[1]

NOVEMBER 28

St Gregory III, Pope and Confessor*

The Calendars record to-day the burial of St Gregory III who died in 741 and was buried at St Peter's. The Liturgy of Rome is greatly indebted to him, for he founded an oratory in the Vatican in honour of all the Saints, and established that the Office should be sung there nightly by monks. He also ordered that in the Masses celebrated in that sanctuary on the feasts of the Saints, these words should be interpolated in the Canon: *Quorum solemnitas hodie in conspectu tuae maiestatis celebratur, Domine Deus noster, toto in orbe terrarum.*

Gregory III also restored the ancient monastery of St Pancratius dating from the time of Pelagius II at the Lateran, and entrusted to the monks the celebration of Divine Office in the Basilica of the Saviour. He founded and richly endowed an abbey near the *Titulus Chrysogoni* in order that the *Opus Dei* should be chanted in the church of the martyr, decreeing that the community should be independent of the jurisdiction of the titular clergy.

There existed no sanctuary in the city or in the cemeteries which was not adorned by this zealous Pope with liturgical gifts, such as embroidered vestments, candelabra, votive lamps and chalices, and patens of precious metal. In many of the sepulchral basilicas, indeed, he carried out vast restorations and rebuilt others from the foundations. He instituted the festive station for the feast of St Petronilla in the Cemetery of Domitilla, and commanded that the monks who, even at that time, officiated at the Basilica of St Paul should celebrate five Masses daily at five separate altars for

[1] Lib. II, 2. *P.L.* XI.

November 28

the benefit of the pilgrims who came in great numbers to visit that sanctuary of the Apostles. This is one of the most ancient examples of plurality of Masses and of altars in the same church. It should, however, be noted that although Gregory III permitted the celebration of several Masses at the Ostian Basilica, only one was offered each day on the same altar.

The Pontificate of Gregory III lasted about eleven years, and was a stormy one, owing to the struggle against the Iconoclasts on the one hand, and on the other to the incursions of Luitprand King of the Lombards, who advanced with his hosts to the vicinity of St Peter's. When the Pope died, his body was interred in the Vatican chapel of the Blessed Virgin and All Saints, which he had built beside the tomb of the Fisherman.

HOLY MASS IN VARIOUS PUBLIC AND PRIVATE CIRCUMSTANCES OF CHRISTIAN LIFE

The notes on the two first parts of the Missal consisting of the *Proprium de Tempore* and the *Proprium de Sanctis* being concluded, the *Commune Sanctorum* should follow in the *Liber Sacramentorum*, with the Masses of those festivals of Saints or Beati which have no special Collect or Lesson in the Sacramentary.

We have, however, preferred to adhere to the ancient traditional order of the *Liber Sacramentorum*, and so have noted in the preceding volumes the feasts with Masses entirely *de Communi*, including them in the body of the Missal. It is well known that the Masses contained in the collection described as *Commune Sanctorum* were originally taken from certain Masses in honour of some saint, which have been used as types or models for other feasts of a later period.

For instance the Mass *Sapientiam Sanctorum*, now used for the feast of two or more martyrs, was first composed for the Roman festival of the " wise doctors," the Anargyri, Cosmas and Damian, when their basilica on the *Sacra Via* was dedicated. The Mass *Sacerdotes tui*, now assigned to many Bishops, was originally the special Mass of Pope St Sylvester. That common to all Virgins, *Vultum tuum*, was chosen formerly for the great festivals of Our Lady such as the Assumption, the Purification, the Annunciation, etc.

This came about in the following manner. In the Middle Ages, as the number of feasts continued to increase, the liturgists, who still regarded the Gregorian Antiphonary as divinely inspired and therefore not to be altered in any way, were afraid of composing new pieces of music, or even new prayers for the more recent solemnities inserted in the Calendar. In order to preserve as far as possible the authentic work of Gregory the Great, they chose some of the more ancient and classic Masses, and repeated these on the feasts recently introduced. This applied not only to the texts, but to the tunes accompanying them in the Antiphonary.

The choice of Collects and Lessons was easy. The Sacramentaries, especially the Leonine, already contained several Masses for each solemnity, these having perhaps been originally intended for use at the different sanctuaries dedicated to SS Peter and Paul, or to certain martyrs in the city. It only

Holy Mass

remained, then, to choose with judgement out of so much ancient material, and to adapt it to later liturgical requirements.

The same happened with regard to the Lessons. The ancient Lists of Epistles and Gospels sometimes assign a choice of Lessons for the greater feasts, recalling a primitive period when three Lessons were read at Mass instead of two. This early collection of Lessons added to the main part of the Sacramentary, or contained in the Lectionary, gradually increased in volume; until in the eighth century we find in the *Indicula*, after the Proper of Saints, a complete series of scriptural Lessons to be used on other festivals or similar stations. Thus in the *Capitula lectionum de circulo anni* of the Würzburg MSS. so often quoted in this work, we find the following indications:

In natali sancti Silvestri: lect. epist. beati Pauli Apost. ad Hebr.: Fratres, plures facti sunt sacerdotes secundum legem ... usque: ... hoc enim fecit semel offerendo se Dominus noster I.C.

This Lesson is now read in the Mass *Sacerdotes* for a Bishop and Confessor.

In natali ubi supra, Lect. epist. beati Pauli Apostoli ad Hebr.: Fratres doctrinis variis et peregrinis nolite abduci ... usque: talibus enim hostiis promeretur Deus. In our Missal this Epistle is read for St Nicholas of Bari.

In natali sacerdotum quorum supra. Lect. libri Sapientiae Salomonis: Ecce sacerdos magnus qui in diebus suis placuit Deo ... usque: ... incensum dignum in odorem suavitatis. This is now part of the Mass *Statuit* for Bishops and Confessors.

In natali quorum supra. Lect. libri Sapientiae Salomonis: Beatus vir qui inventus est sine macula ... usque: ... exaltat omnis ecclesia sanctorum. This belongs now to the Mass *Os justi* for Confessors only.

* * * * *

On the feasts of St Agnes and St Agatha we find this: *In natali sanctarum Agnae et Agathae. Lect. Epist. beati Pauli Apost. ad Corinth. II: Fratres, qui gloriatur, in Domino glorietur; non enim qui seipsum commendat ... usque: ... virginem castam exhibere Christo.* In our present Missal the Mass chosen is *Dilexisti* of Virgins.

In nat. sanctarum suprascriptarum. Lect. libri Sapientiae Salomonis. In omnibus requiem quaesivi et in haereditate Domini morabor ... usque: ... quasi myrrha electa dedi odorem suavitatis. This is now reserved to the Assumption of the Blessed Virgin.

In nat. ubi supra. Lect. libri Sapientiae Salomonis: Confitebor tibi Domine Rex ... usque: ... liberasti eos de manibus gentium. We now find this assigned to the Mass *Loquebar* for martyrs.

In nat. sanctarum ubi supra. Lect. libri Sapientiae Salomonis: Domine Deus meus, exaltasti super terram habitationem meam ... usque ... laudem dicam nomini tuo, Domine Deus noster. This now forms part of the Mass *Me expectaverunt* for Martyrs.

* * * * *

On September 29 for the dedication of the Basilica of St Michael at Castel Giubileo on the Via Salaria we read:

In nat. Angeli. Lect. libri Apocal. Johannis: In diebus illis, significavit Deus quae oportet fieri cito, loquens per Angelum suum ... usque: ... et lavit nos a peccatis nostris in Sanguine suo. This Lesson is now appointed to be read on the double festival of the dedication of the two Basilicas of the Archangel, that on Monte Gargano in May, and that of the Via Salaria at the end of September.

Cuius supra. Lect. Epist. beati Pauli Apostoli ad Corinthios I: Fratres, gratias ago Deo meo semper pro vobis in gratia Dei ... usque ... sine crimine in die adventus Domini nostri Jesu Christi.

In dedicatione Ecclesiae. Lect. Epist. beati Pauli Apostoli ad Corinthios: Fratres, unusquisque propriam mercedem accipiet per suum laborem ... usque ... ipse autem salvus erit, sic tamen quasi per ignem.

In dedicatione Ecclesiae. Lect. libri Apocalypsis Johannis: In diebus illis, vidi civitatem sanctam, Hierusalem novam, descendentem de caelo a Deo ... usque: ... dixit qui sedebat in throno ecce facio omnia nova. This now belongs to the *Commune dedicationis Ecclesiae.*

In dedicatione oratorii. Lect. libri Apocalypsis Johannis. In diebus illis, venit Angelus et locutus est mecum dicens: veni, ostendam tibi uxorem Agni ... usque: ... nisi qui scripti sunt in libro vitae et Agni.

* * * * *

It is easy to discern the rule followed by the compiler of these *Capituli Lectionum.* He has chosen certain types of feasts under which he collects, as it were, in so many categories, the Lessons to be used for other saints of the same type. For instance St Sylvester serves as a type for all Confessors, St Agnes for all Virgins, the encænia of St Michael are used for the dedication of churches and oratories, and so forth. Because of this, the *Commune Sanctorum* of our Missal

Holy Mass

traces its origin from very early times, certainly from the seventh century. At a later date these various types of "common" Masses will no longer form part of the *Proprium Sanctorum*, from which they were derived, but will be placed under the title of *Commune Sanctorum*. This is what we now find in the Missal of Pius V.

After the normal cycle of feasts distributed through the twelve months of the year, even the most ancient Sacramentaries contained a separate collection of Masses for special circumstances, besides the extra Lessons already referred to. There was, for instance, a Mass for the Consecration of a Pope, of priests, and of the minor clergy : a Mass for the bride and for the blessing of a virgin ; a Mass for the dedication of a basilica, for the arrival of the *missi dominici* of the first Carlovingian Emperors ; a Mass in time of public misfortunes ; Masses for the sick, the penitent, and the dead.

Many of these have disappeared from our present Missal, but they have been replaced by others such as the Masses for travellers, for pilgrims, in time of pestilence, against pagans and schismatics, etc., besides that vast collection of votive Masses of various saints named in the Roman Martyrology, which can be said when the rite of the Divine Office of the day is not of double rank.

We may note here a medieval collection of votive Masses arranged for each day of the week, and preserved almost unaltered in our Missal. It is a well-known fact that the *proprium de tempore* consists almost entirely of the Sunday Liturgy. Our forefathers, who appreciated variety and wealth of formulas in the eucharistic Liturgy, did not wish to repeat the Mass celebrated on Sunday during the remainder of the week, nor would this always have been appropriate. As we have seen, the Sunday Mass often contained allusions to the church where the station was celebrated on the Lord's Day. It seems out of place, for instance, to repeat every day in Advent, as many choirs do, the Introit, *Gaudete*, so typical of the night station held formerly at St Peter's on the Sunday before Ember Week in winter. So, too, the daily repetition during Sexagesima Week of the same Mass, *Exsurge Domine*, specially compiled for the great synaxis at the tomb of the Apostle of the Gentiles fifteen days before Lent, appears very inappropriate. Again, our forefathers would have considered it a meaningless ceremony and a monotonous repetition to sing the festive Introit, *Salus populi*, on six consecutive days, since it was chosen for the autumn station celebrated in the Church of the Anargyri at the Forum, on the Sunday nearest to their feast.

The ancients reasoned thus : Let the Sunday Masses be

the solemn stational Masses; but during the week, on days when no *natalis* of a saint is kept, and the Sacramentary contains no special formulas for the eucharistic synaxis, let this lack be filled by means of a collection of votive Masses, or Masses of devotion appointed for every day of the week.

We know that as early as the eighth century Alcuin composed a votive Mass in honour of the most Blessed Trinity. But even before this time, there must have been a Mass in use at Rome, a *missa romensis*, in honour of the Princes of the Apostles. The dedication of Saturday to the Blessed Virgin Mary, subsequently consecrated by a special Mass in her honour, first appears towards the tenth century, and develops in a more definite form chiefly through the agency of St Peter Damian.

Little by little, the days of the week not marked by a festival, acquired votive offices in honour of the most August Trinity, of the Apostles Peter and Paul, of the Holy Ghost, and of the Blessed Virgin *in sabbato*. It is unnecessary to add that periodical Masses for the dead soon came to occupy the devotion of the priests, especially in monastic communities. Besides the traditional *sacrificium pro dormitione* on the day of death or burial, on the seventh or thirtieth days after the decease, and on the anniversary, in Benedictine monasteries from the eighth century at least there were instituted monthly or annual offices for the dead belonging to the community, and also for benefactors of the house.

In order to understand more thoroughly the spirit and character of early Liturgy, it will not be amiss to study a few of these Masses for various occasions, contained in the ancient Roman Sacramentaries. These formulas, as we have said, were the first nucleus of that appendix to our Missal which now contains so many different votive Masses.

Let us begin by examining the so-called Leonine Sacramentary, typical of the Roman Liturgy of the seventh century. Besides the eucharistic Collects for the days of fasting *post infirmitatem*, that is to say after the siege of Rome by Genseric; besides the Masses for the ordination of priests and the consecration of the Pope—where we find a remarkable formula comparing the festival of the new Bishop of Rome to the Paschal feast which was at hand—various offices exist for the burial of Popes and Bishops, for the dedication of virgins, for the Mass following a bridal, and for times of drought, when the Roman Campagna, chiefly consisting of pasture land, was in danger.

The Gelasian Sacramentary is even richer. Besides the Masses for ordinations, for the initiation of various classes of catechumens to the sacrament of baptism, for the reconcilia-

Holy Mass

tion of penitents, for the consecration of the holy oils, we find several formulas for the dedication of altars, of basilicas, and of new baptisteries. The forms of prayer for new churches differed according to whether their *conditor non dedicatam reliquit*, or whether it was merely a matter of transforming a Jewish synagogue into a Christian church. The founder of a church was entitled to the special gratitude of the clergy, even after his death, so there was a special Mass for his funeral : *in ejusdem conditoris agendis*.

The anniversaries of the ordination of bishops, priests, and even of deacons, were distinguished by special Masses. Should a bishop be ill in bed on the anniversary of his consecration, one of his priests was to celebrate the Mass in his place, but in that case a special formula was used.

In the third book of the Gelasian Sacramentary various Collects are contained : *Quotidianis diebus ad missa*, followed by special Masses *ad proficiendum in itinere*, in times of trouble, to increase fraternal charity, in times of sickness either of men or beasts (*pro mortalitate animalium*) ; finally there are Masses against sterility in married women, in order to obtain rain, on the birthday of some member of the congregation (*in natale genuinum*), for peace, in time of war, etc.

There is no lack of different *missae in monasterio*, or of *orationes monachorum*. Further, if a widow should take the veil, a special Mass was said ; if a novice pronounced the vows, there was the *missa pro renunciantibus saeculo*. Even when a young man shaved for the first time, this simple sign of his having attained manhood was celebrated in church by a special Collect.

The extensive collection of the Gelasian Sacramentary is finally brought to a close by the prayers and Masses for the dead. These are often of great beauty, and special ones are dedicated to bishops and to abbots ; we find among them prayers for baptised persons *in extremis*, for those who have lost the power of speech before they were able to confess their sins, and lastly for all the faithful departed.

In these prayers, which describe the eucharistic Liturgy in all the varied circumstances of Christian life, we still see reflected the soul of the Frankish Church of the eighth century, divided as it was into diverse sections or social ranks : the clergy, the monks, the monarchs, consecrated virgins or widows, the multitude of the faithful, and so forth.

The genuine custom of Rome in the Middle Ages is better represented in that part of the Codex of Würzburg edited by Morin and called by him " le plus ancien comes de l'Église Romaine," than by the modified versions of the Sacramentary of Pope Adrian.

In the former important liturgical document, after the five or six Sundays *de adventu Domini*, there follows a vast collection of Lessons for various votive Masses, and for the simple Sundays *infra annum*. It is from this *Comes* of Rome that we shall choose a few titles of special interest to our subject.

First come the various Masses *in ordinatione diaconorum ; in ordinatione presbyterorum ; in ordinatione episcoporum.* Then follows the station *in ieiunio de natali papae ;* with a series of six Lessons *in natali papae*. Of such great importance, then, was the Papal festival to which all the bishops of the metropolitan province of the Roman Hierarch repaired each year. Next come the Masses *ad sponsas velandas ;* the various Masses *in litania tempore belli*, evoking the period disturbed by the wars between Lombards, Romans and Byzantines, a period which embraces a great portion of the history of the Papacy and of Rome in the seventh and eighth centuries.

Special Lessons are also indicated *in sterilitate pluviae, in die belli*, at funerals, on the encænia, and lastly *in adventu judicum*. The latter circumstance probably refers to the Byzantine period, when the arrival of the Greek functionaries in Italy and in the Roman Duchy, must have caused some anxiety to the Pope and the "Commune," who had little faith in the *Danai et dona ferentes*.

The same formula may also have been used during the early Carlovingian period, when, from time to time, there appeared at Rome these *missi Dominici*, come to administer justice in the name of the Emperor with the explicit object, therefore, of recalling to the Pontiff and the too forgetful Romans that, in France, the Eternal City was regarded merely as a town dependent on the Imperial crown of Charlemagne.

When the principle of these votive Masses had once been accepted the later Middle Ages proceeded to develop it. The consequences of this were carried so far, in a period of liturgical decadence, that the Council of Trent was obliged at last to repress such abuses, and to put a stop to grotesque exaggerations. By this we allude to the Masses of the "lunatics," of the "asses," of the judgement of God by fire : to the Mass of the *Sancti Auxiliatores* and other liturgical extravagances, which are proofs, not of faith, but of the superstitious tendencies in a period of decadence of the Catholic spirit.

The Liturgy was in the eyes of the ancients the legitimate expression of their Christian life. Abuses arose when with the decline of the faith which ennobled worship in earlier times, the people attempted to combine the Liturgy with their

Holy Mass 315

buffooneries and with their amusements, however harmless in themselves these might be.

The feast of the Ass, for instance, accompanied with Kyries and chants imitating the donkey's braying, had a sequence: *Orientis partibus adventavit asinus, pulcher et fortissimus, sarcinis optissimus*, in praise of the ass in the Gospel who carried the King of Glory. The Mass of the fire, of the blazing pyre, the red-hot ploughshare, or the boiling water, used during the most barbarous period of the Middle Ages in the Judgement of God, was justified by the test of the poisoned cup prescribed in the Book of Numbers, to establish the guilt of a Jewish wife accused of adultery.[1]

Before the terrible trial took place, Mass was celebrated and the fire was blessed, as we read in the life of Peter Igneus. This holy monk of Vallombrosa, a disciple of St John Gualbert, declared himself ready to endure the trial by fire, in order to prove that he and his companions had spoken the truth when they asserted that the Bishop of Florence had obtained the See by simony. Having assumed the sacerdotal vestments, Peter Igneus celebrated the holy Sacrifice, and, with the blessing of his Abbot, entered the narrow passage between two blazing piles of wood, emerging unhurt at the opposite side amid the acclamations of the monks.

Then as the maniple, which according to the ancient custom he had held in his hand, had fallen in the passage, he entered the furnace a second time, found the maniple, and once more returned unharmed, to be greeted with cries of joy by the Catholic onlookers, who bestowed on him the name of Igneus.

Since we are speaking of the liturgical abuses of the Middle Ages, it is not out of place to mention here an ancient custom derived from that special form of piety by which the votive Masses of the eighth century were inspired. As the centuries passed, effacing the memory of the classic age of the Fathers with their strong doctrinal teaching, Catholic piety became weaker, and expressed itself in a multiplicity of formulas. Whereas, at first, the Sacrifice of our Redemption was offered up by the Bishop alone for the needs of the whole Christian community, later when the celebrants were multiplied, as many Masses were offered as there were special intentions. Therefore in the ninth century, the custom arose that a priest should say more than one Mass each day. He might, for example, say one for the dead, another in honour of the Blessed Virgin, a third in honour of the Holy Cross, a fourth for the convenience of unexpected guests, etc. This habit became so universal that several councils were obliged to

---
[1] C. I, vi, 14–24.

regulate it by means of statutes and canons, forbidding priests to celebrate more than three Masses each day.

If Walafrid Strabo[1] is to be credited, Pope St Leo IV himself confessed that he had sometimes said seven or eight of these votive Masses on one day. There were other saints, such as St Elphege, St Anselm, St Norbert, St Ulderic, who, more discreet than the above-mentioned Pontiff, and more observant of liturgical laws, yet were in the habit of saying two or even three Masses on the same day.

The so-called " missae bifaciatae " or " trifaciatae " had some affinity with this votive polyliturgical custom. Instead of consecrating the sacred mysteries at each of the votive Masses to be offered, in order to evade ecclesiastical prohibition, several of these Masses were said as far as the Preface, which was single, as was the Canon of the Consecration. In this way the law was obeyed. There was only one Sacrifice but the Mass was, in a manner, multiplied.

Besides these we also hear of the *missae siccae* which were celebrated at sea, by the bedside of the sick, on the arrival of unexpected guests, at funerals, more especially if these took place in the afternoon, and on other occasions.

The order of these *missae siccae*, often celebrated by the Carthusians in the solitude of their cell, greatly resembled our Liturgy of the Presanctified on Good Friday. The Introit, Collect, Lessons, and Preface were recited as far as the Sanctus. Then, omitting the entire Canon, the Pater noster was said, and Holy Communion was distributed to the faithful. In some places a relic was held up for the veneration of the congregation, instead of the Elevation of the sacred Host.

This form of Liturgy of the Presanctified, the origin of which dates back in the East beyond the seventh century, was widely diffused in the late Middle Ages, and was long popular in Italy. Martène quotes the example of St Louis IX who, when returning to France from Palestine, caused a *missa sicca* to be said every day on the ship. In the sixteenth century, the *Liber Sacerdotalis*, approved by Leo X, describes the rite, and we know that in 1587, on the occasion of a nobleman's funeral, the *missa sicca*, with the assistance of a deacon and a subdeacon, was celebrated at Turin.

All this exuberance of eucharistic Liturgy, oftentimes admirable, but in some cases irregular, has ceased, in our day; and the liturgical law has gradually become more definite and more severe. In the Latin Church liturgical matters, with very few exceptions, are not decided by the Bishops, but by the Apostolic See. Through this system of centralization the

---

[1] *De Reb. Eccles.* XXI. P.L. cxiv, col. 943.

Holy Mass

greatly desired unity of Liturgy has been at last attained, and in these days when modern means of transport have almost demolished the barriers between states and provinces, the local peculiarities and individual liberty permitted in the Middle Ages seem almost incredible.

The priest when about to offer the holy Sacrifice, now needs only to follow the indications of the Calendar of the diocese. In one case only is he at liberty to choose, and to follow his particular inclination; on certain days when there is no feast of double rank the rubric allows him to say the Mass prescribed in the Office of the day, or else one of the many votive Masses contained at the end of the Roman Missal.

I

FOR THE CONSECRATION OF A POPE

We have seen that the *Capitula Lectionum* of Würzburg places before the Mass for the *Natalis Papae*, one bearing the title *in ieiunio de natali Papae*. This was the Mass accompanying the fast observed by the Romans on the day preceding the vigil at St Peter's, at the conclusion of which the Pope was consecrated. The episcopal consecration of a newly elected Pope rarely takes place in these days, when the greater number of Cardinal electors belong to the episcopacy. Such an eventuality is possible, and, indeed, it occurred at the election of Gregory XVI, but the Roman Missal no longer contains the ancient eucharistic Liturgy for this solemn fast, observed by the whole city before the consecration of the new Pope.

In the ancient Mass of the vigil that passage from 1 Esdras (ix, 4–11) was read, where the Prophet confesses the sins of his people which have called down upon them the anger of God and caused them to lie prostrate and leaderless under a foreign yoke. The allusion to the vacant See is apparent here.

The present Missal, in place of the primitive Liturgy of preparation, contains two separate Masses to be used before the Conclave for the election of the new Pope: one *de Spiritu Sancto*, and the other a more modern one with the Introit *Suscitabo mihi sacerdotem*.

The second Mass must have been rarely used, as the various *Ordines Romani* only mention the Mass *de Spiritu Sancto* for this circumstance, and it is celebrated to this day by the Cardinals assembled in Conclave beneath Michelangelo's dome.

This votive Mass of the Holy Ghost is almost the same as that of Whit-Sunday except the Epistle, which is taken from

Whit-Tuesday, and the Gradual, which is that of the Seventeenth Sunday after Pentecost.

From Septuagesima to Easter a *tractus* derived from Psalm ciii is sung: "Send forth thy Spirit and they shall be created, and thou shalt renew the face of the earth. How sweet and merciful is thy Spirit to us, O Lord. Come, O holy Spirit, fill the hearts of thy faithful and kindle in them the fire of thy love."

As the soul is necessary to our human existence, so in the supernatural order it is by the grace of the Spirit that we are raised to the sublime state of adopted sons of God. In conformity with this exalted rank of partakers of the divine nature, as Peter expresses it, we prepare for our eternal life, our supernatural end.

At Eastertide the double alleluiatic verse is the same as on the feast of Pentecost.

* * * * *

The Pope having been elected in the Conclave, the various *Ordines Romani* of the late Middle Ages thus describe his first Pontifical vesting, in the hall where the election had taken place. The chief deacon removed the newly-elected Pope's "cappa magna," and clothed him with the *alba, rochetum, camisia*, and lastly added the stole, cope, and mitre. A ring was placed on his finger, and he was shod with red sandals. The *camisia*, worn over the other garments, and caught up and fastened about the waist by a red girdle, resembled an alb drawn up and shortened. *Ipsa camisia erit ita longa, quod elevata, competenter super ipsum cingulum reflectatur.*[1] It is represented now by the rochet worn by bishops.

If the new Pope was a deacon or a priest, he was consecrated as a priest or as a bishop, before receiving the tiara. The rites were the usual ones, but the Pope remained seated, whilst the consecrating Bishop, standing before him, recited the sacramental formula and laid his hands upon him, invoking the Holy Spirit.

According to the ancient Roman custom the episcopal consecration of the Supreme Pontiff took place at the tomb of St Peter. So strong was this tradition that when at the death of Gregory VII the Abbot Desiderius of Monte Cassino was chosen to succeed him, the orthodox party seized the Basilica by force of arms, expelling the antipope Guibert. Desiderius was ill, and could not undertake the journey on horseback, but they insisted on his being conveyed by boat, rather than that he should be consecrated elsewhere than at St Peter's,

[1] *Ord. Rom.* XIV. *P.L.* LXXVIII, 1126–27.

Holy Mass 319

and that doubts should be raised as to whether he was the legitimate successor of Gregory VII.

From very early times it had been the privilege of the Bishop of Ostia to consecrate the Pope, and at this ceremony he wore the sacred pallium. He was assisted by the Bishops of Albano and of Porto, and the three performed the consecration of the Pope according to the rite which has been described in our first volume for the consecration of a bishop. The one slight difference occurred in the Anaphora. While in the case of any other bishop the following words are said: *Et idcirco huic famulo tuo N. hanc, quaesumus, gratiam largiaris*, etc., for the Pope's consecration the form runs: *Et idcirco huic famulo tuo N., quem Apostolicae Sedis praesulum et primatem omnium qui in orbe terrarum sunt sacerdotum, ac universalis Ecclesiae doctorem dedisti, et ad summi Sacerdotii ministerium elegisti, hanc, quaesumus, gratiam largiaris*, etc.

The same Mass read for the feast of St Peter's Chair on February 22, is now used for the consecration and for the coronation of the Pope, as well as on the anniversary of the former—*in natale ordinationis*—but with special Collects, whereas formerly the *Ordo Romanus IX* of the Carlovingian period indicates the Introit: *Elegit te Dominus*.

The consecration of the Pope took place immediately after the Introit, and when it was ended, the Pontiff assumed the pallium, and ascending the papal throne intoned the *Gloria in excelsis*, after which the Mass proceeded in the usual order.

The following are the three special Collects which are recited on the anniversary of the election and consecration of the Pope.

Collect: " O God, the shepherd and ruler of all the faithful, mercifully look down upon thy servant N., whom thou hast been pleased to appoint pastor over thy church; grant, we beseech thee, that both by word and example he may edify those over whom he is set, and together with the flock committed to his care, may attain everlasting life."

Secret: " Be appeased, O Lord, we beseech thee, by the gifts we offer: and govern by thy continual protection thy servant N., whom thou hast been pleased to appoint as pastor over thy church."

Post-Communion: " May the partaking of this divine sacrament protect us, we beseech thee, O Lord; and ever save and defend thy servant N., whom thou hast been pleased to appoint as pastor over thy church, together with the flock committed to his care."

In the Middle Ages, the coronation of the Pope took place at the foot of the steps of the Vatican Basilica.

During the ceremony the heads of the Rioni sang three

times the *Laudes: Domnus N. Papa quem sanctus Petrus elegit, in sua sede multis annis sedere;* then the *prior stabuli* placed the *regnum* upon the head of the newly-elected Pontiff, and the procession returned on horseback to the Lateran for dinner.

The *Capituli Lectionum* of Würzburg contain at least six Lessons from which to choose *in natali Papae.* The first is assigned in our present Missal to the feast of St Callixtus on October 14.

II

THE NUPTIAL MASS

The original title of this Mass is: *ad sponsas velandas,* derived from the characteristic rite of the *flammeum* which the priest laid upon the head of the bride during the nuptial benediction. We have already treated elsewhere of the antiquity of the ceremonies accompanying the celebration of Christian marriage, and shall therefore only describe the nuptial Mass. This, however, formed part of the marriage rite, and the eucharistic Sacrifice offered for bride and bridegroom was a symbol of the divine seal set on their conjugal union. We may call to mind the famous words of Tertullian extolling the happiness of that marriage: *quod Ecclesia conciliat, et confirmat Oblatio, et obsignatum Angeli renuntiant, Pater ratum habet.*[1]

The Introit is taken from the Book of Tobias (vii, 15, 19), and alludes to the union of young Tobias with the daughter of Raguel, who until then had been tormented by the devil, in order that no other man than the son of Tobias should take her to wife. Indeed several men who before his coming had been destined by her parents to marry her, had been slain in succession by the angel of darkness on the bridal night. Tobias, warned by the archangel Raphael, espoused Sara in the fear of the Lord, and spent the first night in prayer with her. Thus by prayer and continence he warded off the blows of Satan.

℣. "May the God of Israel join you together: and may he be with you, who was merciful to two only children: and now, O Lord, make them bless thee more fully."

The nuptial Psalm cxxvii follows: "Blessed are all they that fear the Lord, that walk in his ways."

The following Collect is to be found in the Leonine Sacramentary for the classic *Velatio Nuptialis.*

[1] *P.L.* I, col. 1302.

Holy Mass

Collect: "Graciously hear us, almighty and merciful God, that what is done by our ministry may be abundantly fulfilled with thy blessing."

In the *Capitula Lectionum* the Lesson of this Mass is taken from the First Epistle to the Corinthians (vi, 15-20), where the Apostle, affirming the principle that the body of a Christian is the temple of the Holy Ghost and a member of the mystical body of Christ, speaks strongly against the sin of fornication so common among pagans.

In our Missal, however, the Lesson is from the Epistle to the Ephesians (v, 22, 33), in which St Paul explains the duties of Christian marriage, holding up the indissoluble union of Christ and his Church as an example to be imitated.

The Gradual is taken from Psalm cxxvii, and describes the joys of the sacrament of matrimony in beautiful language: "Thy wife shall be as a fruitful vine on the sides of thy house. ℣. Thy children as olive plants round about thy table."

The married state is in a sense a form of priesthood, for by giving birth to children and educating them in the Christian religion, parents contribute to the growth and development of the Church and fill the places left empty in heaven through the fall of the rebel angels. We may note that when the Holy Ghost praises the valiant woman it is in words portraying her as a careful housewife intent on womanly occupations.

The alleluiatic verse is taken from Psalm xix: "Alleluia. May the Lord send you help from the sanctuary and defend you out of Sion. Alleluia."

The majesty of God fills the heavens and the earth, but in condescension to our weakness which needs to express even abstract and spiritual things in material forms, he has chosen consecrated places of worship as his sanctuaries, where the magnificence of his mercy is made known to us.

After Septuagesima this Tract is read, taken from Psalm cxxvii: "Behold thus shall the man be blessed that feareth the Lord. ℣. May the Lord bless thee out of Sion; and mayest thou see the good things of Jerusalem all the days of thy life. ℣. And mayest thou see thy children's children: peace upon Israel."

The fear of God is the beginning of his holy love, and far from straitening or oppressing the heart, it raises it to a great feeling of confidence and draws down many blessings, even in the material order.

At Eastertide the second alleluiatic verse is as follows: Alleluia (Psalm cxxxiii): "May the Lord out of Sion bless you, he that made heaven and earth. Alleluia."

The Church does not tire of invoking blessings on the bride and bridegroom, for the Christian family is the seed from which all society develops. In order to reform nations it is necessary to begin by sanctifying the family. It is the first and most legitimate of natural societies, and the State, inasmuch as it is formed by the union of numerous domestic societies, is intended to protect them and co-operate with them, and not to suppress the special influence and essential rights of the family, as does the modern liberal State in our day.

The Gospel is taken from St Matthew (xix, 3–6). The Pharisees ask our Lord if it be lawful for a man to divorce his wife, as was the custom under the Old Law. Jesus replies that it is not. God has joined together man and wife, and they have become one flesh. What God has joined together, man cannot put asunder.

Mysterious union! Here we see unity and plurality as in the most Holy Trinity, and whilst husband and wife mutually complete each other in the necessities of life, from their union come forth the children who are bound together by the powerful tie of their common parentage, the brotherly love uniting those who have shared one home.

The Offertory is the same as on the Thirteenth Sunday after Pentecost.

The Secret is profound in meaning and beautifully expressed, but the concise strength of the Latin is weakened by translation.

Secret: " Receive, we beseech thee, O Lord, the offering we make to thee on behalf of the holy bond of wedlock; and even as this institution is the gift of thy bounty, so dispose of it according to thy will."

The Gelasian Sacramentary prescribes this Preface: *Vere dignum . . . Qui foedera nuptiarum blando concordiae jugo et insolubili pacis vinculo nexuisti : ut multiplicandis adoptionum filiis, sanctorum connubiorum foecunditas pudica serviret. Tua enim, Domine, providentia, tuaque gratia ineffabilibus modis utrumque dispensat; ut quod generatio ad mundi edidit ornatum, regeneratio ad Ecclesiae perducat augmentum, per Christum.*

In former days, after having read the diptychs, the priest prayed for the bride in the following words: *Infra actionem. Hanc igitur oblationem famulorum (famularum) tuorum N.N.* (the parents of the bride) *quam tibi offerunt pro famula tua N. quaesumus, Domine, placatus accipias; pro qua maiestatem tuam supplices exoramus, ut sicut eam ad aetatem nuptiis congruentem pervenire tribuisti; sic eam consortio maritali tuo munere copulatam, desiderata sobole gaudere proficias : atque ad optatam seriem cum suo coniuge provehas benignus annorum; diesque nostros,* etc.

In this manner does the Church safeguard the honour of

woman, in contrast with the contempt shown towards her in pagan times, and uphold her dignity as a mother, insisting on the principal object of Christian marriage: the bearing of children to complete the mystical body of Christ.

At the end of the Canon of the Mass, at the moment when in ancient times the various blessings of the chrism, of the holy oils, and of the firstfruits took place, the *velatio nuptialis* was performed, with the *flammeum* and the sacerdotal blessing. This rite concerned the bride only, and was composed of two parts. A short Collect was followed by a long prayer resembling a Preface. It recorded the divine origin of marriage, and the numerous blessings bestowed upon it which the sin of Adam and the universal deluge had not obliterated. If man is created in the image of God, the weaker sex, too, rests upon him, partaking in this likeness, for by the union of the weak with the strong comes forth the remedy to the shortness of human life, the bearing of offspring. May the bride then be amiable to her husband as Rachel, wise as Rebecca, may she be faithful and long-lived as Sara, so that she may see her children and her grandchildren in her old age, and at length attain eternal life which shall never end.

Communion: Psalm cxxvii: "Behold, thus shall every man be blessed that feareth the Lord; and mayest thou see thy children's children: peace upon Israel."

By giving life to immortal beings, parents attain a very high honour, and may be said to co-operate with God *a quo omnis paternitas in caelo et in terra nominatur*.

Post-Communion: "We beseech thee, almighty God, to accompany the institutions of thy Providence with thy gracious favour; that thou mayest keep in lasting peace those whom thou joinest in lawful union."

The congregation having been dismissed with the *Ite missa est*, a last special blessing is pronounced over the newly-married couple, in which the same thoughts are expressed as in the *velatio nuptialis*. The priest invokes the divine assistance upon them, and prays that they may see their children and their children's children to the third and fourth generation.

We know from the Gelasian Sacramentary that the nuptial Mass was repeated on the thirtieth day, and on the anniversary of the wedding. This will not cause any surprise when we remember that the dignity and sanctity of marriage is one of the essential pivots of social morality. This dignity is the result of the Church's teaching, for it had no existence before Christianity, and it does not exist now outside the Catholic Church. In spite of the great privileges with which the Church has surrounded the celibacy of the clergy and religious virginity, she has always shown herself in every age and circumstance the fearless defender of the inviolability of the marriage vow. Thus in the sixteenth century the Popes preferred to allow England to fall away from obedience to the Holy See, rather than offend the sanctity of Christian marriage by approving the divorce sought by Henry VIII.

III

IN TIME OF WAR

The Index of the *Capitula Lectionum* mentioned above, notes at least six different Lessons under the rubric: *In litania, tempore belli ;* an indication of the great need of these Masses at the time when that list was compiled. The Masses instituted by Gregory II on the Thursdays in Lent betray the same preoccupation. Indeed the entire Roman stational system reorganized by Gregory the Great, with its litanies and processions to the tombs of the martyrs, was inspired in a measure by the desire to raise a barrier of liturgical prayer between the just anger of God and the Roman Duchy, delivered by Providence into the hands of the Lombard barbarians. St Gregory's addition to the Canon of the Mass: *diesque nostros in tua pace disponas*, was also suggested by the anxiety which filled the mind of the Pope, and the beautiful invocation synchronised with the approach of the hosts of Agilulf about to lay siege to Rome. Consequently when we consider carefully the Roman Liturgy at the moment when it was definitely established under Gregory I, it appears, as a whole, like the solemn, collective prayer of a terrified and afflicted nation, fearing at any moment to be put to the sword by the Lombards, and imploring the protection of him who is called the Lord of Hosts.

These antecedents and this historical background must be remembered when we consider the *missa tempore belli* described in our Missal.

The sung portions are all taken from other feasts in the Sacramentary, a fact testifying to the antiquity of this Mass. In the early Middle Ages the Antiphonary of St Gregory was thought to be inspired and consequently sacred. When a new solemnity was introduced, the ancient compilers preferred to choose some of the venerable chants contained in the Gregorian collection and to repeat them exactly, rather than to compose new melodies and insert them at the end of the Antiphonary.

The Introit *Reminiscere* is taken from the Wednesday after

Holy Mass

the First Sunday in Lent. If, however, the processional Litany preceded this Mass in olden times, as the Würzburg Codex would imply, the liturgical action had no proper Introit or Kyrie, for these were embodied in the penitential procession before the eucharistic synaxis.

Collect: " O God, who bringest wars to nought and shieldest by thy power all who hope in thee, overthrowing those that assail them; help thy servants who implore thy mercy; so that the fierce might of their enemies may be brought low and we may never cease to praise and thank thee."

When these litanical processions (*in litania, tempore belli*) were instituted, the wars then in progress were not, as in our days, political wars, but the help of the Lord was invoked to save the Roman Empire—the only form of Christian government then known—from the invasion of the pagan or Arian barbarians. In the recent great war the highest ecclesiastical authority refused to enter into the question of the justice of military action on either side, and instead of ordering the celebration of the Mass *in tempore belli*, ordered that the Mass *pro pace* should be said.

The Lesson is taken from Jeremias (xlii, 1-2 and 7-12). The people besought the prophet to intercede for them to the Lord that they might be delivered from the vengeance of the Chaldean king. Jeremias then prayed to God, and made his answer known to the children of Israel. If the latter persevered in the spirit of penance, and did not desert their post and the defence of their country to fly to Egypt, the Lord would be their shield against the anger of the Babylonian king.

The *Capitula Lectionum* prescribe six entirely different Lessons taken from Isaias or Jeremias. The third of these is to be found in the Missal on the Thursday after Quinquagesima, the fourth appears on the Thursday in the third week of Lent. This shows even more clearly the relationship between these Masses of Gregory II, and that calamitous period of Roman history when the town was constantly threatened by the Lombards.

The Gradual: *Tu es Deus*, from Psalm lxxvi, is the same as on Quinquagesima Sunday. This was probably another station instituted by St Gregory the Great, to avert the danger menacing Rome from the armies of Agilulf.

The alleluiatic verse *Eripe me*, from Psalm lviii, also appears, on the Ninth Sunday after Pentecost.

After Septuagesima the Tract from Psalm cii is sung: *Domine non secundum peccata nostra*, etc., as on the Mondays, Wednesdays, and Fridays of Lent. In Paschal time besides the alleluiatic verse which we have quoted, a second follows taken from the same Psalm lviii: " But I will sing of thy strength and will extol thy mercy in the morning. Alleluia."

The Gospel is taken from St Matthew (xxiv, 3-8) and also occurs in the Missal on the feasts of SS Marius, Martha, etc., on January 19. Jesus replied to the disciples who invited him to admire the new adornments of the temple, that of all that magnificence no stone would be left standing. When they had left the town and retired to pray on the Mount of Olives, the Apostles desired to know at what time this prophecy should be accomplished. In his reply, Jesus included in a single prophetic vision the immediate event and that which it prefigured, speaking of the destruction of Jerusalem as a symbol and prophecy of what would happen to the entire world on the last day. At that time, there will be wars and seditions; instead of Christian love, the nations who shall have turned from Christ will be divided by mutual hatred. Jesus exhorted his Apostles not to fear, however, and not to listen to those who spread rumours of war (*opiniones proeliorum*). Men cannot put their plans into execution when they choose. God is above Cæsar and is stronger than he.

The Antiphon for the Offertory, *Populum humilem*, from Psalm xvii, is taken from the Eighth Sunday after Pentecost, while the Communion, *Inclina*, from Psalm xxx, is that of the preceding Sunday.

Secret: "Be appeased, O Lord, and look upon the sacrifice which we offer up: that it may deliver us from all the evil of war, and establish us under thy sure protection."

The merit of the divine Sacrifice making satisfaction for our sins restrains the just anger of God, and placating it, draws down upon the faithful, through the divine Victim, the fullness of heavenly graces and benediction.

The following is an interesting Preface, *Tempore belli*, drawn from the Leonine Sacramentary; it describes the devastated Roman Campagna with the crops ravaged by the barbarian hordes.

Vere dignum . . . Agnoscimus enim, Domine Deus noster, agnoscimus, sicut prophetica voce dudum testatus es, ad peccantium merita pertinere, ut servorum tuorum labore quaesita, sub conspectu nostro manibus diripiantur alienis; et quae, desudantibus famulis, nasci tribuis, ab hostibus patiaris absumi. Totoque corde prostrati, supplices exoramus, et praeteritorum concedas veniam delictorum, et ab omni mortalitatis incursu, continuata miseratione nos protegas. Quia tunc defensionem tuam non diffidimus adfuturam, quum a nobis quibus offendimus dignanter expuleris. Per Christum.

Post-Communion: "O God, who hast dominion over all realms and kings, who by striking healest, and by pardoning

Holy Mass

savest ; stretch out over us thy mercy, so that by thy power we may enjoy peace and tranquillity and use them for our healing and amendment."

This prayer sets before us the end for which God prolongs our life and bestows his gifts upon us. *Patientia Dei ad poenitentiam te adducit*, St Paul tells us. God gives us time and opportunity to complete the work he has entrusted to us, the reproduction of the image of Christ in our souls.

We conclude with an admirable Collect, taken from the Leonine Sacramentary, for the feast of Pentecost. It expresses the idea to which we have alluded, that in the minds of the Fathers of the Middle Ages, the enemies of the Roman Empire were, for that reason alone, the enemies of Christianity.

Oratio. Exaudi, Domine, preces nostras, et sicut profanas mundi caligines Sancti Spiritus luce evacuasti ; sic hostes Romani nominis et inimicos catholicae professionis expugna.

IV

MASS FOR THE SICK

We have already spoken, in the first volume of this work, of the Liturgy for the dying. We need only remark here that, as St James, speaking in his canonical Epistle of the Christian in danger of death by sickness, shows that the sacrament of Penance is closely united to that of Extreme Unction, so, too, the early Liturgy of the Church joined together in one magnificent ceremony these three sacraments: Absolution, Extreme Unction, and the Viaticum.

Contrary to the present custom, Extreme Unction was regularly given before Holy Communion, and immediately followed the sacrament of Penance, for the holy Anointing is the final complete purification of the Christian at the end of his life. When he has been thus purified he receives his Viaticum, and prepares to depart.

In many cases the Viaticum was administered to the sick *intra missarum solemnia*. This explains why many ancient manuscripts speak of the sacrament of the Body and Blood of the Lord partaken of by the dying. This custom continued for a long time, and is mentioned in the lives of St Odo and St Hugh, Abbots of Cluny.

Concerning this practice a remark made by Cardinal Rampolla in his notes upon the life of St Melania the Younger, is interesting. The biographer relates that the Saint, being near to death, received the Holy Eucharist for the last time " in conformity with Roman usage " : *Consuetudo autem est*

Romanis, ut cum animae egrediuntur, Communio Domini in ore sit.[1]

The compiler of the notes quotes several cases of the kind, for instance that of St Ambrose : *Qui descendens* (Onoratus) *obtulit Sancto Domini Corpus ; quo accepto, ubi glutivit emisit spiritum.*

In order to realize more completely the spirit in which this *missa pro infirmo* was celebrated, we must remember that in the first centuries, the administration of Extreme Unction was accompanied by magnificent and impressive ceremonies. The faithful were so far from sharing the dread felt in our days for this sacrament of comfort and healing, that they habitually reserved the holy oils for the sick in their own houses. Even apart from its sacramental purpose they made use of it with great faith to anoint wounded or aching limbs. They were in the habit of putting a few drops of this oil into the food prepared for the sick, in order to obtain their cure. This practice must have been very common in the third century, for the Canons of Hippolytus contain the episcopal formula for the blessing of the oil as a ceremony appertaining to the Sunday Mass.

The Eastern custom that the sacrament of the "oil of prayer," as they call it, should be administered by several priests, was also common in the West at one time. Contrary to the present rule, as this sacrament was administered *per modum unctionis medicinalis* to the sick, and not only to those about to die, the ancients sometimes repeated the anointing for seven days, until the sick man had been healed by the sacrament, or had quietly passed away purified from sin to eternal life.

In any case, during the golden period of the Liturgy, corresponding to the age of the Fathers of the Church, when all religious rites were closely connected with the Holy Eucharist, the administration of Extreme Unction was accompanied by Mass, in the same way as blessing of the oils for the sick was performed during the *missa chrismalis* on Holy Thursday. Thus the former was truly the Mass of the Viaticum, as that of the Paschal Eve was to the neophyte the Mass of his first Communion.

It is impossible to suppose that a choir of cantors stood around the bed of a sick man about to be anointed. Consequently the Antiphons and Graduals assigned to this Mass in later time, were not primitive, and have been taken from other parts of the Gregorian Antiphonary. The Introit from

---

[1] Cf. Rampolla. *S. Melania Giuniore* (Roma, Tipogr. Vat. MCCCCV), n. LXVIII.

Holy Mass

Psalm liv: *Exaudi Deus*, is from the Tuesday in the fourth week in Lent.

Collect: "Almighty everlasting God, the eternal salvation of those who believe; hear us in behalf of thy servants who are sick, for whom we humbly crave the help of thy mercy, that being restored to health they may render thanks to thee in thy church."

The return of the sick man to the church is also prayed for in a Collect forming part of the rite of Extreme Unction: *Atque Ecclesiae tuae Sanctae cum omni desiderata prosperitate restituas*. From this it may be seen that the same thought is uppermost both in this Mass and in the *Ordo* of Extreme Unction: the recovery of the patient that he may for many years continue to acquire merit unto eternal life.

If the sick man is near to death, the Collect is as follows:

Collect: "Almighty and merciful God, who bestowest on mankind both the remedies of salvation and the gifts of life everlasting: look mercifully upon thy servant who is afflicted with sickness of the body and refresh the soul which thou madest: so that at the hour of its going hence it may be found worthy to be borne to thee its Maker, free from all stain of sin, by the hands of holy angels."

This prayer, like the preceding one, is from the Gelasian Sacramentary. It is full of beauty and profound meaning. Until a certain moment the remedies given us by God are of use. The time comes, however, when only the grace of eternal life is of any avail. The reason for which God's strengthening help is invoked, is the essential reason of his divine Providence; the most powerful and efficacious reason which can be brought forward. He it is who has created us, and we are the work of his hands, indeed his chief work. Is it possible that God should not love and care for that which he has made?

The Lesson, very naturally, is taken from the Epistle of St James (v, 13–16), where he commands Christians in case of grave sickness to call the priests that they may administer the sacramental unction, whose salutary effects on both body and soul are described.

The Gradual *Miserere mei Domine* from Psalm vi follows; and is taken from Wednesday of the third week in Lent.

The alleluiatic verse, Psalm ci: *Domine exaudi*, is from the Seventeenth Sunday after Pentecost. After Septuagesima the Tract is from Psalm xxx: "Have mercy on me, O Lord, for I am afflicted, my eye is troubled with wrath, my soul and my belly. ℣. For my life is wasted with grief and my years in sighs. ℣. My strength is weakened through poverty and my bones are disturbed."

This Psalm refers to Jesus, who in his blessed Passion took

upon himself our infirmities, and by his most sacred agony rendered ours holy and meritorious.

In Paschal time the second alleluiatic verse is from Psalm xxvii: "Alleluia. In God has my heart trusted and I have been helped; and my flesh has flourished again and with my will I will give praise to him."

The Gospel read is that passage from St Matthew (viii, 5-13) which describes the healing of the servant of the centurion of Capharnaum.

When we turn with confidence to the Lord and importune him with our prayers to obtain deliverance from our ills, we give honour to God, and he is well pleased, according to the words of the Psalmist: *Invoca me in die tribulationis: eruam te, et honorificabis me.*

The Antiphon for the Offertory is taken from Psalm liv: *Exaudi Deus*, as on Monday after the Third Sunday in Lent.

Secret: "O God, by whose decree each moment of our lives passes by, receive the prayers and victims of thy servants on behalf of those for whom in their sickness we crave thy mercy; so that we may rejoice in the safety of those at whose danger we were afraid."

This is an admirable maxim calculated to keep our souls at peace in any circumstances: *Deus cuius nutibus vitæ nostrae momenta decurrunt.* Every moment of our life is ordered by the loving Providence of our heavenly Father.

When the sick man is nigh to death: "Receive, O Lord, we beseech thee, the sacrifice which we offer up on behalf of thy servant who is nigh unto death, and grant that by means of it all his sins may be washed away, so that he who by thy appointment is stricken by thy scourges in this life may win eternal rest in the life to come."

God does not punish twice. If he chastises us in this world, it is in order that he may not punish us in the next.

The Communion *Illumina* from Psalm xxx is also said on Septuagesima Sunday.

Post-Communion: "O God, who art the only defence for the frailty of man; show forth thy might and help thy servants who are sick; so that succoured by thy bounteous mercy they may be found worthy to be restored safe and sound to thy holy church."

The Holy Eucharist, in contrast to the fatal fruit of the earthly paradise, is above all the supersubstantial bread of the soul. But, as we are told in the Gospel, a virtue goes forth from Jesus which heals bodily ills as well, for the Word, the author of all created things, mercifully deigns to restore his chief work, ruined by the devil.

Holy Mass

When the sick man is nigh to death: "We beseech thy clemency, almighty God, that by the virtue of this sacrament thou wouldst vouchsafe to strengthen thy servant with thy grace so that at the hour of his death the enemy may not prevail against him, but he may deserve to pass with thy angels to life."

A man's last hour is solemn and decisive. Upon that moment depends not only his eternity but the very efficacy of the Saviour's Passion, of the sacraments received by the dying man throughout his lifetime, of a treasure of divine graces and love bestowed on a wretched creature. Jesus stands beside the deathbed, for the salvation of that soul is the fruit of redemption and the Sacred Heart yearns to win it. The Church, filled with the spirit of Christ, cannot be indifferent when the last hours of the wayfarer in this land of exile have arrived, and she does all that is in her power to co-operate with the divine Redeemer, in saving the souls of the dying, by the ritual *de visitatione infirmorum*, by establishing pious confraternities for a holy death under the patronage of St Joseph, by indulgenced prayers, and by Masses offered for those about to die. Of all the poor and needy who have a right to our compassion, the souls of the dying are surely those who are in the most dangerous state, even more so than the souls in Purgatory. The latter are sure of their eternal salvation, whereas the souls of the dying, by reason of the assaults of Satan, are in the greatest danger.

This is one of the reasons why the divine mercy, besides the many spiritual remedies offered by the Church to the sick, was pleased to institute a special sacrament to ensure their eternal salvation in that last awful moment, and to enable them to die peacefully in the arms of God.

The sacrament of Penance is the sacrament of spiritual regeneration, and that of Extreme Unction is the final purification and perfection of the Christian.

V

THE EUCHARISTIC SACRIFICE ON OCCASIONS OF PUBLIC PLAGUE

We find among the votive Masses in the Roman Missal one under the following title: *pro vitanda mortalitate, vel tempore pestilentiae*, similar to the one we have just described. It does not show great originality, and the compiler has not succeeded in giving a special character to his work. Indeed in some places there is little to distinguish it from the many Masses *pro infirmo* contained in the medieval Sacramentaries.

The Sacramentary

Apart from these imperfections, the Mass is inspired by a deep sentiment of faith and confidence, and in the first part, before the Offertory, attains to a certain tragic grandeur, especially in the Introit. The teaching to be derived from this Mass is that the best medicine in time of pestilence is purity of conscience; in other words, that we should keep our soul free from any stain of sin.

Although this Mass *tempore pestilentiae* is a comparatively late composition, prototypes of it are to be found in the ancient Liturgies. The Collects are taken from those at the end of the Gregorian Sacramentary, which contains many other alternative formulas. It is not easy to guess on what considerations the composer has based his choice, but it is certain that the prayers given in the first part of the Sacramentary of Adrian I are very beautiful, and appear better suited to the time of plague than those chosen for the occasion in the present Missal, which are couched in general terms, and would be equally appropriate to any other calamity, as, for instance, a fire, an accident, a hailstorm, etc.

It is well to note here that in the early Sacramentaries all the necessities both public and private of the individual, of the family, and of the nation, are expressed through the eucharistic Sacrifice. While, in the Old Testament, a great number of oblations existed for sins, for purification, for pacification, for propitiation, etc., in the New Law the Sacred Victim on our altars comprehends in one perfect Sacrifice the various significations which those former legal oblations partially expressed. It may be said truly, that, in the New Testament, the Holy Eucharist is the entire worship paid to God by the faithful people.

The Antiphon of the Introit of the Mass *pro vitanda mortalitate* is taken from Kings, Book II, 24, where David implores the Lord to stop the plague which for three days had raged among the people. The verse following it is from Psalm lxxix and is appropriate to the occasion, as it is messianic in character.

Introit, Kings II, 24.

Recordare, Domine, testamenti tui, et dic Angelo percutienti : cesset iam manus tua, et non desoletur terra, et ne perdas omnem animam vivam.
 Ps. lxxix. *Qui regis Israel, intende : qui deducis, velut ovem, Joseph.—Gloria Patri.—Recordare.*

Remember, O Lord, thy covenant, and say to the destroying angel : Hold now thy hand, and let not the land be made desolate, neither let every living thing be destroyed.
 Psalm lxxix. Give ear, O thou that rulest Israel : thou that leadest Joseph like a sheep. Glory be. Remember.

Great calamities or public misfortunes are generally inflicted by God as punishments for the sins of the nation. The individual will expiate his faults in the next world, but nations and states cannot do so, and therefore the Lord punishes their social sins here. He desires, by these public scourges, to bring them to repentance, and the surest means to avert the divine justice is the conversion of the people and their return to God. St Gregory had this object in view when he instituted the famous *litania septiformis* with the procession to the Vatican Basilica, in order to stop the plague desolating Rome in 590.

This thought inspires the following Collect:

Deus, qui non mortem, sed poenitentiam desideras peccatorum : populum tuum ad te revertentem propitius respice ; ut, dum tibi devotus existit, iracundiae tuae flagella ab eo clementer amoveas. Per Dominum.

" God, who desirest not the death but the repentance of sinners, mercifully look upon thy people who return to thee ; and grant that they, being devoted to thee, may by thy mercy be delivered from the scourges of thine anger. Through our Lord."

The Lesson is taken from the same chapter as the Introit. The plague was raging throughout the kingdom of David, and slew seventy thousand victims in three days. The angelic minister of the sanctity of God was sent to punish the sin of vainglory committed by the king, when he ordered the census of the nation to be taken. The people suffered for his sin on the principle of solidarity so strongly felt by the ancients, who regarded the sins or the virtues of parents and rulers as drawing down punishment or blessings upon their children and subjects. By permitting this, God commits no injustice, for it is merely a question of temporal goods which he is in no way bound to bestow, and if he deprives certain individuals of these advantages, it is for their eternal welfare. For instance, the plague was in reality ordered to the greater good of the Israelites, for God, who does not punish the same sin twice, allowed them to expiate their sins by that death, and the poor victims were carried away by the pestilence at the moment when it was to the greater advantage of their souls.

Even those who by the inscrutable judgement of God were not saved, were spared from adding to their guilt, and their eternal punishment was less terrible in consequence.

David propitiated the Lord by erecting a votive altar on the spot where he had beheld the angel with the drawn sword ; that altar is a symbol of our Redeemer who reconciles all humanity to God through the merits of his precious Blood.

The Gradual is taken from Psalm cvi : " The Lord sent his

word, and healed them : he delivered them from their destructions. ℣. Let the mercies of the Lord give glory to him, and his wonderful works to the children of men. Alleluia."

Not only did Jesus heal the sick, but he left this power to his Apostles, and we still see miraculous cures performed by the more holy members of the Church even to this day.

The alleluiatic verse taken from Psalm lxviii follows. As we know, it was originally separated from the responsorial Psalm by a second Lesson from the New Testament. " Alleluia, alleluia. Save me, O God, for the waters are come in even unto my soul. Alleluia."

From Septuagesima to Easter the alleluiatic verse is omitted, and the verse from Psalm cii : *Domine non secundum peccata* is sung. This Tract has been sung on Mondays, Wednesdays, and Fridays in Lent since the time of Adrian I. In Paschal time the alleluiatic verse is said instead of the Gradual, and therefore, in the place of the second Lesson now suppressed, another Psalm, curtailed and reduced to a single verse, is added. The verse in this Mass is not taken from the Psalter but from the minor prophets.

Alleluia (Zach. viii, 7-8) : " I will save my people Israel in their evil day, and I will be their God in truth and in justice."

When confronted with some great catastrophe such as an earthquake or a pestilence, the pride of man is brought low ; all his discoveries and his boasted wisdom are powerless before God, whose touch can wither and dissolve the earth. Man raises his towers of Babel, his palaces and monuments, as though they were to endure for ever, but an earthquake of the duration of a few seconds is sufficient to make of a populous city a heap of ruins. Science performs miracles ; man thinks that he has penetrated all the secrets of nature, he boasts that he has mastered creation and has now no need of God. An epidemic breaks out : a mysterious bacillus slays thousands and thousands of victims, and upsets all the calculations of the learned. It is a microbe, an almost invisible organism, which annihilates human pride. Such is our life, the span of which can be shortened by such microscopic enemies. God alone is strong, wise, and good. In him only can we trust, for he alone will never fail us. All other things, science, art, glory, health, and strength, are but vanity.

The Gospel is that of Saturday of the Summer Ember Days (Luke iv, 38-44), and relates the healing of St Peter's mother-in-law, and of the many sick persons who came to Jesus in consequence of this cure. When the Word took flesh he conferred upon that flesh the power to bestow health, grace, and holiness. The Saints, especially in early Christian times, regarded the Holy Eucharist as a remedy not only for the soul but for the body. The Fathers of the Church relate many cases of bodily cures effected by Holy Communion. Indeed St John Chrysostom tells us that many sick people were restored to health after having been anointed with the oil from the lamps which burnt before the altar. We have already mentioned in the preceding pages that since the second century the bishop always blessed the oils for the sick at the Sunday Mass. When, subsequently, the performance of this rite was limited to the *missa chrismalis* of Maundy Thursday, the faithful of Rome in the Middle Ages used to bring their own phials of oil to be blessed by the Pope or the clergy celebrating with him. This *oleum infirmorum* was reverently preserved in every house as holy water is now. A great change has taken place since those days in the mind of Christians, some of whom now appear to have a great fear of Extreme Unction.

The Antiphon accompanying the Offertory Psalm, now no longer used, is taken from the Book of Numbers (xvi, 48), and tells how the people of Israel rebelled against Moses, and how fourteen thousand were destroyed by fire from heaven. The great legislator commanded Aaron his brother to place himself as mediator between the bodies of the dead and the living, and the justice of God. The prayers of Aaron ascended like incense and God was placated. This is the place and the vocation assigned to the clergy. The priest is called away from the multitude to be a mediator between God and man. Among all the ministries and offices he is chosen to fulfil, there is no office more worthy, none more essential, than the offering up of the Eucharistic Sacrifice and liturgical meditation, the psalmody *in loco sancto, in quo orat sacerdos pro delictis et peccatis populi.*

The priest makes prayer and intercession for the sins of others, for it is understood that he must be holy and pure from every sin, or else *si non placet, non placat*, as St Bernard wisely says. St Jerome, too, when speaking of the legal purifications of the Jews, remarks: " Does any man among the people fall into sin ? The priest prays for the culprit and his sin is forgiven. But should the priest sin, who shall make intercession for him ? "

The prayer over the Oblations, which formerly in Gaul accompanied the reading of the diptychs, and at Rome preceded the Canon of the Consecration, is as follows :

Subveniat nobis, quaesumus, Domine, Sacrificii praesentis oblatio: quae nos et ab erroribus universis potenter absolvat, et a totius eripiat perditionis incursu. Per Dominum.	" Let the sacrifice which we now offer up succour us, O Lord, may it wholly release us from sin and deliver us from ruin and destruction. Through."

In time of plague when the chief need is to find the cause and the remedy for the disease, the Church is indeed wise to point out the true source of all evil, sin. When this is removed by a sincere return to God, the epidemic will disappear, God will be placated, and will restore his grace, which will purify the body, too, from every contagion.

The Communion (Luke vi, 17–19), contrary to rule, is not taken from the Psalter nor from the Gospel of the Mass. This proves that it is a composition of a later date when these canons were no longer adhered to. "A multitude of the sick, and those that were troubled with unclean spirits, came to him; for virtue went out from him and he healed them all."

The fruit of the fatal tree poisoned the lives of all mortals, but the fruit of Mary's blessed womb is the medicine of immortality, the antidote against the virus of sin, spread through the soul as well as the body.

The ancient Liturgy always supposed that the faithful, who had offered the Sacrifice to God together with the priest, would also devoutly participate in it by Holy Communion. To people accustomed to pagan sacrifices, a sacrifice in which those present did not participate by means of a sacrificial banquet would have been almost incomprehensible. The following is the prayer after Holy Communion:

Exaudi nos, Deus, salutaris noster: et populum tuum ab iracundiae tuae terroribus liberum, et misericordiae tuae fac largitate securum. Per Dominum.

"Hear us, O God of our salvation, and deliver thy people from the terrors of divine anger, and make them secure by the bountifulness of thy mercy. Through our Lord."

There may well be physical causes for the spread of epidemic diseases, and remedies for combating them. But anyone who considers these scourges, before which human science is conscious of its own impotence, from a supernatural point of view, will easily recognize that they are the consequence of sin—more especially of the sins of Society. The remedy is to be sought in conformity to the Will of God, who disposes and orders all things to our own greater good, in sincere conversion and the amendment of our sins; and, lastly, in an ardent zeal and activity, according to our social influence, in order that our individual conversion and expiation may bear fruit in a sincere return to God of modern society: *generatio mala et adultera.*

EUCHOLOGICAL APPENDIX

Prayers to the Blessed Virgin taken from the Byzantine Liturgy

O Virgin most pure, Mother of Christ the Son of God, a sword of sorrow pierced thy most holy soul when thou didst behold thy Son and God voluntarily nailed to the Cross. Cease not, O Blessed Virgin, to intercede with him for us that he may grant us pardon for our sins in this time of penance.

We dare not speak because of the great number of our sins. Do thou, O Virgin Mother of God, implore thy Son, for the prayers of his Mother are powerful to obtain mercy from the Lord. O purest One, do not despise the petitions of the sinner; for he who deigned to suffer for us will also be merciful towards us and save us.

O Christ, behold thy Mother, she who conceived thee in her womb without the loss of her virginity, and who after she had given thee birth remained a stainless virgin. We present her to thee that she may be our advocate, O thou who art all mercy, thou who dost grant pardon to those who say to thee from their hearts: Be mindful of me, O Lord, when thou art come into thy kingdom.

From the Office of Good Friday.

O most glorious Mother, who gavest birth to the Divine Word, receive the devout homage of our devotion; deliver us from every misfortune, guard us from future condemnation, whilst in thy honour we sing the hymn: Alleluia.

From the Hymnos Akathistos.

We fly to thy patronage, O Holy Mother of God, despise not our petitions in our necessities, but deliver us always from all dangers, O glorious and Blessed Virgin.

Byzantine Prayer
in Form of a Litany

Whilst we sing the glories of thy Son we praise thee, too, O Mother of God, living temple of the Godhead. God, who holds the entire universe in his hand, dwelt in thy womb and sanctified and glorified thee, teaching us to praise thee in this manner:

> Hail, O tabernacle of God and his Word!
> Hail, most holy Lady, holier than the holiest Saint!
> Hail, O golden ark fashioned by the Holy Ghost!
> Hail, O inexhaustible treasure of our life!
> Hail, thou diadem of Catholic sovereigns!
> Hail, thou glory of the priesthood!
> Hail, steadfast tower of Holy Church!
> Hail, impregnable bulwark of the Empire!
> Hail, thou who dost give victory to our standards!
> Hail, conqueror of our enemies!
> Hail, preserver of our bodies!
> Hail, salvation of our souls!
> Hail, O spotless Spouse!

Thou, O Virgin Mother of God, art the refuge of all pure souls, and of all who have recourse to thee. The author of heaven and earth having formed thee without stain was pleased to inhabit thee, that we might hail thee as pillar of virginity, gate of salvation, dispenser of divine bounty, conqueror of the enemy of souls.

From the Hymnos Akathistos.

INVOCATIONS TO THE MOTHER OF GOD

O Mother of God, thy womb is like the sacred table whereon lies the heavenly Bread, of which it is written that he who eats it shall never die.

Thou who wert worthy to carry the great God in thy womb, O holy Spouse and Virgin, spotless Mother, cease not to pray for us, for we have recourse to thee at all times to escape the evils which threaten us.

Thou wert worthy to bear in thy womb the incomprehensible Word: thou didst nourish him who nourishes the whole world. O most pure Mother of God, thou didst hold in thine arms him who assists us in all our necessities.

How was it possible that thou couldst give life to him who is begotten by the Father from eternity, and is adored with the Holy Ghost? He only can understand this mystery, who was well pleased to be born of thee, O holy Mother!

From the Office of Feria IV after Pentecost.

PRAYER OF ST MARTIN FOR HIS PEOPLE.[1]

Dicamus omnes ex toto corde et ex tota mente : Domine, exaudi et miserere. Domine, miserere.

Qui respicis super terram et facis eam tremere. Oramus te, Domine ; exaudi et miserere.

I. Pro altissima pace et tranquillitate temporum nostrorum ; pro sancta Ecclesia catholica, quae est a finibus usque ad terminos orbis terrae. Oramus te, Domine ; exaudi et miserere.

II. Pro pastore nostro N. episcopo (Martino) et omnibus episcopis et presbyteris et diaconis et omni clero. Oramus, etc.

III. Pro hoc loco et inhabitantibus in eo ; pro piissimis imperatoribus (Arcadio et Honorio) et omni exercitu romano. Oramus, etc.

IV. Pro omnibus qui in sublimitate constituti sunt ; pro virginibus, viduis et orphanis. Oramus, etc.

V. Pro peregrinantibus et iter agentibus ac navigantibus : pro poenitentibus et catechumenis. Oramus, etc.

VI. Pro iis qui in sancta Ecclesia fructus misericordiae largiuntur, Domine, Deus virtutum, exaudi preces nostras. Oramus, etc.

VII. Sanctorum Apostolorum et Martyrum memores simus, ut, orantibus iis pro nobis, veniam mereamur. Oramus, etc.

Christianum et pacificum nobis finem concedi a Domino deprecemur. Praesta, Domine, praesta.

IX. Et divinum nobis permanere vinculum charitatis sanctum Dominum deprecemur. Praesta, Domine, praesta.

X. Conservare sanctitatem et catholicae fidei puritatem Dominum deprecemur. Praesta, dicamus omnes : praesta, Domine, praesta.

From the Stowe Missal.

---

[1] The form of this liturgic prayer dates from the most remote antiquity, for the Church borrowed it from the liturgic worship of the synagogues. The text quoted above may easily belong, as its title claims for it, to the time of St. Martin of Tours.

Byzantine Tropes for Sundays

Composed by St Metrophanes of Smyrna for the Union of the Churches.

Τὴν πάντων Βασιλίδα καὶ παντουργόν, ὑπεράρχιον φύσιν, ὑπερχρόνιον, ζωαρχικὴν, εὔσπλαγχνον, φιλάνθρωπον, ἀγαθὴν, ἐναρχικὴν Τριάδα σε νῦν δοξολογοῦντες, ἁμαρτιῶν συγχώρησιν αἰτοῦμεν, τῷ κόσμῳ τὴν εἰρήνην καὶ 'Εκκλησίαις τὴν ὁμόνοιαν.

We glorify thee, O Holy Trinity, sole principle, Sovereign Creator of all things, Supreme nature, eternal, life-giving, entirely good. We ask of thee pardon for our sins, peace for the world, unity among the Churches.

'Η μία Κυριότης καὶ τριλαμπὴς ἐνικὴ θεαρχία τρισήλιε, τοὺς ὑμνητὰς πρόσδεξαι τοὺς σοὺς ἀγαθωπρεπῶς, καὶ τῶν πταισμάτων λύτρωσαι, καὶ τῶν πειρασμῶν καὶ τῶν δυσχερῶν, καὶ θᾶττον τὴν εἰρήνην παράσχου φιλανθρώπως ταῖς 'Εκκλησίαις καὶ τὴν ἕνωσιν.

Sole Lordship, sole Divine Sovereignty in a threefold splendour and a threefold ray; mercifully receive those who glorify thee with their hymns, deliver them from temptation and adversity and in thy mercy grant to the Church a speedy peace and union.

Νηδὺν, Χριστέ, Σωτήρ μου, παρθενικὴν ἐνοικήσας, ἐφάνης τῷ κόσμῳ σου θεανδρικῶς, ἄτρεπτος, ἀσύγχυτος ἀληθῶς, καὶ καθυπέσχου πάντοτε μετὰ τῶν σῶν δούλων εἶναι σαφῶς, διὰ τῆς σὲ τεκούσης πρεσβείαις, τὴν εἰρήνην πάσῃ τῇ ποίμνῃ σου πρυτάνευσον.

O Christ, my Saviour, thou who didst dwell in the womb of the Virgin and who didst appear in this world, made by thy hands, without any change or confusion God and man at once; thou who hast solemnly promised to be for ever with thy servants, through the intercession of her who bore thee, grant peace to all thy flock.

CORRIGENDA
IN PREVIOUS VOLUMES

Volume I.

Page 13, line 40. *for* redemption *read* reception.
Page 139, line 38. *for* name *read* nave.
Page 280, line 40. *for* fifteenth *read* fifth.
Page 294. *delete the whole of line 35, and substitute:* essential, inasmuch as it defines what the Eucharist.

Volume IV.

Page 220, line 29. *for* Synaxis in the Via Ardeatina *read* St Boniface, Bishop and Martyr.

INDEX

Abdon and Sennen, MM., iv, 390
Abundius and Abundantius, MM., v, 116
Abundius and Irenaeus, MM., v, 67
Acontius and others, MM., v, 94
Adalbert, M., iv, 114
Adrian, M., v, 96
Advent:
  1st Sunday in, i, 319
  2nd Sunday in, i, 323
  3rd Sunday in, i, 325
  Ember Days, i, 329
  4th Sunday in, i, 352
Aedistus, M., v, 173
Agapitus, M., v, 59
Agatha, V.M., iii, 410
Agnes, V.M., iii, 363
  Nativity of, iii, 386
Alexander and others, MM., iv, 139
Alexius, C., iv, 354
All Saints:
  Vigil, v, 204
  Feast, v, 208
  Octave, v, 252
All Souls, v, 213
Aloysius Gonzaga, C., iv, 257
Alphonsus Liguori, B.C.D., iv, 402
Ambrose, B.C.D., iii, 293
Anacletus, P.M., iv, 346
Anastasius, M., iii, 370
Andrew, Ap.:
  Vigil, iii, 265
  Feast, iii, 270
Andrew Avellino, C., v, 263
Andrew Corsini, B.C., iii, 408
Angela Merici, V., iv, 202
Angels, Guardian, v, 151
Anicetus, P.M., iv, 107
Anne, Mother of B.V.M., iv, 376
Annunciation of B.V.M., iv, 73
Anselm, B.C.D., iv, 108
Anthony, Ab., iii, 346
Anthony Mary Zaccaria, C., iv, 320
Anthony of Padua, C., iv, 237
Antoninus, B.C., iv, 161
Apollinaris, B.M., iv, 368
Apollonia, V.M., iii, 418

Appearance of B.V.M. at Lourdes, iii, 423
Ascension:
  Vigil, ii, 372
  Feast, ii, 374
  Sunday after, ii, 378
Ash Wednesday, ii, 38
  Thursday after, ii, 47
  Friday after, ii, 49
  Saturday after, ii, 51
Assumption of B.V.M.:
  Vigil, v, 50
  Feast, v, 52
  Octave, v, 66
Asterius, M., v, 183
Athanasius, B.C.D., iv, 137
Augustine of Canterbury, B.C., iv, 194
Augustine of Hippo, B.C.D., v, 78

Balbina, M., v, 155
Barbara, V.M., iii, 280
Barnabas, Ap., iv, 229
Bartholomew, Ap.:
  Vigil, v, 69
  Feast, v, 69
Basil, B.C.D., iv, 239
Basilides, M., iv, 233
Basilla, M., iv, 180
Basilla, V.M., v, 128
Bede, C.D., iv, 192
Benedict, Ab., iv, 65
Bernard, Ab.C.D., v, 61
Bernardine of Siena, C., iv, 179
Bibiana, V.M., iii, 274
Blaise, B.M., iii, 407
Bonaventure, B.C.D., iv, 347
Boniface, M., iv, 171, v, 93
Boniface, B.M., iv, 220
Brice, B.C., v, 272
Bridget, W., v, 169
Bruno, C., v, 160

Caesarius, D.M., v, 206
Cajetan, C., iv, 422
Callistus, P.M., v, 175
Calocerius and Partenius, MM., iv, 176

343

The Sacramentary

Camillus de Lellis, C., iv, 357
Candida, V., v, 154
Canute, K.M., iii, 357
Casimir, C., iv, 33
Cassian, M., iv, 447
Catherine, V.M., v, 302
Catherine of Siena, V., iv, 129
Cecilia, V.M., Dedication of, v, 291
Charles Borromeo, B.C., v, 246
Christina, V.M., iv, 371
Christmas Eve, i, 356
Christmas Day, i, 361
Christmas, Sunday in Octave, i, 388
Christmas, Octave of, i, 395
Christopher, M., iv, 375
Chrysanthus and Daria, MM., v, 192
Chrysogonus, M., v, 299
Circumcision of Our Lord, i, 395
Clare, V., iv, 440
Clement, P.M., v, 294
Cletus and Marcellinus, PP.MM., iv, 121
Cornelius and Cyprian, MM., v, 106
Corpus Christi, iii, 82
   Sunday in Octave, iii, 89
Cosmas and Damian, MM., v, 141
Crescention and Justin, MM., iv, 407
Cross, Holy:
   Finding of, iv, 143
   Exaltation of, v, 108
Crowned MM., v, 249
Cyprian and Justina, MM., v, 140
Cyriac and others, MM., iv, 423
Cyril of Alexandria, B.C.D., iii, 419
Cyril of Jerusalem, B.C.D., iv, 58
Cyril and Methodius, CC., iv, 329
Cyrinus, B.M., iv, 233
Cyrus and John, MM., iii, 391

Damasus, P.C., iii, 306
Denis and others, MM., v, 170
Didacus, C., v, 273
Diogenes and others, MM., iv, 245
Dominic, C., iv, 407
Donatus, B.M., iv, 421
Dorothy, V.M., iii, 415

Easter Sunday, ii, 313
Easter Monday, ii, 318
Easter Tuesday, ii, 322
Easter Wednesday, ii, 325
Easter Thursday, ii, 327

Easter Friday, ii, 331
Easter Saturday, ii, 334
Easter:
   2nd Sunday after, ii, 342
   3rd Sunday after, ii, 345
   4th Sunday after, ii, 348
   5th Sunday after, ii, 351
   Monday of 5th Week after, ii, 371
   Tuesday of 5th Week after, ii, 372
Edward, K.C., v, 174
Eleutherius, P.M., iv, 191
Eleutherius, M., v, 95
Elizabeth of Hungary, W., v, 288
Elizabeth of Portugal, W., iv, 333
Ember Days:
   In Advent, i, 329
   In Lent, ii, 63, 70, 73
   After Pentecost, ii, 402, 407, 410
   In September, iii, 150, 155, 159
Emerentiana, V.M., iii, 373
Ephrem, C.D., iv, 250
Epiphany:
   Vigil, i, 399
   Feast, i, 400
   Sunday in Octave, i, 405
   Octave of, i, 408
   2nd Sunday after, i, 409
   3rd Sunday after, i, 412
   4th Sunday after, i, 414
   5th Sunday after, i, 415
   6th Sunday after, i, 416
Erasmus, B.M., iv, 214
Eugenia, V.M., iii, 322
Euphemia, V.M., v, 113
Euplus, D.M., iv, 439
Eusebius, B.M., iii, 314
Eusebius, P.C., iv, 448
Eusebius, P.M., v, 139
Eustace, B.M., v, 124
Eutropius and others, MM., iv, 350
Eutychius, M., iii, 409
Evaristus, P., v, 195

Fabian, P.M., iii, 359
Family, Holy, iii, 330
Faustinus and Jovita, MM., iii, 430
Felicitas, M., iv, 335; v, 247
Felicola, V.M., iv, 219
Felix, P.M., iii, 336
Felix I, P.M., iv, 198
Felix II, P.M., iv, 384
Felix and Adauctus, MM., v, 84
Felix of Valois, C., v, 289
Fidelis of Sigmaringen, M., iv, 115
Forty MM. of Sebaste, iv, 44
Frances of Rome, W., iv, 41

Index

Francis of Assisi, C., v, 155
  Stigmata of, v, 117
Francis Borgia, C., v, 172
Francis Caracciolo, C., iv, 217
Francis of Paola, C., iv, 91
Francis de Sales, B.C.D., iii, 390
Francis Xavier, C., iii, 277

Gabriel, Archangel, iv, 69
Genesius, M., v, 71
Genuinus and others, MM., v, 170
George, M., iv, 112
Gertrude, V., v, 276
Gervase and Protase, MM., iv, 251
Giles, Ab.C., v, 91
Good Friday, ii, 204
Gordian and Epimachus, MM., iv, 159
Gorgonius, M., v, 99
Gregory the Great, P.C.D., iv, 46
Gregory III, P.C., v, 306
Gregory VII, P.C., iv, 183
Gregory Nazianzen, B.C.D., iv, 158
Gregory Thaumaturgus, B.C., v, 279

Hedwig, W., v, 180
Helena, W., iv, 180
Henry, Emperor, C., iv, 348
Hermenegild, M., iv, 99
Hermes, M., v, 77
Hilarion, Ab., v, 187
Hilary, B.C.D., iii, 339
Hippolytus, M., v, 65
Hippolytus and Pontian, MM., iv, 442
Holy Saturday, ii, 223, 286
Holy Week:
  Monday in, ii, 182
  Tuesday in, ii, 187
  Wednesday in, ii, 193
Hyacinth, M., v, 100
Hyginus, P.M., iii, 328

Ignatius, B.M., iii, 394
Ignatius of Loyola, C., iv, 393
Immaculate Conception:
  Vigil of, iii, 295
  Feast, iii, 298
  Octave, iii, 313
Innocent I, P.C., iv, 382
Innocents, Holy:
  Feast, i, 385
  Octave, i, 398

Irenaeus, B.M., iv, 284
Isidore, B.C.D., iv, 93

James, Ap.:
  Vigil, iv, 372
  Feast, iv, 372
Jane de Chantal, W., v, 62
Januarius and others, MM., v, 122
Jerome, C.D., v, 146
Jerome Emiliani, C., iv, 361
Jesus, Holy Name of, iii, 323
Joachim, C., v, 56
John, Ap.Ev.:
  Feast, i, 381
  Octave, i, 398
  Before the Latin Gate, iv, 151
John Baptist:
  Vigil, iv, 262
  Feast, iv, 265
  Beheading, v, 81
John I, P.M., iv, 193
John Baptist de la Salle, C., iv, 172
John Capistran, C., iv, 82
John Chrysostom, C.D., iii, 384
John of the Cross, C.D., v, 301
John Damascene, C.D., iv, 79
John, Festus and others, MM., iv, 269
John of God, C., iv, 40
John Gualbert, Ab., iv, 345
John of Kenty, C., v, 185
John of Matha, C., iii, 417
John and Paul, MM.:
  Vigil, iv, 272
  Feast, iv, 272
Josaphat, B.M., v, 273
Joseph, C., iv, 61
  Solemnity of, iv, 130
Joseph Calasanctius, C., v, 75
Joseph of Cupertino, C., v, 120
Juliana Falconieri, V, iv, 254
Justin, M., iv, 103

Kingship of Christ, v, 200

Lateran, Dedication of, v, 254
Lawrence, M.:
  Vigil, iv, 427
  Feast, iv, 430
  Octave, v, 58
Lawrence, St., Dedic. of, v, 241
Lawrence Justinian, B.C., v, 95
Lent, 1st Sunday, ii, 53
  Monday after, ii, 58
  Tuesday after, ii, 61
  Wednesday after, ii, 63

Lent, 1st Sunday :
  Thursday after, ii, 67
  Friday after, ii, 70
  Saturday after, ii, 73
Lent, 2nd Sunday, ii, 78
  Monday after, ii, 80
  Tuesday after, ii, 83
  Wednesday after, ii, 85
  Thursday after, ii, 87
  Friday after, ii, 90
  Saturday after, ii, 92
Lent, 3rd Sunday, ii, 95
  Monday after, ii, 98
  Tuesday after, ii, 101
  Wednesday after, ii, 103
  Thursday after, ii, 105
  Friday after, ii, 107
  Saturday after, ii, 111
Lent, 4th Sunday, ii, 113
  Monday after, ii, 116
  Tuesday after, ii, 119
  Wednesday after, ii, 122
  Thursday after, ii, 134
  Friday after, ii, 138
  Saturday after, ii, 141
Leo, B.M., iv, 56
Leo the Great, P.C.D., iv, 94, 282
Leonard, C., v, 248
Liberius, P.C., v, 133
Liborius, B.C., iv, 371
Linus, P.M., v, 137
Litanies, Greater, ii, 355
Louis, K.C., v, 72
Low Sunday, ii, 338
Lucius I, P.M., iv, 32
Lucy, V.M., iii, 310
Lucy and Geminianus, MM., v, 114
Luke, Ev., v, 181

Machabees, MM., iv, 399
Magnus, M., v, 60
Marcellinus and Peter, MM., iv, 211
Marcellus, P.M., iii, 343
Marcellus and Apuleius, MM., v, 163
Margaret, Q.W., iv, 229
Margaret, V.M., iv, 360
Marius and others, MM., iii, 354
Mark, Ev., ii, 355 ; iv, 116
Mark, P.C., v, 161
Mark and Marcellian, MM., iv, 247
Martha, V.M., iv, 388
Martin, B.C., v, 266
Martin I, P.M., v, 117, 271
Martina, V.M., iii, 390
Mary, B.V. :
  Ad Martyres, Dedic. of, iv, 167
  Of Mount Carmel, iv, 351
  Holy Name of, v, 105

Mary Magdalen, iv, 366
Mary Magdalen dei Pazzi V, iv, 197
Matthew, Ap. :
  Vigil, v, 125
  Feast, v, 125
Matthias, Ap. :
  Vigil, iii, 435
  Feast, iii, 436
Maundy Thursday, ii, 199
Maurice and others, MM., v, 130
Melchiades, P.M., iii, 305, 328
Mennas, M., v, 264
Merita, M., v, 129
Michael, Archangel :
  Dedic. of, v, 144
  Appearing of, iv, 154
Monica, W., iv, 146

Nabor and Felix, MM., iv, 344
Nabor and Nazarius, MM., iv, 233
Nativity of B.V.M. :
  Vigil, v, 96
  Feast, v, 97
Nazarius and Celsus, MM., iv, 380
Nemesius, M., v, 87
Nereus and others, MM., iv, 162
Nicholas, B.C., iii, 289
Nicholas of Tolentino, C., v, 101
Nicomedes, M., v, 111
Nicomedes, Dedic. of Basilica of, iv, 209
Norbert, B.C., iv, 225

Optatus, B., v, 305
Our Lady of Ransom, v, 138
Our Lady of the Snows, Dedic. of, iv, 409

Palm Sunday, ii, 171
Pancras, M., iv, 162
Pantaleon, M., iv, 379
Paschal Baylon, C., iv, 174
Passion Sunday, ii, 145
Passion Week :
  Monday, ii, 149
  Tuesday, ii, 152
  Wednesday, ii, 156
  Thursday, ii, 159
  Friday, ii, 163
  Saturday, ii, 167
Patermutius and Copretes, iv, 334
Patrick, B.C., iv, 57
Paul, Ap. :
  Commemoration of, iv, 309
  Conversion of, iii, 378

Index

Paul, First Hermit, C., iii, 339
Paul of the Cross, C., iv, 125
Paulinus, B.C., iv, 260
Pentecost:
  Vigil, ii, 381
  Feast, ii, 388
  Octave, Monday, ii, 396
  Octave, Tuesday, ii, 399
  Octave, Wednesday, ii, 402
  Octave, Thursday, ii, 406
  Octave, Friday, ii, 407
  Octave, Saturday, ii, 410
  1st Sunday after, iii, 78
  2nd Sunday after, iii, 89
  3rd Sunday after, iii, 93
  4th Sunday after, iii, 95
  5th Sunday after, iii, 99
  6th Sunday after, iii, 103
  7th Sunday after, iii, 107
  8th Sunday after, iii, 112
  9th Sunday after, iii, 117
  10th Sunday after, iii, 121
  11th Sunday after, iii, 124
  12th Sunday after, iii, 128
  13th Sunday after, iii, 132
  14th Sunday after, iii, 136
  15th Sunday after, iii, 139
  16th Sunday after, iii, 142
  17th Sunday after, iii, 145
  18th Sunday after, iii, 167
  19th Sunday after, iii, 171
  20th Sunday after, iii, 174
  21st Sunday after, iii, 178
  22nd Sunday after, iii, 182
  23rd Sunday after, iii, 186
  24th Sunday after, iii, 189
Perpetua and Felicitas, MM., iv, 34
Peter, Ap.:
  Chair at Antioch, iii, 433
  Chair at Rome, iii, 348
  Chains, iv, 395
Peter and Paul, App.:
  Vigil, iv, 287
  Feast, iv, 290
  Within Oct. of, iv, 318, 320
  Octave, iv, 324
Peter and Paul, Dedic. of Basilica, v, 280
Peter, M., iv, 128
Peter of Alcantara, C., v, 184
Peter of Alexandria, B.M., v, 303
Peter Celestine, P.C., iv, 177
Peter Chrysologus, B.C.D., iii, 283
Peter Damian, C.D., iii, 435
Peter Nolasco, C., iii, 393
Petronilla, V., iv, 199
Philip and James, App., iv, 133
Philip Benizi, C., v, 68

Philip Neri, C., iv, 188
Pius I, P.M., iv, 343
Pius V, P.C., iv, 149
Placidus and others, MM., v, 158
Polycarp, B.M., iii, 383
Pontian, P.M., v, 287
Praxedes V, iv, 364
Precious Blood of Our Lord, iv, 309
Presentation B.V.M., v, 290
Primus and Felician, MM., iv, 226
Prisca, V.M., iii, 346
Processus and Martinian, MM., iv, 312
Protus and Hyacinth, MM., v, 101
Pudentiana, V., iv, 177
Purification B.V.M., iii, 397
Pygmenius, M., iv, 60

Quinquagesima, ii, 36
Quiricus, M., iv, 215
Quiricus and Julitta, MM., iv, 244, 351
Quirinus, M., iv, 73

Raphael, Archang., v, 189
Raymund Nonnatus, C., v, 89
Raymund of Pennafort, C., iii, 374
Remigius, B.C., Transl. of, v, 151
Rogation Days, ii, 371
Roman Protomartyrs, iv, 278
Romanus, M., iv, 426
Romuald, Ab., iii, 417
Rosary, Holy, of B.V.M., v, 165
Rose of Lima, V., v, 88
Rufina and Secunda, VV.MM., iv, 343

Sabbas, Ab., iii, 286
Sabina, M., v, 80
Sacred Heart of Jesus, iv, 203
Saturninus, M., iii, 260
Scholastica, V., iii, 421
Sebastian, M., iii, 359
Semetrius, M., iv, 187
Septuagesima, ii, 30
Serapia, M., v, 93
Sergius and Bacchus, MM., v, 163
Seven Brothers, MM.:
  Vigil, iv, 335
  Feast, iv, 335
Seven Servite Founders, CC., iii, 426
Seven Sorrows of B.V.M. ,iv, 86
Sexagesima, ii, 33
Silverius, P.M., iv, 255

Simeon, B.M., iii, 433
Simon and Jude, App.:
  Vigil, v, 195
  Feast, v, 197
Simplicius and others, MM., iv, 386
Sixtus II and others, MM., iv, 412
Sosius, M., v, 180
Soter, V.M., iii, 422
Soter and Gaius, PP.MM., iv, 110
Stacteus, M., v, 143
Stanislaus, B.M., iv, 153
Stephen, Protomartyr, i, 378
  Octave, i, 398
  Finding, iv, 406
Stephen, K.C., v, 91
Stephen I, P.M., iv, 400
Susanna, V.M., iv, 438
Sylvester, P.C., i, 393
Sylvester, Ab., v, 304
Sylvia, W., v, 242
Symphorian, M., v, 66
Symphorosa and others, MM., iv, 355

Tarcisius, M., v, 55
Telesphorus, P.M., iii, 327
Teresa, V., v, 179
Thecla, V.M., v, 132
Theodore, M., v, 253
Thomas, Ap.:
  Vigil, iii, 317
  Feast, iii, 319
Thomas Aquinas, C.D., iv, 38
Thomas of Canterbury, B.M., i, 391
Thomas of Villanova, B.C., v, 131
Tiburtius, M., iv, 437

Tiburtius, Valerian and Maximus, MM., iv, 101
Timothy, B.M., iii, 376
Timothy, P.M., v, 63
Titus, B.C., iii, 415
Transfiguration of Our Lord, iv, 418
Trinity Sunday, iii, 74
Trypho and others, MM., v, 262
Twelve MM. of Beneventum, v, 89

Ubald, B.C., iv, 173
Urban I, P.M., iv, 181
Ursula and Companions, MM., v, 187

Valentine, P.M., iii, 429
Venantius, M., iv, 175
Victor and others, MM., iv, 108
Victor I, P.M., iv, 381
Vincent, M., iii, 370
Vincent Ferrer, C., iv, 93
Vincent de Paul, C., iv, 359
Visitation of B.V.M., iv, 314
Vitalis, M., iv, 123
Vitalis and Agricola 'MM., v, 245
Vitus and others, MM., iv, 242

Wenceslas, M., v, 143
Whitsun. See Pentecost
William, Ab., iv, 271
Willibrord, B.C., v, 249

Zeno and others, MM., iv, 333
Zephyrinus, P.M., v, 74

www.ingramcontent.com/pod-product-compliance
Lightning Source LLC
Chambersburg PA
CBHW071950070526
44583CB00015B/1141